CONSTRUCTING EARLY CHRISTIAN FAMILIES

The family is a central topic in recent discussion of Graeco-Roman antiquity. This volume contributes further to that discussion. Interacting with methods and models from sociology and social anthropology it offers original and diverse perspectives on the nature of the family in early Christianity and the use of family terms as metaphors for the relations between members of Christian communities. *Constructing Early Christian Families* presents a comprehensive, well-documented and timely insight into the social structures of the early Christian world.

Halvor Moxnes is Professor of New Testament at the University of Oslo, Norway. He is the author of *The Economy of the Kingdom* (1988) and other studies of social relations in early Christianity.

ALSO AVAILABLE FROM ROUTLEDGE

THE FIRST CHRISTIANS IN THEIR SOCIAL WORLDS
Social-Scientific Approaches to New Testament Interpretation
Philip F. Esler

MODELLING EARLY CHRISTIANITY
Social-Scientific Studies of the New Testament in its Context
Edited by Philip F. Esler

THE SOCIAL WORLD OF JESUS AND THE GOSPELS
Bruce J. Malina

CONSTRUCTING EARLY CHRISTIAN FAMILIES

Family as social reality and metaphor

Edited by Halvor Moxnes

London and New York

First published 1997
by Routledge
11 New Fetter Lane, London EC4P 4EE

Simultaneously published in the USA and Canada
by Routledge
29 West 35th Street, New York, NY 10001

©1997 Halvor Moxnes

Typeset in Garamond by Routledge
Printed and bound in Great Britain by T. J. International,
Padstow, Cornwall

British Library Cataloguing in Publication Data
A catalogue record for this book is available from the British Library

Library of Congress Cataloguing in Publication Data
A catalogue record for this book has been requested

ISBN 0–415–1463–80 (hbk)
ISBN 0–415–1463–99 (pbk)

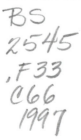

To Arnfinn, family and friend

CONTENTS

CONTENTS

ILLUSTRATIONS

FIGURES

TABLE

Figures 3.1–2 and 3.4–5 are taken from Y. Hirschfeld, *The Palestinian Dwelling in the Roman-Byzantine Period*, Studium Biblicum Fransiscanum, Coll. Minor 34, Jerusalem: Franciscan Printing Press, 1995; Figure 3.3 is from S. Loffreda, *Recovering Capharnaum*, Studium Biblicum Fransiscanum, Guides 1, 2. (ed.) Jerusalem: Franciscan Printing Press, 1993. I am grateful to the Franciscan Printing Press for permission to use them.

CONTRIBUTORS

Reidar Aasgaard is a Research Fellow at the Faculty of Theology, University of Oslo, Norway.

John M. G. Barclay is a Senior Lecturer in the Department of Biblical Studies, University of Glasgow, Scotland.

Stephen C. Barton is a Lecturer in New Testament, Department of Theology, University of Durham, England.

Philip F. Esler is Dean of Divinity and Professor of Biblical Criticism, University of St Andrews, Scotland.

Lone Fatum is Lecturer in New Testament, Department of Biblical Exegesis, Copenhagen University, Copenhagen, Denmark.

Ingvild Sælid Gilhus is Professor of History of Religion, University of Bergen, Norway.

Santiago Guijarro is Assistant Professor of New Testament in the Faculty of Theology, Pontifical University of Salamanca, Spain.

Eva Marie Lassen is a Senior Carlsberg Research Fellow at the Danish Centre for Human Rights, Copenhagen, Denmark.

Dale B. Martin is Associate Professor of Religion at Duke University, Durham, North Carolina, USA.

Halvor Moxnes is Professor of New Testament, University of Oslo, Norway.

Karl Olav Sandnes is Professor of New Testament at the Norwegian Lutheran School of Theology, Oslo, Norway.

Risto Uro is a Docent at the Department of Biblical Exegetics, University of Helsinki, Finland.

PREFACE

Most of the essays in this volume are revised versions of papers presented at the conference on *Family as a Social Reality and Metaphor in Early Christianity* held in Oslo from 28 September to 1 October 1995. The conference was a result of contacts between Biblical scholars in Scotland and the Nordic countries initiated with a Scottish-Scandinavian conference in Glasgow in 1993. This cooperation proved so fruitful that it was decided that it ought to be followed up, this time in a smaller forum and with a more specialised topic. The topic 'Family in early Christianity' was chosen as a fruitful area for historical interpretation and reconstruction, as well as for hermeneutical reflections. Scholars and doctoral students in New Testament, theology, history of religion and classical studies from the Nordic countries, Scotland, England, Ireland, and the United States spent three days on papers and discussions that challenged us to find a new understanding. The paper by Santiago Guijarro on the family in Galilee (an earlier Spanish version was published in *Estudios Biblicos* 53 (1995)) unfortunately could not be read at the conference, but supplements the contributions in an important way.

The conference was made possible through financial support from the Nordic Academy for Advanced Study (NorFA) and the Faculty of Theology, the University of Oslo, through its project on 'The Christian Moral Tradition in Norway'. I am grateful to Troels Engberg-Pedersen, Copenhagen, who initially suggested the topic for the conference and for colleagues at the Faculty of Theology who supported the undertaking. I am particularly indebted to Reidar Aasgaard, doctoral student in New Testament, who with great enthusiasm and hard work carried most of the administrative responsibilities before, during, and after the conference, with help from Birgitte Lerheim, secretary for the 'Moral Project'. Warm thanks are due to my colleagues Sean Freyne, Dublin; Lone Fatum, Copenhagen and Bengt Holmberg, Lund, who made up the editorial committee and provided good advice for the authors and the editor. Thanks are also due to the authors for their willing participation, and for the spirit of generous cooperation that resulted from the conference, in that native English speakers took it upon themselves to read and comment upon the manuscripts of the others.

The Reverend Roger Jensen provided invaluable help in preparing the manuscripts for publication and in compiling the indexes.

I am grateful to the Senior Editor, Mr Richard Stoneman, for his support, and to the staff at Routledge for the competent and friendly way in which they have dealt with this project.

The book is dedicated to Arnfinn J. Andersen, who more than anyone has challenged and stimulated my thoughts on family/ies.

Halvor Moxnes

ABBREVIATIONS

NOTE

All references to Classical works are to *The Oxford Classical Dictionary*, second edn, Oxford: 1992, unless otherwise stated in the relevant chapters.

AB	Anchor Bible
ABD	D. N. Freedman (ed.) *The Anchor Bible Dictionary*
ALGHJ	Arbeiten zur Literatur und Geschichte des Hellenistischen Judentums
ANRW	*Aufstieg und Niedergang der Römischen Welt*
BAGD	W. Bauer, W. F. Arndt, F. W. Gingrich and F. W. Danker *Greek–English Lexicon of the NT*
BARev	*Biblical Archaeology Review*
BASOR	*Bulletin of the American Schools of Oriental Research*
BBB	Bonner Biblische Beiträge
BTB	*Biblical Theology Bulletin*
BZNW	Beihefte zur ZNW
CG	Cairensis Gnosticus
EKKNT	Evangelisch–Katholischer Kommentar zum Neuen Testament
FRLANT	Forschungen zur Religion und Literatur des Alten und Neuen Testaments
HDR	Harvard Dissertations in Religion
HTR	*Harvard Theological Review*
JBL	*Journal of Biblical Literature*
JPOS	*Journal of Palestine Oriental Society*
JRS	*Journal of Roman Studies*
JSNT	*Journal for the Study of the New Testament*
JSNTSup	Journal for the Study of the New Testament – Supplement Series
JTS	*Journal of Theological Studies*
NEAEHL	*The New Encyclopedia of Archaeological Excavations in the Holy Land*

NHS	Nag Hammadi Studies
NovTSup	Novum Testamentum, Supplements
NRSV	New Revised Standard Version
NTS	*New Testament Studies*
RB	*Revue Biblique*
SBFLA	*Studii Biblici Fransiscani Liber Annuus*
SBLDS	Society of Biblical Literature Dissertation Series
SBLMS	Society of Biblical Literature Monograph Series
SBLSBS	Society of Biblical Literature Sources for Biblical Study
SBLSP	Society of Biblical Literature Seminar Papers
SBS	Stuttgarter Bibelstudien
SNTSMS	Society for New Testament Studies Monograph Series
ST	*Studia Theologica*
TDNT	G. Kittel and G. Friedrich (eds) *Theological Dictionary of the New Testament*
TU	Texte und Untersuchungen
TZ	*Theologische Zeitschrift*
WMANT	Wissenschaftliche Monographien zum Alten und Neuen Testament
WUNT	Wissenschaftliche Untersuchungen zum Neuen Testament
ZNW	*Zeitschrift für die Neutestamentliche Wissenschaft*

1

INTRODUCTION

Halvor Moxnes

What happened to family life within the early Christian movement? How did the first Christians react vis-à-vis the social structures of household and kinship in Palestine and the Graeco-Roman world? Why were family metaphors so important for the self-definition of early Christian communities? And why did they choose some metaphors over others to express their identity and the inter-relationships between group members?

Strangely enough, although 'family' is such an important topic in Christianity, there have been few comprehensive studies of family in early Christianity. There has been much interest in certain aspects, in particular in ethical issues concerning marriage or the so-called 'household' codes, but much less in the social behaviour and forms of family as a social institution among early Christians (but see Lampe 1992 and Osiek 1996). This corresponds to the situation in Graeco-Roman studies until a few years ago. Keith R. Bradley speaks of family history as 'virtually a new field of Roman historical scholarship' (Bradley 1991: 5). Under the impact of the new social history it has been possible to study the 'dynamics of Roman family life' as well as to 'understand the family as a social organism'. The result has been a number of exploratory and experimental studies. The same has been the case to a lesser degree concerning Greek and Jewish studies of family.

But the situation for early Christianity as a whole is very similar to J. H. Neyrey's description of studies of the Gospel material in the Q source:

> more serious consideration needs to be given to the basic social institution of antiquity, namely the family and the role of the *paterfamilias*. Further studies in Q would do well to investigate the role of families in socialising new members and exercising social control. Issues of family and (fictive) kinship remain underdeveloped in scholarship.
> (Neyrey 1995: 156–57)

Neyrey also points to the need for further studies of fictive kinship, that is, the ways in which the first Christians regarded and treated each other as 'family'. The goal of this collection of essays is to combine the study of the family as a social institution in early Christianity with a study of Christian communities as examples of 'fictive kinship'. This combined interest was expressed in the title of the seminar in which most of these essays originated: 'Family as social reality and metaphor in early Christianity'. In order to understand the meaning of early Christian use of family terminology to describe groups and inter-relationships between members, we need to know more about their ideals and social experiences of family, and their expectations of kinship relations.

To draw this picture it is not sufficient to study only those early Christian texts that speak explicitly about family, marriage, children, etc. Social structures of family and cultural assumptions and values associated with family underlie many more passages than those which explicitly speak of family relations. Consequently, there is a need for studies which illuminate the family structure of Palestinian and Graeco-Roman societies in which the Christian movement took hold. It follows that studies of early Christianity must be in dialogue with parallel studies of the Graeco-Roman world. In a recent collection of essays on family in ancient Rome, Beryl Rawson points to the need to analyse the social behaviour of Christian groups developing in this period within the Roman world: '*The interaction of Christians and pagans* (my italics), and their influence on each other, are large subjects, and of great relevance to the topics of this book – marriage, divorce and children – but they require a separate study . . . ' (Rawson 1991: v).

Many of the essays in this collection share an interest in this interaction between Christians and the larger Graeco-Roman world. The Jewish and the Graeco-Roman social and cultural worlds do not merely form the 'background' for Christianity, they represent the surrounding milieu, so that we must speak of a continuous interaction, be it in dialogue, in positive exchange or in conflicts and controversies. Studies of social and cultural worlds in ancient societies are today influenced by methods and perspectives from social anthropology. In Biblical studies this approach has been highly influential in attempts to establish the historical context of literary texts. This interaction between classical and Biblical studies on the one hand, and anthropology on the other, is visible in several of the essays in this collection.

The first group of essays deals with family within the social context of Palestine and the larger Graeco-Roman world, that is, with family as a social reality. But what do we mean by 'family'? Did 'family' mean the same in Mediterranean societies in the first century CE as it does today, in the Western world of the twentieth century? In the opening essay (Chapter 2), Halvor Moxnes situates the present study within the context of modern family studies. He suggests that studies of early Christian families should draw on various social sciences and the different perspectives they have developed. Since ancient language did not have a word that is equivalent to the modern '(nuclear) family', it is necessary when studying early Christian texts about 'family' to use various perspectives: household, kinship, marriage, inter-relations between members. Moreover, the study of early Christian families should situate them in their appropriate social and cultural context: Mediterranean societies in antiquity with their honour and shame culture.

Whereas Moxnes attempts to provide a basis for methodological approaches to the study of family, Santiago Guijarro, in Chapter 3, provides a material basis for the study of family in one area of early Christianity by focusing on Galilee. His study combines several approaches: literary, historical and sociological. Most important is his use of archaeological evidence based on recent excavations of domestic architecture in Galilee and Palestine. Combining the evidence from these various sources, Guijarro is able to reconstruct four different family types in Galilee in the first century. They are set apart by the type of house they inhabited, by the number of family members, their capacity for mutual support, the amount of land they possessed, and the social group they belonged to. This reconstruction forms the basis upon which to discuss the ways in which the Jesus movement interacted with 'family'. It is not a matter of just one type of family – different family situations must be studied:

> perhaps the consideration of their family situation, which is indicative of privilege or of dependency, may help to understand their reaction towards Jesus: on the one side, the people that followed him and acclaimed him and on the other, their rulers and their retainers that questioned his message.
>
> (Guijarro: this volume, 63)

Guijarro has described the material, social and economic basis and function of families as households. John M. G. Barclay, in his study (Chapter 4), adds the dimension of the religious function of the household, and shows how religion is embedded in family, understood as household and kinship. Barclay addresses the question to what extent religion was embedded in the lives and ideologies of families in the ancient world, especially Judaism and the early Christian movement. He pays special attention to the question of socialisation of children and focuses on the central role of the family in the preservation of Jewish tradition.

By contrast, Barclay claims, the early Christian movement was ambiguous in its attitude to family life and the relationship between the household and the faith. Thus, Barclay distinguishes between two trends, one that was 'anti-familial', and another that attempted to re-embed Christian discipleship within the household. With his study Barclay presents a picture of early Christianity where these trends occur as separate tendencies and developments which need not be forced into one harmonious picture. The following chapters focus more clearly on one or the other of these trends: those by Barton, Martin, Uro, and Gilhus on the 'anti-familial' trend; those by Esler, Sandnes and Aasgaard on the attempts to re-embed discipleship in some forms of family structures.

Stephen C. Barton (Chapter 5) explores the topic, hitherto little discussed, of subordination of mundane ties, among these family ties, to be found in Jewish monotheism as well as in demands addressed to the philosopher in Graeco-Roman traditions. This material is of obvious relevance for an understanding of the 'anti-family' material in the Gospels. It is particularly helpful to see how rejection of the social family is often combined with joining groups with a family-like character. Jewish writers like Philo of Alexandria and Josephus often describe conversion to Judaism in terms of its effect on family ties. The model communities, the Therapeutae and the Essenes, lived an ascetic life in renunciation of family ties, but their communities are described as alternative groups, modelled after the household.

There is enough material from Jewish and Graeco-Roman sources to indicate that the Gospel tradition relativising family ties could resonate against a wider background of well-known religious and philosophical topics. However, there were differences: the Cynic tradition renounces kinship ties to emphasise individual freedom and self-sufficiency, whereas in the Gospel tradition their subordination is the price of the eschatological mission started by Jesus.

The descriptions by Philo and Josephus of the Essenes and the Therapeutae in terms of 'spiritual kinship' or 'spiritual household' are similar to those used of Christian groups by various New Testament authors as well as in Gnostic scriptures. Thus, household and kinship/family metaphors provided a powerful idiom for 'chosen' groups, as well as for the larger society.

In the second section of the book, 'Family as metaphor', the focus moves towards the use of family language to denote fictive kinship, that is, the use of family terminology for Christian communities. But these essays also keep the social situation in mind, and relate the use of family terminology in fictive kinship to that of 'real' kinship. The close relationship between the two is also visible in Stephen Barton's study in the first section. In Chapter 6 Eva Marie Lassen provides a broader context to the function of fictive kinship terminology in early Christianity. Her essay is a study of some of the ways in which the Roman family served as an ideal as well as a metaphor in the classical Roman period, especially in the first century CE. Family metaphors played an important role in Roman society; especially important was the metaphor of father–son. It is significant that the Romans saw themselves not as a society of mothers and daughters or of brothers, but of fathers and sons. The father image became particularly significant in the form of the title *pater patriae* used of the emperor. And the family of the emperor became the state family and reinforced the image of the emperor as the father of the state.

It is into this context of a society described by the means of family

4

metaphors that Christianity entered – as a religion and a social group that also used family metaphors, both to describe relations between God and the faithful, and to describe internal relations within the group. Thus, family metaphors constituted a well-known means of communication with Roman society, but at the same time the content of the metaphors was partly unfamiliar. In light of the Roman tradition of describing society as a 'father–son' relationship, it is striking that the most popular term to describe interrelationships among the first Christians was 'brother'.

Why did this term, which describes only a relatively small segment of the full system of family relations, gain prominence? Several studies in this volume focus on the use of 'brothers' (*adelphoi*), three of them focus on a Pauline letter or section of a letter: Galatians (Esler), 1 Thessalonians (Fatum) and Philemon (Sandnes); the last one (Aasgaard) makes a general comparison between brother terminology in Plutarch and Paul.

Philip F. Esler (Chapter 7) studies the way in which Paul uses family images, especially that of relations between brothers, in his exhortations in Gal 5:13 to 6:10. It is Paul's purpose to create an identity for the Christian groups in Galatia. Esler's study is an example of the use of models from social sciences. He employs findings from studies of social psychology into the formation of group identity through inter-group conflict, as well as anthropological studies of honour and shame in a Mediterranean context. In a Mediterranean society the sense of collective honour within a family meant that it was particularly shameful if members of a family publicly displayed inter-family strife. In addition to the social science models, Esler also provides Greek and Roman texts which illustrate the importance of upholding family honour and avoiding strife. Moreover, Esler finds that the meetings in family houses, in contrast to Gentile collegia and Jewish synagogues, enhanced the familial dimension of Christian identity, and stimulated . the adoption of the language of kinship in their interrelationships. In his study Esler establishes a methodology to study Paul's use of the 'brother' language as part of the social dynamics of the formation of group identity.

In Chapter 8 Karl Olav Sandnes also situates Paul's use of brotherhood terminology within a wider context of the development of social structures and relations within the first Christian communities. Sandnes enters into a discussion with the views of K. Schäfer (1989), who considers household and brotherhood to be contrasting models in Pauline ecclesiology: the one represents a patriarchal model, the other an egalitarian and participatory one. Similarly E. Schüssler Fiorenza (1983) sees the two models as two different stages of development within early Christianity: an egalitarian brotherhood came first, followed later by the hierarchical household. Sandnes claims that the social reality of early Christianity was more patriarchal and household-like than most modern theologians are happy with. His thesis is that there was a convergence of household and brotherhood structures. The brotherhood-like nature of Christian fellowship was not a first stage – rather, it was embedded in household structures. Household structures underwent some modifications when their members became Christians. Sandnes studies an example of such modifications in Paul's letter to Philemon. It concerns Philemon's slave, Onesimus, who had become a Christian, and Paul's use of 'brother' terminology to describe the relations between the master and his slave. The juxtaposition of two types of terminology: master–slave and brotherhood, leaves us with a picture of ambiguity and tension; egalitarian structures are emerging, but the patriarchal structures of the household are still in place.

Esler and Sandnes presupposed that there were links between the brotherhood terminology in Christian texts and their socio-historical context. In his essay on Paul and Plutarch, Reidar Aasgaard (Chapter 9) makes an explicit study of these links. He investigates the brotherhood ideas in Paul's letters, and attempts to understand them on the basis of their social context in family life. The main example of a contemporary understanding of brotherhood in Antiquity is the treatise 'On brotherly love' by Plutarch. Plutarch was a popular moral philosopher and his ideas often represent a general mentality in Hellenism. Aasgaard argues (against H. D. Betz 1978) that Plutarch's brotherhood ethics can be distinguished both from family ethics and friendship ethics, that is, it has a distinctive character. Much of Plutarch's discussion is concerned with conflicts between brothers, which should be avoided at all costs. Aasgaard finds many similarities between Plutarch and Paul. Paul likewise is concerned with brotherhood, in the form of fictive brotherhood applied to relations within the Christian community. This raises interesting questions about Paul's situation within the Hellenistic world (see T. Engberg-Pedersen 1995) – is he strongly embedded in this world, so that when he discusses conflicts between brothers in a Christian community, he participates in a discussion of a topos of general interest?

In Chapter 10 Lone Fatum adds a new perspective to the study of Paul's brotherhood terminology when she undertakes a 'gender hermeneutical reading' of 1 Thessalonians. Fatum, too, relates Paul's use of the brotherhood terminology to the social context of his readers, in particular to the divisions based on *gender*. She argues that 1 Thessalonians must be read as an example of an androcentric and patriarchal perspective: Paul addresses a group of male Christians. His main form of address to them is as 'brothers', and Paul applies the moral obligation of brotherhood in order to create a strong sense of community. Fatum argues that Paul strives to organise the brothers according to the social and moral obligations of the patriarchal family, in which Paul represents the fatherly authority. In this male world, there is almost no indication of a female presence, it is the patriarchal, male pattern of social values and virtues that is taken for granted. In partial contrast to other feminist interpreters, Fatum finds it difficult to imagine how

Christian women could be integrated into the Thessalonian community. According to the patriarchal ideology, women could be among the converts, but not among the brothers of Christ, and not members of the new community. Fatum's interpretation seriously undermines the understanding of the Bible as a source of equality for women and thereby challenges our hermeneutical capacities.

The third section of essays focuses on one of the most important factors that influenced attitudes to family life as well as metaphors of family among the early Christians: the impact of asceticism and the rejection of sexual desire. Among New Testament authors, the most explicitly ascetic statements are found in Paul's writings. Dale B. Martin's purpose, in Chapter 11, is to show the precise structure of Paul's asceticism, and to compare it to that of other ancient writers. Main texts are 1 Cor 7, 1 Thess 4 and Rom 1. Paul argues that Christians should experience sexual intercourse only in the context of marriage, and only in absence of sexual desire. The passion of desire is part of the dirty, polluted cosmos in opposition to God. Sexual desire is connected with the Gentile world. Martin compares Paul to two major groups of contemporary writers: medical and Aristotelian as well as Stoic writers. Martin discusses critically M. Nussbaum's position in *Therapy of Desire* (1994). She holds that only the Stoic position is the rational one, whereas the others are 'irrational'. Martin criticises her concept of 'rational', and proceeds to show that the various positions are carried by different systems characterised by their own internal logic.

Paul simply follows a different rationality from the Stoics. For Paul, every human being receives his identity by his place, either in 'this cosmos' or 'in Christ'. Thus, the free will and free moral agency that is a necessary precondition for the Stoic position is absent from Paul. Paul saw man threatened by cosmic forces, coming from outside, which could possibly enter the body as pollution. Thus, Paul feared sexual desire as a polluting force that threatened the Christian's body.

Paul's view on desire is not just an individual position on a single topic, it is part and parcel of his total world view of human beings and their position in the world, cosmology, theology and anthropology. This rejection of desire shows a different 'logic' from modern positions, but it shows how marriages and family can be conceived of in very different categories from those that we know and take for granted. Martin's exposition of Paul's rejection of desire illuminates the development towards the Gnostic perception of desire (see Gilhus, Chapter 13).

Risto Uro's purpose, in Chapter 12, is to pose the question of the specific nature of asceticism in the Gospel of Thomas, through a study of passages related to marriage and sexuality. The Gospel of Thomas has been the subject of widely diverging interpretations, from an extreme emphasis on the encratic nature of the Gospel to an almost complete rejection of this view. Uro undertakes a careful investigation that provides a nuanced view.

He finds that the general background of the book is the ascetic tendencies that were prevalent in Thomas' environment. But how is this ascetic tendency expressed in the Gospel of Thomas and how far does it go? The Gospel of Thomas represents not just one trajectory, but several, and is a witness to that Syriac Christianity that was later to produce explicitly encratic books. Uro points out that metaphorical language about family can have several functions. A criticism of 'biological procreation' and the setting up of 'true mother/father' as an alternative in a description of the disciples' identity does not necessarily imply social consequences like rejection of marriage and sexuality. The purpose may be to put up a contrast between 'this-worldly' and 'other-worldly'.

In her essay on family structures in Gnosticism Ingvild S. Gilhus (Chapter 13) introduces us to a strange mythological world in Sethian Gnosticism. In the mythological world of mainstream Christianity the 'divine family' is conceptualised as a 'father–son' relationship. The female element is subordinate. In Sethian Gnosticism the female element is much more prominent, but as a bridge between the material and the spiritual, in an ambivalent position. There is also a tension between the pronounced ascetic tendency of Gnostic texts and their symbolic language, where sexual relationships play a prominent part.

Since we know so little about the social structure of Gnostic groups, is it possible to say something about the outcome of this mythology for social families? The Gnostic texts frequently speak against sexual desire and procreation. Gilhus outlines some possible alternative views of procreation: first, continence is the ideal, procreation is evil; second, procreation is allowed, in order to multiply the spiritual race, but sexual desire is not; third, sexuality is allowed, but not in order to bear children. There are similarities between these possible forms of logic and Paul's discussion of desire (Martin, Chapter 11). Gilhus' propositions show how views of desire and views on procreation and family life are connected.

BIBLIOGRAPHY

Betz, Hans D. (ed.) (1978) *Plutarch's Ethical Writings and Early Christian Literature*, Studia ad Corpus Hellenisticum Novi Testamenti, vol. 4, Leiden: Brill.

Bradley, Keith R. (1991) *Discovering the Roman Family*, New York: Oxford University Press.

Engberg-Pedersen, Troels (ed.) (1995) *Paul in his Hellenistic Context*, Minneapolis: Fortress.

Fiorenza, Elisabeth Schüssler (1983) *In Memory of Her. A Feminist Theological Reconstruction of Christian Origins*, New York: Crossroad.

Lampe, Peter (1992) ' "Family" in Church and Society of New Testament Times', *Affirmation* (Union Theological Seminary in Virginia) 5: 1–20.

Neyrey, Jerome H. (1995) 'Loss of Wealth, Loss of Family and Loss of Honor', in P. F. Esler (ed.) *Modelling Early Christianity: Social-Scientific Studies of the New Testament in its Context*, London: Routledge: 139–58.

Nussbaum, Martha. C. (1994) *The Therapy of Desire: Theory and Practice in Hellenistic Ethics*, Princeton, NJ: Princeton University Press.

Osiek, Carolyn (1996) 'The Family in Early Christianity: "Family Values" Revisited', *Catholic Biblical Quarterly* 58: 1–24.

Rawson, Beryl (1991) 'Introduction', in B. Rawson *Marriage, Divorce and Children in Ancient Rome*, Oxford: Clarendon Press: 1–5.

Schäfer, K. (1989) *Gemeinde als 'Bruderschaft'. Ein Breitrag zum Kirchenverständnis des Paulus*, Europeische Hochschulschriften, R. XXIII, vol. 333, Frankfurt am Main: Peter Lang.

Part I

THE SOCIAL CONTEXT OF EARLY CHRISTIAN FAMILIES

2

WHAT IS FAMILY?

Problems in constructing early Christian families

Halvor Moxnes

'Do you have a family?' This is a very common question at a certain stage in conversations with 'relative strangers', e.g. colleagues we meet at conferences or meetings, fellow travellers on train journeys, acquaintances made on holidays. I sometimes respond to that question by saying, 'Yes, my parents are alive, and I have two brothers and a sister, who are married and who have children'. Then I go on to speak about my childhood summers spent on my grandparents' farm. My grandparents lived with my uncle and aunt and their children in two separate households in a large farmhouse. Each summer the house was filled with several cousins, with uncles and aunts, and even great-uncles and great-aunts and second cousins were occasional visitors. We all made up a large, extended family. From the bewildered look this response evokes, I know that I have not answered the question they posed. I have told them about my 'family of origin', the family in which I grew up. But they meant to ask about my 'family of procreation', i.e. 'Are you married? Do you have children?'

My response to that question is 'no', and that would appear to end the conversation. But from my family in a wider sense I know something about the many possible positive answers to such questions. The traditional answer, implying a married couple with one or two children is just one alternative. Divorce has become quite common, resulting in split families. But a divorce may be followed by remarriage to a new spouse, who may or may not have been married before, with or without children from a previous marriage. To complicate matters further, at least in the Scandinavian countries, couples living in co-habitation without formal marriage are so common that they as a matter of course are considered to constitute 'family'. And to continue the list of possible answers, again with the Scandinavian countries in the forefront, some countries have established a legal 'partnership' between individuals of the same sex, with similar rights and obligations as married couples without children. So, to say that 'I don't have a family of my own' might imply a great variety of possible paths that I have not chosen. In order that people should not pity me as a person who has failed in an area with strong cultural expectations, I sometimes add: 'But I have a family of friends!' I then tell them about

13

my close network of male friends who share many of the same functions as family members do: emotional and practical support, celebrations of holidays and personal feast days, long time commitments.

I have used this question 'Do you have a family?' and some of my own experiences, to remind us of the great variety of social groups that can be covered by the name 'family' and the many different meanings implied by 'family'. In this way our own experiences may introduce us to the variety of ways in which 'families' are studied. This is now frequently mentioned and discussed in many studies of 'family', but I want us to be aware of and to reflect upon what implications this insight has. I am not looking for a universal definition of what family *is*.[1] I think our goal should be more modest: try to be clear about what it is that we are studying, and how we are going about this study. And in a study of 'family' in early Christianity, we should not look just for what *we* think of as 'family'. I shall therefore attempt to raise questions that correlate modern presumptions about the study of family and questions relevant to the ancient world, i.e. the world of early Christianity. Thus, I hope that these sets of questions will help us to see where we are coming from with our questions, and to see both the similarities and the differences concerning family between our post-modern world and that of Antiquity. This is also a necessary precondition for any hermeneutic reflection on the relevance of Biblical statements concerning family for modern society.

MODERN STUDY OF FAMILY

Few if any areas of study have been so politically, ideologically and emotionally sensitive as the study of family. In social theory the development of family was closely associated with the development of modernisation. The idea of the 'nuclear' family as the modern form of family, in contrast to the pre-modern large, extended family, was for a long time the predominant paradigm. This concept also played a large part in political ideology and public consciousness. The stable, nuclear family was associated with an idea about a stable society. Uneasiness about changes in society is often voiced as concern for 'the family'. A report on families to the Church of England sums it up in this way:

> Families are so fundamental to society that they easily become a focus for society whenever society is anxious about itself. During the last half century, phenomena such as the increase in female employment in the 1970s, the questioning of authority and new experiences of affluence and freedom in the 1960s, the emergence of a teenage culture in the 1950s, and wartime displacement in the 1940s have all been accompanied by fears for the future of families.
>
> (*Something to Celebrate* 1995: 1)

14

It is not, therefore, sufficient to study what 'family' is 'in itself': it is always part of a wider social context and has a cultural meaning. In order to understand the function and the place of the family, we must have a grasp of the larger social pattern of which it is a part. A cross-cultural and cross-temporal comparison of functions and meanings of families, e.g. between Antiquity and modern societies, must be undertaken within a wider context of social analysis. How can we understand society, what theories can best illuminate the complexities of social life and the role of families?[2] Especially if we try to do comparative studies or to discuss the relevance of ancient family patterns, it is important to take into consideration the full social context. The main difference between traditional and modern societies may not be so much in the group of people who form a 'nuclear family' or a household, but in its function and relevance within the total social system. In traditional societies the family and the larger kinship group or lineage form the model and basis for other social relations. This is not the case in modern societies in which the role of a citizen is based on the individual rather than on membership in a family (Giddens 1991).

This does not mean that 'families' are without interest for modern societies, but that they are integrated into society in new and different ways. To indicate the complicated structure within which 'family' is found in a modern society, let us take a brief look at the way in which family is studied in various programmes of the Norwegian Research Council. First, one aspect of family studies is covered by the Welfare State Programme. Family is an important recipient of the politics of the Scandinavian welfare state system. Education and social welfare, especially the responsibility for children and the elderly, have become the responsibility of society and state. State and local authorities have entered a sphere earlier dominated by the household, and demanded taxation, control and information about the life of the family/household to a previously unheard of degree. Thus, the family is more private than before, as the arena of 'affective' relationships, but at the same time more public, directly influenced by the public sphere. And gender roles have been greatly influenced by the influx of women into the workforce and by a politics of equal rights for women in the public arena. In its research on families the Welfare State Programme addresses questions like: How is family embedded in society? How has the development of the welfare state affected families? What changes have taken place in the economy, in divisions of labour between men and women, with regard to role models within the family as a result of these policies?

But there is also a special programme (*Child, Youth and Family* 1996), which represents an attempt to integrate earlier programmes on children and young people, respectively, with a focus on 'the family' as an institution in itself. After some decades when more interest has been shown in the role and development of individual family members rather than in the family as an institution, the family as a totality has come back into focus for research.

That does not mean that family as an institution can be taken for granted. It is a central concern of the programme to study changes in family, especially through the break up of relations, divorce, and reorganisation through the establishment of new relations. Another aspect is the cultural and ideological meaning of family: what are the cultural connotations associated with it? Finally, the programme is concerned with the ways in which the family interacts with other institutions or segments of society. What is the interrelationship between family and state agencies, local authorities and institutions (like schools and kindergartens), market economy and the mass media, etc.?

These two programmes do not cover all aspects of family life. Therefore, a new area of study has been discussed, on kinship or the extended family, focusing on the role of history, tradition and the larger network of which families and individual persons are part. Whereas in traditional societies these groups formed the backbone of society, in modern societies they have become 'invisible' institutions. Or it may be that they have been invisible for scholars and not been made subjects of study, whereas for many families they have been a living part of their life.

What are family, kinship and household?

The study of family has traditionally been the arena of sociologists. It is now an area of study under change (Finch 1993; K. Moxnes 1993). There is a break with the structural-functionalism of earlier family sociology and its unified concept of 'family', in which the centrality of the family was assumed. In this view, the concept of 'family' was based on the theory of modernisation, with the 'nuclear family' representing the ideal form. The main problem with this was that 'family' was used as if it were an analytical concept with a distinct meaning, whereas now it is regarded much more as a cultural construction. The reason for this break with earlier assumptions was that the sociology of family was challenged from various sides. One challenge was the argument that the family is a social construct and that to treat it as an organic unit is to obscure the manifold interests represented within families (Dixon 1992: 24). One of the most serious challenges was that of feminism, with its criticism that the term 'family' obscured patriarchal control as a central factor in the relationship between men and women. Instead of family one should speak of gender relations (Finch 1993:17–19). The result of these various forms of criticism is that the paradigm of family studies has been deconstructed. Instead of building upon an idea about 'family' or even different 'families', sociology ought to turn to people's usage when they speak of 'family'. 'Family' is not a given entity, it cannot be taken for granted, so investigations should start by asking people how they define their family and what meaning they ascribe to family (Finch 1993: 25; K. Moxnes 1993: 97–107).

16

This focus on family by the sociologists is but one perspective; a related area of research is that of households. Students of the household have discussed whether it is a significant unit in the analysis of human societies, and the relationship between 'household' and 'family'. In a review of recent discussions R. McC. Netting, R. R. Wilk and E. J. Arnould make the following distinction:

> While both households and families are culturally defined, the former are task-oriented residence units and the latter are conceived of as kinship groupings that need not be localised. ... The point to be made is that physical location, shared activities, and kinship need not be empirically or logically overlapping.
>
> (Netting, Wilk and Arnould 1984: xx)

Studies of households focus more on economic and functional perspectives, i.e. on observable behaviour, than on the affective qualities of the relations, e.g. between parent and child. Studies of family, on the other hand, put more emphasis upon the symbols, values and meanings that characterise family. This distinction cannot be absolute, however. Netting, Wilk and Arnould conclude the discussion at this point with the observation that 'the household cannot be divorced from ideas that people have of the domestic group and from symbolic concepts like family and home ... that influence decisions and guide actions' (p. xxi).

Still another perspective is provided by social anthropologists. With their traditional concentration on 'primitive cultures' they have focused on kinship. Kinship studie sees family as part of a larger structure, and 'kinship' as a word which is 'an abstraction relating to the network of relationships based upon birth (either real or fictive) and marriage' (Hanson 1994: 183). In modern Western societies kinship does not play an important institutional or structural role. That does not mean that kinship is emotionally or socially unimportant, an interest in genealogy and large family reunions may indicate a growing interest in historical roots and networks, but it means that we relate to authorities and to the state as individuals or as members of a nuclear family, not via membership in a clan or extended family. At least, that is the ideal in societies based on a universalistic ethics code. In primitive and pre-modern societies kinship is one of the primary means to structure social life (see Bohannan and Middleton 1968). A study of kinship is therefore the best way to investigate the relations between families and the political power in society.

Finally, 'family history' is a relatively new sub-discipline of social history (Goody 1983; Herlihy 1985), which first focused on family as the household unit. From there it branched out to consider family as a process in the lives of its members. Likewise, it broadened its approach from the internal relations and structures of the family to the nuclear family's interaction with the wider kinship group, and its interaction with a wider net of institutions:

17

work, education, welfare institutions. There are different attempts to set up models for the most characteristic aspects of family systems, so as to distinguish between various types of families. Emmanuel Todd (1985) has proposed a typology that can be used in cross-cultural comparisons. The typology is based on some important variables, like forms of marriage (who chooses, parents or prospective partners), relationship between partners, division of inheritance, and cohabitation of married sons with parents. In a comparison of 'Eastern' and 'Western' (Muslim and Christian) structures of families around the Mediterranean, Goody (1983: 10–33) discusses a model with a few more aspects, e.g. the strength of the conjugal pair vis-à-vis the larger kinship group, the position of women and the notion of honour.

After this very brief overview of different research areas related to 'family', we may conclude that kinship, household and families are not objective facts, they are social systems that are human constructions. As cultural constructs they are given 'meanings' that might also be overlapping. When these terms are used in scholarship they indicate various perspectives that are used to study human groups and their interactions. They are not mutually exclusive but rather overlapping so that we see different aspects according to which perspective we choose.

HOW TO STUDY FAMILY/IES IN EARLY CHRISTIANITY: METHODOLOGICAL PROBLEMS

What are the sources for studies of family in the context of early Christianity? The major sources are texts, Christian as well as Jewish, Greek and Roman authors. It is common among all these sources that they offer statements of ideals and norms, not just data on people's actual behaviour. This is a particularly difficult question concerning the position of women, since most of the sources are written by elite men. Family as an institution is not an issue that is treated in a systematic way by New Testament authors, it is rather taken for granted as a presupposition which forms the basis for many underlying assumptions. Therefore it will be useful to outline how this system might be studied, in order better to understand hidden assumptions, and also to see what parts of the system played a significant role for the early Christians.

The goal is to present a model for the study of families in early Christianity, using the approaches outlined above: the study of households, family in its relation to kinship, and family as a group established by marriage. This is an outline for a study of social groups, not only with a view to their social composition and function, but also with a view to the meanings attached to them. What were the social and cultural patterns of 'families' provided by the Jewish and Graeco-Roman environment of the first Christians as reflected in New Testament texts? The emphasis is upon these shared presuppositions, not upon the specific types of social behaviour regarding families or different attitudes to marriage in various early

Christian groups (see chapters by Barclay, Barton and Uro in this volume). The use of family terms as metaphors in early Christian texts is another large and important area of study, which is covered by many other studies in this volume (see chapters by Esler, Fatum, Gilhus, Sandnes and Aasgaard), but it falls outside the main scope of this chapter.

The larger context of interpretation: the Mediterranean region in the first century

What is the larger social and cultural context of families in early Christianity? What type of socio-economic and political system were they part of? And what was the cultural system of norms and values that regulated life, or the religious universe within which individuals and families found their place? When we study families in early Christianity the primary context must be that of Mediterranean society and culture in Antiquity. Anthropological studies of the present Mediterranean cultural and social context have proved to be very helpful both for Classical studies and for the study of early Christianity.[3] Moreover, a number of cross-cultural, historical studies of family and family development focus particularly on family in the context of the Mediterranean (Goody 1983: 6–33; Saller and Kertzer 1991: 8–19).

Various aspects of the Mediterranean context are important for a study of families. One is that of the political and economic system of this area in Antiquity, in sociological terms characterised as 'advanced agrarian societies' (Lenski and Lenski 1987: 176–91). What form did the relations between the state and family take within this type of society? In societies with simple social structures, kinship is the most important social system. More advanced societies often have rather complex kinship systems, but also a centralised political system and associations that are not based on kinship ties. The Roman Empire, with the Hellenistic city states and Jewish Palestine, represent types of 'advanced agrarian societies' in which the dominant social spheres were *politics* and *kinship*. The other spheres that regularly form part of a social description of society are *religion* and *economics*. But in Antiquity these spheres had not yet become separate institutions in the way they have in later periods; instead they were embedded in politics and kinship. That an area is 'embedded' in another means that 'its definition, structures, and authority are dictated by another sphere' (Hanson 1994: 183). From this it follows that kinship and politics were institutions that had important economic and religious functions and, so to speak, included economy and religion within them (see Barclay, this volume, 66–72).

Another aspect is that of the dominant cultural presuppositions, according to which these societies are characterised as 'honour and shame societies' (Peristiany 1966; Gilmore 1987a; Malina 1993: 28–62; H. Moxnes 1993). The main cultural context of the family in the Mediterranean area of Antiquity is that of honour and shame. When the Mediterranean was established as a specific area of study among the social anthropologists, the main hypothesis was that this region had a social and cultural unity, and that honour and shame formed an important element of that culture (Peristiany 1966; Gilmore 1987a). The honour and shame system is based on presuppositions concerning human nature which differ markedly from a modern, western society that places much emphasis upon individuality and autonomy. In Mediterranean Antiquity the individual was far more dependent upon the group, and part of the group, so that we may speak of the concept of a 'dyadic personality' (Malina 1993: 63–89). The individual is dependent upon the group for recognition of his or her honour, and conversely, the honour of the group depends upon the behaviour of any member of the group. Thus, people were more oriented towards the group than is the ideal in modern, individualistic societies. Interaction between individuals and between groups was characterised by a competition for recognition.

There is in the Mediterranean a special emphasis on the honour of the family associated with sexuality, status and gender distinctions. Especially important was 'the notion that a family's honour is tied to the virginity and sexual fidelity of its daughters and wives' (Saller and Kertzer 1991: 17). Thus, women's behaviour was directly linked to men's honour. The focus was on relations between men and women, in the social context, as well as related to sexuality and procreation. The cultural value system was dualistic, built around the dichotomy of honour and shame, purity and cleanness, male and female. C. Delaney has suggested that this dichotomy is ultimately related to cosmology and to notions of creation, and to the participation of each sex in creation and procreation (Delaney 1987). Thus, she finds that the three monotheistic religions that originated in the Middle East each have a male creator god, and therefore a male role as primary in creation and procreation, sharing in the power and honour of the god. Women, on the other hand, do not share in this power. They are inferior, and therefore subjected to shame.

How did this honour and shame culture influence the relations between the individual and the family, as well as relations between family members? These aspects will be described in their relevant sections below.

Terminology

Neither in Greek nor in Latin is there a term for our word 'family' in the meaning of 'husband and wife with one or more children' (i.e. 'the nuclear family'). In Greek literature we find extensive discussions of *oikonomia*, that is, the management of households (Finley 1973: 17–21). 'Economics' of the household was the counterpart to 'politics', the management of city life. 'Economics' was thus concerned with the house, *oikos* (Elliott 1981:

170–82). This word could be used with two different meanings, relative to property: some used it to refer to the material possessions of the head of the household, but other writers, like Aristotle, used *oikos* to include all the members of the household, those who were under the authority of the head: wife, children, and other blood relatives, as well as slaves and servants.

In Latin we find a similar situation: the words we commonly think of as terms for 'family' – *familia* and *domus* – do not carry this connotation (Garnsey and Saller 1987: 127–29; Herlihy 1985: 2–4; Dixon 1992: 1–5) . *Familia* indicated things and possessions, but it could also be used of persons. In the latter meaning, it could include all those who were under the authority of the *paterfamilias*, wife and children as well as slaves, and also all agnates (related through male blood from the same house), or all those related through males to a common ancestor. *Domus* was used in the meaning of 'household', so that it included husband, wife, children, slaves and others living in the house. In a broader sense it could also be used of the descent group, and was larger than *familia* since it also included descendants through women.

Since Greek and Latin languages did not have a terminology that identified 'family' in the sense it is most commonly used today, viz. 'the co-residential, primary descent group', it is important that when we encounter 'family terms' we try in each case to identify what type of social group we are dealing with. What was the meaning attached to it, and what place did it have within the total social and cultural system of the Graeco-Roman and Jewish world of the first century?

Plurality of contexts

The terminology that we do find, *oikos*, *domus*, *familia*, is primarily used of the large households of prosperous people, who had slaves, servants and other dependants. This terminology indicates that the Roman family must be understood in the context of a slave society, a situation that affected paternalism, the raising of children and sexual relations (Garnsey and Saller 1987: 127–29). Thus, we are left with a terminology that identifies only some households, in particular the prosperous ones. We know much less about the family life and structure of poor people, and even less of the possibilities that slaves had to form family-like groups. M. Peskowitz makes similar observations concerning Jewish families. She says that it is basic for studies of the Jewish family to recognise that families come in the plural, depending upon the various socio-economic contexts in Palestine. Likewise, it is necessary 'to investigate the relations of families to other social institutions and to the production of culture' (Peskowitz 1993: 16). This plurality is associated not only with the social composition of the family; one's location as well as social power influences the 'meaning of family', therefore it must be spoken of in the plural, as 'multiple meanings'.

Gender perspectives

Students of early Christianity and Biblical texts have over the last decades become well aware of the male bias of scholarship, and there have been many efforts towards a 'feminist reconstruction of early Christianity' (E. Schüssler Fiorenza 1983, 'Feminist Reconstruction of early Christianity', *ST* 1989). However, it is clearly recognised that it is not only male-biased modern scholarship that is the problem, but that the texts themselves are written by men and from a male – that is, from a patriarchal – perspective. This of course colours descriptions of family and household: they are always ideological. The result is that we must ask not only what the texts say about male authority, but also what the actual balance of power between males and females has been. And is it at all possible to gain access to the perspectives of women, children and slaves?

To say that gender perspectives are important in the study of families must obviously mean more than adding chapters on the role of women or on the relations between husband and wife. It is a matter of new perspectives that focus on 'the different ways in which social life is structured by gender differences and on the different ways in which gender divisions are conceptualised and symbolised' (Saller and Kertzer 1991: 13). It is a major problem that conceptions of 'family' contain within them unexamined conceptions of women and gender. The result is that families of ancient times are described in the light of contemporary gender relations. Peskowitz' observations concerning the study of families in early Rabbinic Judaism is relevant for early Christian groups as well. She says that the Jewish family 'should not be construed as an essential, timeless and unchanging or biologically determined entity'. Instead it should be recognised as 'a site of male and female activity and as a site for the ideological construction of gender' (Peskowitz 1993: 10–12).

Archaeology as a source for family history

In addition to literary documents, archaeology is increasingly becoming more important as a source for family history. In Roman archaeology the excavations of Ostia, Pompeii, Herculaneum (Wallace-Hadrill 1991) and more recently Ephesus have brought to light a wide variety of houses and apartments. Together with finds of villas and large estates, these provide a good picture of the environment for elite families. As a result of recent excavations in Palestine we now know about a number of different types of houses and, in combination with literary and historical sources, can reconstruct the types of families that inhabited them, and their possible position in a socio-economic structure of Palestine. Archaeology and architecture are useful not only to determine economic level, but also to inform us about the social composition of households, about social interaction between members, as well as about their relations with the larger society outside of the house. The house often held others as well as family members, especially slaves and other dependants (freedmen, workers, lodgers, friends) that made up the household (Wallace-Hadrill 1991: 214–27). Keith R. Bradley has made some suggestions about the social implications of the use of space in his study of Roman families. To the Roman elite the house was not 'private', rather, it was 'multi functional, a place of constant social, economic, and sometimes political intercourse, not simply a place of habitation' (Bradley 1991: 8–9). In this volume S. Guijarro shows how information about different types of houses can be used together with other information to reconstruct different household patterns in Galilee.

HOUSEHOLD

Palestinian households as support systems

What will we see if we study 'family' under the perspective of 'household'? Let us first look at the Gospels and their descriptions of village life in Palestine, especially Galilee. We often say somewhat imprecisely that in order to follow Jesus, disciples were required to leave their 'families', and that he predicted that there would be conflicts in the 'family'. But what did they actually leave? And what was the group like where there was a conflict? If we look more closely at the texts, we find that Mark 10:29–31 speaks not just of brothers, sisters, mother and father, but of their 'house' (*oikia*) and 'fields' (*agrous*). This statement focuses on the importance of the house and farm as the centre for a group of people. In the passage in Mark 10:29–31 we meet the family as a household, a group of people bound together by close kinship, who live together and make a living together. This is a pattern found in many peasant communities, in which the place of residence and subsistence takes precedence and defines the group that lives and works there. This perspective focuses on the family as a co-resident group that performs various tasks: production, distribution, transmission, reproduction, and that serves as the primary group of identification.

It is not the family as an 'emotional unit' that we encounter in the Gospel descriptions of households in Galilee, but rather as a group that lives and works together within the context of socio-economic inter-relations. This is a perspective that is found in all synoptic Gospels, especially in the parables, and is particularly well developed in Luke–Acts (Moxnes 1988; Scott 1989; Elliott 1991; Love 1993). The household is part of a larger social structure, the village; people come into the picture as relatives, neighbours, friends, participating in one another's lives. Household and village also relate to the elite: to the rich, often absentee-landlords and their deputies, and they are affected by rents, tolls and taxes. The usual experience recorded in the Gospels is that the household is affected in a negative way. As a cultural unit the household was also the centre of religious life and of transmission of values (Barclay, this volume). In the Gospel parables it is the family as household, situated in the land, that comes to the fore. It is the questions of subsistence, of how to manage small resources, of finding what people need to live, of quarrels over inheritance, that stand at the centre of Luke's narratives. Thus, it is the household as a unit of production and support that is important.

Some relevant questions when we look at the household as a unit of production and of sharing and support should be mentioned here: what are the typical activities of the household? How do they divide into male and female activities? Who are the members of the household: one or more generations, one or more family groups? Are both men and women mentioned? Does it include slaves or servants? What is the role of children? What types of hierarchy or relational structures are there between different members or groups of members, e.g. between 'lord of the house' and servants, between husband and wife, father and sons and daughters, mother and sons and daughters? What are the resources of the household? What are the relations with those outside the household: other kin, neighbours, friends, village members and people beyond the village? Does the household stand in a dependent relationship to others, e.g. landowners or their representatives?

We have now tried to raise questions that are relevant to the 'institutional logic' of the household. But it is even more important to ask about the 'moral logic' of the household, that is, the meanings ascribed to it. What is the moral system of this household, i.e. what types of behaviour are expected from its various members? What are the norms and values that are taken for granted, e.g. in terms of the sharing of resources? One way to attempt to grasp this, not just as individual norms, but as a system, is by applying the insights from studies of 'peasant economics' to the Gospels (in particular Luke) and their descriptions of Galilee as the setting for Jesus, his works, speeches and parables (Moxnes 1988: 75–98). The ideals of peasant economics, as a protest against economic exploitation from outside forces, were based not on hoarding or selling for profit, but on the principle that everybody should receive according to need, and that members of the household should share, without demanding a quick or equal return. In the Gospels the household becomes a model for human society and for the ideals associated with the Kingdom of God. Thus, the household and its economy are used as moral examples and models for the renewal of Palestine, in contrast to the negative leadership exemplified by the exploitation by the rich elite and the temple (Elliott 1991; Moxnes 1988: 139–53).

The household in the historical context of Palestine

Is there a historical scenario behind the Gospels and their descriptions of the household? David A. Fiensy (1991: 119–53) has described how changes in land ownership and the growth of large estates in Palestine in the Herodian period affected the position and structure of peasant households. These changes, which made many farmers into tenants or forced them off the land altogether, started in Hellenistic times, but increased in Herodian times. This had considerable impact on the peasant household and kinship and neighbourhood structure. Most scholars agree that there was a gradual break-up of this system which they ascribe to scarcity of land, diminished landholdings, and the fact that many farmers were forced into an existence as wage labourers. This was a process of disintegration that gradually made it impossible for the extended family to fulfil its function, to secure the subsistence of its members. As a result the village and neighbours became more important as socio-economic relationships. Thus, a study of peasant household relations in the Herodian period indicates that they were under pressure, that the traditional clan network had disappeared, and that the extended family complex in most areas was severely threatened. This situation in many ways corresponds to that which is described in the Gospels, concerning both the pressures upon peasant households and the attempt to revive the 'old' morality based on household sharing and village solidarity.

Households in an urban Hellenistic setting

In most New Testament writings apart from the Gospels, the scene is no longer Palestine but the cities of the Eastern Mediterranean. Here, too, the household is taken for granted as a social institution, but viewed from a different perspective. Focus is no longer on the village household unit in Palestine as a unit of production and sharing, but on the urban household in the cities of the empire, their social structure and their relations to the larger social contexts (Verner 1983: 27–81). As in Graeco-Roman sources we hear mainly of large, but not necessary elite households, for instance that of a Roman officer or a woman who runs her own business (Acts 10–11; 16:13–15). From many sources we learn that slaves, as a matter of fact, were part of such households (e.g. 1 Cor 7: 21–24; Philemon; Eph 6:5–9; Col 2:2–4:1; 1 Pet 2:18–25).

Both in narrative sections (e.g. Acts 10–11; 16:25–34) and in normative exhortations like the household codes (Eph 5:22 to 6:9; Col 3:18–4:1; 1 Pet 2:18 to 3:7) the head of the household, almost always a man (but for Acts 16:13–15), plays a dominant role, both towards the other members of the household and towards the outside world. He is the master (*kyrios*) and acts on behalf of the household. Whether historically reliable or not, Luke's descriptions of conversions illustrate this social convention: when the master of a household converts, his household follows suit (Acts 11:14; 16:33–34; Matson 1996). Heads of large households could play the role of patrons in the town and towards visiting missionaries, or to a group of believers. Hospitality was a central expression of such patronage. In this way the large household was part of the patronage structure whereby social relations are governed by personal relations between a patron and his clients (Garnsey and Saller 1987: 148–54). New Testament references to patronage, e.g. in the form of gathering a group of believers in one's house, show how this patronage system with its system of benefices and obligations was part of life for early Christian groups (Moxnes 1991). Moreover, the household was embedded in the larger social structures of the city and the Roman Empire; as the microcosmos was headed by the master of the house, the macrocosmos, the larger social system, was headed by elected officials, but above all by the emperor and his representatives (Rom 13:1–7; 1 Pet 2:13–15).

It was this urban context, with the institution of the household within a system of patronage and structures of personal authority, which provided the setting for the first Christians and which circumscribed their possibilities for social behaviour. This was also an arena of interaction between Christians and pagans. It is therefore of great interest to study how Christians related to this household structure. What were the main issues that were discussed in early Christian texts? Especially in the household codes, the focus is upon the authority structures of the household and internal relations between household members (Balch 1981; Verner 1983). Thus, we gain insight into issues like 'What was the hierarchy or relation between different members or groups of members (e.g. servants, children) of the household?'

Of particular interest is the situation and status of slaves compared to that of other members of the household, especially sons: what was their relation to the head of the house? (See Lassen, this volume, 108–9.) Some scholars find but little distinction between the two in regard to the authority of the father in the Roman household (Veyne 1987: 9–31, 51–69). Others, especially R. Saller (1991) have argued, and I think convincingly, that this authority took very different forms: the master–slave relationship was basically exploitative whereas the father–son relationship, although asymmetrical, was reciprocal. The household codes seem to confirm the latter view: slaves were warned of the danger of being exposed to bad masters. But it is obvious that there was a tension between social conventions concerning the place of slaves in a household and their status as 'brothers' within a household in which the master (and the rest of the house) had converted (Sandnes, this volume). Another set of questions relates to the authority and privileges within Christian communities: should household heads who acted as patrons to the community house-churches enjoy a special authority? Should the social patterns of community gatherings follow the social rules based on household and distinctions between patrons and clients, or ought these to be modified? And finally, we find discussions of the role of wives within the household, and also their role outside the household, in public or in the semi-public atmosphere of gatherings of Christian groups. Here we only hear male voices speaking, most of the time restricting the role of women in the Christian community, and emphasising their role in the household (1 Tim 5:9), and making that role into a model for their function in the community as well (Seim 1994: 249–60).

KINSHIP

In the Graeco-Roman world of the first century CE, kinship played a significant role, although it was no longer the only form of social organisation. With the arrival of the Roman Empire in the former Hellenistic areas and Greek city states, relations of power shifted away from a rule based on families towards a form of power that was more dependent upon the Roman emperor or the emperor's representative. This was also a form of power that was oriented towards people, especially the patron–client relationship that structured dependent relations (Garnsey and Saller 1987: 148–59). And in Rome itself, the development from republic to rule by an emperor weakened the power of the large senatorial families, who were drawn more into the bureaucracy and into dependence upon the emperor.

As far as Palestine is concerned, it has been suggested that the old clan and tribe system had been in gradual decline over a longer period. The clans were groups of households with a mutual obligation to assist each other in times of need, which thus was a form of subsistence guarantee. However, in Hellenistic times references to clans disappear. David Fiensy suggests that there were economic and administrative reasons for this (1991: 127–32). Since the country was reorganised in regional toparchies for tax purposes, the old clan system lost its importance. A relevant question for a description of first century Palestine in the Gospels is whether the clan, the larger kinship system, any longer played a role as a 'support system' for families. On the elite level, however, it is obvious that the larger kinship group continued to play an important role regarding marriage, inheritance and power sharing (Hanson 1989–90).

Kinship and the honour of Jesus

Kinship continued to play an important part on the cultural and social level, in terms of collective identity. The larger kinship group as a collective group with a common history formed the link between the individual as a member of a household and the larger community and the people. The statement in Mark 6: 4 explicitly positions Jesus within the context of these three groups: 'A prophet is not without honour, except in his own country (*patris*), and among his own kin (*syggeneis*) and in his own house (*oikia*).' Moreover, the

27

reference to honour in this statement places Jesus squarely within a Mediterranean context of honour and shame.

The conflicts between Jesus and his opponents must be read in light of this honour culture, for they are often examples of challenge and riposte with the outcome as honour or shame (Malina 1993: 34–37). These exchanges are examples of honour that can be acquired. But honour could also be ascribed on the basis of membership of a group, especially a kinship group. This membership had to be established, and the primary means was through genealogies. In the most immediate form it was expressed through 'segmented genealogies' that describe the immediate relations of an individual (Wilson 1992: 930–32). An example of this form is the question about Jesus: 'Is this not the son of the carpenter? Is he not the son of Mary . . . ' (Matt 13:55–56). Jesus is here questioned about his origin and about his family background; he is identified by his descent. It is a primary function of kinship systems and genealogies to create structure. In a kinship system everybody has their place. This system replicates other systems like the contrast between inside and outside, pure and impure, etc. Thus, the question of origin becomes a question of social control. The individual is considered first and foremost as part of a family, not only of the small, 'nuclear' group, but of a lineage. Family is the main source of honour, and consequently it becomes important to uphold the family honour, to behave according to the family honour. Within this system it is a fault to diminish one's family, but also to overextend oneself, to go beyond that which is acceptable. The story in Mark 3:21–35 about the conflict between Jesus and his mother and brothers, who consider him to be possessed by demons, and therefore come to bring him back home, is a story of how they attempt to protect the family honour.

The evangelists defend Jesus by using a strategy that shows the importance of genealogy for a person's identity and claim to honour. The genealogies of Jesus (Matt 1; Luke 3) as well as the birth story in Luke 2 link Jesus to the lineage of David and even Adam (Rohrbaugh 1995). The purpose is to ground in an earlier ancestor a claim to power, status, rank, office or inheritance. This strategy was not only valid vis-à-vis Jews; it was well known in the Graeco-Roman world, e.g. in the way in which the Roman emperors were associated with Roman gods and goddesses.

'Descendants of Abraham': the genealogy of faith

From the polemics of early Christian writers we learn something about presuppositions about kinship in the Jewish environment. In addition to the polemics in the Gospels about the genealogy of Jesus, there is another group of polemics that is concerned with the role of Abraham as ancestor of the Jews, and which reflects an early period in the relationship between Jews and non-Jews in the emerging Christian communities. Examples of this are discussions in the Gospels about 'who are the children of Abraham?' (Matt 4:8–9; Luke 3:7–9; Joh 8:33–44), but the most extended discussion we find is Paul's reinterpretation of the Abraham story in Romans 4 and Galatians 3 (Moxnes 1980: 207–82).

Why was Abraham so important to Jewish identity? In order to understand that, we must realise that it was an identity based on kinship categories. In an ideological construction the nation was divided into twelve tribes descended from the sons of Jacob, and ultimately from Abraham who was the ancestor of all Jews. Thus, kinship and nation were the same and the claim to descend from Abraham was a focal point for Jewish identity. This is Paul's point of reference when he starts Romans 4 by characterising Abraham as 'our forefather according to the flesh' (Rom 4:1). As the ancestor of all Jews Abraham embodied the ideals of Jewish identity for all generations. In Romans 4 this is related to the honour which Abraham possessed as a just man, associated with the exclusive identity mark of circumcision, which linked Abraham as the ancestor to Jewish men only. In Paul's reinterpretation he associates Abraham's honour with his belief in God, a belief which could be shared also by non-Jews. And Paul does not only describe their faith as similar to that of Abraham – they became related to Abraham in a deeper sense. Paul draws on the promises to Abraham that he should have many descendants, and makes Abraham the ancestor not only of Jews but also of believing non-Jews (Moxnes 1980: 241–53). In this way Paul transformed the Jewish notion of kinship by introducing a distinction between descending from Abraham and the ethnic identity associated with that descent. The relations between kinship and ethnic identity become ambivalent. In Paul's discussion in Galatians 3 it is less ambivalent, since the descent from Abraham (and ultimately from God) is clearly established by 'faith in Christ Jesus', with no distinctions between Jews and Greeks (3:15–29). In this way Paul has taken a central Jewish family term and moved it into the area of 'fictive kinship' which also included non-Jews (Esler, this volume).

FAMILY AS INSTITUTION : MARRIAGE

As mentioned above, there is in the New Testament, as in other Greek literature, no specific word for 'family' in the sense of 'a group consisting of wife, husband, children', what we find is the terminology of 'household' which includes a larger number of people. But does that mean that there was no consciousness of a small, 'core group' within the household or within the larger kinship group? This question has been much discussed within studies of the Roman family. There seems to be a growing consensus that the most typical family form was that of the 'core nuclear family', and that the father–son relationship had social and affective qualities that set it apart from that of the master–slave relationship (Rawson 1991: 2; Saller 1991:

164–65). In their discussion of family and household in the Roman empire, Garnsey and Saller (1987: 126–47) focus on the various aspects of the husband–wife and parent–child bonds.

There is good reason, therefore, to look at early Christian texts with a view also to what they say about relations between husband and wife and between parents and children, that is, in terms of the family that was established through marriage. In contrast to modern, 'romantic' marriages between two individuals, marriage in Antiquity took place within the context of the kinship group (Malina 1993: 117–48). It was a matter of linking two kinship groups and two households. Thus, it is possible to see it as something which was primarily part of the life of the lineage and household. But it was also an act that united two members of separate households, a man and a woman, two different genders, with the purpose of procreating children and often of setting up a new household. Marriage represented the start of one basic social function of the family: the formation of a group with the tasks of production and reproduction, sharing, social protection, worship, etc. Another social function was inheritance, that is, to transmit wealth – in Palestine, land especially – to the next generation, and, also very important, to transmit status and honour.

Marriage was 'a social contract negotiated between families, with economic, religious, and (occasionally) political implications beyond the interests of sexuality, relationship , and reproduction' (Hanson 1994: 188). Whom one married was therefore an important matter of family strategy to protect or enhance its economy, status and power. Jewish families practised different strategies in this area from those of Greek and Roman families. The dominant Jewish marriage was one within the kin group, *endogamy*, whereas the Greeks and Romans practised *exogamy*, i.e. marriage between close kin was excluded. For Jews, the barrier against marriage with non-Jews was also very high; this was one of the most important indicators of Jewish identity.

When we go to New Testament texts we find that there is no systematic discussion of institutional aspects of marriage, e.g. questions like endogamy or exogamy, cohabitation of a married son with his parents, or bride-wealth. All we find are splinters of information – even less than we find on matters of household and kinship. And in passages discussing matters that pertain to marriage, e.g. levirate marriage (Mark 12:18–27), we cannot be certain if the question is important in itself, or if it is used as a foil to frame the opponents of Jesus. Thus, we must distinguish between what information we can find about marriage and marriage institutions of a socio-historical character, and discussions of the *meaning* of marriage.

We can only guess what happened to marriage rules among early Christian groups. We learn that there were Christians who were married to non-believers (1 Cor 7:12–16; 1 Pet 3:1–2), but clearly this was a matter of concern and controversy (Deming 1995). But strangely enough, nothing is said about marriage between Jews and non-Jews. If this happened during this period, e.g. as a result of Paul's mission 'without law', it would be one of the most important results of breaking with ethnic Jewish boundaries, and a radical break with the rule of endogamy. Commensality between Jews and non-Jews created a distinct form of Christian community (Esler 1994: 52–69), and mixed marriages would have been even more influential in establishing the Christians as a group with a new identity. How should we understand the silence in this area?

Divorce, on the other hand, is discussed in a few instances (e.g. Mark 10:2–12; Matt 5:31–32; Luke 16:18; 1 Cor 7:10–16). The words of Jesus imply stricter rules against divorce than those found in Judaism, and it is noteworthy that the context of these sayings is conflict with the Jewish community, so that they serve as 'identity-markers' for the Christian group. Also the institution of inheritance is spoken of as something that is taken for granted. The examples show that the conflicts that often followed from inheritance were well known, cf Luke 12:13–15; 15:11–32.[4]

FAMILY AS A SYSTEM OF RELATIONS

Another way to study family is as a system of relations. This approach makes it possible to distinguish between various types of relationships: 'spousal, parental, parent–child, and sibling relationships, and to inquire what characterise such relationships, how do they change, and to what degree do family relations differ from other kinds of relationships' (K. Moxnes 1993: 106). In modern society we take for granted that the relationship between husband and wife is the most important social and familial relationship. But we cannot take that for granted in other types of societies, present or historical. In classical Greece, for example, it may well be that a man's friendships were more important than his relationship with his wife. Likewise, within the family itself other relations may have been more important than that between the married couple. What type of relations figure most prominently in New Testament texts? A cursory study shows that in relations between the generations, 'fathers' and 'sons' dominate the picture whereas 'mothers' and 'daughters' are very rare. In relations between members of the same generation, those between 'brothers' outweigh all others. It may be that some of these terms express 'inclusive language', but still the gender imbalance is considerable.

Marriage as the relations between husband and wife

Instead of discussions of the institutional aspects, New Testament authors concentrate upon the relations between husband and wife, and other internal relations between members of the family. There is a strong tendency to emphasise the unity of the couple: that is the reason given why a marriage should not be dissolved by divorce (Mark 10:1–9; Matt 19:1–9). Jesus' statement on the union between husband and wife is contrasted to the attitudes of Jewish law. This unity, which is God-willed, is stronger than the laws and customs of marriage laws. Likewise, statements about marriage by Paul and in the Pauline tradition, are set against the attitude of the Gentiles (Yarbrough 1985). Again, it is not institutionalised forms, but the content of marriage that is focused upon. The contrast is one of 'impurity' versus 'holiness'; Christians are urged to behave 'not like the Gentiles', but to take a wife in 'holiness and honour' (1Thess 4:6–7). The problem here is sexuality and desire (Martin, this volume). It is the fear of filthy, unbridled sexuality that comes to the fore – so that marriage is regarded as a protection against this desire (1 Cor 7) and as an expression of holiness (1 Cor 7; 1 Pet 1:14ff; cf Rom 12:2ff; 1 Thess 4:6–7; Eph 5). The unity of husband and wife is strongly emphasised, but the basis for the union should not be 'carnal desire', but Christian love and holiness. This again makes for a strong emphasis on mutual love and respect, the way we find it in the household codes.

What shall we make of these observations on the character of the relationship between husband and wife? When we evaluate statements on such relations, we must be careful not to read them in the light of a modern, romantic ideal of marriage and love.[5] But is there something in the contemporary culture of the New Testament writings that can explain this interest in relations between the couple, rather than in the institutional framework? Foucault (1986: 147–85) has pointed out that in this period – late first and early second century CE – we find new perspectives on love and marriage that emphasise the conjugal nature of marriage. His main witness is the moral philosopher Plutarch, who, although he retained many traditional ideas, e.g. about the inferior position of women, still emphasised the equality between men and women in terms of friendship, a category which in Classical Greece was not applied to a man's relationship to a woman. Moreover, it is characteristic of Plutarch's writings about marriage in the *Moralia* that he focuses on the relation between husband and wife, separate from a social context. This stands in marked contrast to Stoic philosophers, like his older contemporary, Musonius Rufus, who views marriage in terms of household, and as a social institution in the city.

Husband and wife: an honour and shame relationship

The emphasis upon the unity between husband and wife and (some sort of) equality between them, represents only one aspect of a description of relations between a couple. The relative value of that aspect must be measured against the background of more traditional and deeply rooted cultural structures. In the discussion of kinship, we have mentioned the paramount importance of honour and shame as cultural values in the ancient Mediterranean world, especially in the area of sexuality and gender relations within the family. The distinction between men's honour and women's shame does not result only in a dual pattern, but in a hierarchical system in which the husband has the most powerful role, closer to God (Moxnes 1993: 70–72). Pauline and post-Pauline texts in particular (1. Cor 11:1–16; Eph 6:23; Col 3:18) describe the relations between husbands and wives in this way, although they sometimes may be modified by statements about 'equality'.

The expectations inherent in this cultural pattern are recognisable in *male* descriptions of the good wife in the Pastoral letters. A good wife shows 'modesty' in dress and appearance and is deferential towards her husband (1 Tim 2:9–12; 1 Pet 3:1–5; Tit 2:4–5) (Balch 1981: 95–105). An anthropological study of the world of Bedouin women by Lila Abu-Lughod (1986) provides a key to understanding the implications of this 'modesty' or 'shame' (*aidos*). The central term in Arabic is *hashama*, which 'involves both feelings of shame in the company of the more powerful and the acts of deference that arise from these feelings' (1986: 107). Abu-Lughod traces the links between female sexuality, modesty and patriarchal social structure. The bonds of sexuality between a young couple are a threat to the social hierarchy of this society, and modesty codes, e.g. in dress that covers the body, are a way of denying sexuality and of showing acceptance of social structures. These aspects are part of the description of the 'proper' wife in Hellenistic popular philosophy and are found also in some New Testament passages. They point to the cultural integration of early Christians in their local communities. The Pastoral letters in many ways represent a position of 're-patriarchising' early Christian communities, e.g. in relation to the relatively independent position of communities of women, the so-called 'widows' (Bassler 1982).

Intra-familial relations: parents–children and between brothers

We can only indicate here different types of inter-familial relationships. Within the parents–children relationship it is necessary to distinguish between different types of relationships (Saller and Kertzer 1991: 8–19). This reflects a Mediterranean society in which all relations are gender-based. Therefore, instead of using the gender-neutral term 'parents', we ought to speak of the relations between a father or mother, respectively, and their sons or daughters, respectively (Malina 1990: 57–59).

Relations between parents and small children are characterised by care and concern on the part of the parents. The most central concern is that of providing food (Luke 11:11–13). The central figure in these narratives is the father, not the mother. The father is described as provider, nurturer and in general has a caring role, e.g. vis-à-vis a sick son or daughter (Mark 5:21–43; 9:17–27). Only rarely does a woman enter into the public arena to demand help from Jesus for a sick daughter (Mark 7:24–30). There is little said directly by New Testament authors about the role of children in the family (see Müller 1992), but the use that Jesus makes of children in his 'reversal' statement about entry into the kingdom of God points to something unexpected and highly unusual. The use of children as 'role models' in the Gospels most likely represents a break with the traditional role of children within the family.

The reverse side of the relation between parents and children is described in terms of relations between adult sons and daughters and their parents. The commandment 'honour thy father and mother' is directed towards situations in which parents are old and need help (Mark 7:9–13; Matt 15:6–9). It is towards adult sons and daughters that the hierarchical and patriarchal character of the family becomes most visible. A husband and father has the right to expect obedience (Eph 6:1–3; Col 3:20; 1 Tim 2:3–7).

The relationship that is most spoken of in New Testament texts is that between father and son. Some parables highlight this relationship (Matt 21:28–32, 33–40; Luke 15:11–32) with emphasis upon the obedience that a son owes his father. Another dominant motif in these parables is the question of inheritance. The right of the son to inherit not only the property of his father, but also his role and authority upon his death, emphasises the special character of this relationship. These aspects of the father–son relationship play a decisive role in the description of the relationship between God and Jesus in John's Gospel. The place of the father–son relationship within the total family structure may be interpreted in light of a study by Fredrik Barth (1981: 83–92) of the father–son relationship in Middle Eastern societies. He suggests that this is 'the dominant kinship relationship' in these societies, with the result that other relationships, especially that of husband and wife, have less importance and are partly suppressed. The result is that the son always remains son vis-à-vis his father, so that this relationship takes precedence over his relationship with his wife.

This suggestion helps us to see the radicalism of the break with fathers in some New Testament narratives, especially in narratives about the disciples who are called to follow Jesus and who in the process pointedly leave their fathers (Mark 1:17; Matt 4:21–22). This might indicate a stronger countercultural attitude and behaviour by at least some of the first Christians than we have tended to think. Destro and Pesce (1995) have made an observation that points in the same direction. When we study the New Testament, especially the Gospels and Acts, with a view to family relations, we find many mothers of disciples and community leaders, but no fathers associated with the group of Jesus' followers. This may support the findings of Barth: a son always remains son vis-à-vis his father: consequently, it would be impossible for a father to join a movement led by a 'son'.

The mother and son relationship is rarely described or alluded to in parables or narratives about social life in Palestine (but see Luke 7:11–17). However, it plays a significant role in the description of Jesus and his family relations, and likewise we find several mothers of his disciples. It is significant that when we encounter the family of Jesus, it is his mother and his brothers who are mentioned (Mark 3: 20–21; 31–35). And it is his mother who is the central authority figure, the father is never mentioned. The special relationship between Jesus and his mother is an important aspect of John's description of Jesus and his family. In the crucifixion scene John is the only evangelist to mention 'his mother and the mother's sister' standing under the cross, and this 'underlines the matrilineal and female character of Jesus' kinship world' (Destro and Pesce 1995: 276). Thus, although kinship relations continued to play a part in the Jesus movement as described by John, the dominant, male agnatic line is not represented. Also, several mothers of disciples are mentioned, especially the mother of the sons of Zebedee who plays a role in Matthew 20:20–28 in attempting to promote her sons within the Jesus movement.

These descriptions are made more intelligible if we consider the role of the mother–son relationship in Mediterranean societies. Malina (1990: 60) suggests that 'the mother–son bond is perhaps the closest Mediterranean equivalent in intensity of what people in the US expect in the "love" of a marriage relation'. And Gilmore suggests that the result of the upbringing of sons by mothers is 'the consequent emotional closeness and affective "symbiosis" of mothers and sons – a pan-Mediterranean trait'. This is supported by a wide range of anthropological studies which speak of the mother–son bond as 'the strongest possible bond between two human beings' (Portugal) or as the 'primary axis of family continuity' (Italy); it may even be described as 'indestructible' (Greece) (Gilmore 1987b: 14–15). It may be that this special relationship between sons and mothers can help explain the particular character of the Jesus movement: some mothers followed their sons into the discipleship group, whereas we hear of no fathers who did the same.

Thus, we see a distinct difference in character of the two most important close relationships: the father–son relationship is based on the father's (benign) authority and the son's right to inherit his role; a mother–son relationship has more emotional affinity and support from the son.[6]

We also hear of some relationships between brothers and between sisters (Luke 10:38–42), also of sisters and a brother (John 11). The first disciples whom Jesus called were two pairs of brothers (Mark 1:16–20), and at least two of them, James and John, form a dyadic pair where the kinship relation according to Mark's narrative (10:35–41) became stronger than the solidarity with the disciple group. But in several narratives and parables we learn about conflicts between brothers (Luke 12:13–14; 15:11–32; Matt 21:28–32), obviously intended as a negative example. The cultural expectation was that of unity and harmony. But the most prominent use of 'brother' in the New Testament is as metaphor, or a fictive kinship term, especially used in addressing a Christian community or addressing the members concerning their relationship to one another (Duling 1995; Aasgaard this volume).

CONCLUSION

It is time to sum up our findings after this attempt to look at 'family' in the context of early Christianity, from the perspectives of household, kinship and family as institutions and as systems of relations. There appear to be two groups of patterns. One is found primarily in Gospel material describing the Palestinian setting, the other is found primarily in New Testament letters set in an urban, Hellenistic setting. As both groups of texts probably are written outside of Palestine, most of them probably in the Eastern Mediterranean, the two patterns should not necessarily be ascribed to different settings, but may be due more to differences with regard to the influence of the Jesus tradition and conflicts with the surrounding milieu. In the picture of Galilee in the Synoptic Gospels 'family' is described primarily as 'household' in terms of a social, caring unit where resources are shared. In Acts the main role of the household is that of a unit which follows its head. Central areas of concern in portrayals of the family as a system of social relations are the father–son relationship, the question of inheritance, and the responsibility of sons to support their parents in old age. That is, the overarching concern is with family relations in the area of support and sustenance. The issue of kinship is broached as a question of the legitimacy of Jesus and his credentials as a 'son of David'.

With Paul and the post-Pauline authors we move into a different social setting. The social structure as 'household' is found here also, but the main focus is upon the household as a pattern of authority structures and relations between various members of the household. Moreover, the household is not viewed as an ideal in contrast to elite or political authorities; rather, the household with its patriarchal structure is portrayed as an integral part of the macrocosmos, ruled over by the emperor. Slaves are members of the household as a matter of fact, although their relationship to their master is different from that of husband and wife or father and son. Thus, although we find no specific terminology, there might have been an awareness of a special relationship between husband and wife and their children.

POSTSCRIPT: WHAT HAPPENED TO 'FAMILY' WITH THE RISE OF CHRISTIANITY?

The purpose of this chapter was to describe social and cultural *patterns* of family, household and kinship which were presupposed in the early Christian world, patterns which should be considered in studies of what happened to 'family' among the first Christians (see Barton, Barclay, Uro, this volume). Here I can only indicate some possibilities for studies building on these patterns. I suggest that the best way to start is to locate areas of conflict, i.e. where we find tensions within given patterns (see Verner 1983: 9–12, 64–70).

In the Gospels these areas are related to the dominant pattern of *household*. First, the life and relations of the household are viewed as an ideal in contrast to exploitation from 'outside', be it from rich absentee landlords or under the symbol of 'Mammon'. This places the household and its relations against the oppressive structures of the elite and political authorities. The household images in the Gospels also have elements of a break with patriarchy: the central tasks of nurturing and life-giving are characteristic of the roles of women (Jacobs-Malina 1993). Second, the description of Jesus and his followers also represents a break with the household pattern, but of a different sort, as for instance in the calling of disciples and the situation of discipleship (Mark 1:16–20; 10:28–31; Barton 1994). Since the household was of fundamental importance for economic and social support, and for integration into the local community as well as for participation in religious and cultural life, leaving this community was a much more drastic rupture than it seems in today's world. Did it imply not only losing the support system of the household, but also leaving the authority of one's father, as well as the authority of tradition and the association with lineage and ethnic identity (Neyrey 1995)? In such cases, discipleship was an alternative, a counter-cultural social structure, so to speak, in which the only influence of kinship structure may be in the form of brothers and mothers as disciples (Destro and Pesce 1995).

In the Pauline and post-Pauline letters we find conflict areas related to all three aspects of 'family' that we have discussed: household structures, kinship, and marriage and relations between husband and wife. The authors of the New Testament letters, apparently arguing against 'local' views, do not advocate leaving households upon becoming Christians, even if some believers apparently lived with non-Christian husbands or wives. Also, in households in which all members became Christians there were problems; the main areas of conflict concerned the role of slaves and relations between husbands and wives. Although it is difficult to pinpoint, it may be that the most important changes in Christian households compared to pagan ones happened in these areas (Sandnes; Esler this volume).

Written in the earliest part of this period, Paul's letters reflect a conflict over the larger Jewish kinship system associated with descent from Abraham and vital for Jewish identity. This continued importance of Jewish kinship is mirrored in Paul's use of it as fictive kinship terminology applied to non-Jewish believers. Likewise, a relatively small segment of the system of family as relations – the relationship between brothers – gained prominence as a terminology used of relations between community members (Esler; Fatum; Sandnes; Aasgaard, this volume).

The last conflict area lies in the inter-relationship between what was considered pagan influence and individual desire. External dangers were not described in terms of 'Mammon' or oppression by authorities, but instead in terms of *porneia* and the dangers of sexuality, against which marriage was an antidote (Martin, this volume). It is noteworthy that Paul does not speak of marriage as a means of procreation or as an important social institution, but primarily in relation to sexuality. This lack of interest in the institutional aspects of marriage leads to the question of the status of marriage among the first Christians. It appears that marriage was not prescribed or taken for granted as an institution for all Christians. Both in Jewish tradition and in Roman regulations in the first century CE, marriage was strongly encouraged, sometimes even prescribed. In the early Christian community, opinion was divided: there was a strong tendency to encourage asceticism, a non-married life. On the other hand, the Pastoral letters are witnesses to a patriarchal wish to curtail asceticism. Women who chose an ascetic life, without marriage, escaped the patriarchal household and thereby threatened the authority structures of society. Marriage and the renunciation of marriage created a long discussion and an ambivalent attitude to sexuality and marriage as an institution among Christians throughout Antiquity. The roots of this ambiguity are to be found in early Christian texts, not least in Paul's writings (Brown 1988: 44–59). This contributed to a situation in which *attitudes* to sexuality, to the body and to asceticism, more than existing social patterns, made up the cultural paradigm for discussions of marriage (Gilhus; Marti; Uro, this volume).

NOTES

1 For an attempt at a 'universal' definition, see Reiss: 'The family is a small kinship structured group with the key function of nurturant socialization' (Reiss 1971: 19).

2 See the discussion by Mann ('Persons, Households, Families, Lineages, Genders, Classes and Nations', in *The Polity Reader in Gender Studies* 1994: 177–94) in which he argues for a more complete social theory, adding inter alia household/family/lineage and nation to the three nuclei of social stratification used by Marx and Weber: social class, social status and political power.

3 For an overview of the influence of anthropology in Classical studies, see Humphreys 1978; for early Christinianity, e.g. Malina 1993; Esler 1994: 19–36; many examples can be found in the collections of essays edited by Neyrey 1991 and Esler 1995.

4 'Inheritance' is also a term that is much used in a metaphorical sense, e.g. inherit kingdom, Matt 5:5; 25:34; Gal 4:30; 5:21, identity of being a son versus a slave Gal 4:1–7; 30–31, cf Rom 8:17.

5 In a study of the Roman family, Bradley (1991: 6–10) points out significant differences: rather than the modern emphasis on intimacy and romantic ties, the ideal characteristic of a Roman marriage was *concordia*, a state of harmony between husband and wife, something which one hoped for in marriages that might have been arranged without much previous knowledge between husband and wife. Likewise, in a modern perspective it is odd to have the relationship between husband and wife described as asymmetrical.

6 This difference in the character of the relationship is continued in the relationship to uncles on the father's side and on the mother's side, respectively; see the

study of these types of relations (also father's sister and mother's sister) by Bettini 1991: 5–114.

BIBLIOGRAPHY

Abu-Lughod, Lila (1986) *Veiled Sentiments: Honor and Poetry in Bedouin Society*, Berkeley: University of California Press.

Balch, David L. (1981) *Let Wives be Submissive: The Domestic Code in 1 Peter*, SBLMS 26, Chico: Scholars Press.

Barth, Fredrik (1981) 'Role Dilemmas and Father–son Dominance in Middle Eastern Kinship Systems', *Selected Essays* vol. 2, *Features of Person and Society in Swat*, London: Routledge and Kegan Paul: 83–92.

Barton, Stephen C. (1994) *Discipleship and Family Ties in Mark and Matthew*, SNTSMS 80, Cambridge: Cambridge University Press.

Bassler, Jouette (1982) 'The Widows Tale: A Fresh Look at 1 Tim 5:3–16', *JBL* 103: 23–41.

Bettini, Maurizio (1991) *Anthropology and Roman Culture: Kinship, Time, Images of Soul*, Baltimore and London: Johns Hopkins Press.

Bohannan, Paul and Middleton, John (eds) (1968) *Kinship and Social Organization*, American Museum Sourcebooks in Anthropology, Garden City, NY: Natural History Press.

Bradley, Keith R. (1991) *Discovering the Roman Family*, New York: Oxford University Press.

Brown, Peter (1988) *The Body and Society: Men, Women, and Sexual Renunciation in Early Christianity*, New York: Columbia University Press.

Child, Youth and Family (1996) Oslo: The Research Council of Norway: Culture and Society.

Delaney, Carol (1987) 'Seeds of Honor, Fields of Shame', in D. D. Gilmore (ed.) *Honor and Shame and the Unity of the Mediterranean*, American Anthropological Association Special Publication 22, Washington, DC: American Anthropological Association: 35–48.

Deming, Will (1995) *Paul on Marriage and Celibacy: The Hellenistic Background of 1 Corinthians 7*, SNTSMS 83, Cambridge: Cambridge University Press.

Destro, Adriana and Pesce, Mauro (1995) 'Kinship, Discipleship, and Movement: An Anthropological Study of John's Gospel', *Biblical Interpretation* 3: 266–84.

Dixon, Suzanne (1992) *The Roman Family*, Baltimore: Johns Hopkins Press.

Duling, Dennis C. (1995) 'The Matthean Brotherhood and Marginal Scribal Leadership', in P. F. Esler (ed.) *Modelling Early Christianity: Social-Scientific Studies of the New Testament in its Context*, London: Routledge: 159–82.

Elliott, John H. (1981) *A Home for the Homeless: A Sociological Exegesis of 1 Peter, Its Situation and Strategy*, Philadelphia: Fortress (rev. edn 1990).

—— (1991) 'Temple versus Household in Luke–Acts : A Contrast in Social Institutions', in Jerome H. Neyrey (ed.) *The Social World of Luke–Acts : Models for Interpretation*, Peabody: Hendrickson: 211–40.

Esler, Philip F. (1994) *The First Christians in their Social World*, London: Routledge.

—— (ed.) (1995) *Modelling Early Christianity: Social-Scientific Studies of the New Testament in its Context*, London: Routledge.

'Feminist Reconstruction of Early Christianity' (1989) Special issue, *ST* 43: 1–163.

Fiensy, David A. (1991) *The Social History of Palestine in the Herodian Period*, Studies in the Bible and Early Christianity 20, Lewiston: Mellen.

Finch, Janet (1993) 'Problems and Issues in Studying the Family. International

Perspectives', in A. Leira (ed.) *Family Sociology – Developing the Field* (Report 93: 5) Oslo: Institute for Social Research: 16–33.

Finley, M. I. (1973) *The Ancient Economy*, London: Chatto & Windus.

Fiorenza, Elisabeth Schüssler (1983) *In Memory of Her. A Feminist Theological Reconstruction of Christian Origins*, New York: Crossroad.

Foucault, Michel (1986) *The History of Sexuality*, vol. 2, *The Use of Pleasure*, New York: Pantheon.

Garnsey, Peter and Saller, Richard (1987) *The Roman Empire. Economy, Society and Culture*, London: Duckworth.

Giddens, Anthony (1991) *Modernity and Self-Identity*, Cambridge: Polity Press.

Gilmore, David D. (ed.) (1987a) *Honor and Shame and the Unity of the Mediterranean*, American Anthropological Association Special Publication 22, Washington, DC: American Anthropological Association.

—— (1987b) 'Introduction: The Shame of Dishonor', in *Honor and Shame and the Unity of the Mediterranean*, American Anthropological Association Special Publication 22, Washington, DC: American Anthropological Association: 2–21.

Goody, Jack (1983) *The Development of the Family and Marriage in Europe*, Cambridge: Cambridge University Press.

Hanson, K. C. (1989–90) 'The Herodians and Mediterranean Kinship' I–III, *BTB* 19: 75–84, 142–51; 20: 10–21.

—— (1994) 'BTB Readers Guide: Kinship', *BTB* 24: 183–94.

Herlihy, David (1985) *Medieval Households*, Cambridge: Harvard University Press.

Humphreys, S. C. (1978) *Anthropology and the Greeks*, Boston and London: Routledge and Kegan Paul.

Jacobs-Malina, Diane (1993) *Beyond Patriarchy. The Images of Family in Jesus*, New York: Paulist Press.

Lenski, Gerhard and Lenski, Jean (1987) *Human Societies: An Introduction to Macrosociology*, fifth edn, NewYork: McGraw-Hill.

Love, Stuart L. (1993) 'The Household: A Major Social Component for Gender Analysis in the Gospel of Matthew', *BTB* 23: 21–31.

Malina, Bruce J. (1990) 'Mary – Mediterranean Woman: Mother and Son', *BTB* 20: 54–64.

—— (1993) *The New Testament World*, rev. edn , Louisville: Westminster.

Mann, Michael (1994) 'Persons, Households, Families, Lineages, Genders, Class and Nations', in *The Polity Reader in Gender Studies*, Cambridge: Polity: 177–94.

Matson, David Lertis (1996) *Household Conversion Narratives in Acts: Pattern and Interpretation*, JSNTSS 123, Sheffield: Sheffield Academic Press.

Moxnes, Halvor (1980) *Theology in Conflict. Studies in Paul's Understanding of God in Romans*, NovTSup 53, Leiden: Brill.

—— (1988)*The Economy of the Kingdom: Social Conflict and Economic Relations in Luke's Gospel*, Philadelphia: Fortress.

—— (1991) 'Patron–Client Relations and the New Community in Luke–Acts', in Jerome H. Neyrey (ed.) *The Social World of Luke–Acts : Models for Interpretation*, Peabody: Hendrickson: 241–68.

—— (1993) 'BTB Readers Guide: Honor and Shame', *BTB* 22: 167–76.

Moxnes, Kari (1993) 'Changes in Family Structure. Challenge for Theory Formation', in A. Leira (ed.) *Family Sociology – Developing the Field* (Report 93: 5) Oslo: Institute for Social Research: 91–109.

Müller, Peter (1992) *In der Mitte der Gemeinde: Kinder im Neuen Testament*, Neukirchen-Vluyn: Neukirchener.

Netting, Robert McC., Wilk, R. R. and Arnould, E. J. (1984) 'Introduction', in R. McC. Netting, R. R. Wilk and E. J. Arnould *Households, Comparative and*

Historical Studies of the Domestic Group, Berkeley: University of California Press: xiii–xxxviii.

Neyrey, Jerome H. (ed.) (1991) *The Social World of Luke–Acts : Models for Interpretation*, Peabody: Hendrickson.

—— (1995) 'Loss of Wealth, Loss of Family and Loss of Honor', in P. F. Esler (ed.) *Modelling Early Christianity: Social-Scientific Studies of the New Testament in its Context*, London: Routledge: 139–58.

Peristiany, J. G. (ed.) (1966) *Honour and Shame. The Values of Mediterranean Society*, London: Weidenfeld and Nicolson.

Peskowitz, Miriam (1993) 'Family/ies in Antiquity: Evidence from Tannaitic Literature and Roman Galilean Architecture', in S. J. D. Cohen (ed.) *The Jewish Family in Antiquity*, Brown Judaic Studies 289, Atlanta: Scholars Press: 9–36.

Rawson, Beryl (1991) 'Introduction', in B. Rawson (ed.) *Marriage, Divorce and Children in Ancient Rome*, Oxford: Clarendon Press: 1–5.

Reiss, I. (1971) *The Family System in America*, New York: Holt, Rinehart & Winston.

Rohrbaugh, Richard L. (1995) 'Legitimating Sonship – A Test of Honor. A Social-Scientific Study of Luke 4:1–30', in P. F. Esler (ed.) *Modelling Early Christianity: Social-Scientific Studies of the New Testament in its Context*, London: Routledge: 183–97.

Saller, Richard (1991) 'Corporal Punishment, Authority, and Obedience in the Roman Household', in B. Rawson (ed.) *Marriage, Divorce and Children in Ancient Rome*, Oxford: Clarendon Press: 144–65.

Saller, Richard P. and Kertzer, David I. (1991) 'Historical and Anthropological Perspectives on Italian Family Life', in R. P. Saller and D. I. Kertzer (eds) *The Family in Italy from Antiquity to the Present*, New Haven: Yale University Press: 1–25.

Scott, Bernhard Brandon (1989) *Hear Then the Parable: A Commentary on the Parables of Jesus*, Minneapolis: Fortress Press.

Seim, Turid Karlsen (1994) *The Double Message. Patterns of Gender in Luke–Acts*, Edinburgh: T. & T. Clark.

Something to Celebrate. Valuing Families in Church and Society (1995) General Synod Board for Social Responsibility, London: Church House Publishing.

Todd, Emmanuel (1985) *The Explanation of Ideology. Family, Structures and Social Systems*, Oxford: Blackwell.

Verner, David C. (1983) *The Household of God: The Social World of the Pastoral Epistles*, SBLDS 71, Chico: Scholars Press.

Veyne, Paul (1987) 'The Roman Empire', in P. Veyne (ed.) *A History of Private Life*, vol. 1, English tr. by A. Golhammer, Cambridge: Harvard University Press: 5–205.

Wallace-Hadrill, Andrew (1991) 'Houses and Households: Sampling Pompeii and Herculaneum', in B. Rawson (ed.) *Marriage, Divorce and Children in Ancient Rome*, Oxford: Clarendon Press: 191–227.

Wilk, Richard. R and Netting, Robert McC. (1984) 'Household: Changing Forms and Functions', in R. McC. Netting, R. R. Wilk, E. J. Arnould *Households, Comparative and Historical Studies of the Domestic Group*, Berkeley: University of California Press: 1–28.

Wilson, Richard R. (1992) 'Genealogy, Genealogies', *ABD* 2: 929–32.

Yarbrough, O. Larry (1985) *Not like the Gentiles: Marriage Rules in the Letters of Paul*, SBLDS 80, Atlanta: Scholars Press.

3

THE FAMILY IN FIRST-CENTURY GALILEE

Santiago Guijarro

Nineteen miles northeast of Capernaum the traveller can find the archaeological park of Qatzrin. Qatzrin was a flourishing town during the Mishnaic period if we judge by the splendid synagogue that its inhabitants built there. The visitor is pleasantly surprised at the sight of a house which the team of excavators had the brilliant idea of reconstructing as it was fifteen centuries ago (see Figure 3.1).

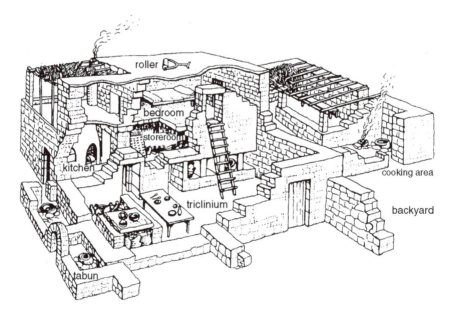

Figure 3.1 Reconstruction of the talmudic house at Qatzrin, fourth–fifth centuries CE (after A. Killebrew and S. Fine)

Ann Killebrew, who conducted the works over a period of nine years, says that, in order to complete the reconstruction, they had to take into account three different types of data. In the first place, archaeological data, which

42

had to be complemented with the results of similar excavations when the remnants were incomplete or non-existent. In the second place, the texts from the Mishna which, directly or indirectly, talk about the houses of the time, about their construction, arrangement, decoration, etc. Finally, in order to have a more precise idea of what the house they were reconstructing would look like, they compared it with today's houses in the Druse villages of the Golan Heights, which have preserved the traditional architecture (Killebrew and Fine 1991: 45–46).

The reconstruction of this house is an illustration of the way social scenarios of past times can be reconstructed. The contemporary texts, the archaeological data and the study of similar societies are also the pillars on which the recent studies of Galilee and the historical Jesus rest (Freyne 1994: 75; Horsley 1994: 91–92; Oakman 1994: 220–22). In fact, these studies have advanced as a result of the great number of archaeological excavations undertaken in that region in the last few years.

Recent studies on the Galilee of the time of Jesus have pointed to themes related to 'public life', such as the process of urbanisation (Overman 1988), the relationship between urban and rural (Edwards 1988; Freyne 1992), commerce and communications (Edwards 1992; Strange 1994), population numbers (Reed 1994). In contrast little attention has been given to 'private life', the life that revolves about the house and the household. Yet the family was the central institution of the Mediterranean society of the first century. Through the family, the wealth and the social status were transmitted; in the family, the individual found support, solidarity and the protection that the state could not give (Garnsey and Saller 1991: 151–52).

In this chapter I attempt an initial exploration of this theme. I will begin by recalling some of the external factors that could have affected the traditional family in first-century Galilee. Then I will consider some of the existing contemporary texts and the archaeological data. Finally I will 'read' this data against the framework of the social stratification which is characteristic of agrarian societies, in order to describe the different types of families that could be found in Galilee at that time.

EXTERNAL FACTORS

Oakman (1986), Fiensy (1991) and Freyne (1994) have called attention to some of the factors that had a bearing on the composition and the functions of the traditional family in Palestine during the Hellenistic and Roman periods. The most important of these was, no doubt, the accumulation of land in the hands of the elites. In first-century Palestine, as in all agrarian societies, land was the main source of wealth, and it constituted the basis of the domestic economy. For this reason, the traditional inheritance laws sought to keep the land within the 'house' or, at least, within the wider circle of the 'kinship group' (Wright 1990: 44–65); and for the same reason, the possession of land was indicative of social status. The combination of both elements (economic and social) made land the most sought after possession in ancient times, to the point that those who acquired land through commerce or by other means were normally trying to improve their status by investing in land (Oakman 1991: 35).

This is exactly what had been happening in Palestine since the beginning of the Hellenistic age, although the phenomenon of the concentration of land in the hands of a few families was more intense during the Roman and Herodian periods. According to Oakman (1986: 49–53) the most common procedure was to lend money to peasants with economic troubles, thus forcing them to pledge their land as guarantee of repayment. Taking into consideration the structure of the agrarian economy as well as the expenses the peasants would incur (Wolf 1966: 5–10), it was very difficult for a family caught up in the snares of debt ever to free itself. In most cases the peasant was unable to repay his debt and lost the land. Then, if he was lucky, he would remain as the tenant of his own hereditary land, with the obligation to give the new owner a part of its produce; the less fortunate ones would end up as paid labourers. In other cases the elite families would use less 'legal' methods such as coercion, deception or threats to force peasants to sell or to abandon their plots of land (Oakman 1986: 72–77; Fiensy 1991: 79).

The tendency of elite families to increase their economic resources and their prestige by the acquisition of land was bolstered by a set of political circumstances that affected the economy of the peasant families. Galilee was governed, in a period of less than one century, by the Hasmoneans, the Romans and the Herodians. According to Josephus the change from one government to another followed devastating confrontations, such as the destruction of Magdala in 63 BC by the army of Casius (*BJ* I. 8, 9: 180; *Ant.* XIV. 7, 3: 120) and that of Sepphoris in 4 BC by Varo's son (*Ant.* XVII. 10, 9: 288–89), in this latter instance, with serious effects on the economy of the peasants. Due to the ownership conception of the state which is characteristic of the agrarian societies, the new rulers felt that they had the right to seize a portion of the land for themselves and to exact a tribute for the use of the rest. We learn from Josephus that the land properties of Herod Antipas in Galilee paid him an amount of 200 talents a year (*Ant.* XVII. 11, 4: 319), and that Herodias (*Ant.* XVIII. 7, 2: 253) and Bernice (*Vita* 24. 119) too, had properties in Galilee.

There are also some indications that, during the tenure of Herod the Great, first as governor of Galilee and later as client-king of Rome over all Palestine, his economic pressure on the farmers was very severe (MacMullen 1974: 34; Oakman 1986: 66–72; Freyne 1994: 87–93). On top of the ordinary taxes on land, people, harvest and commercial transactions, we know that Herod collected special contributions when he was the governor of Galilee (one hundred talents: *Ant.* XIV. 11, 12: 272–74), and special taxes for his building projects, specially for the Jerusalem temple (*Ant.* XV. 11, 2: 389–90); he also sent troops to Galilee to be billeted there for the winter at the expense of the local population (*Ant.* XIV. 15: 411), which was one of the most dreaded impositions of all. Those special contributions and his building programme must have had a tremendous impact on the economy of the peasants, because – as in the case of the expropriation of land – the pressure on the elite families produced a cascade reaction similar to the one produced by the collection of taxes; the peasant families were probably the most affected (Fiensy 1991: 99–103).

The repercussion of Herod's policies for the lower classes of society explains the social instability of Palestine during his reign, and the revolts that took place at his death. Josephus refers to this situation when he says that 'at this time there were ten thousand other disorders in Judea' (*Ant.* XVII. 10, 4: 269), and that 'Judea was full of robbers' (*Ant.* XVII. 10, 8: 285). To this context belong also the petition of a tax reduction addressed by the population to Archaelaus at the time of the death of his father (*Ant.* XVII. 8, 4: 204–5), the disorders that ensued after the death of Herod (*Ant.* XVII. 10, 9–10: 286–98; XVII. 10, 10: 295), and the revolt at the time of the census, which was the means of controlling the population in order to enforce the payment of taxes (*Ant.* XVIII. 1, 1: 1–2).

Freyne has pointed out another economic factor that had an influence on the composition and the functions of the family: the process of marketisation of the economy (Freyne 1994: 105–9). This process started in the Hellenistic period, but increased during the Herodian period. One important consequence of this process was the development of intensive cultivation in order to meet the needs of a wider market. This intensive production was the cause of important changes in the structure of the traditional peasant family, because production was no longer limited to answering the needs of the family, but was intended to expand the market. The traditional family ceased to be the basic unit of production and became the instrument of the economy of redistribution under the control of the powerful landowners and the ruling class. To this type of economy seem to belong the farms of the Herodian period, similar to the one unearthed in Ramat Hanadiv, near Caesarea, where indications of intensive agricultural activity have been found (Hirschfeld and Birger-Calderon 1993).

To get a more accurate picture of what the situation of peasant families was like, we have to add to the preceding account the natural disasters that constitute a threat to any agrarian economy. During the Herodian period, the land of Palestine went through two seasons of famine and seven earthquakes, not counting the devastating effect of the locusts, the heavy winds and other catastrophes (Fiensy 1991: 98).

The repercussion of all these factors on the economy of the peasants has been documented by archaeology: the possessions of big landowners increased, while those of peasant families decreased. Jesus' saying: 'to the one who has, more shall be given; from the one who has not, even what he has will be taken away' (Mark 4:25; par. Matt 25:29) – which probably was a popular proverb – reflects the situation from the point of view of the peasants. The same can be seen in Jesus' parables where the 'latifundia' appear frequently to be cultivated by tenants (Mark 12:1–8) or by day labourers (Matt 20:1–15). The policies of Herod as well as the rise of a local elite who accumulated lands as sources of wealth and prestige, resulted in the loss of land on the part of many peasant families; they would either lose their property entirely, or see their estate drastically reduced. Thus in Galilee, as well as in the rest of the Hellenistic-Roman world, most of the peasant families did not cultivate their own lands, but those of propertied families, and most of the peasants were on the edge of subsistence (MacMullen 1974: 21; Fiensy 1991: 93).

The impact of these factors on the family is still a disputed question, but everything seems to indicate – taking into consideration the relationship between the family and the land in agrarian societies – that the accumulation of land in the hands of the elites not only increased their numbers but also enabled them to become more capable of supporting each other. On the other hand, as the peasant families lost their land, they diminished in size and in their capacity for mutual support. The scarcity of land contributed to the reduction and the dispersion of many peasant families when their plots of land were no longer sufficient to feed all their members. For the same reason, only one of the sons of the impoverished peasant families could inherit land; the rest had to look for employment as tenants or as day labourers on the lands of other people.

Although there are indications that the traditional Israelite family was still in existence in the Herodian period, the above data indicate that it was going through a process of disintegration due to lack of an economic basis. It was not a homogeneous process and it did not take place at the same time in all regions; it was rather a gradual process that began during the Hellenistic period. The two main consequences of the disintegration were that the power of the head of the family was weakened considerably, and that the peasant families lost the capability to help and support their relatives, due to the fact that they themselves were living at the margin of subsistence (Goodman 1987: 68–70).

DATA FROM THE TEXTS

Analysis of the external factors shows that the concentration of land in the hands of some upper-class families affected significantly the composition and functions of the family in first-century Galilee. A study of the textual and archaeological data in their proper social framework can help to make this first observation more specific.

Given the nature of the present contribution, I will consider only two representative and complementary examples: the autobiography of Josephus and the parables of Jesus. The first presents a view 'from above', the view of a member of the ruling class coming from an urban environment. Jesus' parables, on the other hand, may be considered as representative of the vision 'from below', the view of an artisan from a rural area. Both Josephus and Jesus knew Galilee very well; both had travelled the region from one end to the other several times and taken a close look at people and situations; but they contemplated the Galilee of their time from different perspectives.

The data about the family that we find in the autobiography of Flavius Josephus (Rajak 1984: 24–26, 118–26) makes reference almost exclusively to the families of the elite. In the first paragraphs of the book, he presents himself as a descendant of a priestly family on his father's side, and of a royal family on his mother's side, thus showing the social level he belonged to (*Vita* 1. 1–2). Later on, when he talks about the situation he found in Tiberias when he arrived in Galilee, he makes reference to three factions he found in the city. The first, whose leader has the Roman name of Julius Capellus, consisted of the prominent persons (*hoi euschêmonoi*); the second was that of the people from the lowest level (*hoi asêmotatoi*); whereas the third consisted of the bulk of the population of the city (*hoi politai*).

The description he gives of these groups is representative of the social stratification of Galilee and also of his own point of view. Writing about the first group he mentions seven persons by their first and last names (*Vita* 9. 32–35). He only dedicates one short sentence to the second group most certainly composed of peasants and disinherited people; he does not even mention their leader (*Vita* 9. 35b). He gives more attention to the third, not to the group itself, but to its leader, Julius, the son of Pistus, one of the group of prominent persons, whose party was integrated by the low classes of the city (*Vita* 9. 36–42). In the whole description, Josephus mentions only the names of the people who belong to the first group. The same is true for the rest of his book, which mentions only the names of the influential families of Jerusalem (*Vita* 38. 191: *genous sfodra lamprou*; *Vita* 39. 197: *hieratikou genous . . . ex archiereôn*) and of Galilee (*Vita* 14. 79: *hoi en telei*; 44. 220: *hoi prôtoi*). The data of Josephus on these families indicate two things: that they were very few in number (seventy according to *Vita* 14. 79 and 44. 220), and that their members were united by strong bonds of solidarity and mutual support.

A few examples can be useful to illustrate the characteristic solidarity among the influential families. The relatives (*syggeneis*) of Philippus, the son of Jehoiakim, prefect of King Agrippa, intervened to save him when he was in danger (*Vita* 11. 47). Josephus kept the objects stolen from the wife of the procurator of King Ptolemy in Taricheae, in order to return them to her, because he was a relative (*homophylos*: *Vita* 26. 128). His father, warned by a friend, told him about the snares that Simeon was setting for him in

Jerusalem (*Vita* 41. 204). Josephus himself helped a good number of relatives and friends after the destruction of Jerusalem, asking Titus for the liberation of fifty of them, bringing out of the temple another 190 who were there as prisoners, and pleading for the life of three relatives who were crucified on the way to Tekoa (*Vita* 75. 419–21). These data portray the image of large families, comfortably situated in the social system who, because of their numbers and connections, were capable of defending their members and of helping each other.

From Josephus we turn now to the parables of Jesus, which are an exceptional document, in order to reconstruct the situation in Galilee during the first half of the first century. In contrast with Josephus, who represents the view of the upper class, these short sketches depict the point of view of the peasants to whom Jesus addressed his teaching (Dodd 1983: 23). One would expect to find in them a portrait of the families of peasants, fishermen or day workers. But that type of story would not have captivated the attention of his listeners. As a matter of fact, in the parables of Jesus we find a significant number of individuals who belong to the elite families: rulers or aristocrats, who lived in big mansions, had servants to perform different tasks, and owned large amounts of land.

In some parables the main character is a 'paterfamilias' (*oikodespotês*). In the parable of the wheat and the tares (Matt 13:24–30), for example, the servants tell the 'paterfamilias' that one of his enemies has sowed darnel in his land. In the parable of the 'wicked' husbandmen (Mark 12:1–12 par.) we are told of another 'paterfamilias' who sends his 'servants' to collect his share of produce from the tenants to whom he had leased the vineyard. Another parable is about the 'paterfamilias' who should be awake and not let the thieves steal his possessions (Matt 24:43–44 par.). Yet another parable is about the 'lord' (*kyrios*) who went away leaving his household in the care of his 'servant' (Matt 24:45–51 par.). Finally, there is one about a man who travels abroad and leaves his doorkeeper in charge of the house, and the rest of his 'servants' in charge of his affairs (Mark 13:34 par.).

In two parables in Matthew's Gospel, one from his special source and the other from the Q source, the person in question is a king (*anthrôpos basileus*). In the parable of the two debtors (Matt 18:23–34) the king is such a wealthy person that he can forgive an enormous debt; in the one about the guests invited to the wedding (Matt 22:1–10; par. Luke 14:6–24), the king has lots of servants and a huge hall to accommodate all the invited guests.

Luke makes reference to the elements that defined the social status in ancient times: genealogy and property. In the parable of the talents (Luke 19:12–27; par. Matt 25:14–30) the owner of the house is of noble birth (*anthrôpos eugenês*) and owns a large amount of money that he distributes among his servants to do business with. In the parables of the crafty steward and of the rich man and the poor Lazarus (Luke 16:1–8; Luke 16:19–31) the protagonist is a rich man (*anthrôpos plousios*), and this is confirmed by the fact that in the first parable he has a servant who administers all his possessions and debts, and in the second the man could afford to feast magnificently day after day. Although it is not explicitly said, the father of the prodigal son (Luke 15:11–32) had to be a very rich person because, after giving the younger son his share of the estate, he still had a splendid house in which to celebrate a great feast, as well as cattle and fields with servants to work on them. He also mentions a judge (Luke 18:2), who was a prominent representative of the local leadership (Moxnes 1988: 55–58).

Even if we take into consideration that many of the details are to be attributed to the tradition of the early Church and to the Evangelists, it is evident that in the parables we hear quite often of families from the upper level of society: privileged rulers, propertied landowners and wealthy persons. Those families had spacious houses to celebrate banquets and feasts, and they had large numbers of servants with specific duties: stewards, porters, investors, collectors of the family's share of the produce of the land; they also had many fields to be cultivated by tenants (Mark 12:2: *geôrgoi*) or day labourers (Matt 20:1: *ergatai*; Luke 15:17: *misthioi*). These families, who in all probability lived in cities, appear in the parables in connection with 'latifundia' and absenteeism (Mark 14:34; Matt 25:14: *apodêmos*). For them, land no longer had the meaning that it used to have for peasant families, but rather was an investment, the produce of which was handled by slaves.

Although from different perspectives, both Flavius Josephus and Jesus make reference to wealthy families. Persons from other social strata are mentioned here and there: the inhabitants of Tiberias (*politai*), the people of lower classes (*asêmotatoi*), the tenants (*geôrgoi*), the day labourers (*ergatai* and *misthioi*). They, too, had their own families, but very little is said about them. It should be obvious that, because of their social and economic position, these families had to be very different from the families that appear in the parables of Jesus and in the autobiography of Josephus. This conjecture has been confirmed by the different kinds of houses from that time that archaeologists have discovered in the region.

ARCHAEOLOGICAL EVIDENCE

Compared to that of former and subsequent periods, the domestic architecture of Galilee – and of Palestine in general – during the Roman-Byzantine period had a wide variety of forms. According to Stager, in the traditional architecture of Israel we find two types of house: the simple house, which was the usual type in rural areas, and the courtyard house that was more frequent in urban settlements (Stager 1985: 17–18). These two types of house are well documented without interruption in Palestine from the second millennium BC until our own day (Canaan 1933: 33–47). Only during the Roman-Byzantine period can we find another three types of house: the big mansion or '*domus*', the farmhouse, and the shop-house. The differences between these types of houses are not only architectural, they also extend to the size, the materials used in their construction, and their furnishings. Such differences reflect very distinct social and economic levels,

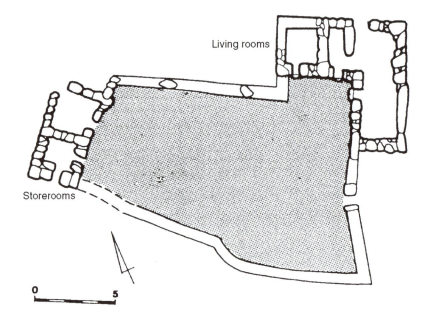

Figure 3.2 Plan of a farmhouse near Umm Rihan, first century BC–first century CE
(after S. Dar *et al*)

as well as the existence of different types of families. The following classification is done for the purpose of exhibiting these differences.

The first type is the *simple house*. This was the most common kind of house, in which most of the population lived. It was a quadrangular building joined to an external courtyard, where some of the domestic tasks were performed; the interior was divided into three or more rooms. The size could oscillate between 20 and 200m^2, but most of them were very small. The houses of this type that have been uncovered were made of stone or excavated in the rock. Some of the stone houses have been found in Gamala and in Meron (Hirschfeld 1995: 29–34). Among the houses excavated in the rock, the most representative are the ones of Nazareth, in the interior of which there used to be a silo to store grain and other products (Bagatti 1954–55: 11). These two kinds of simple houses are the ones that have survived until our own day, but in all probability they were not the only

50

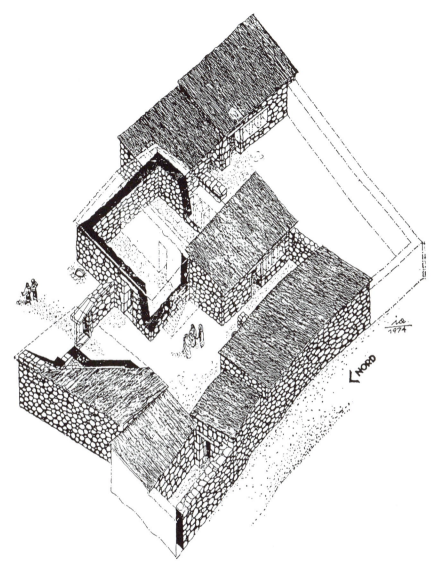

Figure 3.3 Isometric view of the insula sacra at the time of Jesus

ones, not even the most frequent ones. Studies on the domestic architecture in Palestine at the beginning of the first century show that, besides the stone houses and those excavated in the rock, there was a third kind of simple house: the sand-dried brick house. Although they have not stood the passage of time, they were probably the most common among the peasants (Canaan 1933: 33–39).

Some of these simple houses were enlarged later in order to accommodate the new families of sons as they got married, so that a complex structure would eventually result which was an intermediate kind of house between this type and the next one (Hirschfeld 1995: 44–50).

The second type was the *courtyard house*, which consisted of several houses with a common courtyard. This was the most characteristic type of domestic architecture in Palestine. The complex was surrounded by an external wall with a single entrance that gave access to the courtyard. Around it were the family houses with two or more rooms each. In the common courtyard the domestic tasks were performed – grinding the grain, cooking, spinning, washing – as well as some of the agrarian and occupational tasks. Courtyard houses from the Herodian period have been found in Dor, Bethsaida and in Capernaum. Those found in Dor were built in the Persian period, but were in use during the Herodian period (Raban 1993: 364). The building identified at zone B in Bethsaida was probably owned by a well-to-do family of fishermen (Kuhn and Arav 1991: 100–1; Arav and Rousseau 1993: 422–23). In the 'insula sacra' of Capernaum, as well as in the rest of the insulae (see Figure 3.3), the houses are of this type, with an average of four dwellings per complex. Insula II has gone through a lesser number of modifications than the 'insula sacra' and has been studied in more detail than insula III and insula IV (Corbo 1971: 269–72 and 280–83; Corbo 1976: 176–94).

It is commonly said that these houses were inhabited by members of the same family or by related families; this is suggested by the fact that there was a common courtyard with a single entrance to the complex. In favour of this theory stands the fact that, at the beginning of the first century, houses of this same type were inhabited in Palestine by members of the same family or by related families (Canaan 1933: 40–42). Each of the conjugal families that lived in these houses had two or more rooms at their disposal. The size of these houses – between 200 and 300m^2 – shows that the dwellers were families with a good economic situation.

The third type of house was the *big mansion* (*domus*). This type of house was introduced to Palestine at the end of the Hellenistic period (Arav 1989: 166–67). The oldest example found in Galilee are the four villas discovered in Philotheria/Bet-Yeraj (see Figure 3.4). The best preserved one is a 22- by 12-meter building with eleven rooms of different sizes, for different purposes, richly decorated with marble, stucco and mosaics (Arav 1989: 98). The entrance to these villas opens to a colonnaded yard surrounded by rooms for different functions. On the other side of the yard were the private rooms: the triclinium, the dormitories and the women's quarters.

Big mansions from the Herodian period have been found in Tel Anafa, Tel Auwaiad, Sepphoris, Magdala and, probably, in Gamala. The one of Tel Anafa was built in the Hellenistic period and remodelled during the Herodian period. The stucco of the walls, the mosaics and the zone reserved for the baths are indicative of the high social level of the family that lived

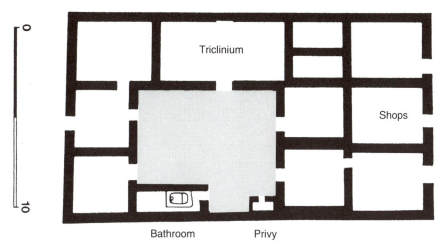

Figure 3.4 Plan of a house at Beth Yerah, third–second centuries BC

there (Herbert 1993: 59–60). Details of the excavation of Tel Auwaiad, near Tel Anafa have not been published yet, but Professor Vasilios Tzaferis, director of the Department of Excavations of Israel Antiquities Authority informed me last summer that a big mansion of the Herodian period has been uncovered there. The actual configuration of the Roman '*domus*' of the acropolis of Sepphoris is from the third century AD, but the two teams that have excavated the site agree that this house was built on top of another building of similar characteristics from the Herodian period (Strange 1992: 334; Netzer and Weiss 1994: 30–33). In Magdala, the building identified as a '*domus*' of this period was found in zone C, north of the synagogue (Corbo 1976: 362–64). Finally, in Gamala a big house has been found in the residential area, together with a spacious courtyard that seems to be the entrance to a '*domus*' (Gutman 1993: 463).

These mansions had space enough to house a large family and a good number of servants, as well as to receive clients and friends, and to conduct the business transactions and social gatherings that were frequently held in the large houses in Antiquity (Vitrubio, *De Architectura* 6: 5, 1–12). The existence of this type of house in relatively high numbers is one more indication of Graeco-Roman influence in Galilee during the Hellenistic and Roman periods.

Farmhouses can be listed as the fourth type of house. The farmhouse was a rural dwelling attached to an area of intensive cultivation. To date, three of these farmhouses have been found in Palestine, and all of them belong to the Herodian period: one in Judea (Kalandiya); another in Samaria (Qasrl-e-Leja) and the third on the sea shore, close to Caesarea (Ramat Hanadiv, see Figure 3.5) (Hirschfeld 1995: 50–55). None has been found yet in Galilee, but it seems probable that this type of farmhouse also existed there. The farmhouse in Ramat Hanadiv had a surface of 2,800m², and was surrounded by a wall. The living quarters were on the opposite side from the entrance, but most of the space was used as storage room for the farm tools and for the produce of the land (Hirschfeld and Birger-Calderon 1993: 1257–60). The living quarters could have housed a large family, but the storage capacity indicates that other people, probably peasants from the surrounding area, were working in the same farmhouse and on its lands.

Finally, some examples of *houses with shops* (*tabernae*) have been found. This type of construction, a very common one in the cities of the Roman empire, consisted of one room facing the street, and connected to an interior room that was used as living quarters. The number of 'house-shops' that have been

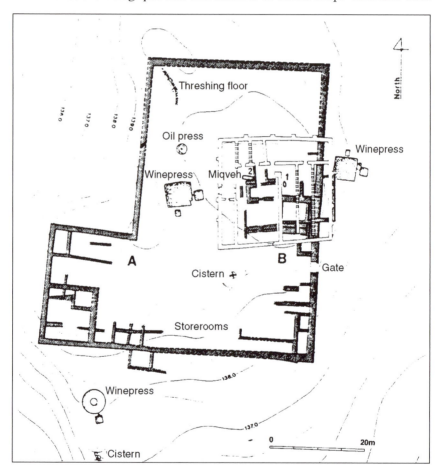

Figure 3.5 Plan of an extended farmhouse at Ramat Hanadiv, first century BC–first century CE

found in diverse places in Palestine lead us to believe that this kind of house was very common (Hirschfeld 1995: 107). In Galilee, this type of house was found in the main streets of the big cities, for the most part (Foerster 1993: 1464).

To date, no examples of big apartment buildings (*insulae*), which were very common in other cities of the Roman Empire, have been found in Palestine. This could be due to the fact that most of the buildings of the Roman period have been preserved only up to a certain altitude. It is highly possible that, as in other cities where this type of house has been better preserved, the apartment buildings were on the top of the houses with shops (Packer 1967: 83–85).

SOCIAL STRATIFICATION

From the archaeological point of view, the most significant phenomenon of the Hellenistic-Roman period is the introduction of the big mansions of Roman style (*domus*). This type of house was a foreign import not found before in the local architecture. This fact is indicative of the level of Hellenisation in the cities, as well as of the economic and social level of the well-to-do families of Galilee in the first century, and of their connection to and resemblance with the upper classes of other parts of the empire. Moreover, the presence of this type of house in the Hellenistic-Roman period coincides with the phenomenon of the accumulation of land observed by Fiensy (1991) and Oakman (1994), because each one of these big mansions required a vast area of intensive cultivation for its subsistence (MacMullen 1974: 38). Both phenomena in turn coincide with the prominent place that elite families have in the autobiography of Flavius Josephus and in the parables of Jesus.

Now, both the texts and the archaeological discoveries show that not all families of Galilee were of this type. Some families lived close to their relatives in courtyard houses; others lived in one-room houses that could accommodate no more than one 'nucleated' family, and there were probably poor families that could not afford to have a house at all. In order to have a more accurate idea of how many and what kind of people belonged to each one of these categories of families we need to resort to comparative studies of similar societies. The texts of ancient times, as well as the archaeological discoveries, are representative of the voice of the 'Great Tradition' which is the one that dominated the culture and left the most durable evidence. The other voice, the voice of the 'Little Tradition', can only be heard in this context by means of comparison with similar societies of past and present times.

The Galilean society, as well as that of the rest of the Roman Empire, can be described as agrarian. Sjoberg (1960) and Lenski (1969) have studied this type of society and give estimates of the number of persons who belonged to each of the component social groups. The social stratification proposed by Lenski has been applied more recently by Fiensy to the case of Palestine in the Herodian period (Fiensy 1991: 156–70). The conclusions of these studies help in a significant way to reconstruct the social situation in Galilee and to describe the different types of families and of houses in connection with the different social groups.

As we have seen, the main source of wealth in agrarian societies is land, which, cultivated by human and animal labour and using rudimentary techniques, yields a limited amount of produce. In spite of this – and this is an important difference between agrarian and horticultural societies – farmers produce more than they need to cover their basic needs, and thus they generate a modest surplus which is transferred to those who do not farm (Lenski 1969: 201–5). This concept of 'surplus' is important in order to understand the social stratification of the agrarian societies, because it is at the root of the economic relationship between peasants and rulers (Wolf 1966: 4).

In the most developed agrarian societies – which is the case of the Roman Empire and of Galilee – the rulers and their retainers take possession of this surplus on the basis of their right to taxation for the use of the land, and they tend to extract as much as possible from the peasants, resorting if necessary to pressure and physical force. According to Sjoberg this relationship between rulers and peasants generates a social stratification where three large groups can be distinguished: (a) the rulers and their retainers; (b) the peasants and craftsmen; (c) the unclean and degraded (Sjoberg 1960: 110–35). Lenski differentiates nine social classes that can very well be fitted into these three groups (Lenski 1969: 226–95).

The first group is small by nature, given the fact that the surplus produced by the peasants is limited, and that those at the summit of the social pyramid live for the most part in luxury. In this group we find the supreme ruler, the ruling class, the high rank retainers, and the elite of the priests and the prominent merchants with their families. The ruler and the ruling class, which amount to 1 per cent of the population, control one half of the total produce. In Palestine the rulers consisted of the members of King Herod's family and the families of the high priestly class (Fiensy 1991: 156–59). The rest of the components of this privileged group serve the supreme ruler and the ruling class in different ways, and they receive part of the surplus taken from the peasants; all together they amount to less than 5–10 per cent of the total population (Sjoberg 1960: 110). The second group comprises the peasants and craftsmen: they generate most of the produce in agrarian societies. The peasants, small landowners and day labourers are the majority of the population (about 70 per cent), whereas the craftsmen make up 5 per cent (Lenski 1969: 278 and 290). Finally, the group of those at the margins of society, consisting of the unclean and degraded, accounts for about 15 per cent of the total population.

Characteristic of this social structure is the lack of upward mobility and the separation between the social classes. The differences between the high and the low classes were enormous in terms of access to economic resources and to education. The privileged classes lived in the cities, which offered them protection, services and the possibility of contact with the privileged classes of other cities (Sjoberg 1960: 113–15), whereas most of the peasants lived in the rural areas with none of those advantages. This is what we find in the Galilee of the first century, the situation of which was not different from other regions of the Roman Empire. In the words of Fiensy: 'Palestinian society was divided. It was divided horizontally by the enormous chasm between the wealthy and the common masses and vertically by the cultural gap between the urban and rural populations' (Fiensy 1991: 170).

Another characteristic of agrarian societies, which has its origin in the method of production, is that goods are limited, and as a consequence, if one is to become rich, it must be at the expense of other people losing some of their previous possessions. In this context, the emergence and the progress of a well-to-do class in Galilee necessarily had, as a consequence, a worsening in the quality of life among the peasants and craftsmen, and their families.

When we place the data provided by the literary texts and the archaeological discoveries in this framework, their features become more precise. On one hand, we are able to relate the different types of houses found by the archaeologists to the families on different levels of the social ladder, whose style of life, occupation and percentage of the population can be determined with a certain degree of accuracy. On the other hand, the model we have described may help us to bring to light the corner of the stage that the Great Tradition has left in the penumbra: the corner comprising the lower classes, which made up the great majority of the population. Precise information on their way of life, and the type of houses they lived in, has not withstood the passage of time, yet any description of Galilean society that fails to include this immense silent majority is doomed to be an incomplete one.

DIFFERENT FAMILY TYPES

Putting all the above data together, we can identify in the Galilee of the first century four types of families, set apart by the type of houses they inhabited, the number of members comprising the basic family unit, the capability of mutual support and solidarity, the amount of land they possessed and the social group they belonged to (see Table 3.1).

Only a small percentage of the population belonged to *large families*. The houses they inhabited show that not all large families were equal either in their composition or in their life-style or economic position. Large traditional families (*bet av*) probably lived in simple houses of large proportions and in some of the courtyard houses, whereas the most Hellenised and

Table 3.1 Family types in first-century Galilee

Family type	Large	Multiple	Nucleated	Scattered
House style	Palace; big mansion (*domus*)	Courtyard house	Insulae? A single room house	Homeless
Components of the basic family group	Father, mother, unmarried children and married sons with their families	Two or more conjugal families	Father, mother, one or two sons and some other relatives	Hard to tell
Support from the kinship group	Mutual support and solidarity; interchange of favours	Support and solidarity in cases of need	Little capability to help because they live on the margin of subsistence	No support from their relatives
Access to resources; ownership	They control most of the revenue (taxes) and own big pieces of land	Some possess land or other resources (fisheries); some receive part of the surplus of the elite (retainers)	Some own small pieces of land; some have lost lands (tenants, day labourers)	They have neither land nor jobs; many are beggars
Social level	Rulers, high clergy, prominent landowners, business owners	Retainers, priests, military men, modest landowners	Peasants, craftsmen	Unclean and degraded; expendable
Resident in	Big cities	Cities and towns	Country (peasants)	Cities and country
Approximate percentage	1 per cent	9 per cent	70–75 per cent	15–20 per cent
Examples	Herod and the important people in Galilee (Matt 6:21)	Fishermen, tax collectors (Mark 1: 16–20: 2:14)	Jesus, farmers and day labourers (Mark 12:1–11; Matt 20:1–16	Beggars and sick people (Mark 5:25–34; 10:46–52)

wealthy ones would live in the Roman style '*domus*' which, in addition to be used as living quarters, were convenient for other social purposes: to receive clients (*atrium*), to invite friends (*triclinium*) or to store products from the land (silos, store room).

The basic family group living in the same house consisted of the father, the mother, the unmarried children, probably one or more married sons with their own wives and children, and other family members, to whom we have to add the servants and the slaves. The capability of mutual support and the solidarity between these family members was very significant and was supported by a network of patronage relationships that allowed the flow of favours to reach all members of the group. For these families, ownership of land was not only a source of income, but also of social prestige; hence their tendency to accumulate and to exploit it. These families were in the upper echelon of the social pyramid, where the supreme ruler and the ruling class could be found. According to Mark 6:21 (Freyne 1994: 96–100) in this group we can find the family of Herod Antipas (Hanson 1989a; 1989b; 1990), the great ones (*megistanes*), the military chiefs (*chiliarchoi*) and the leading class of Galilee (*hoi prôtoi tês Galilaias*), about seventy families, according to Josephus (*Vita* 14. 79; 44. 220).

A more significant group of people belonged to *multiple families*, a very common type of family in the whole of the Near East. The basic unit consisted of two or more conjugal families that were related to each other (usually two or more brothers), with independent living quarters but sharing other areas of the same house. The type of house in which this type of family lived was the courtyard house; the distribution of the space is indicative of the relationship between the members. While in the case of large families the rooms of the house were occupied by members of the same family, in the case of courtyard houses there is a definite separation between the space occupied by each conjugal family (living quarters) and the common space shared by all (yard, barn, silo, etc.). The relationship between the kinsmen living in the same house was strong in all respects, and their capability of mutual support was also considerable.

The families living in this type of house had moderate access to resources, and it is not by chance that the majority and the most representative houses of this type have been found in towns of medium size, like Capernaum and Bethsaida. Both Capernaum and Bethsaida were border towns and were on the 'Via Maris'. They were inhabited not only by tax collectors (Mark 2: 14 par.) but also by soldiers (Luke 7:1–10 par.) and businessmen (Loffreda 1985: 18–20). Fishing was an important source of income in both cities, and could provide for a multiple family, especially fishing with a sweeping net which needed a boat and between ten and sixteen people (Nun 1990: 16–22). Finally, the lake, which was the boundary between Galilee, Decapolis and Philip's Tetrarchy, was in all probability the channel for a large part of the commercial relationship between the cities of these territories. The boats, which were used for fishing only two months of the year, could be used for commercial purposes, thus increasing the income of the owners. The insula sacra in the vicinity of Capernaum, as well as the one found in zone B of Bethsaida, were owned by fishermen, which indicates that the social and economic position of fishermen was similar to those of the retainers. The farmhouse of Ramat Hanadiv could have accommodated a rural version of this type of family.

This places the multiple families at a social level immediately below those of the 'prominent'; they were the families of the retainers (tax collectors, soldiers, low clergy, etc.) and those which had a certain access to wealth through fishing, commerce or intensive agriculture. If the percentage of people belonging to this type of family in Galilee was similar to that in other agrarian societies, it would not surpass 10 per cent of the total population. It is worth observing that at least five of Jesus' disciples came from this type of family: Peter and Andrew, whose house seems to have been identified in Capernaum (Loffreda 1985: 52–66), James and John, whose father owned a boat and had workers (Mark 1:18–20), and Levi, a tax collector from Capernaum (Mark 2:14).

The great majority of the inhabitants of Galilee were members of *nucleated families*. I call them 'nucleated' and not 'nuclear' to avoid the identification of this type of family with the nuclear individualistic family which is characteristic of post-industrial western societies. The nucleated family can be described as a nuclear collectivistic family which has been forced to loosen its ties with other relatives because of external factors, but that still keeps some of those ties, especially with the closer relatives.

The houses in which these families lived consisted, as a rule, of a single room, both in urban and in rural areas. The majority of the houses of the peasants were not of stone, but of sun-dried brick, and for this reason they have not been preserved. Nevertheless, the traditional domestic architecture of Palestine offers a parallel model that can be used to reconstruct the form and the percentage of this type of house. According to Canaan (1933: 33–39), the majority of the peasant houses of Palestine at the beginning of the first century were sun-dried brick houses that were covered with tree branches; the interior gave shelter to animals (first floor) and to people (upper floor); they were unhealthy and small. The houses of the poor inhabitants of the cities (craftsmen?) were no different in any way from those of the peasants.

The size of this type of family is a matter of debate. Packer (1967: 83–85) estimates that the apartments of the *insulae* found in Ostia could house a family of no more than four people. According to MacMullen the average family size of the lower classes in Egypt was six people (1974: 27), and the same figures are suggested by Fiensy for Roman Palestine (1991: 87). Sometimes modern parallels of peasant families of more than six (husband, wife, four children and husband's parents) living in the same one-room house are proposed, in order to visualise the size of nucleated families in Antiquity, but we have to consider the difference between pre-industrial and post-industrial peasant families. W. T. Sanders, after a study of several pre-industrial societies, makes this clarifying assertion:

It seems obvious that the average nuclear family size, particularly of the bottom of the social pyramid in stratified societies must have been low, considerably below the average nuclear family size in twentieth-century peasant populations. The completed fertility of the average woman would have been comparable, with the difference lying in the survivorship of children. A census of such populations taken in a given year would show an average family size of not much more than four people.

(Sanders 1984: 12)

Poor hygiene, disease and malnutrition, which come with lack of resources, contributed to keeping the size of families of peasants and craftsmen within these limits. The capacity for relatives to offer and receive support was small, because each nucleated family lived on the margin of subsistence. This type of family was the most frequent among the lower classes, which, in agrarian societies, often reach 75 per cent of the total population.

To the preceding types of families, we have to add another type, of which the Gospels speak indirectly: those who, for different reasons, had descended the social scale to the lowest level: the slaves, the sick, beggars, thieves, bandits, impoverished widows, orphans, the disinherited. Most of these did not have a house or a family, and they could not count on support from any relatives. The political situation of Galilee in the first century (confiscations, debts, mortgage of land) leads us to think that this group of people was no less numerous than in other agrarian societies, where they made up from 15 to 20 per cent of the population.

CONCLUSION

The study of the external factors that affected the composition and the functions of the family in first-century Galilee, together with the texts and the archaeological evidence placed within the framework of the stratification of agrarian societies, has unveiled some aspects of the family that cannot easily be discovered when only one of these perspectives is taken into account. Nevertheless, the description of the different types of family is not an exact reproduction of reality. It is only a hypothetical reconstruction, a social scenario, intended to underline the most characteristic features. Reality was, no doubt, more diversified and more complex.

What has been said about the different types of families in first-century Galilee can be used as a 'reading scenario' (Malina 1991: 17–23) that may help towards a better understanding of the Galilean society of the first century and also of the texts produced by people who shared this social scenario, in particular those produced within the Jesus movement, which were included in the Gospel tradition.

First, the scenario that we have described warns us against a reading of the texts which may project onto them images of the family and home in the society in which we live, or the elitist image of the family that has been handed down to us by the ancient texts. The differences between the social groups that are reflected in the distinct types of families, provide us with a framework in which to examine the texts of the Gospel tradition to find out about the situations of the people they talk about as well as those who brought it about.

Second, in the traditional Mediterranean culture, the family was the basic reference of the individual, and the channel through which he or she was inserted into social life. To be born in a certain family was a decisive factor, because family was the depository of 'honour' and of position in society, and the transmitter of economic resources. If we wish to know the people of the New Testament and the way they were known by their contemporaries, we have to ask ourselves the same question they asked, the question that is still asked today in traditional Mediterranean societies when someone wants to know someone else: 'What family do you come from?' The answer will tell us his or her position on the social scale, possible way of life, religious attitudes, etc. Every piece of information about a person's family can help towards a better understanding of that person. Thus, the fact that a woman was a widow tells worlds about her situation of helplessness; in the same way, the fact that a peasant is working as a day labourer indicates, in all probability, that his family is small and he cannot count on the support of his kinsmen.

Third, the omnipresence in the literary texts of families of the highest class, together with the widely attested evidence of big mansions of Hellenistic-Roman origin indicate that Galilee was deeply Hellenised, and that the families of this social class – who lived in cities – were not substantially different from those who lived in cities in other parts of the empire. The growth of this group had enormous influence on the whole of society from several points of view. These families, being in control of the power and the resources, effected a change in the relationship between the traditional family and the land. The new relationship replaced the ideal of economic self-sufficiency with the ideal of maximum productivity. At the same time the relationships of reciprocity that governed the family circle gave way to the relationships of redistribution that placed the control of productivity in the hands of a few, through the market and the tax system. The families most affected by these changes were undoubtedly those of the peasants, whose economic and social basis of subsistence as well as their capability of mutual support were significantly reduced.

Fourth, the proposed scenario is appreciative of the echoes of the 'silent majority': the poor. A reconstruction of the situation of the poor is, of necessity, hypothetical, since we only possess at best faint echoes of their existence. Their voice has not been handed down to us in written literary texts, because most of them could not read or write. Furthermore, whatever the elite may say about them is highly suspect of partiality, because it may reflect stereotypes of social groups that are very distant from – or perhaps in confrontation with – each other and entertain very negative opinions of each other. Neither do we have the remains of their houses, constructed as they were of perishable material. Only a comparison with similar societies (the *fellahim* of Palestine of the beginning of the century, for example) can help us to have an idea of their situation, their life-style, their family type and the support they could expect from their kinsmen.

Finally, the proposed scenario may contribute to the study of Jesus' ministry in Galilee, because it helps to clarify some of the themes, like the polemic about his humble origin which comes up several times in various passages of the Gospel (Mark 6:1–6a; par. John 7:41–42; 1:45–46) or the question of the brothers of Jesus and of his relationship with his family (Mark 3:20–21; 31–35 par.). The contrast between the origin of Jesus and that of his disciples, of whom at least five came from well-to-do families (Mark 1:16–20; 2:14 par.), raises interesting questions about the people to whom he addressed his calling and what he was intending to accomplish by calling those people. The type of families to which these disciples belonged gives a precise meaning to the words of Jesus about the need to renounce their own relatives (Luke 9:59–60; 14:26; 12:51–53 par.), a rupture all the more difficult the larger the size and the closer the ties of the family to which the disciples belonged (Mark 10:17–22 par.).

This scenario also permits us to identify more precisely the different kinds of people encountered by Jesus, and perhaps the consideration of their family situation, which is indicative of privilege or of dependency, may help us to understand their reaction towards Jesus: on the one side, the people who followed him and acclaimed him, and on the other, the rulers and their retainers who questioned his message.

BIBLIOGRAPHY

Arav, R. (1989) 'Hellenistic Palestine Settlement Patterns and City Planning 337–37 BCE', *BAR* International Series, 485, Oxford.

Arav, R. and Rousseau, J. (1993) 'Bethsaïde, ville perdue et retrouvé', *RB* 100: 415–28.

Bagatti, B. (1954–55) 'Ritrovamenti nella Nazaret evangelica', *SBFLA* 5: 5–44.

Canaan, T. (1933) 'The Palestinian Arab House. Its Architecture and Folklore', *JPOS* 13: 1–83.

Corbo, V. (1971) 'Aspetti urbanistici de Cafarnao', *SBFLA* 21: 268–85.

—— (1976) 'La città romana di Magdala. Rapporto preliminare dopo la quarta campagna di scavo: 1 ottobre–8 dicembre 1975', in *Studia Ierosolimitana in onore del P. Belarmino Bagatti*, Jerusalem: Franciscan Printing Press.

Dodd, C. H. (1983) *The Parables of the Kingdom*, Glasgow: Collins.

Edwards, D. R. (1988) 'First Century Urban–Rural Relations in Lower Galilee: Exploring the Archaeological and Literary Evidence', in E. D. Lull (ed.) *SBLSP*, Atlanta: Scholars Press: 169–82.

—— (1992) 'The Socio-Economic and Cultural Ethos of the Lower Galilee in the First Century: Implications for the Nascent Jesus Movement', in L. I. Levine (ed.) *The Galilee in Late Antiquity*, New York: The Jewish Theological Seminary of America: 53–73.

Fiensy, D. A. (1991) *The Social History of Palestine in the Herodian Period. The Land is Mine*, Lewiston: The Edwin Mellen Press.

Foerster, G. (1993) 'Tiberias', in E. Stern (ed.) *NEAEHL*, 4: 1464–73.

Freyne, S. (1992) 'Urban–Rural Relations in First-Century Galileee: Some Suggestions from the Literary Sources', in L. I. Levine (ed.) *The Galilee in Late Antiquity*, New York: The Jewish Theological Seminary of America: 75–91.

—— (1994) 'The Geography, Politics and Economics of Galilee and the Quest for the Historical Jesus', in B. Chilton and C. Evans (eds) *Studying the Historical Jesus. Evaluations of the State of Current Research*, Leiden: E. J. Brill.

Garnsey, P. and Saller, R. (1991) *El imperio romano. Economía, Sociedad y Cultura*, Barcelona: Crítica.

Goodman, M. (1987) *The Ruling Class of Judea. The Origins of the Jewish Revolt against Rome AD 66–70*, Cambridge: Cambridge University Press.

Gutman, S. (1993) 'Gamala', *NEAEHL* 2: 459–63.

Hanson, K. C. (1989a) 'The Herodians and Mediterranean Kinship. Part I: Genealogy and Descent', *BTB* 19: 75–84.

—— (1989b) 'The Herodians and Mediterranean Kinship. Part II: Marriage and Divorce', *BTB* 19: 142–51.

—— (1990) 'The Herodians and Mediterranean Kinship. Part III: Economics', *BTB* 20: 10–21.

Herbert, S. (1993) 'Anafa, Tel', *NEAEHL* 1: 58–61.

Hirschfeld, Y. (1995) *The Palestinian Dwelling in the Roman-Byzantine Period*, Jerusalem: Franciscan Printing Press.

Hirschfeld, Y. and Birger-Calderon, R. (1993) 'Ramat Ha-Nadiv', *NEAEHL* 4: 1257–60.

Horsley, R. (1994) 'The Historical Jesus and Archaeology of the Galilee: Questions from Historical Jesus Research to Archaeologists', in E. Lovering (ed.) *SBLSP*, Atlanta: Scholars Press: 91–135.

Killebrew, A. and Fine, S. (1991) 'Qatzrin. Reconstructing Village Life in Talmudic Times', *BARev* 16, 3: 45–56.

Kuhn, H. W. and Arav, R. (1991) 'The Bethsaida Excavations: Historical and Archaeological Approaches', in A. Pearson (ed.) *The Future of Early Christianity. Essays in Honor of Helmut Koester*, Minneapolis: Fortress Press: 77–106.

Lenski, G. (1969) *Poder y Privilegio*, Barcelona: Paidós.

Loffreda, S. (1985) *Recovering Capharnaum*, Jerusalem: Franciscan Printing Press.

MacMullen, R. (1974) *Roman Social Relations 50 BC to AD 284*, New Haven: Yale University Press.

Malina, B. J. (1991) 'Reading Theory Perspective. Reading Luke-Acts', in J. H. Neyrey (ed.) *The Social World of Luke-Acts. Models for Interpretation*, Peabody, MA: Hendricksson: 3–23.

Moxnes, H. (1988) *The Econonomy of the Kingdom. Social Conflict and Economic Relations in Luke's Gospel*, Philadelphia: Fortress Press.

Netzer, E. and Weiss, Z. (1994) *Zippori*, Jerusalem: Israel Exploration Society.

Nun, M. (1990) *El Mar de Galilea y sus Pescadores*, Kibbutz Ein Gev.

Oakman, D. E. (1986) *Jesus and the Economic Questions of his Day*, Lewiston: The Edwin Mellen Press.

—— (1991) 'The Ancient Economy in the Bible', *BTB* 21: 34–39.

—— (1994) 'The Archaeology of First-Century Galilee and the Social

Interpretation of the Historical Jesus', in E. Lovering (ed.) *SBLSP*, Atlanta: Scholars Press: 220–51.

Overman, J. A. (1988) 'Who were the First Urban Christians? Urbanization in Galilee in the First Century', in D. E. Lull (ed.) *SBLSP*, Atlanta: Scholars Press: 160–68.

Packer, J. E., (1967) 'Housing and Population in Imperial Rome', *JRS* 57: 80–95.

Raban, A. (1993) 'Dor', *NEAEHL* 1: 357–71.

Rajak, T. (1984) *Josephus. The Historian and his Society*, Philadelphia: Fortress Press.

Reed, J. L. (1994) 'Population Numbers, Urbanization, and Economics: Galilean Archaeology and the Historical Jesus', in E. Lovering (ed.) *SBLSP*, Atlanta: Scholars Press: 203–19.

Sanders, W. T. (1984) 'Pre-industrial Demography and Social Evolution', in T. Earle (ed.) *On the Evolution of Complex Societies. Essays in Honor of Harry Hoijer*, Malibu: Undena Publications.

Sjoberg, G. (1960) *The Preindustrial City*, New York: The Free Press.

Stager, L. E. (1985) 'The Archaeology of the Family in Ancient Israel', *BASOR* 260: 1–35.

Strange, J. (1992) 'Six Campaigns at Sepphoris: The University of South Florida Excavations, 1983–1989', in L. I. Levine (ed.) *The Galilee in Late Antiquity*, New York: The Jewish Theological Seminary of America: 339–55.

——(1994) 'First-Century Galilee from Archaeology and from the Texts', in E. Lovering (ed.) *SBLSP*, Atlanta: Scholars Press: 81–90.

Wolf, E. R. (1966) *Peasants*, Engelwood Cliffs, NJ: Prentice Hall.

Wright, C. J. H. (1990) *God's People in God's Land: Family and Property in the Old Testament*, Grand Rapids, MI: Paternoster.

4

THE FAMILY AS THE BEARER OF RELIGION IN JUDAISM AND EARLY CHRISTIANITY

John M. G. Barclay

I recently came across the following prayer while on holiday in the Republic of Ireland. It was framed and hung on the wall of a farmhouse in Kells and was entitled, 'A Centenary Tribute to Our Lady from the Davis Family'.

> Eternal Father, we give you thanks that she who is the Mother of your Son is our dear mother also, by Divine Decree. *A Naoimh Mhuire, Mháthair Dé* [Holy Mary, Mother of God], for centuries you have not failed those who trusted in you. You brought us the peace of Christ in the midst of all our trials and sanctified our daily lives through the Family Rosary. *Céad mile buiochas leat A Mhaighdean Ghlormhar* [One hundred thousand thanks to you, Glorious Virgin]. The future holds no fears for those who trust you. So be a mother in our homes and in those of future generations. Let the peace of Christ be known to our children's children. May the pledge we make today of Daily Family Prayer consecrate our home to you always.

That prayer encapsulates something deeply significant about the conception of religion within the Irish Catholic tradition. It represents a piety which reaches back through past generations and forward into the future *through the medium of the family*. Each new generation is heir to a sense of loyalty to Our Lady, expressed in the Family Rosary and the Daily Family Prayer, and these function to sanctify the 'daily lives' of members of the family in every detail. Family life is thus held within a strong web of piety, and the persistent use of familial metaphors in this prayer serves to reinforce its sacred significance: God is addressed as the 'Eternal Father', while Mary is honoured as 'our dear mother'. Religion is here deeply embedded in the life of the family, permeating its traditions, expectations and daily practices.

My purpose in this chapter is to ask to what extent religion was embedded in the lives and ideologies of families in the ancient world, and to compare, in particular, the Jewish tradition with some features of the early Christian movement. By 'family' I mean inter-generational social units which shared a domicile (although, of course, the ancient 'household' did not generally correspond to our current idealisations of 'family'), and in pursuing our topic I wish to pay particular attention to the place of religion in the socialisation of children. A brief survey of domestic cult in the Greek and Roman worlds will lead into a fuller analysis of 'ancestral customs' within Jewish homes of the early imperial era. The third and final section will focus on early Christianity, which, by contrast to Judaism, will prove to be ambiguous in its attitudes to family life and varied in its capacity to embed its religious convictions within the domestic sphere. Throughout we will be forced to rely on evidence which is both sparse and sporadic, since ancient literature generally takes family life for granted and rarely bothers to describe its rituals and routines. But I hope at least to formulate some significant questions, and to point in fruitful directions for further research.

DOMESTIC CULT IN THE GREEK AND ROMAN WORLDS

Scattered literary references and the archaeology of domestic architecture do not afford as detailed evidence as we would like, but certain outline characteristics of domestic religion are clear enough. In the Greek world, and from time immemorial, the hearth was the site of veneration and the associated goddess, *Hestia*, was accorded great respect. The hearth represented the centre of family life; it was thus the appropriate site for domestic offerings and for rites which integrated the family (e.g. at the birth of a child). Also of fundamental significance was the deity, typically Zeus, who was associated with the food supply and with the boundaries of the domicile, honoured (though we know not how) as *Zeus Ktesios* and *Zeus Herkios*. Such domestic cult was usually distinct in focus from public and state cults. For instance, we find Athena everywhere in public places in Athens, as the tutelary deity of the city, but rarely in the private homes of Athenian citizens (Rose 1957). But prayers, libations and the simple offerings of portions of food and incense appear to have been regular and ubiquitous features of domestic routine. It was a rare family that did not feel the need to respect the powers which, for good or ill, influenced their welfare.[1]

Roman households also honoured the hearth (*Vesta*) and the *Penates*, the deities who watched over the store-house and guaranteed the food supply. In addition, they worshipped gods of the household known as the *Lares* (probably deified spirits of dead ancestors), who were often represented by small statues or paintings. Roman literature sometimes alludes to domestic sacrifices to these household gods (e.g. Horace, *Odes* 3.22) and archaeology has unearthed numerous *lararia* – household shrines – in niches in the dining room or kitchen, or as independent shrines in the atrium or garden (Orr 1978; Clarke 1991: 6–12). Roman habit often associated these gods with the figure of Fortuna and the Genius of the family – specifically the Genius of the *paterfamilias* – so that the domestic cult was intimately linked with the honour and prosperity of the head of the household. *Lararia* paintings show the *paterfamilias* flanked by the *Lares* offering sacrifice (e.g. Orr 1978:

plate IV) and the prologue to Plautus' *The Pot of Gold* indicates that other pious members of a family might offer daily gifts of incense or wine (Prologue 23–25). It was probably in relation to this domestic shrine in particular that the prayers and libations associated with meals were offered on a regular basis (Gooch 1993: 29–38).

Prudentius (the fourth-century CE Christian writer) gives an unusually full description of this domestic 'superstition' which 'runs continuously through a thousand generations, one after another', noting in particular its influence on children (*Ad Symmachum* 1.197–211). The young heir of the family shudders as he bows in respect to whatever his ancestors have designated as worshipful. Infants drink in such 'error' with their milk (*puerorum infantia primo/errorem cum lacte bibit*), partaking of the sacrificial meal and gazing at the statuettes of the deities dripping with oil.

> The little one had looked at a figure in the shape of Fortuna, with her wealthy horn, standing in the house, a hallowed stone, and watched his mother pale-faced in prayer before it. Then, raised on his nurse's shoulders, he too pressed his lips to the stone and rubbed it with them, pouring out his childish petitions . . . convinced that all one's wishes must be sought from thence.
>
> (*Ad Symmachum* 1.205–11, Loeb translation)

Such piety was, as Prudentius says, a matter of custom (*usus* 1.213): there were no sacred texts to regulate the prayers and sacrifices or to interpret the meaning of such rituals. But we may well appreciate the profound effect of the socialisation described by Prudentius. Infants learnt very early which powers to propitiate in the home, and the demands of *pietas* to one's forebears, living or deceased, made it unthinkable that a child would wish to break the time-honoured traditions or show less than full respect for the *paterfamilias*. Family loyalty constituted a cardinal virtue, and the routine domestic ritual, associated with the Genius of the head of the household, served to reinforce that loyalty by the subtle and powerful influence of religion. There were also special festivals which took place in a Roman family, in association with birth, at a boy's adoption of the *toga virilis* and in connection with marriage, and these embedded religion in the high points of family life (Ogilvie 1969: 99–105; Harmon 1978). Finally, the participation of the whole household in honouring its deceased members at their tombs and at the anniversaries of their deaths served to bind the family together in its multiform *pietas* (Harmon 1978: 1600–3).

THE FAMILY AND THE JEWISH TRADITION

Judaism of the first century CE was a greatly variegated phenomenon, but all our evidence suggests that the Jewish religious tradition was deeply woven into the fabric of Jewish family life, with connections as intricate and profound as those we have observed in the Gentile world. Although Judaism could embrace Gentile converts (proselytes), it was fundamentally an ethnic tradition: it fostered a conception and practice of religion which was bound up with Jewish ethnic identity, so that to be Jewish and to practise the 'ancestral customs' (*ta patria ethê*) involved a range of distinctive family practices which were of profound religious significance. As we have seen, Greek and Roman household cult was also an ancestral and therefore, in a sense, an 'ethnic' tradition, but the Jews' minority status and their fear of intermarriage heightened their sense of ethnic identity and made the family a crucial bulwark against social and cultural assimilation. Moreover, at least in the Diaspora, Judaism knew no significant distinction between domestic and public cult. The familial celebration of festivals and the observance of food and Sabbath laws closely matched the practice of Jews in the public domain. In this way, Jewish consciousness of difference permeated many aspects of domestic routine. Children were born into a tradition which it was assumed they would perpetuate, and they learnt from their parents what it meant to be a Jew. The family constituted the key arena for the socialisation of each new generation, who would be equipped to raise the following generation, in turn, as Jews.[2]

It comes as no surprise that the *Shema'*, a pivotal text in early Jewish liturgy, reminds Jews of their unique commitment to the 'one Lord' and to the commands which

> shall be upon your heart; and you shall teach them diligently to your children, and shall talk of them when you sit in your house, and when you walk by the way, and when you lie down and when you rise up.
>
> (Deut 6:4–7; cf 11:13–21)[3]

In this reference to 'commands' lies a significant difference between the practice of 'religion' in a Jewish and in a Gentile home. Judaism is not only a matter of 'custom' (though, as we shall see, 'unwritten laws' played an important role in the home): it is also founded upon texts and sacred laws, held to be of divine origin. That gives to the domestic practices both a greater degree of seriousness and an expectation of exactitude, since it is as important here as in any other sphere to know and to follow precisely what God has commanded. In Judaism, children could be taught not merely to follow the example of their 'pale-faced' mothers and nurses: they could be expected also to learn – and perhaps to read and study – the divine decrees which were promulgated for the ordering of their domestic routine.

Josephus claims that the Jewish tradition is distinguished by the care it devotes to the instruction of children (*paidotrophia*; cf Paul, Rom 2:20), and he makes that claim in a context where he emphasises the special character of the Jewish life-style and the commitment of Jews to preserve their inherited piety as 'the most important duty in life' (*Contra Apionem* 1.60–61). Jewish wisdom literature is, of course, replete with instructions about the raising and disciplining of children (e.g. Proverbs 13:24; 19:18; Sirach 7:23–25; 22:3–6; 30:1–13). Such texts illustrate the attitude, typical in the ancient world, that disobedient children who fail to follow in the ancestral ways bring very great shame on their parents. A number of passages indicate the specifically Jewish aspect of this process of socialisation. Susannah is recorded as having been taught by her parents 'in accordance with the laws of Moses' (Susannah 3), and the seven martyred brothers immortalised in *4 Maccabees* are said to have been taught by their father 'the law and the prophets', with the recital of famous biblical stories, the singing of psalms and the pronouncement of biblical proverbs (*4 Macc* 18:10–19). Josephus, in a later passage of the *Contra Apionem*, also claims that Jewish children are taught to read, and so learn 'both the laws and the deeds of their forefathers' (2.204). That claim may be somewhat idealised, as are also the later rabbinic passages which assume that children will learn to read in the home and will be given there an elementary education in the Jewish law.[4] Nonetheless, there is ample evidence that the law formed the core of Jewish identity and was the focus of weekly instruction in the synagogue, whence it was transmitted to the home (Philo, *Hypothetica* 7.14). Thus there is no good reason to doubt Philo when he claims that Jews have been trained 'from a very early age', even 'from the cradle', to honour the One God alone and to observe the Jewish law (e.g. *Legatio* 115, 210; *Praem* 162; *Spec. Leg.* 1.314; 2.88; 4.149–50). Indeed, both he and Josephus speak of the laws and the 'ancestral customs' as having been 'engraved' on the soul of every young Jew (*Legatio* 210; *Spec. Leg.* 4.149; Josephus, *Contra Apionem* 2.178).[5]

It is not difficult to imagine how this 'engraving' took place when one thinks in concrete terms about the daily and weekly routines of a Jewish household. Once again, Josephus provides some important clues when he describes how the Jewish constitution, in distinction from all others, combines words with deeds in inculcating its virtuous life-style. In particular, the commands of the law are put into routine practical effect within the home:

> Starting from the very beginning of our upbringing and from the mode of life practised by each individual in the home (*kai tês kata ton oikon hekastôn diaitês*), he [Moses] did not leave anything, even the minutest detail, free to be determined by the wishes of those involved. Even in relation to food, what we should refrain from and what we should eat, in relation to the company we should keep in our daily lives, in relation to alternate periods of strenuous work and rest, our legislator set the law as the rule and boundary, so that we might live under it as our father and master and not commit any sin either wilfully or from ignorance.
>
> (*Contra Apionem* 2.173–74, my own translation)

This passage seems to me particularly revealing of the sociological realities of the Jewish home. Josephus mentions in particular three aspects of home-life ruled by the Torah: food, company and the rhythm of work and rest. Each is worth considering in concrete terms.

The production, purchase, preparation and consumption of food is, of course, one of the primary activities of the household and it was crucial for the socialisation of Jewish children that, from the very beginning of their consciousness, such matters were known to be governed by their ancestral customs. Jewish *difference* in this matter from their Gentile neighbours – their peculiar abstentions from foods which others ate without qualm – reinforced their sense of ethnic particularity and made the daily meals occasions when Jewish identity was reinforced precisely by the fare that was, or was not, provided (see further Barclay 1996: 434–37). As 3 Maccabees makes clear, 'because they honoured God and were governed by his law, Jews created a distinction in the matter of foods' (3 Macc 3:4; cf *Letter of Aristeas* 139–42) and this close connection between religion and food must have been reinforced in each family meal with the giving of thanks to God.

Closely associated with food was the second factor mentioned by Josephus: the company which was kept. Both Jews and non-Jews recognised the importance of the social distinctions created by Jewish dietary laws, which typically (though not in every circumstance), inhibited social inter-course between Jews and Gentiles.[6] To be brought up in a Jewish home was thus to be made repeatedly aware of who were 'your own' folk and who were not, with whom one could risk meal associations and who would not be admitted to the primary circle of friends. It is here, in the home, that those limits are set by which 'casual visitors are not allowed to associate with us on an intimate level' (*anamignysthai tê synêtheia*, Josephus, *Contra Apionem* 2.210). Most importantly, the Jewish home defined whom a young Jew could or could not expect to marry, that crucial decision of 'company' which would determine the manner in which the next generation was raised.

The third aspect of home life mentioned by Josephus is the rhythm of work and rest, in which he is no doubt thinking primarily of the Sabbath. Although Gentiles also had lucky days in the month on which they might sacrifice to the *Lares*, there is no parallel in the Graeco-Roman world to the devotion of one whole day in seven to rest. The regularity of the Sabbath, and the special rituals in the home associated with its observance (Josephus elsewhere mentions the lighting of the Sabbath lamps, *Contra Apionem* 2.282), gave to the domestic sphere a particular importance in Judaism, which is still evident to this day (see further Barclay 1996: 440–42).

In such practical ways, and many others not mentioned by Josephus, Judaism was woven particularly deeply into the fabric of family life, and Jewish children raised in an ethos in which their ethnic distinctiveness was continually reinforced. Less regular than the Sabbath, though important highlights of the family calendar, were the festivals – especially Passover,

Tabernacles and the Day of Atonement – which Jews celebrated both in public gatherings and in private domestic settings. Passover was pre-eminently a domestic occasion, its 'hymns and prayers' an important family event lasting several days (Philo, *Spec. Leg.* 2.145–49). Indeed, built into the Biblical prescription for the occasion is a particular rule about instruction to children (Exod 13:8; cf m. Pesahim 10.4). Tabernacles similarly causes a dramatic change in the domestic routine and forms a family celebration in which even very small children can take part (cf m. Sukkah 3.5). Finally, the solemnity of the Day of Atonement, and its striking rule of abstention from food (perhaps not required of children, m. Yoma 8.4), surely made a big impression on children in Jewish homes. What is important here is the matching of the public and domestic spheres. Whereas festivals in Graeco-Roman religion were public events which might have minimal effect on the domestic routine, Jewish festivals were simultaneously communal and domestic occasions. They bound Jews both to their own families and to the larger community of fellow Jews with whom they shared such ethnic traditions.

Indeed, since it was as 'ancestral custom' (*ta patria ethē*) that the Jewish tradition was preserved, it was natural that the family, the conduit of ancestral traditions, should be the principal carrier of Judaism. References in Philo to the 'unwritten customs' observed by children from infancy (*Legatio* 115; *Spec. Leg.* 4.149–50) suggest that a good deal of what was passed down through the generations was that body of tradition concerning 'how things are done' which is powerful precisely because its origins are unknown and therefore (in Antiquity) taken to be unquestionable. In any case, it is clear that to a degree perhaps even deeper than in Gentile homes religion was comprehensively embedded within the structures, practices and ethos of the Jewish family. The family thus constituted one of Judaism's greatest strengths in the sometimes hostile atmosphere of the Graeco-Roman world.

THE FAMILY AND EARLY CHRISTIANITY

By contrast to the Graeco-Roman and Jewish traditions we have surveyed, the early Christian movement proved to be remarkably ambiguous in its attitude to the structures of family life and to the relationship between the household and the faith. On the one hand, certain trends in the new movement constituted a challenge to the common assumptions of family solidarity and loyalty, a challenge which endured beyond the first convulsive generation in the form of a powerfully persistent ascetic ideal. On the other hand, the household soon came to constitute the main locus of gathering for urban churches, and the later documents of the New Testament show how some branches of early Christianity began to invest much in the creation of Christian families and in the associated socialisation of Christian children. We may trace these two trends separately.

The challenge to the family

The pattern by which early Christianity spread and took root ensured that it could not function simply as an ethnic tradition rooted in the patterns of family life. To begin with, for those who were converted from a Gentile background, belief in Christ caused a fundamental rupture with their 'ancestral customs', abruptly and offensively breaking that religious tradition which had 'run continuously through a thousand generations, one after another'. The author of 1 Peter celebrates the fact that his addressees had been 'ransomed from the futile ways inherited from your ancestors' (*ek tês mataias hymôn anastrophês patroparadotou*, 1 Peter 1:18), but, as van Unnik pointed out (1969), that was a process bound to be viewed as a shameful act of disloyalty. For such Gentile converts, the Christian movement fundamentally undermined their family loyalties, and, as we shall see, frequently caused tensions with family members. For Jewish believers, the rupture with ethnic tradition was by no means so sharp, and in some cases may have been felt to be non-existent: such believers simply continued their 'ancestral customs' with an additional commitment to the Messiah. But as it emerged that the majority of their fellow Jews did not believe in this Christ, and as the Christian movement increasingly crossed ethnic boundaries and bound believers together in communities in which 'there is neither Jew nor Greek', Jewish ethnic identity was inevitably relativised in its significance (see Boyarin 1994).

Moreover, the early Christian movement brought into question not only ethnic but also family solidarities. Paul indicates the existence of Christians in mixed households – a Christian spouse, for instance, with a non-Christian partner (1 Cor 7:12–16) – and encourages them to make the best of their present situation. They are not required to separate themselves to create a new 'Christian family'. The advice to Christian wives of 1 Peter 3:1–6 also accepts the reality of isolated Christians in families hostile to the Christian faith. We may appreciate the pressure on such women if they refused as Christians to take part in the domestic cult (which honoured the Genius of the husband, the *paterfamilias*); they are told to hope, somewhat optimistically, that they may 'win' their husbands by their exemplary behaviour (see Balch 1981). Yet it is clear in any case that Christian identity did not require the creation of a Christian household. The Christian message embraced *individuals*, who were bound together, to be sure, in a new metaphorical family as brothers and sisters in Christ, but did not necessarily live, and were not required to live, within the solidarity of a 'Christian family'. Even children may be brought within the sphere of the Christian community without the acquiescence of their parents. In the second century, Celsus provides a vivid cameo of children being instructed by Christian 'cobblers' and 'washerwomen' not to pay attention to their fathers (or teachers) since they do not know the truth or the secrets of a happy life

(Origen, *Contra Celsum* 3.55); Celsus reacts with the outrage of a man whose cultural assumptions are greatly threatened by such behaviour.[7]

Similarly, the Gospels indicate the expectation that believers will be subject to hostility and even ostracism from their families. Mark warns his converts that 'brother will deliver up brother to death, and the father his child, and children will rise against parents and have them put to death' (Mark 13:12). Even if this passage reflects an apocalyptic *topos* concerning the chaos of the last days, there are enough indications in Mark that this to some extent reflects social reality as well (e.g. Mark 10:30). The same theme recurs in Matthew, and is even sharpened, with Jesus' mission portrayed as bringing 'not peace but a sword': 'a man's foes will be those of his own household' (Matt 10:34–36). As Barton notes in his analysis of these passages, the fact that Matthew includes such material in his Jewish-Christian context suggests that domestic strife was an important aspect of the parting of the ways between Christian believers and the Jewish mainstream (Barton 1994: 222).

Thus the practical effect of the early Christian movement was not to solidify but to undermine family loyalties for a significant proportion of its adherents. Whatever partial parallels there may be outside Christianity to the notion that commitment to God (or philosophy) might take precedence over family ties (Barton 1994: 23–56), the fact remains that early Christianity became distinguished by this characteristic, whose importance led to a fundamental reconsideration of the worth of family loyalties and of the family as such. This reconsideration could express itself in more or less radical forms. At the less radical end of the scale, Christians could be encouraged to reckon that their commitment to Jesus and the demands of his mission might require them to forego family commitments and to forge alternative 'kinship' relations with fellow believers outside the family circle. That, as Barton shows (1994), is the thrust of much of the Synoptic material, which portrays Jesus' tension with his own kin and his call of the disciples to give his mission a higher priority than the love of their family (e.g. Mark 1:16–20; 3:21–35; 10:28–31; 13:9–13; Matt 10:16–23; 34–39; Luke 14:25–27). Its most pointed expression is the demand that the disciple not bury his father, but 'leave the dead to bury their own dead' (Matt 8:21–22), a saying so counter to the family values of the ancient world that it is practically unparalleled in all ancient literature (Hengel 1981).[8]

At the more radical end of the scale, early Christians might reckon that they should refrain from creating their own families, thus challenging (in Halvor Moxnes' terms) not only 'family of origin' but also 'family of procreation'. Some Christians maintained that marriage and sexual relations were to be shunned on principle, in some cases because of their polluting effect, in others due to their encouragement of insatiable desires, or again because the chief function of the family, the propagation of the race and of the family name, was rendered pointless by the imminence of the kingdom of God. The power of these ascetic and eschatological motives is evident in many parts of the New Testament. 1 Corinthians 7 shows that Paul encountered ascetics in Corinth who advocated abstention from all sexual activities, and it is striking to what degree he agreed with them, on the grounds of eschatology: 'the form of this world is passing away' (1 Cor 7:29–31). It is largely for this reason that he considers marriage a second-rate option and, despite a passing reference to children (1 Cor 7:14), shows no discernible interest in the raising of the next generation.[9] He is, in part, overwhelmed by the importance of 'serving the Lord', just as a Cynic might ask who does humankind the greater service, 'those who bring into the world some two or three ugly-snouted children to take their place, or those who exercise oversight, to the best of their ability, over all humanity' (Epictetus 3.22.77; see Deming 1995). But the fact that he regards 'being anxious for the affairs of the Lord' as incompatible with anxieties for one's spouse suggests that Paul regards marriage, in principle, as less than helpful to the Christian cause. It is not, he insists, a sin, but neither is it, or the establishment of a Christian family, a positive contribution to the creation or preservation of the Christian tradition.

It was perhaps only a radicalised version of Paul's viewpoint which surfaced as the object of attack by the later 'Paulinist' in 1 Tim 4: here there is mention of those who forbid marriage, apparently out of Christian commitment (1 Tim 4:3). A comparable sense that celibacy was the better option 'for those to whom this saying is given' is suggested by the Matthaean respect for those who 'make themselves eunuchs for the sake of the kingdom of heaven' (Matt 19:10–12).[10] Such texts indicate that the principled renunciation of marriage and family life was an influential option in some circles in earliest Christianity, and (shockingly) not just for men but for women too (1 Cor 7:32–35; 40). While Christians might form fellowships which celebrated an alternative 'family' ethos, such communities could hardly secure the future of the Christian tradition into the next generation. Thus, the experience of domestic ostracism, the demands of Christian mission, the sense of an impending end and the first signs of a principled Christian asceticism combined to frustrate the routine embedding of the Christian tradition with the structures of the family.

The creation of a Christian family ethos

On the other side, the most important countervailing factor was the gathering of Christian communities within the households of their socially significant members, those *oikos*-fellowships which we hear about in Acts and in the letters of Paul (Meeks 1983). Here, since the household became the locale of Christian fellowship, it was bound to be affected by its participation in this special experience. Even so, it did not necessarily follow that all the members of a host-household were fellow-believers (Onesimus was not a 'brother' to Philemon until he encountered Paul elsewhere, Philemon 10), and for those who belonged to other households it must have been less obvious that the ethos of the Christian movement was to infiltrate the daily routines of family life. Indeed, it is not altogether clear *how* Christianity was to become embedded in that sphere. Christian households had no *Lares* or *Penates* before whom family members could express their solidarity by honouring the beneficent deities of the house. Nor, by contrast to Judaism, was it obvious where Christian belief should influence the customs of the house. Gentile Christians rarely bothered about Jewish food-laws – except in some cases in relation to food 'offered to idols' – so the daily production, purchase and consumption of food was far less obviously a 'Christian' activity. Perhaps specifically Christian prayers of thanksgiving for the food, which may be hinted at in 1 Corinthians 10:30–31 and Romans 14:6, are the most that could be expected here. If Christians did not observe the Sabbath, or Jewish festivals, where was their Christian tradition 'ritualised' within the annual cycle of family life? And in what context were children to experience that 'engraving' of the Christian tradition on mind and soul of which Philo and Josephus spoke in relation to Jewish children? Primitive Christianity appears to have been remarkably weak in this social sphere and ill-equipped to ensure its propagation from one generation to the next.

The first indication of a concern to embed the Christian tradition within the structures of the family is to be discerned in the New Testament household codes. These may represent, in general terms, the 'community-stabilizing institutionalization' of early Christianity (MacDonald 1988), but we should not miss their specific function in yoking Christianity to the household as the locus of its routine expression. To be sure, the habit of meeting in houses made such a development natural, but it is only in Colossians and Ephesians that these instructions first emerge, constituting a large proportion of the paraenetic material in each letter (see Crouch 1972; Lincoln 1990: 350–428). The trend which these codes represent is most clearly evidenced in Ephesians. Here God is hailed as the father from whom every family (*patria*) is named (3:14–15) – a prayer which suggests the sanctification of *lineage* as a divinely-ordained gift. More specifically, the household code assumes the solidarity of a Christian family (there is no hint here of religious tensions, as there is in 1 Peter),[11] and projects an image of the household as the context in which Christian discipleship is given practical expression.

Most significantly, it is here for the first time in Christian literature that instructions are given about the Christian socialisation of children: fathers are to raise their children 'in the discipline and instruction of the Lord' (*en paideia kai nouthesia kyriou*, 6:4). The precise nuance of the two nouns here – *paideia* and *nouthesia* – is difficult to determine. *Paideia* can mean formation in the educational sense ('training') or merely 'discipline'; the two were closely associated in Antiquity by the assumption that lessons were best beaten into children! *Nouthesia* can mean merely 'warning', but it seems to have the sense here of 'instruction' in more than merely a negative sense.[12] In any case, the combination of these two nouns with the genitive *kuri/iou* signals a perception that there is a specifically Christian way of raising children, and perhaps a specifically Christian body of instruction to be imparted to them. Indeed, the direct address to children (*ta tekna*) in both the Colossian and the Ephesian Haustafeln (Col 3:20; Eph 6:1–2) indicates their inclusion in the sphere of Christian education and the expectation that they will fulfil their family obligations (*en paideia kai nouthesia kyriou*). Not much later, Clement can talk of children sharing in 'our *paideia* which is in Christ' (1 Clement 21.8; cf 21.6; Didache 4.9; Polycarp, *Phil* 4.2), a notion which is given specific moral content in terms of humility, love, the fear of God and a pure mind. In Clement, as here in Ephesians, the family has become a key site for the practice of a distinctly Christian life-style.

This new grafting of Christianity onto the pattern of family life is beginning to be taken for granted by the time of the Pastoral epistles. The designation of the church as 'the household of God' (1 Tim 3:15) here determines the conception of the household itself as a church in microcosm (Verner 1983). Only those who manage their own households in an exemplary fashion can be trusted to manage the church (1 Tim 3:5), and they must set an example in having 'submissive and respectful children' (1 Tim 3:4), that is, specifically, children who are 'believers' (Titus 1:6). Women are expected to run a household marked not just by the common virtues of domesticity and sexual faithfulness (Titus 2:4–5) but also by the specifically Christian virtues of charity and hospitality: a widow, for instance, is to be honoured if she has 'brought up children, shown hospitality, washed the feet of the saints, relieved the afflicted and devoted herself to doing good in every way' (1 Tim 5:10). Perhaps here, in the routine practice of charity and the relief of fellow Christians, we have a notion of the specific customs by which the family would embody a distinctly Christian ethos. Certainly for the Pastor the identification of the Christian faith with the duties of the family is so close as to lead him to declare that 'if any one does not provide for his relatives (*idioi*) and especially for his own family (*oikeioi*) he has renounced the faith and is worse than an unbeliever' (1 Tim 5:8). We have travelled a long way here from when Jesus' disciples left the dead to bury their own dead!

The Pastor emphasises such conventional rules of family loyalty partly because he is engaged in a bitter struggle with other Christians (perhaps other 'Paulinists') whose ascetic gospel threatened to undermine the household structures on which the Christian tradition was beginning to rely (1 Tim 4:3). Indeed, here in the Pastorals we see played out the tension between the two opposing trends in early Christianity which we have traced above. The struggle engendered by this tension was to last for many centuries. Many strands of early Christianity display the strength of the

conviction that the 'new creation' brought by Christ must involve a fundamental renunciation of family life, with its social and physical constraints,
its enthralment to the desires of 'the flesh', and its compromised commitment to procreation and to the continuation of the 'present age'. As Peter
Brown comments in his brilliant elucidation of this stream of thought, such
Christians operated on the conviction that 'only by dissolving the household
was it possible to achieve the priceless transparency associated with a new
creation. It is the great hope which, in all future centuries, would continue
to flicker disquietingly along the edges of the Christian church' (1988: 53).
On the other hand, the Pastoral letters, and their subsequent canonisation,
show the concern of the 'Great Church' to secure its future, economically
and demographically, through the conventional medium of family life and
by means of networks of households and 'elders' who were to provide the
leadership of the urban churches (see Campbell 1994). The legacy of early
Christianity was sufficiently ambiguous on this issue to make the eventual
identification of Christianity with 'family values' by no means self-evident.
But the eventual re-embedding of the Christian tradition within the ethos of
the family was to have lasting effects which remain to this day, not least in
that moving Irish prayer with which I began.

NOTES

1 See further Jameson 1990: 192–95, noting that in time 'the hearth' often
became a portable brazier and that 'household ritual made do with the simplest
equipment'. Nonetheless, 'the daily consumption of food was accompanied by
simple offerings burnt in the household fire (whenever it was lit) and poured
on the ground' (p. 193). Wachsmuth 1980 provides the fullest survey of
domestic cult in Antiquity.

2 See further Barclay 1996: 402–13 on family and ethnicity in Diaspora
Judaism. D'Antonio and Aldons note that 'ethnic religion reinforces all levels
of family loyalty as sacred' (1983: 31).

3 The early significance of the *Shema'* is well-documented (e.g. from amulets and
mezuzoth), though the extent of its recitation (i.e. whether it included the whole
paragraph, Deut 6:4–9, and how early Deut 11:13–21 was added) is not clear;
see Reif 1993: 63, 83.

4 The passages are discussed by Safrai 1976: 945–70. Cf Rajak 1983: 26–29 (on
the provision of education in Judaea) and, more generally, Yarbrough 1993:
39–59.

5 Philo notes by contrast the dangers for those who are away from home on their
own without any 'monitor' from their parental home: they are liable to change
to 'alien ways', *Jos* 254.

6 On the extent of the social demarcation created by Jewish food laws see the
debate between Esler 1987: 71–109 and Sanders 1990.

7 Eva Marie Lassen's essay in this volume has rightly drawn attention to the
ready comprehensibility of Christian family metaphors in the Roman world.
But Christian social practice was probably more significant than Christian
vocabulary in shaping the reaction of Romans to the new Christian movement.

8 I do not think that this saying can be neutralised either by spiritualising it

('leave the spiritually dead to their own devices') or by appeal to the Corban pericope (Mark 7:9–13; Matt 15:1–6). If the latter can be traced back to Jesus, it only indicates that he advocated the application of the fourth commandment in one sphere while radically suspending it in another.

9 The reference to children is introduced only to bolster an argument against the need to divorce an unbelieving spouse (7:12–14). Paul claims that children of one believing parent are 'holy', though what this means in terms of expectations of their salvation or future discipleship is unclear; against his normal usage, Paul says that even the unbelieving spouse is 'holy' (7:14), though he/she may not be saved (7:16). The fact remains that Paul never mentions the raising of children as a reason for marriage.

10 I side with the majority of commentators who take this saying as referring to voluntary celibacy (e.g. Beare 1981: 390–91; Gnilka 1988: 154–58), *pace* Barton 1994: 191–204 who implausibly takes the 'eunuchs' to refer to those who do not marry again after divorcing an unfaithful wife (19:9). The final phrase in the paragraph, 'he who is able to receive this, let him receive it' (19:12), indicates that something is being required beyond the ruling of 19.9.

11 Best 1994 suggests that the author is being unrealistic here.

12 See *BAGD* ad loc.; Abbott 1897: 178 and Lincoln 1990: 407.

BIBLIOGRAPHY

Abbott, T. K. (1897) *A Critical and Exegetical Commentary on the Epistles to the Ephesians and to the Colossians*, International Critical Commentary, Edinburgh: T. & T. Clark.

Balch, D. (1981) *Let Wives be Submissive. The Domestic Code in 1 Peter*, Chico, CA: CA: Scholars Press.

Barclay, J. M. G. (1996) *Jews in the Mediterranean Diaspora from Alexander to Trajan (323 BCE–117 CE)*, Edinburgh: T. & T. Clark.

Barton, S. C. (1994) *Discipleship and Family Ties in Mark and Matthew*, SNTSMS 80, Cambridge: Cambridge University Press.

Beare, F. W. (1981) *The Gospel according to Matthew*, Oxford: Blackwell.

Best, E. (1994) 'The Haustafel in Ephesians (Eph 5.22–6.9)', *Irish Biblical Studies* 16: 146–60.

Boyarin, D. (1994) *A Radical Jew. Paul and the Politics of Identity*, Berkeley: University of California Press.

Brown, P. (1988) *The Body and Society*, London: Faber & Faber.

Campbell, R. A. (1994) *The Elders. Seniority within Earliest Christianity*, Edinburgh: T. & T. Clark.

Clarke, J. R. (1991) *The Houses of Roman Italy, 100 BC–AD 250. Ritual Space and Domestication*, Berkeley: University of California Press.

Crouch, J. E. (1972) *The Origin and Intention of the Colossian Haustafel*, FRLANT 109, Göttingen: Vandenhoeck & Ruprecht.

D'Antonio W. V. and Aldons, J. (1983) *Families and Religions. Conflict and Change in Modern Societies*, Beverly Hills: Sage Publications.

Deming, W. (1995) *Paul on Marriage and Celibacy. The Hellenistic Background of 1 Corinthians 7*, SNTSMS 83, Cambridge: Cambridge University Press.

Esler, P. F. (1987) *Community and Gospel in Luke-Acts*, SNTSMS 57, Cambridge: Cambridge University Press.

Gnilka, J. (1988) *Das Matthäusevangelium*, vol. 2, Freiburg: Herder.

Gooch, P. D. (1993) *Dangerous Food. 1 Corinthians 8–10 in Its Context*, Waterloo: Wilfrid Laurier University Press.

Harmon, D. P. (1978) 'The Family Festivals of Rome', in *ANRW* II, 16.2: 1592–603.

Hengel, M. (1981) *The Charismatic Leader and his Followers*, Edinburgh: T. & T. Clark.

Jameson, M. (1990) 'Private Space and the Greek City', in O. Murray and S. Price (eds) *The Greek City from Homer to Alexander*, Oxford: Clarendon Press: 171–95.

Lincoln, A. T. (1990) *Ephesians*, Word Biblical Commentary, Dallas: Word Books.

MacDonald, M. Y. (1988) *The Pauline Churches. A Socio-historical Study of Institutionalization in the Pauline and Deutero-Pauline Writings*, SNTSMS 60, Cambridge: Cambridge University Press.

Meeks, W. A. (1983) *The First Urban Christians*, New Haven: Yale University Press.

Ogilvie, R. M. (1969) *The Romans and their Gods in the Age of Augustus*, London: Chatto & Windus.

Orr, D. G. (1978) 'Roman Domestic Religion: The Evidence of the Household Shrines', in *ANRW* II, 16.2: 1557–91.

Rajak, T. (1983) *Josephus. The Historian and His Society*, London: Duckworth.

Reif, S. (1993) *Judaism and Hebrew Prayer*, Cambridge: Cambridge University Press.

Rose, H. J. (1957) 'The Religion of a Greek Household', *Euphrosune* 1, 95–116.

Safrai, S. (1976) 'Education and the Study of the Law', in S. Safrai and M. Stern (eds) *The Jewish People in the First Century*, Compendia Rerum Iudaicarum ad Novum Testamentum I.2, Assen: Van Gorcum; Philadelphia: Fortress Press: 945–70.

Sanders, E. P. (1990) 'Jewish Association with Gentiles and Galatians 2:11–14', in R. T. Fortna and B. R. Gaventa (eds) *The Conversation Continues. Studies in Paul and John in Honor of J. Louis Martyn*, Nashville: Abingdon Press: 170–88.

van Unnik, W. C. (1969) 'The Critique of Paganism in 1 Peter 1:18', in E. E. Ellis and M. Wilcox (eds) *Neotestamentica et Semitica. Studies in Honour of Matthew Black*, Edinburgh: T. & T. Clark: 129–42.

Verner, D. C. (1983) *The Household of God. The Social World of the Pastoral Epistles*, Chico, CA: Scholars Press.

Wachsmuth, D. (1980) 'Aspekte des Antiken Mediterranen Hauskults', *Numen* 27: 34–75.

Yarbrough, O. L. (1993) 'Parents and Children in the Jewish Family of Antiquity', in S. J. D. Cohen (ed.) *The Jewish Family in Antiquity*, Atlanta: Scholars Press: 39–59.

5

THE RELATIVISATION OF FAMILY TIES IN THE JEWISH AND GRAECO-ROMAN TRADITIONS

Stephen C. Barton

INTRODUCTION

The Gospel traditions provide clear evidence that Jesus' call to discipleship explicitly sanctioned the relativisation of kinship and household ties:

> He who loves father or mother more than me is not worthy of me; and he who loves son or daughter more than me is not worthy of me; and he who does not take his cross and follow me is not worthy of me.
>
> (Matt 10:37–38; par. Luke 14:26–27)

The aim of this chapter is to show that this kind of demand was not unprecedented in the traditions and practices of either Judaism or of the Graeco-Roman world as a whole. On the contrary, there is a wide range of evidence, not yet sufficiently explored, which indicates that subordinating mundane ties of all kinds was a rhetorical theme and a mode of action deeply rooted in the traditions of Jewish monotheism. Nor was it without analogy in Graeco-Roman traditions to do with the cost of conversion to the life of the philosopher. Without such roots and analogies, it is doubtful that the Gospel material relativising family ties could have been meaningful or persuasive to its hearers and readers.

In the space available, I can only be selective: I have given a more detailed account elsewhere (Barton 1994). An awareness of the various forms of 'hostility' to family in the ancient sources will render more intelligible what we find in the Gospels and provide a comparative historical setting within which to interpret the nuances of the Gospel material more adequately. My own view is that the 'anti-family' material in the Gospels is primarily a rhetorically powerful metaphorical way of calling for the displacement of every obstacle to true discipleship of Jesus in the light of the imminent coming of the kingdom of God.

THE EVIDENCE OF PHILO OF ALEXANDRIA

Family ties constitute a recurrent theme in the writings of Philo (c. 20 BC –50 CE) and provide a major idiom in terms of which Philo expresses his fundamental religious and philosophical preoccupations (cf Baer 1970). What is striking, for our purposes, is how frequently family ties become an idiom of discourse or a focus of attention in their own right and how common is the idea of the subordination or redefinition of family ties for the sake of a greater good.

Presuppositions

In a significant comment upon the scriptural warning against going after false prophets in Deut 13:1–11, Philo expresses a conviction fundamental to Judaism as a whole, that the observance of the command not to go after other gods is a mandatory obligation which transcends family allegiance:

> And if a brother or son or daughter or wife or a housemate or a friend, however true . . . urges us to a like course, bidding us fraternize with the multitude, resort to their temples, and join in their libations and sacrifices, we must punish him as a public and general enemy, taking little thought for the ties which bind us to him. . . . For we should have one tie of affinity, one accepted sign of goodwill, namely the willingness to serve God, and that our every word and deed promotes the cause of piety . . .
>
> (*Spec. Leg.* I.316–17)[1]

Here is a transparent statement of religious absolutes in the light of which natural and social ties are relativised profoundly. First, conjugal and consanguinal ties are made subordinate to the 'one tie' of devotion to God, summed up in the word *eusebeia*. Second, this one tie provides the basis for a higher kinship, where kinship relations are redefined in spiritual terms. So Philo goes on to describe as sons of God those 'who do "what is pleasing" to nature and what is "good"'; and the corollary of this spiritual kinship is to regard God as a father (*Spec. Leg.* I. 318). Third, whereas the deuteronomic law is concerned primarily with the penalties to be exacted upon all who transgress the commandment, Philo draws a positive implication, as well, namely, that just as *eusebeia* takes precedence over ties of natural kinship, so there is a bond uniting the pious which is also superior to bonds of marriage and blood. This then becomes a basis for patterns of association no longer determined solely by family ties, such as the Therapeutae and the Essenes, as we shall see.

Proselytes

It is not surprising that a thoroughly Hellenised Jew like Philo, an inhabitant of the large and cosmopolitan city of Alexandria, should refer frequently to what was involved for a proselyte in converting to Judaism. What is significant is the extent to which the transfer to Judaism is cast in terms of its effect on family ties. The proselyte is characterised as one who has left his home and native land and become incorporated into a new family.

Especially interesting is Philo's interpretation of the Biblical law concerning hospitality to the sojourner (*LXX*, *prosêlytos*), in *Spec. Leg.* I. 51–53 (cf Lev 19:33–34; Deut 10:18–19). According to Philo, Moses is referring to the treatment to be accorded converts; and it is noteworthy that family ties are invoked, not only as representative of what the proselyte has left behind, but also as an essential aspect of what he has converted to: 'they have left, he [*sc.* Moses] says, their country, their kinsfolk and their friends for the sake of virtue and religion. Let them not be denied another citizenship or other ties of family and friendship . . . ' (p. 52). This is not an isolated example. There are at least three others,[2] and in each case the transfer from paganism to Judaism is expressed in terms of family ties and their corollaries – homeland, native customs and deities, ancestors and friends.

What Philo says about proselytes is quite consistent with what we found earlier about his presuppositions. Clearly, Philo's commitment to family ties is not absolute. There are motives and circumstances which allow, indeed require, their subordination. What is significant for our purposes is how frequently religious and philosophical conversion is depicted with reference to its social, and above all familial, corollaries. The change of belief involves a change of community as well. It is important to add that such beliefs and practices do not go unnoticed from outside Judaism, either. For Tacitus, for example, they exemplify the misanthropy of the Jews and the social irresponsibility of those who convert to Judaism.[3]

Model communities

In depicting the Therapeutae as philosophers devoted to the pursuit of *eusebeia* through the life of contemplation, Philo emphasises both the asceticism of their life-style and the character of their community as a spiritual family. Both of these aspects are of interest for our study.

Their asceticism is seen in many ways. First, in the abandonment of property. Unlike the Essenes, who pool their resources upon entry, the Therapeutae leave their property to their heirs as an early inheritance. This shows that the Therapeutae are not antagonistic to family ties as such: only that the call to contemplation and the worship of *to on* (the self-existent) is a higher priority, that of the spiritual over the material. Second is their separation from family, which Philo describes in *De Vita Contemplativa* 18:

> So when they have divested themselves of their possessions and have no longer aught to ensnare them they flee without a backward glance and leave their brothers, their children, their wives, their parents, the wide circle of their kinsfolk, the groups of friends around them, the fatherlands in which they were born and reared, since so strong is the attraction of familiarity and very great its power to ensnare.

Samuel Sandmel has pointed out that Philo here ascribes to a group of his contemporaries behaviour which elsewhere he ascribes to an individual contemplative of the past, namely Abraham (Sandmel 1971: 95). This is certainly true, for on numerous occasions Philo draws attention to Abraham's departure from homeland and native kin in obedience to the higher demand of God, piety and the things of the spirit.[4] So Philo's depiction of the Therapeutae is idealising. They are made to exemplify the platonic elevation of the immaterial above the material and of the soul above the body, an ideology for which Abraham serves as the primary type from amongst the patriarchs. Property and family ties serve in such discourse as a fundamental instance of the kind of material and sensory concerns which can distract the pious from the spiritual quest. The abandonment of property ties and the subordination of family ties are part of the rhetoric of Philo's argument for the pursuit of piety through a life of contemplation.

Although the Therapeutae live a life of ascetic renunciation,[5] their philosophy is not anti-social. Rather, they constitute an alternative society, many in fact congregating in a community near Alexandria on a hill above the Mareotic Lake. Contemplation in solitude and living in community are held together. Significantly, this alternative society is depicted partly in familial terms. The Therapeutae live in houses (*oikiai*) either singly or in small groups (of men or women): Philo does not specify. They regard their place of settlement 'as their fatherland' (*kathaper eis patrida*). At the communal meal every sabbath, those who serve, says Philo,

> give their services gladly and proudly like sons to their real fathers and mothers, judging them to be the parents of them all in common, in a closer affinity than that of blood, since to the right minded there is no closer tie than noble living.

(Vit. Cont. 72)

Here, as elsewhere in Philo, it is spiritual kinship which is of greatest importance, and this transforms normal patterns. In consequence, the household patterns of the wider society are turned on their head. There are no slaves to serve at meals; seniority is determined by the length of time spent in the contemplative life rather than by natural age; women and men live together in community, but do so as celibates; and household-based economic practices have been given up.

Here, then, we have a community of religious *virtuosi* in which the power of household ties and sexual identity is redirected – or better, *reinterpreted* – to form the basis of an alternative society where the pattern of relationships is determined by training in wisdom and piety rather than property-owner-ship and consanguinity, and where sexual differences are transcended both in the ascetic quest for virtue and in ecstatic worship (cf *Vit. Cont.* 83–89). Putting it sociologically, the shift is from social relations based on ascribed status (related to 'natural' circumstances like birth and marital alliance) to social relations based on achieved status (related to individual or group initiative).

One effect of this transformation of household norms is worthy of note. In concluding his account, Philo says that the Therapeutae 'have lived in the soul alone, citizens of Heaven and the world (*ouranou men kai kosmou politôn*), presented to the Father and Maker of all by their faithful sponsor Virtue' (*Vit. Cont.* 90). Clearly, the abandoning of family and possessions – ties parochial in scope, distracting in demand, and divisive (or at least differenti-ating) in practice – makes possible a universalism of appeal otherwise unavailable or severely limited. This is why adherents of both sexes gathered 'from every side (*pantachothen*)' to a new 'fatherland' (*Vit. Cont.* 22). The extent to which the subordination and redefinition of household ties in early Christianity was related to its universalistic ethos is likely to have been significant also. In Philo, it is a matter of philosophical ideal and social pragmatism: in early Christianity, it is a matter of eschatological mission and inclusive community.

The communalism of the Essenes is well known (cf Schürer 1973ff: II: 562–74), and Philo is one of our primary sources, describing their ethos and life-style in two places: *Quod omnis Probus Liber sit* 75–91 and *Hypothetica* II. 1–18. Once more, the relativisation of family ties for the sake of group membership is an all-pervasive concern. To establish and maintain group identity, it appears that the household pattern which is so central to main-stream social relations is shifted to the periphery. Briefly, we note the following points.

First, membership is voluntary rather than guaranteed by birth: 'zeal for virtue and desire to promote brotherly love' are the prime conditions (*Hyp.* II. 2). Second, only mature male adults are eligible to join (*Hyp.* II. 3). Third, Philo categorically states that Essenes 'eschew marriage', and that 'no Essene takes a wife' – and this, out of a concern to maintain their communal life (*koinônia*), to escape the guiles of women, and to practise *egkrateia* (*Hyp.* II. 14–17). The fact that Philo refers three times here to the threat posed by marital and paternal ties to the corporate life of the Essenes shows the extent to which he views the Essene way as an alternative to normal, household-based community. Fourth, like their attitude to women, their view of

85

property is negative, at least in so far as the possession of property involves them in economic and social relations from which they seek release (cf *Omn. Prob. Lib.* 77–78). The money, land and slaves, together with wife and children, all constitute the household ties with which membership of the Essene community is incompatible.

Nevertheless, when we turn to consider the nature of the Essene alternative, it seems clear that the household remains to some extent a model for their communalism. This is seen in the use of the imagery of kinship to describe relations between members. For example, part of the rationale for not owning slaves is the egalitarian doctrine that Nature 'mother-like has born and reared all men alike, and created them genuine brothers (*adelfous gnêsious*), not in mere name, but in very reality' (*Omn. Prob. Lib.* 79). There is a sense also, in which the household pattern is expanded in Essenism. In an important statement, Philo says:

> First of all then no-one's house is his own in the sense that it is not shared by all, for besides the fact that they dwell together in communities (*kata thiasous synoikein*), the door is open to visitors from elsewhere who share their convictions.
>
> (*Omn. Prob. Lib.* 85)

In sum, what Philo says about the Therapeutae and the Essenes gives good grounds for suggesting that the early Christians were not alone in attempting to develop patterns of sociability that were alternative or (better) *complementary* to that of the household and those based on marital and kinship ties. Such evidence also confirms that household and kinship relations provided a powerful idiom in first-century Judaism for expressing personal dedication to transcendent religious and philosophical commitments. It seems reasonable to infer that converts to one or other of the various 'sects' within formative Judaism (including early Christianity) would be familiar with the idea of the renunciation of family and property.

Heroic individuals

In Philo's representations of the patriarchs and other leaders of the people of Israel, it is significant for our purpose that their distinction is illustrated frequently by their willingness to subordinate family ties for a greater cause. What Philo says of model communities recurs in what he says of holy and heroic individuals.

As we have seen already, Abraham is an exemplary figure in the Philonic corpus. One aspect of the Abraham story upon which Philo places great weight is that of his departure from Ur. This is elaborated in a number of places. Most hyperbolic is *De Abrahamo* 67:

And so taking no thought for anything, either for his fellow-clansmen, or wardsmen, or schoolmates, or comrades, or blood relations on father's or mother's side, or country, or ancestral customs, or community of nurture or home life, all of them ties possessing a power to allure and attract which it is hard to throw off, he followed a free and unfettered impulse and departed with all speed . . . .

This radical separation from kinsfolk and homeland is cited by Philo as proof of Abraham's obedience to the divine command, and of his being a wise man. At the allegorical level, it represents a migration from a Chaldean cosmology based on observable phenomena to a cosmology derived from consideration of 'the intelligible and invisible' (*Abr.* 69). But the language of kinship is used, not only to show what is left behind by God's true servant, but also to convey his new allegiance. So, for instance, Abraham's status as an exile from his homeland is complemented by the assertion that God is a surrogate for the things lost, and that Abraham belongs instead to a spiritual family: 'But Thou, Master, art my country, my kinsfolk, my paternal hearth, my franchise, my free speech, my great and glorious and inalienable wealth' (*Rer. Div. Her.* 27). In other words, in a manner somewhat analogous to a Gospel tradition such as Mark 3:31–35, the language of kinship functions as a way of expressing fundamental allegiances and commitments and the transfer from one set of allegiances, beliefs and society to another.

Another case in point is the account Philo gives of Phineas, whose zeal for the law and horror of the pollution to the nation brought by the idolatrous contact with the Midianites, led him to execute judgment without regard to ties of natural kinship (*Vit. Mos.* I. 300–4). Together with others 'zealous for continence and godliness (*tines . . . tôn tên egkrateian kai theosebeian ezêlôkotôn*) . . . [they] massacred all their friends and kinsfolk who had taken part in the rites' (*Vit. Mos.* I. 303). The model for Philo's presentation of Phineas and his colleagues is undoubtedly the Levites, the priestly tribe to whose ranks Phineas is appropriately added. Philo refers to the Levites on at least six occasions with respect to their special eminence in remaining 'on the Lord's side' (cf Exod 32:26), free from the pollution of worshipping the Golden Calf, a holiness finding ultimate expression in their willingness to bring the divine vengeance upon even members of their own kin. Thus, in *De Specialibus Legibus* III. 124ff, Philo says: 'They began with their nearest and dearest, for they acknowledge no love nor kinship but God's love . . . ' (126). This motif is repeated in *De Vita Mosis* II. 171 and 273. On each occasion, what comes to the fore is the radical subordination of the bonds of natural affection under the influence of an all-consuming sense of obligation to God, an obligation expressed in terms of the language of inspiration and ecstasy, and justified by reference to platonising notions of virtue, holiness and the divine nature (cf *Rer. Div. Her.* 68–70).

What, in sum, do these examples of Philo's treatment of heroic individuals contribute to our theme? First, we note the recurrence of the motif of the subordination of natural ties in the characterisation of the heroes. It is as if, by appearing to stand outside, above, or against ties of natural kinship, they gain in holiness and in proximity to God. Separation at one level makes possible identification at another. Second, Philo uses the powerful idiom of kinship ties to speak metaphorically about religious and philosophical allegiance, and in particular to convey certain *priorities*: the mental over the physical, thought over sense, nature over culture, piety over lawlessness, the love of God over idolatry, and so on.

The metaphorical uses of kinship convey a 'programme' which touches on issues religious, philosophical, ethical and social and for which the heroes serve as focal instances, representing the truth in these areas to a quintessential degree. The force of the metaphor lies in the *shock* which comes from the identification of what is normally valued negatively, with the sphere of the holy: the wise man is the one who quits his ancestral home, the Levite is like the homicide. It may be no coincidence, therefore, that in the Gospel stories about Jesus and the disciples, stories of kinship enmity and teaching about the subordination of family ties are not infrequent. It is highly likely that, as in Philo, such stories and teaching carry a significant metaphorical load with strong social corollaries.

THE EVIDENCE OF JOSEPHUS

From the writings of the Alexandrian Jew Philo, we turn to the slightly later writings of the Palestinian Jew Josephus (c. 37–93 CE). As with our discussion of the Philonic corpus, our concern here is to illustrate the extent to which, and the manner in which, the subordination of family and household ties feature in Josephus' writings.

Presuppositions

Perhaps our best access to the presuppositions of Josephus about family ties is via his autobiography (Rajak 1983: 11–45). *Vita* 1–6 shows that family ties are supremely important to Josephus' sense of personal and social identity. His genealogy is adduced as proof of his nobility of birth – he comes from lineages both priestly and royal – and constitutes an argument available against character assassination. His paternity, as the father of three sons, is a further mark of his prestige. The chronology of Josephus' ancestry has strong social and political significance: it is not neutral information. Hence, the mention of his great grandfather's contemporaneity with Hyrcanus and of Josephus' own birth in the year of Gaius' accession to the principate in Rome, as well as of the birth of his three sons during the principate of his patron Vespasian. So Josephus is able to tie his lineage both to the

Maccabean line of royal priests of Judaism and to the rulers of the Roman empire of whose ascendancy he himself is a beneficiary.

The material covering his first nineteen years is noteworthy for making no reference to marriage.[6] In fact, Josephus appears not to have married until after 67 CE, at the age of about thirty (*Vita* 414). He therefore delayed marrying, and did so for reasons of education and public affairs (and the prestige accruing therefrom), upon which he elaborates in *Vita* 7–12. His *curriculum vitae* includes the claim to have engaged in a thorough study of the three main Jewish 'sects' – the Pharisees, Sadducees, and Essenes – as well as spending three years as *zêlôtês* of the eremitical holy man, Bannus. In relation to his period of attachment to Bannus, the strongly ascetical aspects of his life-style are given special emphasis. In all this, there is an implicit acceptance of the idea that delaying marriage and adopting an ascetic life-style for the sake of the pursuit of *paideia* is thoroughly honourable.

The circumstances of Josephus' marriages, the first some ten years after his becoming a Pharisee, illumine further our grasp of his presuppositions about family ties. In *Vita* 414–15, he says that his first marriage was an honour bestowed on him by Vespasian: 'it was by his command that I married one of the women taken captive at Caesarea, a virgin and a native of that place'. So, as with his treatment of his lineage, marital ties are related to an all-embracing concern with prestige. The woman remains anonymous while the patron is named repeatedly. She is important primarily for her gift status in the patron–client relationship between Vespasian and Josephus, as well as for her reputation as a virgin (*parthenos*) and native Jewess, factors important to Josephus' reputation as a Pharisee. This marriage was short-lived and no offspring are mentioned. Josephus' second wife, whom he married in Alexandria, bore him three children of whom only Hyrcanus survived. Josephus then divorced her, 'being displeased at her behaviour', and subsequently married a Jewess 'of distinguished parents (*goneôn eugenes-tatôn*)' by whom he had two more sons (*Vita* 426–27).

On the basis of the foregoing, Josephus' presuppositions may be summarised in two main points. First, Josephus regards genealogy, ancestral history, marriage and paternity as basic mechanisms for attaining and enhancing social prestige, by establishing connections over time and by blood or marriage to those people and institutions constitutive both of Judaism and the Roman *imperium*. In this he is entirely conventional. Second, religious zeal and educational training provide legitimate justification for subordinating kinship ties and delaying marriage, even for a substantial period of time. The same system of values applies here also. Just as conjugal and consanguinal ties can be a source of prestige, so too, the subordination of these ties (if only temporarily, and for a legitimate cause) engenders respect – otherwise Josephus would lose face by including in his *Vita* accounts of his dalliance with Essenism and his ascetic life under Bannus.

89

Model communities

Josephus gives two accounts of the Essenes, the most comprehensive in *Bellum Judaicum* II. 119–61, and an abbreviated account in *Antiquitates* XVIII. 18–22. It is remarkable that he begins his first and longest account by commenting upon the Essenes' attitude to marriage:

> Marriage they disdain, but they adopt other men's children, while yet pliable and docile, and regard them as their kin (*syggeneis*) and mould them in accordance with their own principles. They do not, indeed, on principle, condemn wedlock and the propagation thereby of the race, but they wish to protect themselves against women's wantonness, being persuaded that none of the sex keeps her plighted troth to one man.
>
> (*Bell.* II. 120–21)

Equally remarkable is the fact that Josephus also ends his account of the Essenes with another extended comment on their marriage customs (*Bell.* II. 160–61). These comments on Essene marriage customs invite a number of observations.

First, the extent of Josephus' attention to their marriage customs, together with the pivotal location of his comments whereby they effectively bracket his entire characterisation of Essene beliefs and practices, illustrates the potential contribution of marriage customs to community self-definition generally. It also illustrates how important to Josephus himself as author is the subject of marital relations for his representation of the Essene sect – to whom, interestingly, he gives far more attention than to either the Pharisees or the Sadducees (cf Moehring 1961: 124–27).

Second, the Essenes are represented as being distinctive by virtue of the fact that some, at least, of their number do not marry. This distinctiveness is something of which Josephus clearly approves, since it is motivated by the right reasons – above all, the quest for virtue and the goal of a united communal life, both reinforced by (what is regarded as) a justifiable misogyny.[7] Of the former, he says: 'They shun pleasures as a vice and regard temperance and the control of the passions (*tēn de egkrateian kai to mē tois pathesin hypopiptein*) as a special virtue' (*Bell.* II. 120). The communal motive is reflected in Josephus' claim that 'they show greater attachment to each other than do the other sects' (*Bell.* II. 119); and it seems clear that marital alliances are viewed as constituting a distraction or, even worse, a source of rivalry and general 'dissension' (*stasis*) (*Bell.* II. 121).

Third, Essene marriage rules as depicted by Josephus are elitist in ethos. Although Josephus refers at the end to a branch of Essenes who do marry – but for the sole purpose of procreation of the race, and not at all for reasons of *hēdonē* (pleasure) – it is clear that marriage is legitimate rather for others, who thereby run the risk of moral dissipation, sexual rivalry and household strife, not to mention the pollution associated with menstruation and sexual intercourse. The process of augmenting the community by means of adopting the children of others is elitist also, since it involves a process of selection: of children who are 'yet pliable and docile' (*Bell*. II. 120). Here we have a mechanism of control which is quite of a piece with the rigorous probationary period of three year-long stages through which the initiate has to pass in order to qualify for full membership of the community (*Bell*. II. 137ff). The principle of control is that of merit, evident in the tests of character applied at each stage of entry, and in the Essenes' reputation generally for cultivating sanctity (*semnotês*). What we have, then, is a community of religious *virtuosi* where membership and status are a matter, not of what is ascribed according to marital and household ties, but rather of what is achieved by means of the renunciation of marriage and family and by initiation into the Essene order itself.

Fourth, the renunciation of marriage is all of a piece, in Josephus' presentation, with other obligations laid upon members (*Bell*. II. 122ff). Rights of property-ownership are surrendered, along with the associated differences of status. Members' houses and possessions become available for the use of other members, quite free of charge. Meals are taken with the community rather than with one's kin group. Members are forbidden explicitly to make gifts to their kinsfolk, except by permission. All members wear uniform clothing. Also, contact with outsiders, such as for the purpose of commercial enterprise, is restricted severely. All these are forms of sacrifice which function as proofs of loyalty and heighten members' mutual inter-dependence. There is a definite sense in which the renunciation of kinship ties and household patterns makes Essene communalism viable and allows the members of the community to relate to each other as 'brothers' (*Bell*. II. 122).

Josephus' account of the Essenes confirms and reinforces what we found in Philo's accounts of the Essenes and the Therapeutae. Both writers express high regard for these groups of religious *virtuosi*, and neither finds it unusual that zeal for virtue and a unified and holy common life should find expression – be made possible, even – through the subordination of family and household ties. By analogy, it seems reasonable to infer that the subordination of family ties to become a follower of Jesus was not at all unprecedented and could be justified along similar lines.

Enemies vilified

Confirmation of what we have found in Josephus about the importance of family ties and their subordination for defining personal and group allegiance and identity, comes in negative form in the hostile account he gives of the various groups of rebels opposed to Roman authority in the period leading up to the outbreak of war in 66 CE. Significant for our purpose is the fact that Josephus vilifies the enemies of Rome by citing their treatment of neighbours and kinsfolk as an indicator of their depravity and disloyalty.

Thus, in describing the power struggle in Jerusalem in 67 CE between the pro- and anti-war factions, Josephus says:

> Between the enthusiasts for war and the friends of peace contention raged fiercely. Beginning in the home (*kai prôton men en oikiais*) this party rivalry first attacked those who had long been bosom friends; then the nearest relations severed their connections (*epeita aphêniazontes allêlôn hoi philtatoi*) and joining those who shared their respective views ranged themselves henceforth in opposite camps.
>
> (*Bell.* IV. 131–32)

The image of household relations breaking down and dividing along political lines is a powerful rhetorical means for conveying the acute social instability which Josephus attributes to the war party.

More pertinent still is the digression depicting the extent and character of the depravity of the fomentors of rebellion against Rome, in *Bellum Judaicum* VII. 254–74. Of the Sicarii and their leading men, for example, Josephus asks rhetorically:

> What ties of friendship or of kindred (*poia d' autous philia, poia de syggeneia*) but rendered these men more audacious in their daily murders? For to do injury to a foreigner they considered an act of petty malice, but thought they cut a splendid figure by maltreating their nearest relations (*en tois oikeiotatois*).
>
> (*Bell.* VII 266)

Interestingly, in view of the saying attributed to Jesus in Matt 8:22b; par. Luke 9:60a, one of the most potent ways in which Josephus maligns the Zealots (to take another example) is to cite their refusal to allow the burial of the dead during the internecine struggle for control of Jerusalem prior to the siege by the advancing Roman army. He says:

> The Zealots, however, carried barbarity so far as to grant interment to none, whether slain in the city or on the roads; but as though they had covenanted to annul the laws of nature along with those of their country (*tois tês patridos sygkatalysai kai tous tês physeôs nomous*) . . . they left the dead putrefying in the sun.
>
> (*Bell.* IV. 381–82)

The historical veracity of Josephus' hostile report need not detain us here. What is important to note is the fact that, whereas in his depiction of the Essenes the subordination of family ties is given as evidence of their virtue and piety, the opposite is the case in his depiction of the Jewish revolutionaries. Their subordination of family ties is represented as a sign of their utter depravity. Putting Josephus' perspective in terms of the metaphor of 'centre and periphery' used by anthropologist Clifford Geertz (Geertz 1993), we may say that, in the case of the Essenes, the shift of social and symbolic location to the periphery via the renunciation of marriage and household is a movement in the direction of holiness and order (of a higher kind than found in everyday life); but for the revolutionaries, the shift to the periphery via the subordination of natural ties is a movement in the direction of profanity and disorder.

Heroic individuals

Examination of Josephus' accounts of leading figures of the Biblical and post-Biblical periods of Israel's history shows that, as is the case with Philo, a willingness to subordinate ties of natural kinship is a recurring motif and is presented as a sign of greatness and true piety.

The testing of Abraham is the classic instance, depicted at length in *Antiquitates* I. 222–36 (cf Feldman 1982). Especially noteworthy are the points where Josephus elaborates and embroiders the much more terse Biblical account (cf Gen 22:1–19). First, Josephus emphasises the obedience and full cooperation of Isaac with Abraham in the sacrifice. Isaac, we are told, is 25 years old (227); and he goes to the altar willingly and with joy (232). So the episode is as much the story of the testing of the mature filial piety of Isaac as it is of the obedience of Abraham. Second, Josephus makes more explicit the grounds on which God tests Abraham and on which Abraham shows himself willing to sacrifice his son. This is made plain at the beginning: 'thus would he manifest his piety towards Himself (*houtôs gar emphanisein tên peri auton thrêskeian*), if he put the doing of God's good pleasure even above the life of his child' (224). It is elaborated in the middle, in Abraham's long farewell speech to Isaac (228–31). It recurs at the end, in the *ex post facto* justification given to Abraham by God (233–35). Third, the extent of Abraham's obedience is augmented, even to the point where Abraham conceals the task from his wife and his household lest they hinder him from performing it, 'deeming that nothing would justify disobedience to God and that in everything he must submit to His will' (225). The entire episode assumes and exemplifies the legitimacy of subordinating family ties for a purpose of transcendent religious value, summed up in the text by the term *thrêskeia* (piety) (cf 222, 223, 224, 234).

As one other instance, mention should be made of Josephus' account of the resistance to Antiochus Epiphanes led by Mattathias (*Ant.* XII. 265–86). His zeal for the laws and customs of the Jews, over against Antiochus' attempts at enforced Hellenisation, leads him to depart into the wilderness, 'leaving behind all his property (*katalipôn hapasan tên autou ktêsin*) in the village' (*Ant.* XII. 271). The motivation for so placing at risk his family and the families of his followers, as well as giving up his household goods, is expressed quite explicitly in his rallying call: 'Whoever is zealous for our country's laws and the worship of God (*ei tis zêlôtês estin tôn patriôn ethôn kai tês tou theou thrêskeias*), let him come with me!'

The way Josephus portrays the willingness of the heroic individual to subordinate his family and household ties out of devotion of a higher kind – to God and the will of God – is consistent with what we found in the positive account he gives both of his own rather ascetic *paidveia* and of the common life of the Essenes of whom he claims first-hand knowledge. It is consistent also, but by contrast, with the negative account he gives of the Jewish revolutionaries whose hostility to their own kin is seen as a mark of their depravity and devotion to disorder. Overall, the evidence from Josephus' writings gives further weight to the claim that the subordination or relativisation of natural ties is a by no means uncommon idea in the Jewish milieu of early Christianity, and that it is an idea well suited to serve as an idiom for expressing claims to religious devotion and allegiances of a transcendent kind.

THE CYNICS

From important first-century Jewish sources which illustrate the motif of the subordination of family and household ties, we turn to Graeco-Roman sources which speak of conversion to philosophy and its social implications.[8] The outstanding examples of the socially disruptive effects of the philosopher's vocation – particularly the effects on the family – come in the accounts of the Cynics. Most explicit is the witness of the Stoic philosopher Epictetus (c. 55–135 CE), himself a pupil of the first century Stoic, Musonius Rufus.

In *Dissertationes* III. xxii, Epictetus gives a detailed and certainly Stoicising account of the ideal Cynic, in which he warns an interlocutor against the unpremeditated taking up of the Cynic philosopher's strenuous calling to be a 'scout' (*kataskopos*) of what is good for man and what is evil. Significantly, the cost of the Cynic vocation is presented repeatedly in relation to the philosopher's family ties. In order to be free for the task, what is required is radical detachment from family, property and all social customs and conventions; and to be a Cynic philosopher is to accept the call to live that out in practice. As Epictetus puts it:

> And how is it possible for a man who has nothing, who is naked, without home or hearth, in squalor, without a slave, without a city, to live serenely? Behold, God has sent you the man who will show in practice that it is possible. 'Look at me,' he says, 'I am without a home, without a city, without property, without a slave; I sleep on the ground; I have neither wife nor children, no miserable governor's mansion, but only earth, and sky, and one rough cloak. Yet what do I lack? Am I not free from pain and fear, am I not free?'
>
> (*Diss.* III. xxii. 45–48)

A little later, Epictetus' interlocutor asks specifically if the Cynic philosopher marries and has children. His reply is noteworthy, among other things, for its length. Clearly, the idiom of marital and family ties allows Epictetus considerable scope to address the issue of the philosopher's true goal and allegiance. To quote once more:

> But in such an order of things as the present, which is like that of a battle-field, it is a question, perhaps, if the Cynic ought not to be free from distraction (*aperispaston*), wholly devoted to the service of God, free to go about among men, not tied down by the private duties of men, nor involved in relationships which he cannot violate and still maintain his role as a good and excellent man, whereas, on the other hand, if he observes them, he will destroy the messenger, the scout, the herald of the gods, that he is. For see, he must show certain services to his father-in-law, to the rest of his wife's relatives, to his wife herself; finally, he is driven from his profession, to act as a nurse in his own family and to provide for them . . .
>
> (*Diss.* III. xxii. 69–72)

From these passages we may draw the following inferences about Epictetus' view of the vocation of the Cynic philosopher. First, it is a demanding vocation which requires total commitment as 'the messenger, the scout, the herald of the gods'. Second, this vocation necessitates freedom from distracting ties and obligations, especially ties of family, property and a settled existence. Whereas for the majority, marriage is the norm, for the Cynic it is the exception – that of Crates and Hipparchia being a case in point (cf *Diss.* III. xxii. 76). Third, the Cynic calling involves the renunciation of a particular family and an identifiable citizenship in order to benefit the common good and to foster the ideal of the unity of mankind. Significantly, the renunciation of a particular family makes possible participation in a universal family. As Epictetus says:

> Man, the Cynic has made all mankind his children; the men among them he has as sons, the women as daughters; in that spirit he approaches them all and cares for them all. Or do you fancy that it is in the spirit of idle impertinence he reviles those he meets? It is as father he does it, as a brother, and as a servant of Zeus, who is Father of us all.
>
> (*Diss.* III. xxii. 81–82)

There are other sources which confirm the picture from Epictetus about the incompatibility of the Cynic way of life and normal ties of marriage, family and household. In particular, in the *Cynic Epistles*, there is a letter to Zeno attributed to Diogenes (Epistle 47), but coming probably from the first century BC, which deals exclusively with the question of marriage and child-rearing. Its opposition to both is unequivocal:

> One should not wed nor raise children, since our race is weak and marriage and children burden human weakness with troubles.

Therefore, those who move toward wedlock and the rearing of children on account of the support these promise, later experience a change of heart when they come to know that they are characterized by even greater hardships. But it is possible to escape right from the start. Now the person insensitive to passion, who considers his own possessions to be sufficient for patient endurance, declines to marry and produce children.

(Malherbe 1977: 178–79)

What conclusions may we draw from this evidence of the Cynic hostility to marriage and family ties? First, it is important to register the fact that we have here a philosophical tradition, going back well into the Hellenistic period and lasting through to the first centuries of the Common Era, in which the quest for freedom and a life of simplicity, in harmony with nature and indifferent to the throes of fortune, has an explicitly anti-social and anti-familial corollary. So if the subordination of family and household ties in the Gospels is not unprecedented in the Biblical and Jewish traditions, it is not unprecedented in Hellenistic and Graeco-Roman traditions either. Followers of Jesus both before and after Easter will not necessarily have been surprised, therefore, at the obligation laid upon them to be willing to subordinate kinship ties and household duties.

Second, while the similarities appear to be strong – especially between, say, Epictetus' portrait of the homeless, vagabond existence of the ideal Cynic, on the one hand, and the Gospel traditions about the Son of Man who has nowhere to lay his head and who calls disciples to abandon their kin and follow him, on the other – it is important equally to acknowledge the differences (cf Hengel 1981: 30; Downing 1984: 588–89). For example, where Cynicism is explicitly anti-social and opposed (or at best, indifferent) to marriage and family ties, the Gospels take household institutions and family ties for granted (even if relativising them at the same time) – witness Jesus' prohibition on divorce or the teaching on respect for parents. Where Cynicism involves renunciation of kinship ties as the price of individual freedom (*eleutheria*) and self-sufficiency (*autarkeia*), the Gospels call for their subordination as the price of the eschatological mission inaugurated by Jesus. Where the Cynics adopt a deliberate asceticism as an integral part of the wise man's revolt against culture and his return to nature, the Gospels speak more of involuntary deprivation and hardship in consequence of faithful missionary discipleship. And where the Cynics seek to reform the individual by a highly provocative onslaught on civilised conventions and popular opinion, there is in the Gospels a positive summons to Israel and the nations to personal and social reform in preparation for the advent of God.

THE STOICS

If Cynicism may be characterised as a kind of 'left-wing Stoicism', it is useful also to illustrate attitudes to family and household ties in the writings of Stoics from the relevant period. What we find, in general terms, is a greater social conservatism on the part of the Stoics: a commitment to do one's duty as a citizen, a corollary of which is a willingness to marry and raise sons. In fact, as Balch has shown, advice 'concerning marriage' is a recurring topos of Stoic literature (Balch 1983). We will refer briefly to two Stoic writers, Musonius Rufus, the 'Roman Socrates' (born c. 30 CE) and (once more) his pupil Epictetus.

In the teachings of Musonius Rufus, the question of marriage is addressed no less than three times (Musonius Rufus XIIIA, XIIIB, XIV, in Luz 1947). What is striking, in comparison with the Cynics, is how positive is Musonius towards marital ties and the raising of children, and this, not only for the mutual benefit marriage brings to the partners involved, but also for the contribution it brings to the life and good order of the *polis*. In particular, in relation to the question, 'Is marriage a handicap for the pursuit of philosophy?', Musonius' denial that it is so is clearly a polemic against the Cynic position. Musonius even uses the example of the Cynic philosopher Crates to support his argument: 'Crates, although homeless and completely without property or possessions, was nevertheless married; furthermore, not having a shelter of his own, he spent his days and nights in the public porticoes of Athens together with his wife' (Musonius Rufus XIV). What for the Cynic position is an exception, for the Stoic becomes exemplary of the norm.

Nevertheless, it is also the case that, for Musonius, the philosophical quest for the good takes precedence over other ties of allegiance, including ties of filial piety. He addresses this in relation to the question, 'Must one obey one's parents under all circumstances?' Here, while careful to defend the moral norm of obedience to parents, Musonius argues that there is a higher norm which justifies a son studying philosophy against the wishes of his father:

> If, then, my young friend, with a view to becoming such a man, as you surely will if you master the lessons of philosophy, you should not be able to induce your father to do as you wish, nor succeed in persuading him, reason thus: your father forbids you to study philosophy, but the common father of all men and gods, Zeus, bids you and exhorts you to do so. His command and law is that man be just and honest, beneficent, temperate, high-minded, superior to pain, superior to pleasure, free of all envy and all malice; to put it briefly, the law of Zeus bids man be good. But being good is the same as being a philosopher. If you obey your father, you will follow the will of a man; if you choose the philosopher's life, the will of God.
>
> (Musonius Rufus XIV)

Not surprisingly, the position adopted by Epictetus is similar to that of his teacher Musonius. While more approving of the Cynic option than Musonius, Epictetus also holds that marriage is a duty, and for the same reason: the welfare of the *oikos* and the *polis* (*Diss.* III. vii. 19–28). Nevertheless, the philosopher's commitment to the good transcends even ties of filial respect:

> That is why the good is preferred above every form of kinship. My father is nothing to me but only the good. 'Are you so hard-hearted?' Yes, that is my nature. This is the coinage which God has given me. For that reason if the good is something different from the noble and the just, then father and brother and country and all relationships simply disappear.
>
> (*Diss.* III. iii. 5–6)

Here then are clear examples of a justification for the relativisation of family – and specifically filial – ties in the thought of a leading Roman Stoic philosopher of the first century and his pupil. By comparison, the call to subordinate family ties to be a disciple of Jesus is a justification of a quite different kind, and reflects a different – that is, eschatological – mood and ethos altogether. Nevertheless, that conversion to philosophy, like conversion to Christianity, involved an allegiance higher than ties of kinship and household can fairly be acknowledged.

CONCLUSION

There is no lack of additional material from the Biblical and Jewish sources which provides further evidence for what we found in the analysis of Philo and Josephus: that, fundamentally speaking, allegiance to the one true God transcends family ties and legitimates their subordination.[9] Indeed, given the powerful Biblical precedents of Abraham and the Levites – both willing to subordinate family ties at crucial turning points in Israel's history – such a tradition in Judaism and in the Gospels should come as no surprise at all. When to this are added the anti-familial and subordinationist materials from the Cynic and Stoic sources, there is good reason for claiming that the Gospel traditions relativising family ties resonate against a wider Graeco-Roman background as well.[10]

Awareness of this background is important historically and exegetically. It helps us to understand how Jesus may have been heard by some, at least, of his contemporaries: not as some kind of social fringe-dweller engaged in an idiosyncratic campaign to undermine the fabric of society, but as an inspired leader of the people in the tradition of Jewish monotheism and the eschatological prophets, calling for the renewal of Israel in preparation for the coming of God – a task whose urgency could be dramatised by the demand to subordinate all other responsibilities, even those of family and household. So, when Jesus says to a disciple who would go 'first' to bury his father, 'Follow me, and leave the dead to bury their own dead' (Matt 8:21–22; par. Luke 9:59–60), this is not a summons from piety to impiety, let alone to law-breaking.[11] Rather it is a summons from a lesser piety to a *greater piety*, since what is at stake is Jesus' eschatological mission to prepare the people for the coming of God.[12]

NOTES

1 All quotations of Philo and Josephus, unless otherwise indicated, are from the Loeb Classical Library edition.

2 See *Virt.* 102f, 219; *Spec. Leg.* IV. 178.

3 'Those who come over to their religion . . . have this lesson first instilled into them, to despise all gods, to disown their country, and set at nought parents, children, and brethren' (Tacitus, *History*, V. 5).

4 Cf *Abr.* 60–67; *Migr. Abr.* 1ff; *Rer. Div. Her.* 276–83, 287–88; *Leg. All.* III. 83.

5 In addition to leaving property and family, their asceticism is evident in their escape from the cities for a life of solitude (*Vit. Cont.* 19–20), the careful segregation of the sexes (ibid: 32–33), the rule of celibacy (ibid: 68), the practice of fasting and abstinence from meat and wine (ibid: 34–35, 73–74), and the general frugality of their dietary practices on the principle of *egkrateia* (*ibid.* 34).

6 Cf Schürer, *History*, II, 578, n.14, which refers to the fact that the recommended age of marriage for a man is 18 years, according to Mishnah *Aboth* 5.21, as against 20 years, according to the *Community Rule* from Qumran (I QSa 1.10–11).

7 For the explicit misogyny, perhaps legitimated for the Essenes by scriptural statements such as Prov 25:24, see *Bell.* II. 121 and *Ant.* XVIII. 21.

8 See, in general, Nock 1961: 164–86; also, Hengel 1981: 25–33.

9 For Biblical examples, consider: the call of Abraham (Gen 12:1ff); the Levites at Sinai after the people's apostasy (Exod 32:25–29; Deut 33:9); the call of Elisha (I Kings 19:19–21); the oracle given to Jeremiah prohibiting him from marrying and having children (Jer 16:1–2); and the command to Ezekiel not to mourn his deceased wife (Ezek 24:15–27). From apocryphal and pseudepigraphical sources, note *inter alia*: the case of Tobit (in Tob 1:10–12); the conversion of Asenath (esp. Joseph and Asenath 11:4–6); and the zeal of Judas Maccabeus and his followers (esp. 2 Macc 15:18).

10 Limits of space prevent consideration here of an important issue that our survey of the ancient sources throws up: namely, why does the tradition of 'hostility' to family appear to be so much stronger in the Bible and Judaism than in the Graeco-Roman sources? In particular, what is it about Jewish *monotheism* (by comparison with Graeco-Roman polytheism) that gives such impetus to this tradition? Perhaps it is the case that the transcendence of God in Judaism makes the relativisation of mundane ties possible in a way that the pursuit of philosophy or the worship of the domestic and civic gods, in Graeco-Roman civilisation, do not.

11 *Pace* Sanders 1985: 252–55.

12 For discussion relevant to the hermeneutical dimensions of our theme, see further Barton 1995; 1996: 3–23.

BIBLIOGRAPHY

Baer, R. A. (1970) *Philo's Use of the Categories Male and Female*, Leiden: E. J. Brill.

Balch, D. L. (1983) 'I Cor 7:32–35 and Stoic Debates about Marriage, Anxiety and Distraction', *JBL* 102: 429–39.

Barton, S. C. (1994) *Discipleship and Family Ties in Mark and Matthew*, Cambridge: Cambridge University Press.

—— (1995) 'Marriage and Family Life as Christian Concerns', in C. S. Rodd (ed.) *New Occasions Teach New Duties?* Edinburgh: T. & T. Clark: 159–72.

—— (ed.) (1996) *The Family in Theological Perspective*, Edinburgh: T. & T. Clark.

Downing, F. G. (1984) 'Cynics and Christians', *NTS* 30: 584–93.

Feldman, L. H. (1982) 'Josephus' Version of the Binding of Isaac', in K. H. Richards (ed.) *SBL 1982 Seminar Papers*, Atlanta: Scholars Press: 113–28.

Geertz, C. (1993) *Local Knowledge*, London: Fontana Press.

Hengel, M. (1981) *The Charismatic Leader and his Followers*, Edinburgh: T. & T. Clark.

Luz, C. (1947) 'Musonius Rufus "The Roman Socrates"', *Yale Classical Studies* X: 3–147.

Malherbe, A. (ed.) (1977) *The Cynic Epistles. A Study Edition*, Atlanta: Scholars Press.

Moehring, H. R. (1961) 'Josephus on the Marriage Customs of the Essenes', in A. Wikgren (ed.) *Early Christian Origins*, Chicago: Chicago University Press: 120–27.

Nock, A. D. (1961) *Conversion*, Oxford: Oxford University Press.

Rajak, T. (1983) *Josephus. The Historian and his Society*, London: Duckworth.

Sanders, E. P. (1985) *Jesus and Judaism*, London: SCM.

Sandmel, S. (1971) *Philo's Place in Judaism*, New York: KTAV.

Schürer, E. (1973ff) *The History of the Jewish People in the Age of Jesus Christ* (175 BC–AD 135), Edinburgh: T. & T. Clark.

Part II

FAMILY AS METAPHOR

6

THE ROMAN FAMILY: IDEAL AND METAPHOR

Eva Marie Lassen

Metaphorical language forms an important part of any culture.[1] Its main function is, in the words of two leading linguists: 'to provide a partial understanding of one kind of experience in terms of another kind of experience' (Lakoff and Johnson 1980: 154). In Antiquity, as today, metaphors constituted an efficient way of communicating religious beliefs, political attitudes, and social values. The first Christians also made use of metaphorical language to provide understanding of fundamental Christian concepts. They developed metaphorical language stemming from notions as different as pilgrimage, slavery, and warfare.[2] Metaphors of the family played a central role in this metaphorical network developed by the first Christians. The metaphors 'God the Father', 'Jesus the Son', 'children of God', 'brothers and sisters in Christ', along with a number of other family metaphors became a means by which to develop and communicate a Christian theology as well as constructing a church community with a certain kind of leadership and certain patterns of interactions between its members.

In the first centuries AD, Christianity spread throughout the Roman world. As family metaphors constituted one of the ways in which to speak about the new religion, it follows that the Romans would relate to Christianity partly by relating to the Christian use of family metaphors. In other words, the Romans would understand one kind of experience, the Christian religion, by means of another kind of experience, the family. The meaning of a metaphor, however, may change radically within a culture as well as from culture to culture (Lakoff and Johnson 1980: 142). Therefore, in order to understand how the Romans related to the new Christian religion, it is important to know about the family in *pagan* Rome. Only then do we have the Roman point of departure, the framework within which the Romans would comprehend Christian family metaphors.

This chapter offers an analysis of some of the more important characteristics of the pagan Roman family in the Classical Roman period (from approximately the end of the second century BC to the end of the second century AD); special emphasis is on the Principate in the first century AD. Focusing on the interaction between ideal and metaphor, the first part of the chapter concerns the family as *ideal*, as expressed in legal as well as non-legal norms. The legal concept *patria potestas* is discussed and we examine how *patria potestas* would be expressed in areas such as the marital arrangements and economic conditions of those family members subjected to a *pater-familias*. Then follows an analysis of the Augustan family laws, which contained a legal idealisation of a specific kind of family patterns. Finally in the first section of the chapter, the interactions between owner and slave, and between patron and freedman are examined, especially with a view to sentiments and legal bonds found in these relationships which bore resemblance to or were compared with the sentiments and legal bonds belonging to the inner circle of the *familia*.

Based on ideals of the Roman family, *metaphors* of the family were created; they were used outside the Roman family, in the religious, social, and political sphere. This is the topic of the second part of the chapter. Included in this section are examples of the interplay between private and public, as seen in the political system. Here the metaphor of the head of state as 'Father of the Fatherland' gained increased importance at the beginning of the Principate, and at the same time the imperial family began to be presented as a model for all Romans.

THE FAMILY AS IDEAL

Patria potestas: power and powerlessness

According to Roman tradition, the family was the heart of pagan society; it was the basis of society and its most important part. Despite great economic, political, and social changes taking place during the Republic and Principate, this traditional view was largely maintained throughout the Classical period. A deeply rooted respect surrounded the family.[3]

The Roman *familia* was headed by the *paterfamilias*. He was the oldest male in direct line and exercised his power, *patria potestas*, over members of his *familia*: children, grandchildren, and great grandchildren. In legal terms, persons in *potestas* were called *alieni juris*, 'in another's right', and, depending on their sex, named *filius (familias)* and *filia (familias)* in legal documents.

Biological paternity was not a *necessary* condition for constituting *patria potestas*. A person, minor or adult, might become a member of a *familia* through adoption; if the adopted person had a *paterfamilias* already, the adoption was called *adrogatio*, if he did not have one, it was called *adoptio*. The scale of adoption is not known but it is reasonable to assume that adoption was, at the very least, a well-known concept.[4] Biological paternity, on the other hand, was not a *sufficient* condition for creating *patria potestas*. *Pater naturalis*, the father of a child born outside marriage, had little to do with his illegitimate offspring. He did not have *potestas* over the child, and he was not required to support it (Girard 1924: 191ff; Rawson 1991: 26).

Legal fatherhood was most often created through the Roman marriage, *iustum matrimonium*: '*pater is est, quem nuptiae demonstrant*' (e.g. *Dig.* 2.4.5). In principle, however, the husband in his capacity of the *paterfamilias* – or, if one of them was still alive, his father or grandfather – might decline to accept a newborn child into the *familia*. In order to acknowledge the paternity and admit the child into his *familia*, *paterfamilias* was required to perform an ancient rite, which involved lifting the newborn from the floor.[5]

Patria potestas was a legal concept which gave the head of the family an almost omnipotent position, as expressed by the lawyer Gaius in the second century AD: 'virtually no other men have over their sons a power such as we have.' (Gai. *Inst.* 1. 55).[6] A *paterfamilias* even had *ius vitae necisque*, the right of life and death over the members of his *familia* (Thomas 1984: 448ff). Moreover, the modern idea of growing up, in the sense of *growing away* from parental guidance and control, did not exist in Rome: *patria potestas* was exerted over children and adults alike. Only when a *paterfamilias* died did *patria potestas* end – unless terminated by the *paterfamilias* himself, for instance by *emancipatio* or by the adoption of a *filius* into another family (Dixon 1992: 40).

The fact that *patria potestas* did not end when the children grew up had major consequences, one of which was that adults with a living *paterfamilias* were not capable of ownership. They could not take part in financial transactions without the consent of their *paterfamilias*, and everything they earned would automatically fall to the head of the family (Dixon 1992: 40).

Another area, in which the *paterfamilias* was legally entitled to exercise a near total control over the lives of his children, regardless of their age, was entry to marriage.[7] A *filius* or *filia* could not marry against their father's wishes: 'Marriage cannot take place unless everyone involved consents, that is, those who are being united and those in whose power they are' (*Dig.* 23.2.2; see also Paulus *Sent.* 2.19.2).

In the Principate and the later Roman Empire, a *filius* and *filia* could only get married if they themselves consented. That, at least, was the leading principle; but the law gave room for enforced marriages. A *filius* could find himself married against his will (*Dig.* 23.2.22), and a *filia* had even less chance to resist the marital arrangements of her father:

> But if she does not oppose her father's wishes, she is held to consent. A daughter can only refuse to give her consent where her father chooses someone who is unfit for betrothal because of his bad behaviour or character.
>
> (*Dig.* 23.1.12)

The control of the *paterfamilias* did not stop at the doorstep of the married couple. The *filius* remained subordinate to the *potestas* of his *paterfamilias*. In the late Republic and the Principate, the same applied in most cases to the married *filia*. A *paterfamilias* even had the right to dissolve the marriage of his *filius* or *filia*, even if the couple lived happily together. Only in the second part of the second century AD was the *paterfamilias* legally forbidden to break up a marriage in which the couple lived harmoniously together, *bene concordans* (Paulus *Sent.* 5.6.15 and 2.19.2. *Cod. Iust.* 5.17.5).

Controlling patria potestas

The dependence of *alieni iuris* on the *paterfamilias* in financial matters and marital arrangements are just two examples of the vast power invested with the head of the family. Certain legal and non-legal factors, however, paved the way for alleviating the burden imposed on the *filius* and *filia* by *patria potestas*. First, *patria potestas* belonged to the oldest male in direct line, but a large number of Romans, perhaps even the majority, set up their own nuclear families at marriage.[8] Living apart, the *paterfamilias* would most likely have experienced practical difficulties in controlling his grown-up children.

Second, the life expectancy of the Romans diminished the average length of *patria potestas*. It has been suggested that only one in five adults over 30 years old had a living father.[9] Such estimations, which are results of computer calculations based on inscriptional material, are subject to uncertainty. However, despite reservations about demographic studies of the Roman family such as these, most scholars today agree that a large proportion of adult men were themselves *paterfamilias* at a fairly young age.

In the late Republic and the Principate, most women were married *sine manu*; in legal terms they were not subordinate to the authority of their husbands but remained in the *potestas* of their original *paterfamilias*. A woman whose *paterfamilias* died would – like a *filius familias* – become *sui juris*, in her own right. She could now own and undertake legally valid transactions, for instance concerning financial matters. In principle, all women who were *sui juris* had to have a *tutor* – unless exempted, in the Principate typically as a reward for having reared a number of children (Dixon 1992: 120). However, a number of sources from the Principate describing the lives of individual women, indicate that their freedom of action was not seriously challenged by the *tutor*. Thus many women depicted in the literature and inscriptional material, behaved actively and independently, often handling large fortunes (Gardner 1986: 16; Rawson 1991: 28; Dixon 1992: 43f, 59).

Third, certain legal regulations made it possible for a relationship between a *paterfamilias* and his adult sons to work in a fairly smooth manner. This applied to the economic sphere, where a *paterfamilias* could offer a *filius* a *peculium*, a share in the family fortune. The son administered the *peculium* – in the form of real estate, movables, money, and slaves – as though it was his own; in this way, a *filius* could live in relative economic independence (Schulz 1951: 154; Crook 1967a: 110). Insofar as a man would set up a new home at the time of his marriage, this system of *peculium* is likely to have been widely practised. It should be noticed, however, thàt the *peculium* still belonged to the *paterfamilias* in a legal sense, and that he could withdraw it at any time. Moreover, it was not legally possible for women to receive a *peculium*.

Fourth, certain ideals attached to Roman family life worked to counterbalance the massive power of a *paterfamilias*. Most importantly, parents and children should relate to each other in accordance with *pietas*, a bond of 'reciprocal, dutiful affection', as accurately expressed by Richard Saller (Saller 1991: 150). Latin literature and inscriptions convey with lucidity that love was part of the ideal of paternal *pietas* and that this ideal reigned across classes and throughout the Roman Republic, the Principate, and the late Roman Empire.[10] One example is the writings of Cicero. In his legal speeches, he made rhetorical use of the ideal of parental love (e.g. Cic. *Clu.* 12; *Rosc. Am.* 53; *Ver.* II.44.112), and in his own life he expressed great love for his own young children (Cic. *Att.* 1.18).[11] Another group of sources consists of burial inscriptions, which in a stereotyped conformity convey the love of parents for their children (e.g. Hopkins 1983: 225f). It is impossible to know the extent to which the ideal of paternal love was actually practised, but the sentiment clearly formed a significant part of the father *ideal*.

As *pietas* partly was a state of mind, the concept is elusive. Nonetheless, *pietas* was regulated by the state. During the Republic, one of the functions of the Roman *censor* was to ensure that a *paterfamilias* acted in accordance with *pietas* and *mos majorum*, the tradition of the forefathers. More particularly, the censor was entitled to ensure that the head of family did not abuse his power by maltreating his wife, children, and slaves (Pieri 1967: 100, 105); for *pietas* in the case of the father meant that he exercised *patria potestas* over members of his *familia* within reason and with moderation. Whether, in fact, the abuse of *patria potestas* would normally cause the intervention of the censor is questionable. At any rate, the role of the censor as a keeper of Roman morals declined towards the end of the Roman Republic. This can be observed in connection with another area of Roman family habits traditionally under censorial jurisdiction, namely the obligation to marry and beget children (Pieri 1967: 104ff). In the beginning of the Principate, this area ceased to belong to the domain of the censor; instead, it became the subject of the Augustan family laws.

The Augustan family laws

The Augustan family laws are crucial for the understanding of Roman family life and ideals in the Principate. These *leges* launched a new and major legal regulation of Roman family life. The first family laws appeared in 29 or 28 BC, but neither their name nor exact content are known. *Lex Julia de maritandis ordinibus* and *Lex Papia Poppaea* were issued in 18 BC and AD 9 respectively; in *Corpus Iuris Civilis*, the two laws are often seen together as *Lex Julia et Poppaea*.[12]

By granting economic, social, and political privileges to married couples with children, the Augustan family laws encouraged citizens to marry and beget children. A freeborn woman with three children, for instance, was freed from *tutela mulierum*, and her rights of inheritance were improved (Gai. *Inst.* I.145, I.195). Conversely, the laws imposed major sanctions against unmarried people (including widows and divorcees), notably in the area of inheritance (e.g. *Reg. Ulp.* 22.3; Gai. *Inst.* II.111; II.144; II.286). Certain types of marriages, on the other hand, were branded as misalliances, for instance a marriage between a senator and a former slave woman and a marriage between a freeborn person and a prostitute (e.g. *Reg. Ulp.* 13.1; *Dig.* 23.2.23; 23.2.44). Finally, *Lex Julia de adulteriis coercendis* from 18 BC made a number of sexual relationships outside marriage a criminal offence, such as *adulterium* (an affair between a man and a married woman) and *stuprum* (a sexual relationship between a man and an unmarried woman or a boy) (*Dig.* 48.5.35). People who indulged in *adulterium* or *stuprum* took the risk of being exiled (Paulus *Sent.* 2.26.14. For punishment by exile, see Garnsey 1970: 116).

A number of sources indicate that the laws were valid in the centuries following the reign of Augustus and, moreover, that the lawgivers attempted to see them made effective or amended if necessary (Humbert 1972: 177). It is difficult to assess the impact of the family laws on the marriage patterns of the Romans. Although the sources show that the sanctions and privileges of the laws were sometimes brought into effect, the government must obviously have had difficulties in implementing the laws. Even to the extent that the laws were enforced, it was perfectly possible to defy them and live with the legal sanctions which might follow (the legislation concerning adultery is different in this respect, as a woman's extra-marital affair was a *crimen*). Should, for instance, a senator choose to marry a former slave – even if it meant that sanctions would be imposed against him because he had married *contra legem* – the state could not prevent it.

Notwithstanding these reservations concerning the implementation of the Augustan family laws, it is clear that the laws marked a dramatic attempt on behalf of the state to intervene in the life of the Roman family. The pressure to get married, beget children and exercise sexual virtue – all part of old Republican ideals attached to the family – was intensified by means of legal measures taken by the political leaders of Rome.

At the outskirts of the family: slaves and freedmen

A picture of the Roman family is not complete without mentioning two groups which were placed within or at the outskirts of the family: slaves and freedmen.[13] The slaves belonged to the *familia*, and their position vis-à-vis the owner resembled to some extent the relationship between the *filius familias* and the *paterfamilias*. The master had *ius vitae necisque* over his slaves just as the *paterfamilias* had vis-à-vis his *filii*. Similarly, neither *filii* nor slaves were able to own, but both might administer a *peculium* (Bradley 1994: 27). Still, in contrast to slaves, the *filius* and *filia* were sometimes treated as individuals with legal rights, as we have seen with the requirement of their consent to marriage.

Occasionally, the father–child imagery found its way into the non-legal aspects of the relationship between master and slave – although it should be emphasised that the attitudes existing in the relationship between master and slave undoubtedly varied very considerably, and hence no conclusion of general validity can be drawn.[14] Some Italian inscriptions, for instance, reveal that slaves described their masters as *parens*. This can be seen as a sign that the slave–master relationship occasionally acted as a kind of affectionate substitute for kinship (Wilkinson 1964: 360; Maurin 1975: 221ff). Such close relationships must have been limited to the favourite few, probably household slaves.

Manumission of slaves was a commonplace occurrence in Roman society (Bradley 1994: 162). At this point the owner became *patronus* (or *patrona*) of the former slave. In a few, quite exceptional, legal cases the freedman was placed next to the *filius*. If, for instance, a man killed his patron, he was called *parricida* and in the *Lex Pompeia de parricidi* placed next to him who had killed his parent, grandparent or another close relative (Lassen 1992: 151, 157). However, the *filius* was *alieni juris* whereas the freedman was *sui juris*, and hence their legal position was substantially different. Moreover, the Roman jurists did not acknowledge a proper kinship between patron and freedman, one sign of which is that marriage between a patron and his freedwoman was legally valid and not in any sense considered an incestuous relationship. Another sign is that the former slave was not considered *in loco filii* (or *filiae*) to his patron in matters of inheritance (Kaser 1939: 102).

On the other hand, the patron had an obligation to care for and protect his freedmen as a father cared for his children (e.g. Rawson 1986: 13 and 43). In return the patron could expect filial *pietas* and *honor*. The freedman's *pietas* was regulated by law, notably *Dig.* 37.15, entitled '*De obsequiis parentibus et patronis praestandis*' (see also Joshel 1992: 33ff). The freedman was also capable of replacing a son, in the sense that he could prevent the *nomen* of the patron from dying out (Veyne 1985: 25f; Dixon 1992: 114).

The relation of power and sentiments, then, between the two parties involved in slavery and patronage – slaves and masters, freedmen and patrons – were sometimes compared with, and sometimes described by means of, family concepts.

THE ROMAN FAMILY AS METAPHOR

The family in the public sphere

Metaphors of the family held a strong position among metaphors in Roman society and can be found in the religious as well as the social and political spheres. Several factors help explain the popularity of family metaphors. First, since the family formed an important social unit and held a prominent place in Roman tradition, metaphors of the family had the capacity to form very powerful, and to the Romans meaningful, images. Second, the occasional detachment, as described above, of paternal power from biological fatherhood as well as the exercise of *patria potestas* over adults not living together with the *paterfamilias* meant that the Romans would easily take to the use of family metaphors for describing relationships between *adults outside* the family sphere.

Naturally, different metaphors do not have the same metaphorical significance, and similarly, the value of a particular metaphor is likely to change from context to context. Metaphors can be divided into the following categories.[15] At one end of the scale we find *new* metaphors, followed by *familiar* metaphors which are not new but not well-established either. *Standard* metaphors are established ones which the users still regard as metaphors. When metaphors are *hidden*, their metaphorical meaning has largely been forgotten, until finally, dead or retired metaphors are literal use for most people, for instance, 'the arm of the chair'. It is not always possible to determine where on this scale a particular metaphor should be placed at a particular point of time. During the Roman Republic, to take an example, the metaphor Father of the Fatherland, *Pater Patriae*, was a *familiar* metaphor used for describing certain leaders of the Roman people. In the Principate, the title became a *standard* metaphor for the emperor but when exactly this transformation was completed is not clear.

Family metaphors can be found in all areas of Roman culture. In the context of religious tradition, the father-name, *Pater*, was affiliated with gods such as Mars, Jupiter, Saturn, and Neptune (e.g. Gell. *NA* 5.12). Ancestral family cults were copied and transformed into state cults. Most importantly, this applied to the Vesta cult, but the *lares*, *penates*, and *Janus*, which also belonged to the religious life of the family, were transferred into public religion (Lacey 1986: 125ff).

The Vestal virgins were central to the Vesta cult, and women played important roles in some other traditional cults, for instance in the *Mater Matuta* cult (Gagé 1963). In other areas of Roman culture outside the family, women also held prominent positions, reflected in the occasional use of female metaphors. The metaphor *Mater* was used – probably as a honorific title given to a sort of patroness – in connection with Roman *collegium*, a society of craftsmen, for instance, or a burial society.[16] Compared to men, however, women played a smaller role in the public life of Rome and female metaphors held a significantly less prominent position than male metaphors.

In most cultures, ancient and modern, members of a society are at times described as brothers of one another. In ancient Rome, the civil wars which took place towards the end of the Roman Republic were systematically described as wars between brothers. In this context, the use of the brother metaphor put across the meaninglessness, tragedy and absurdity of civil wars (Jal 1963: espec. 407f). The Romans, however, do not seem to have been particularly occupied with the concept of brotherhood and we do not find the brother metaphor used very frequently. The Romans did not view themselves as a society of mothers, daughters, and brothers but rather as a society of fathers and sons (an aspect of Roman society, particularly stressed by Yan Thomas 1986: 195–230).

This is particularly apparent in the political life of Rome. The *paterfamilias* was placed at the top of the hierarchy within the family. Similarly the father metaphor played the most prominent role amongst family metaphors used in the aristocratic Republic and later on in imperial Rome. By integrating the family metaphors – the metaphors of father and son in particular – into the political and administrative system, some of the attitudes and ideals connected with the family were transferred to the attitudes and ideals connected with certain public offices. An example is found in the relationship between the quaestor and his superior: a praetor or consul or – in the provinces – the propraetor or the proconsul. Traditionally a very tight bond existed between the quaestor and his superior, and this bond was likened to the union of a father and son. Cicero referred to this tradition in his speech against Caecilius: according to tradition the praetor was like a father to his quaestor, ' . . . sui parentis loco' (Cic. *In Caecil.* 61; see also Hellegouarc'h 1963: 72). A similar understanding is expressed in a letter, in which Cicero wrote about a young man who as a quaestor was going to work for the governor of Cisalpine Gaul. The quaestor's relationship with his superior, Cicero said, resembled that of a son to his father (Cic. *Fam.* 13.10.1). *Pietas* formed the basis for the relationship between the quaestor and his superior, a parallel to the family relationship acknowledged by Cicero when he said that Caecilius could not proceed against his former praetor without violating the obligation to show a son's *pietas* (Cic. *In Caecil.* 62).

One hundred and fifty years later, Pliny, by using exactly the same metaphorical language in connection with the relationship between a consul-elect and a quaestor, referred to the same tradition. Pliny wrote to the consul-elect: 'I will only say, he is a young man, who deserves you should look upon him in the same relation, as our ancestors used to consider their quaestors, that is, as your son (*more maiorum in filii locum*)' (Pliny *Ep.* IV.15; see also X.26.1).

The father metaphor was also used in connection with the highest office within the *cursus honorum*, the consulate. The consul was regularly compared with or explicitly called a father of the Romans. Cicero said that the consul ought to act towards the Senate as a good father, *parens bonus* (Cic. *Or.* III 1.3), and when he himself was a consul, he claimed to act as a mild father, not as a cruel tyrant (Cic. *Dom.* 94). Members of the Roman Senate were called *patres*; this was possibly a 'retired' metaphor, that is, the senators were not actually thought of as fathers when so addressed.[17]

Father of the Fatherland

At the beginning of the Christian era, the politically most significant family metaphor was Father of the Fatherland, *Pater Patriae*.[18] This notion probably originated in a Greek context (Strasburger 1976: 96), but the Romans themselves appear to have seen the paternal leader-figure as closely linked to Roman tradition. According to this tradition, Romulus, the founder of Rome, was the first to be called Father of Rome (recorded in a fragment of Ennius, handed down in Cicero's *Rep.* I.64.) The public father-figure was connected with ideas of rescuing the Roman people, typically in time of war, and it was traditionally claimed that a number of military commanders were called 'father' by their army or the whole population (see for instance Livy I.16.3; II.7.4; II.60.3; V.49.7; XXII.29.10–30.3). Towards the end of the Republic, Cicero was offered the title *Parens Patriae* by the *Princeps Senatus* when he had rescued the Republic from Catiline's treason (Cic. *Pis.* 3.6). As Cicero presumably was the first to receive the title by a *Senatus Consultum*, it was only then that it gained a significant official status (Weinstock 1971: 202f).

Caesar also made use of the father metaphor on his rise to power. In contrast to other images used by Caesar, notably kingship and divine political leadership, the notion of *Pater Patriae* harmonised perfectly with Roman tradition. In fact, by using the image of the Father of the Fatherland, he disguised to some extent the novelty of his reign. The title *Pater Patriae* was conferred on him in either 45 or 44 BC, the official reason being that Caesar had saved the country (Weinstock 1971: 200). The Romans also began to celebrate his *genius* in public (Alföldi 1971: 89). In the family cult the *genius* of the *paterfamilias* (a kind of attendant spirit) was celebrated, but this was the first time that a man's *genius* was celebrated in public. Also certain paternal characteristics were attached to Caesar, particularly paternal *clementia*. Even his enemy Cicero, when asking for pardon on behalf of Ligarius, pleaded, not as if Caesar were a jury, but as to a father: '*ego apud parentem loquor: . . . ad clementiam tuam confugio*' (Cic. *Lig.* 10.30).[19]

After the murder of Caesar, various groups of Roman society put a strong emphasis on the fact that Caesar had been Father of the Fatherland. The Roman *plebs* put up a marble column in the Forum, with an inscription reading '*Parenti Patriae*', 'To the Father of his Country'. For a long time they made vows and settled disputes in Caesar's name at this column (Suet. *Iul.*

85. See also Cic. *Fam.* 12.3.1). The Roman Senate named the day of the murder *Parricidium*, and it was resolved that the Senate was never to hold a meeting on that day (Suet. *Iul.* 88). In this context *parricidium* should be translated 'The Day of the Murder of the Father of the Fatherland' (Lassen 1992: 156f).[20]

The state father and the state family of Augustus

More political changes took place under the rule of Caesar's stepson, Octavian. In order to make his transformation of Roman politics more acceptable for the Romans, Octavian (from 27 BC Augustus) evoked – to a much larger degree than his stepfather – political and religious images which belonged to Roman tradition. He made extensive use of traditional leader-images, and the image of *Pater Patriae* became increasingly important (Premerstein 1937: 36 and 166; Alföldi 1971: 47, 70, 95ff; Salmon 1982: 147ff).

Only in 2 BC, when his power over Rome, Italy, and the provinces was at its peak, did Augustus officially receive the title of *Pater Patriae* from the Roman Senate and the people.[21] There are many indications, however, that he was portrayed as father of his country several decades before this event. In a coin from 20 BC, for instance, celebrating the recovery by Augustus of the military standards from the Parthians, he was proclaimed *parens* and *conservator* of the Roman people: '*SPQR PARENTI . . . CONS(ervatori) SUO*'.[22] In the early propaganda, Augustus was also pictured as saviour and a new founder of Rome, both aspects of the traditional political father-figure. Horace, the poet, was one of those who, many years before Augustus officially was called Father of the Fatherland, made use of this metaphorical connection between the father of the family and Augustus (Hor. *Carm.* I.2; I.12; III.24). Also in the religious cults Augustus broke down the barrier between himself, his family and the people. The public Vesta cult became intertwined with Augustus' own family cult (Liebeschuetz 1979: 70), and the emperor initiated a reconstruction of the *Lares compitales* cult in such a way as to make his *genius* and the imperial *lares* central to the cult (Ross Taylor 1931: 184f).

By way of representing his family as a state family, Augustus reinforced the image of himself as state leader and father-figure. During the Republic, the role of officials' wives and families as public figures was limited. Augustus rendered his wife and family visible to the public eye, and although the imperial family was tarnished by scandals he tried to represent its members as models for Roman wives, husbands, and children.[23] On the altar *Ara Pacis*, dedicated in 9 BC, to take a famous example, the imperial family is shown as the incarnation of harmony and, with numerous couples and children, the Roman family *par excellence* (Dixon 1988: 74ff; 1992: 80 and 177).

Most of Augustus' successors bore the title *Pater Patriae* and the paternal aspect of the imperial reign continued to form an important part of the political ideology of Rome. In Strabo's view, indeed, the very nature of the imperial reign was paternalistic:

> it were a difficult thing to administer so great a dominion otherwise than by turning it over to one man, as to a father; at all events, never have the Romans and their allies thrived in such peace and plenty as that which was afforded them by Augustus Caesar, from the time he assumed the absolute authority, and is now being afforded them by his son and successor, Tiberius, who is making Augustus the model of his administration and decrees.
>
> (Strabo 6.4.2)

CHRISTIANITY AND THE ROMAN FAMILY

To sum up: at the beginning of the Christian era, the Roman family had a remarkably strong impact on society – as ideal and as metaphor. The Roman family was strictly hierarchical. *Patria potestas* was a legal concept which gave the *paterfamilias*, the oldest male in direct line within the *familia*, an almost omnipotent power over his *filii* and *filiae*. Although *patria potestas* was curtailed in a number of ways, and despite the fact that the ideal *paterfamilias* would exercise his *potestas* with love and in moderation, both men and women under *potestas* were severely restricted in their freedom of action. Only after the death of the *paterfamilias* did his *filii* and *filiae* become *sui juris*, in their own right. The traditional ideal of the Roman family was legally reinforced by the Augustan family laws, which accentuated the idealisation of marriage, procreation, and sexual virtue.

This family ideal was used as a point of departure for the creation of metaphors outside the family sphere. Family metaphors flourished in Roman society and helped to underline its hierarchical nature. A predominant – though not exclusive – function of Roman family metaphors was to evoke images of authority: authority of Gods over humans, senior officials over junior officials, state leaders over subjects. The Romans seem to have viewed themselves as, above all, a society of fathers and sons, and the metaphor of the father held a particularly important position among family metaphors in the aristocratic political system of the Republic and later on in imperial Rome.

Roman family metaphors were in many respects dissimilar to the metaphorical family introduced by the first Christians. Whereas the Roman family signalled, first and foremost, hierarchical power relationships, the family metaphors as used by the first Christians did not primarily support a hierarchical order on earth. When in the Gospels, to take the most prominent Christian texts, family metaphors were used to describe inter-human relationships, their function was primarily to create equality and a new sense of belonging. From the point of view of pagan Romans, then, there was a contrast between the Roman use of family metaphors, most often conveying authority, and the family metaphors used by the first Christians, expressing equality.

As family metaphors constituted one of the means by which the Christian religion was communicated to the Romans, this difference is important. The use of family metaphors, on the one hand, made Christianity understandable, recognisable – and, in every sense of the word, familiar to the Romans. The frequent use of family metaphors in pagan Roman ideology only added to the familiarity. The contrast, on the other hand, between the old Roman family – as an ideal and a metaphor – and the new Christian family of metaphors, must have meant that the Christian metaphorical language would have been often surprising, or even shocking, to the Roman ear.

As, in the first three centuries AD, the Christian religion expanded within the Roman world, the increased interplay between the Roman family – as ideal and metaphor – and the use of family metaphors in Christian communities opened up new developments. In some areas the Christian message would maintain its original content, emphasising equality. In other areas, it would be distorted, eventually adopting the hierarchical nature of pagan Rome.

NOTES

1 But the exact importance of metaphorical language to the life of a culture is a matter of vivid debate. At one end of the scale of scholarly views on the functions of metaphors we find scholars who believe that metaphors mostly serve rhetorical functions and thus could be omitted easily and converted into literal language. At the other end of the scale are positioned scholars according to whom almost all our experiences are spoken of by means of metaphors; this view has been particularly articulated by Lakoff and Johnson 1980: 22 and 56. For a summary of this debate, see Macky 1990: 163.

2 Studies of religious metaphorical language are numerous. See e.g. Soskice 1985; Crabtree 1991; Macky 1990.

3 Parallel to and connected with the growing scholarship on women's history, the Roman family has been the subject of keen interest throughout the 1970s, 1980s and 1990s. Major issues have been – and continue to be – the size of the Roman family – did the Romans live in something like nuclear families? – and the relationship between the *paterfamilias* and the *filii* and *filiae* from the point of view of legal as well as social history. See notes 4 and 6 below. See also Dixon 1988: 13ff 'Defining the family' and Dixon 1992: 1ff 'Defining the Roman family', in which much of the debate on these issues is summed up.

4 For the importance of adoption in the different levels of society, see e.g. Prevost 1949: 61ff; Hopkins 1983: 49f and 194f; Corbier 1991: 63ff; Dixon 1992: 113. Probably adoption was not immensely widespread, even within the upper classes. Out of the 400 knights registered by Nicolet 1966 and 1974, for example, less than ten were adopted.

5 Dixon 1988: 23ff. On exposure of the newborn child, see e.g. Dixon 1992: 122.

6 The research on the legal concept of *patria potestas* is extensive, carried out by both lawyers and historians. Since Crook wrote his pioneering article *'Patria potestas'* (1967b), in which he put the legal concept of *patria potestas* into the context of social history, a large number of scholars have followed in his footsteps, exploring the impact of *patria potestas* on various aspects of Roman family life. For the more recent and important studies, combining a legal and social approach, see e.g. Saller 1984a; 1986; 1988; 1991; Lacey 1986; Thomas 1986; Wiedemann 1989; Rawson 1991; Treggiari 1991; Dixon 1992.

7 A major part of the legal regulations contained in the *Corpus Iuris Civilis* claim to belong to the Classical period. It is a matter of on-going discussion whether a number of these regulations were in fact interpolated, that is, changed from the original by the sixth-century compilers. Since, however, Volterra in the 1940s carried out his analysis of the Roman law of marriage it is generally agreed that the rules concerning the requirement of the consent of *filiae* and *filii* were not interpolated (Volterra 1940 and 1948: 224ff). See also Gaudemet 1949: 318. The debate about the marriage arrangements includes major questions such as the age at marriage of the *filius* and *filia* (a debate summed up by Treggiari 1991: 398ff) and the importance of dowry (see e.g. Humbert 1972: 99; Saller 1984b: 202f; Crook 1990; Treggiari 1991: Ch. 10).

8 Although most scholars now agree that the Romans lived in some kind of nuclear families – but with differences according to different regions and classes – the actual size of the family in ancient Rome is still a topic of on-going scholarly discussion. See e.g. Saller and Shaw 1984: 124–56, 134f; Saller 1984a: 336–55; Dixon 1988: 8; Treggiari 1991: 410f; Dixon 1992: 6ff; Martin (forthcoming).

9 Saller 1986: 7–22. See also Hopkins 1983.

10 For a further discussion of paternal feelings, see e.g. Wiedemann 1989: 34; Veyne 1985: 25; Hallett 1984: XI, 32, 146ff, 168ff, 219, 255f, 346; Reinhold 1976: 48f, Saller 1988: 393–410; Bradley 1991: 139f; Eyben 1991: 116ff. For examples of *pietas* shown to the mother and senior members of the family, see Saller 1988: 399ff.

11 For the ideal of fatherly love in the Principate, see e.g. Sen. *Prov.* 2.5 (idealising a corrective and guiding love) and Pliny, *Ep.* V.16 (portraying tenderness and indulgence in the relationship between a young girl and her father).

12 The best discussion of each regulation contained in the Augustan laws is still Humbert 1972: 138ff. See also Dixon 1992: 78ff.

13 The relationship between former masters and slaves, now freedmen, formed part of the *clientela* system, which played an essential role in society. The research on *clientela* is vast and far too extensive to enter into in this context. Only those clients who were former slaves will be focused upon, but it should be noticed that by forming links to persons outside the limited *familia*, a vital bond was formed between the family and society, between the private and the public sphere.

14 Scholars have held very different views on the motives behind using family terms in connection with the relationship between master and slave. Such scholarly differences are expressed in relation, for instance, to the fact that slaves were addressed with children's terms: *puer* and *puella*. Moses Finley believed that it showed their deeply inferior role (1980: 73ff and 96ff). According to Paul Veyne, the terminology signified that the slave was an integrated part of the family – a child – as well as an inferior being, 'un

sous-homme' (Veyne 1985: 61). Today probably no one would agree with the sentimental view of Strasburger that slaves were called *puer* and *puella* because the owner cared for his slaves as if they were his own children (1976: 89).

15 I use the terminology and categorisation of Macky 1990: 72f .

16 The titles 'Mother' and 'Father' of a *collegium* are especially found in inscriptions, e.g. *CIL* III. 7505; VI. 8796, 10234; IX. 2687, 5450; XIV. 37, 2408. Liebenam 1890: 218. For *collegium*, see e.g. Hopkins 1983: 211f.

17 But see Sall. *Cat.* 6.6. Florus I.1.15. Livy I.87, for explanations offered by ancient writers as to why the senators were addressed as *Patres*.

18 The Pater Patriae title is most often debated by scholars who are interested in the role of the title in the transformation from Republic to Principate. The paternal leader-figures of the Republic are rarely the object of discussion; but see Alföldi 1971; Weinstock 1971.

19 Also other writings of Cicero make it clear that the *clementia* of the father-figure formed an essential part of Caesar's leader-image, e.g. Cic. *Deiot.* 34, 40; *Lig.* II. 6; *Marcell.* 12; Alföldi 1971: 88; Weinstock 1971: 239.

20 For other references to the perception of Caesar as Father of the Fatherland after his death, see Alföldi 1971: 89f.

21 Augustus himself refers to the event in the culminating passage of his *Res Gestae*: 'In my thirteenth consulship, the senate, the equestrian order and the whole people of Rome gave me the title of Father of the Fatherland, and resolved that this should be inscribed in the porch of my house and in the *Curia Julia* and in the *Forum Augustum* below the chariot which had been set there in my honour by a *Senatus Consultum*' (*Res Gestae* 35). For the importance of *Pater Patriae* in the context of *Res Gestae* as a whole, see especially Ramage 1987: 104–10. Ramage (1987: 20, 25) convincingly argues that *Res Gestae* indicates that for Augustus the title of *Pater Patriae* was the culmination of many years' continuous development. See also Salmon 1982: 150ff.

22 Trillmich 1988: Catalogue no. 344 and p. 486. For a slightly later date, see Alföldi 1971: 48.

23 See e.g. Suet. *Aug.* 34, where Augustus exhibits his nephew Germanicus with his children, as an example to be followed by young Roman men. See also Dixon 1992: 125. Bauman argues that the *maiestas* of Augustus came to include the entire imperial family (Bauman 1967: 218).

BIBLIOGRAPHY

Alföldi, A. (1971) *Der Vater des Vaterlandes im Römischen Denken*, Darmstadt: Wissenschaftliche Buchgesellschaft.

Bauman, R. (1967) *The Crimen Maiestatis in the Roman Republic and Augustan Principate*, Johannesburg: Witwatersrand University Press.

Bradley, K. (1991) *Discovering the Roman Family*, Oxford: Oxford University Press.

—— (1994) *Slavery and Society at Rome*, Cambridge: Cambridge University Press.

Corbier, M. (1991) 'Divorce and Adoption as Roman Familial Strategies', in B. Rawson (ed.) *Marriage, Divorce and Children in Ancient Rome*, Canberra: Humanities Research Centre: 47–78.

Crabtree, H. (1991) *The Christian Life: Traditional Metaphors and Contemporary Theologies*, Harvard Dissertations in Religion, Minneapolis: Fortress Press.

Crook, J. A. (1967a) *Law and Life of Rome*, Ithaca, NY: Cornell University Press.

—— (1967b) '*Patria potestas*', *Classical Quarterly* 17: 113–22.

—— (1990) 'Financial Responsibility in a Roman Marriage', in J. Andreau and H. Bruhns (eds) *Parenté et Stratégies Familiales dans l'Antiquité Romaine*, Collection de l'École Francaise de Rome 129.

Dixon, S. (1988) *The Roman Mother*, London and Sydney: Croom Helm.

—— (1992) *The Roman Family*, Baltimore and London: Johns Hopkins University Press.

Eyben, E. (1991) 'Fathers and sons', in B. Rawson (ed.) *Marriage, Divorce and Children in Ancient Rome*, Canberra: Humanities Research Centre: 114–43

Finley, M. (1980) *Ancient Slavery and Modern Ideology*, London: Chatto and Windus.

Gagé, J. (1963) *Matronalia. Essai sur les Dévotions et les Organisations Cultuelles des Femmes dans l'Ancienne Rome*, Paris: Coll. Latomus 60.

Gardner, J. (1986) *Women in Roman Law and Society*, London: Croom Helm.

Garnsey, P. (1970) *Social Status and Legal Privilege in the Roman Empire*, Oxford: Clarendon Press.

Gaudemet, J. (1949) 'Iustum Matrimonium', *Revue Internationale des Droits de l'Antiquité* 2.

Girard, P. (1924) *Manuel Élémentaire de Droit Romain*, Paris: Rousseau.

Hallett, J. (1984) *Fathers and Daughters in Roman Society*, Princeton, NJ: Princeton University Press.

Hellegouarc'h, J. (1963) *La Vocabulaire Latin des Relations et des Parties Politiques sous la République*, Paris: Les Belles Lettres.

Hopkins, K. (1983) *Death and Renewal*, Cambridge: Cambridge University Press.

Humbert, M. (1972) *Le Remariage à Rome. Étude d'Histoire Juridique et Sociale*, Milan: Dott. A. Giuffre Editore.

Jal, P. (1963) *La Guerre Civile à Rome. Étude Littéraire et Morale*, Paris: Presses Universitaires de France.

Joshel, S. R. (1992) *Work, Identity, and Legal Status at Rome: A Study of the Occupational Inscriptions*, Norman: University of Oklahoma Press.

Kaser, M. (1939) 'Die Geschichte der Patronsgewalt über Freigelassene', *Zeitschrift der Savigny-Stiftung für Rechtsgeschichte* RA 58.

Lacey, W. K. (1986) '*Patria potestas*', in B. Rawson (ed.) *The Family in Ancient Rome: New Perspectives*, London: Croom Helm.

Lakoff, G. and Johnson, M. (1980) *Metaphors We Live By*, Chicago: Chicago University Press.

Lassen, E. M. (1992) 'The Ultimate Crime: *Parricidium* and the Concept of Family in the Late Roman Republic and Early Empire', *Classica et Mediaevalia* 43: 147–61.

Liebenam, W. (1890) *Zur Geschichte und Organisation des Römischen Vereinswesens*, Leipzig: B. G. Teubner.

Liebeschuetz, J. (1979) *Continuity and Change in Roman Religion*, Oxford: Clarendon Press.

Macky, P. (1990) *The Centrality of Metaphors to Biblical Thought: A Method for Interpreting the Bible*, Studies in the Bible and early Christianity, vol. 19, Lewiston: Mellen.

Martin, D. (forthcoming) 'Family structures from funerary inscriptions', *Journal of Roman Studies*.

Maurin, J. (1975) 'Remarques sur la Notion de '*puer*' à l'Époque Classique', *Bulletin de Assn. Guillaume Budé*, Ser. 4, 2: 221–30.

Nicolet, C. (1966 and 1974) *L'Ordre Équestre à l'Époque Républicaine (312–43 av. J-C)*, vol. 1–2, Paris: Boccard.

Pieri, G. (1967) *L'Histoire du Cens à Rome de ses Origines à la Fin de la République*, Paris: Université de Paris.

Premerstein, A. (1937) *Vom Werden und Wesen des Prinzipats*, Munich: Abhandlungen der Bayerischen Akademie der Wissenschaften, Philosophisch-Historische Klasse 15.

Prevost, M.-H. (1949) *Les Adoptions Politiques à Rome sous la République et le Principat*, Publications de l'Institut de Droit Romain, Paris: L'Université de Paris.

Ramage, E. S. (1987) *The Nature and Purpose of Augustus' 'Res Gestae'*, Historia Einzelschriften, Stuttgart: Franz Steiner Verlag.

Rawson, B. (1986) 'The Roman Family', in B. Rawson (ed.) *The Family in Ancient Rome: New Perspectives*, London and Sydney: Croom Helm.

—— (1991) 'Adult–child relationships in Roman society', in B. Rawson (ed.) *Marriage, Divorce and Children in Ancient Rome*, Canberra: Humanities Research Centre: 7–30.

Reinhold, M. (1976) 'Introduction. The Generation Gap in Antiquity', in S. Bertram (ed.) *The Conflict of Generations in Ancient Greece and Rome*, Amsterdam: B. R. Grüner.

Ross Taylor, L. (1931) *The Divinity of the Roman Emperor*, Middleton, CN: American Philological Association.

Saller, R. (1984a) '*Familia, Domus*, and the Roman Conception of the Family', *Phoenix* 38: 336–55.

—— (1984b) 'Roman Dowry and the Devolution of Property in the Principate', *Classical Quarterly* 34: 195–205.

——(1986) '*Patria Potestas* and the Stereotype of the Roman Family', *Continuity and Change* I, I: 7–22.

—— (1988) '*Pietas*, Obligation and Authority in the Roman Family', in P. Von Kneissl and V. Loseman (eds) *Alte Geschichte und Wissenschaftsgeschichte: Festschrift für Karl Christ zum 65. Geburtstag*, Darmstadt: Wissenschaftliche Buchgesellschaft.

—— (1991) 'Corporal Punishment, Authority, and Obedience in the Roman Household', in B. Rawson (ed.) *Marriage, Divorce and Children in Ancient Rome*, Canberra: Humanities Research Centre: 144–65.

Saller R. and Shaw, B. D. (1984) 'Tombstones and Roman Family Relations in the Principate: Civilians, Soldiers and Slaves', *Journal of Roman Studies* 74: 124–56.

Salmon, E. (1982) *The Making of Roman Italy*, London: Thames and Hudson.

Schulz, F. (1951) *Classical Roman Law*, Oxford: Clarendon Press.

Soskice, J. (1985) *Metaphor and Religious Language*, Oxford: Clarendon Press.

Strasburger, H. (1976) *Zum Antiken Gesellschaftsideal*, Abhandlungen der Heidelberger Akademie der Wissenschaften, Heidelberg: Winter.

Thomas, Y. (1984) '*Vitae necisque potestas*', in Y. Thomas (ed.) *Du Châtiment dans la Cité. Supplices Corporels et Peine de Mort dans la Monde Antique*, Rome: École Française de Rome.

—— (1986) 'A Rome, Pères Citoyens et Cité des Pères (IIe Siècle Avant J-C–IIe Siècle Après J-C)', in A. Burguière *et al.* (eds) *Histoire de la Famille*, vol. 1, Paris: Armans Collin.

Treggiari, S. (1991) *Roman Marriage. Iusti Coniugi from the Time of Cicero to the Time of Ulpian*, Oxford: Clarendon Press.

Trillmich, W. (1988) 'Münzpropaganda', in *Kaiser Augustus und die Verlorene Republik*, Eine Ausstellung im Martin-Gropius-Bau, Berlin, 7 June–14 August, Mainz am Rhein: Philipp von Zabern.

Veyne, P. (1985) 'L 'Empire Romain', in Ph. Ariès and G. Duby (eds) *Histoire de la Vie Privée*, vol. 1, Paris: Éditions du Seuil.

Volterra, E. (1940) *La Conception du Mariage d'après les Juristes Romains*, Padua: La Garangola.

119

—— (1948) 'Quelques Observations sur le Mariage des *filii familias*', *Revue Internationale des Droits de l'Antiquité* 1: 213–42.

Weinstock, S. (1971) *Divus Julius*, Oxford: Clarendon Press.

Wiedemann, T. (1989) *Adults and Children in the Roman Empire*, London: Routledge.

Wilkinson, B. (1964) 'A Wider Conception of the Term *parens*', *Classical Journal* 59: 358–61.

7

FAMILY IMAGERY AND CHRISTIAN IDENTITY IN GAL 5:13 TO 6:10

Philip F. Esler

THE PROBLEM OF GAL 5:13 TO 6:10 AND ITS FAMILY IMAGERY

The very existence of 5:13 to 6:10 in the letter to the Galatians constitutes one of the great conundrums of Pauline research. Debate rages as to why in a letter focusing mainly on a problem originating in the external environment, the pressure being exerted on the Gentile members of the Galatian congregations to be circumcised, accept the Jewish law and become Jews, Paul turns away from this subject in 5:13 to 6:10 to something internal to the congregations, the issue of the qualities, values and behaviour which should and should not characterise the lives of the members, especially with respect to one another.

Existing answers to this question range from the suggestion of O'Neill that this passage is actually a non-Pauline interpolation (O'Neill 1972), to that of Dibelius (1934: 238–39 and 1976: 1–11) who thought it was by Paul but quite unrelated to the letter as a whole, representing early Christian paraenesis rather than anything specifically Pauline, to the approaches of Lütgert (1919) and Ropes (1929) who argued that Paul had two entirely different types of problem to deal with in Galatia; on to more recent work by Betz (1979), Howard (1979) and Barclay (1988), all of whom favour regarding the passage as integrated into the rest of the letter, though for different reasons. Almost all existing scholarship on 5:13 to 6:10 insists on categorising it as 'ethical', although commentators rarely define or justify such usage.

My own broad approach, which I have recently developed elsewhere (Esler 1996a) and will only mention here, employs anthropology and social psychology to argue for two propositions. First of all, the passage is tightly integrated into the letter, in that it illustrates the close nexus which often exists between the impact of boundaries which members have crossed to join a group, and the group's internal conditions. Second, a helpful theoretical framework is that of social identity generated under conditions of intergroup tension and conflict, since this approach covers issues which are referred to in existing New Testament scholarship as 'ethical' and 'eschatological' while recognising that they form only a part of a larger complex of meaning constituted by group identity. In this perspective, any behavioural norms in Gal 5:13 to 6:10 serve to reinforce for the Galatian believers their sense of who they are, especially in contrast to Jew and idolatrous Gentile, rather than having an independent function as ethical prescriptions.

My aim in this chapter is to take up a different aspect of the passage, namely, the extent to which this sense of identity is created through the use of family imagery. The most striking instance of this theme comes in Gal 6:10, where Paul issues an injunction to his audience, the congregations of Galatia (1:2), to do good to everyone, 'but especially to the house members of the faith (*oikeioi tês pisteôs*)'. There are also express references to the 'brethren' (*adelphoi*) in 5:13 and 6:1 and I will propose below that the presence of kinship ideas can also be found in the passage by extensive negative implication – in Paul's attribution to the Galatians of behaviour and attitudes diametrically opposed to that expected of family members in this culture. My principal thesis is that Paul uses family imagery to create an identity for his congregations very different from that of the dominant groups outside their boundaries, especially in his rejection of the usual struggle for honour in this culture. Accordingly, I must oppose commentators like Betz (1979: 311) who counsel against reading too much into the expression *oikeioi tês pisteôs* in 6:10. It is worth noting that Halvor Moxnes has recently produced results consonant with those in this chapter, in the form of a persuasive case that in Romans 12 Paul delineates a new community in which one does not seek one's own honour and where, instead, one acts towards other members like a brother (1995: 223–29).

I will deal first with aspects of family life in the Mediterranean region which would have operated as a primary level of socialisation for Paul's audience and which must be appreciated if the general thrust of Paul's message to his audience is to be understood. Second, I will employ findings from social psychology into the creation of group identity through inter-group conflict to proffer a more focused explanation of the family imagery in the other parts of Galatians. Third, I will consider, in the light of the foregoing discussion, how family imagery in Gal 5:13 to 6:10 contributes to the creation and maintenance of a group identity for Paul's addressees which is both differentiated from other groups and also satisfying in itself. Fourth, I will relate my proposal to the demands of contemporary theology and lifestyle.

FAMILY HONOUR IN MEDITERRANEAN CULTURE: AN ANTHROPOLOGICAL MODEL

To the extent that our interest in Galatians is an historical one, in assessing the significance of Paul's message on *oikeioi* to his original audience we must try to set out what these first-century Galatians would have meant by 'family' or 'household', the cultural norms which governed relations with family members and how these differed from relations with people not connected by ties of kinship. If we do not attempt to come to terms with likely Galatian understandings in these areas we run the risk of imposing modern North Atlantic notions of family onto a text where they are quite inappropriate, of falling into the maws of those twin monsters of anachronism and ethnocentricity.[1]

Still the best way to begin this enquiry is with reference to the model of first-century Mediterranean kinship based on contemporary anthropological research in the region which was developed by Bruce Malina in his 1981 book, *The New Testament World: Insights from Cultural Anthropology*, a revised edition of which appeared in 1993. I stress at once that this is a model, operating at a particular level of generality, not a description of empirical reality, and that we not should expect to find that a particular case will correspond with it in every respect. Using a model like this in no way involves ignoring the diversity of types of family across the Mediterranean in the first century CE. Moreover, even if it were suggested that a model based on contemporary Mediterranean culture is so remote in time from the Biblical texts as to cast doubt on whether it can be used with respect to them at all (a claim I reject), it is clear that merely going through the process of applying Malina's model fulfils the vital purpose of establishing a set of scenarios on the family which, if not quite the same as those of the ancient Mediterranean, must necessarily be much closer than those we derive from our modern North Atlantic social systems and often unconsciously employ. In any event, I will seek to illustrate the applicability of central aspects of the model to ancient Mediterranean family arrangements with respect to some selected literature from Greece and Rome. There is a growing body of secondary literature on ancient Mediterranean family life.[2]

According to the Malina model, the primary good in the Mediterranean world is honour, meaning the value of a person in his or her own eyes together with the acceptance of such an assessment by a relevant group. Honour resides in proper public behaviour or demeanour, and is attached to positions of eminence in family, village, city or nation. It may also be lost, to be replaced with its opposite, shame. Honour may either be ascribed to someone, for example by being born into an aristocratic or illustrious family, or acquired, actively gained in various forms of social interchange which anthropologists refer to as 'challenge and response'. Like all goods in this culture, honour is thought to exist only in limited quantities, so that an accretion of honour to one person in such an interchange means that the other party has been dishonoured, or 'shamed', in consequence. Mediterranean culture is fiercely competitive, or 'agonistic', and virtually any social interchange, such as business affairs, politics, sport, literary contests, dinner invitations or even arranging a marriage, constitutes an arena in which people strive to enhance their honour at someone else's expense. Cooperation usually takes place only within groups, of which families are the most important, and collaboration outside existing groups is a rare event.

John H. Elliott has amplified this aspect of the model in a significant respect (1988; 1990; 1991). Given the stakes at issue in any social contest, those who are unsuccessful, and even the onlookers, tend to develop an extremely negative attitude towards the winners which is best described as 'envy' (*phthonos*; *invidia*). Associated with envy is the evil eye, a powerful force to injure or beset with sickness which can be discharged by such envy in the direction of the person who has been successful.[3] The linked phenomenon of envy and the evil eye reminds us of the extremely serious, almost pathological, dimension to the Mediterranean striving for honour.

Honour is not only possessed by individuals, however. In Mediterranean culture the groups to which one belongs are of far more decisive importance in social relations and in the development of human personality than in our modern individualistic setting. Corresponding to this is the fact that groups are carriers of honour and this is particularly the case with the most important group of all, the family. Few aspects of Mediterranean culture are more pervasive or central than family honour. Outside the family the battle for the acquisition of honour goes on, but inside it the family members work to maintain and extend their collective honour. Malina puts it like this:

> Honor is always presumed to exist within one's own family of blood, that is among all those one has as blood relatives. Outside that circle all persons are presumed to be dishonorable, guilty, if you will, unless proved otherwise. It is with all these others that one must play the game, engage in the contest, put one's honor and one's family honor on the line.
>
> (Malina 1993: 38)

An important consequence of this is that honour gained by one member accrues to the family as a whole, while the family is dishonoured if any of its members acts shamefully. Thus, the family is shamed if a son acts violently or inappropriately in public, or if a daughter is seduced before marriage. Any act which constitutes disobedience to the father of the family will dishonour it and him.

This sense of collective honour within a family means that it is particularly shameful if the members themselves fall out and fail to present a united front to a harshly judgmental public. Yet sometimes there are conflicts within families and to assess their impact it is helpful to consider Malina's description of the three degrees of events in which individuals or groups might be dishonoured: first, the extreme and total dishonour that arises from murder, adultery or kidnap, which demands vengeance since revocation is not possible; second, the significant deprivation of honour where revocation might yet be possible, as in the restitution of stolen items or a verbal insult; and, third, the regular and ordinary social interactions which require some response, as with dinner invitations, for example. Malina points out that first degree dishonour within a family is considered sacrilegious and would constitute a transgression quite out of the ordinary. Murdering a parent is not just homicide, it is parricide, and murdering a brother, fratricide. These are extremely serious crimes which are seen as involving a rift in the sacred order of the universe (Malina 1993: 46–47). Yet examples of inter-family strife falling within the second degree of dishonour, such as where brothers are publicly at odds, for example, in politics or love or sport, are also likely to have serious consequences for the family's honour.

I will now discuss some Greek and Roman texts which illustrate various aspects of this model and which will prove helpful in commenting upon Gal 5:13 to 6:10.

GREEK AND ROMAN ILLUSTRATIONS OF FAMILY HONOUR

The Adelphoe of Terence

A good text for illustrating the essential connection between family honour and the behaviour of individual members in the ancient Graeco-Roman world, and one not inappropriate in relation to Galatians with its ten references to *adelphoi*, is the *Adelphoe* of Terence.[4] This play was first performed in Rome in 160 BC, although it is based on a Greek original (or originals) composed by Menander over a century earlier. The fact that this type of comedy reflects stock morals makes it very helpful for our purpose. The plot revolves around two elderly brothers, Demea and Micio, and their two sons, Ctesipho and Aeschines; both of them are actually the natural children of Demea but he has given Aeschines to Micio for adoption. Demea lives on a farm out of town and is very strict, especially with Ctesipho. He is a *senex durus*. Micio, on the other hand, lives in town and is easy-going and very indulgent with the rather wayward Aeschines. He is a *senex lepidus*. There are two events which propel the plot. First of all, the apparently virtuous Ctesipho harbours a passion for a slave-girl and as the play starts Aeschines has just helped him break through the front door of her owner's house, kidnap her and bring her back to Micio's house. Second, Aeschines loves an otherwise respectable woman who is about to bear his baby and whom he has promised to marry, a plan put into peril by her family learning of the kidnapping and forming the view that it is Aeschines who is interested in the slave-girl. In the end, both young men get their girls, but the issue of family honour is a very critical one as the play proceeds. That this is a deliberate aspect of the plot is indicated by the fact that Aeschines means 'shame' in Greek.

Demea is horrified when he learns of Aeschines' exploits and then discovers that the dutiful Ctesipho was also involved. Demea is almost a mouthpiece for the Malina model. For most of the play his views are continually subverted, but they triumph in the end. Virtually the first remark that Demea makes to Micio about Aeschines is that 'nothing causes him shame' (*quem neque pudet quicquam*: 84). He then goes on to complain about the assault on the slave-dealer's house, saying: 'The whole town is shouting that this was a completely disgraceful act! Scores of people told me this on my way here, Micio. It's on everyone's lips' (*clamant omnes indignissime factum esse. hoc advenienti quot mihi, Micio, dixere! in ores omni populo*: 91–92). At one point Demea and Micio argue over whether what Aeschines has done does amount to a *flagitium*, a grievously shameful act (ibid.: 100–12), but after Demea's departure even the tolerant Micio concedes that Aeschines has injured the family (ibid.: 148). Later on a slave falsely suggests to Demea that he heard Ctesipho rebuking his brother in these words: 'Really Aeschines, how can you perpetrate these shameful acts! How can you disgrace our family in this way' (*o Aeschine, haecin flagitia facere te! haec te admittere indigna genere nostro*: 407–9). There are many other references to the way the family's honour has been besmirched, has suffered *pudor*, by Aeschines' behaviour, or is under threat of this happening (ibid.: 457–59, 485, 489, 504). Similarly, a slave of the family of the pregnant woman who takes the view that all of them (including himself) have been dishonoured, have suffered *infamia* (ibid.: 303), by the apparent desertion of Aeschines, expresses a wish that he could have the young man's whole family in front of him so that he could spew forth his anger over all of them (ibid.: 310–12). In the end, Demea softens his demeanour and takes charge of affairs, somewhat to Micio's detriment. Thus, the old order of morality is confirmed.[5]

Aeschylus' *Seven Against Thebes*

Yet in the *Adelphoe* the brothers, although dishonouring their family, are actually on good terms with one another. To illustrate ancient Mediterranean views on a situation in which there was dissension between brothers I will briefly refer to Aeschylus' *Seven Against Thebes*. The plot concerns a dispute between Eteocles and Polyneices, the two sons of the now dead Oedipus. Eteocles has seized power in Thebes for himself and Polyneices has come to attack the city with six other champions and an army. One of these champions is richly aware of the gravely disordered and dishonourable nature of brother seeking to supplant brother and denounces Polyneices for seeking to destroy his father's city and his native gods, to quench his maternal spring and to imprison his paternal soil (ibid.: 580–85). Not for this champion such a dishonourable fate (*atimos moros*: 589). In due course, Eteocles, having sent off six Thebans to face six of the attackers, announces that he himself will fight his brother. Not surprisingly the prospect of fratricide produces a gasp of horror from the chorus:

So do you wish to cull your own brother's blood?

(ibid.: 717)

Yet Eteocles persists and in due course the brothers kill one another. The chorus comments:

> When men die by a kinsman's hand,
> When brother is murdered by brother,
> And the dust of the earth drinks in
> The crimson blood that blackens and dries,
> Who then can provide cleansing?
> Who can wash it away?
> O house, whose guilty agonies,
> The old vintage and the new, mingle together!
> (ibid.: 735–41; trans. Vellacott 1961: 110)

Although this type of event falls within the first degree of dishonourable act as set out by Malina, the model suggests that dissent between brothers even on matters of lesser importance will be regarded as a serious affront to family honour.

Plutarch's *Peri Philadelphias*

The last classical work to which I will make reference is Plutarch's *Peri Philadelphias* ('On Brotherly Love'), which has been usefully discussed by Betz (1978). This is particularly useful since it was written in the first century CE and its author essentially offers a collection of stock morality covering both Greece and Rome on the subject of how brothers should treat one another. It is the only extended and systematic presentation of what Antiquity had to say about what Betz calls the 'ethics' of brotherly love (Betz 1978: 232), although Hierocles, a second-century CE Stoic, devoted part of his *Elements of Ethics* to the treatment of brothers.[6] We will see later that there are some very close parallels in Plutarch's treatise to views which Paul expresses in Gal 5.13 to 6.10. Plutarch bemoans the fact that brotherly love is actually far rarer in his day than brotherly hatred (478C) and offers detailed and shrewd advice as to how and why it might be encouraged.

As far as the Malina model is concerned, it is worth noting that the idea of brothers needing to be at harmony because of the damage that would otherwise be done to the family honour, is not dealt with at any length, but is mentioned occasionally and may be said to underlie the discussion. The clearest case occurs when Plutarch quotes Sophocles to the effect that the relationship between brothers 'is yoked in honour's bonds not forged by man' (*aidous achalkeutoisin ezeuktai pedais*: 482A, trans. Helmbold 1939: 269). Similarly, he notes that any strife between brothers is analogous to the disharmony among an animal's limbs which bring it to a most shameful end

(479A). Related to this sentiment is the fact that honour is owed by children to parents and by brother to brother (479D) and that parents are owed the greatest honour after the gods (479F). Particular aspects of Plutarch's discussion will be taken up later in this chapter.

THE LETTER TO THE GALATIANS IN CONTEXT: INTER-GROUP CONFLICT AND FAMILY IMAGERY

Prior to employing this material on family honour in the ancient Mediterranean in a detailed consideration of Gal 5:13 to 6:10, we need to bring into the discussion certain general issues concerning the connection between the letter *as a whole* and its context in Galatia. This involves, first, considering the identity of the groups present there and the nature of the boundaries and relationships between them and, second, in the light of this discussion, as enriched by theoretical perspectives drawn from the social psychology of inter-group conflict, demonstrating the importance of family institutions and imagery in the letter outside the passage in question.

Groups and inter-group boundaries in Galatia

It is necessary first, however, to say something of my understanding of 'boundary' in this context, since many New Testament commentators employ this important term, or the related expression 'boundary-markers', without clarifying the notion of 'boundary' which informs their exegesis. Following Fredrik Barth, I see boundaries between groups not as walls or barriers but as zones of interaction which are permeable to the extent that they allow some movement across them, for example, for the purposes of communication or trade, but which are impermeable in the way they proscribe other types of interaction, such as with respect to inter-marriage and inter-commensality (Barth 1969: 9–16; Esler 1996a: 224–26). Second, insiders envisage a boundary separating them from out-groups in two quite separate ways. On the one hand, they have a sense of how the boundary will be perceived by outsiders; this is the public face and typical mode of the boundary and normally involves some of the more visible features of their beliefs or practices. On the other hand, however, they perceive the boundary as it relates to all the complexities of their life and experience; this is the private and idiosyncratic mode (Cohen 1989: 74–75; Esler 1996a: 223–24).

I will now briefly restate my understanding of the Galatian context of Paul's letter, much of which I have set out in more detail elsewhere (Esler 1994: 52–69; 1996a), but here with regard to the diagram in Figure 7.1, which highlights the three groups critical to the discussion: Gentiles, Jews and Christ-followers, and the boundaries between them:

The segment CBAC represents the congregations, drawing members from both Jews and Gentiles, which have only come into existence as a result of

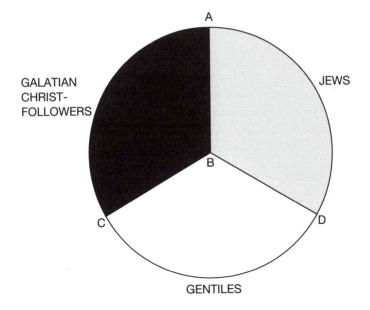

Figure 7.1 The boundaries between Gentiles, Jews and Christ-followers in Galatia

Paul's missionary activities. From the perspective of a particular theory of inter-group conflict and identity formation, which I will discuss below, these Christ-followers constitute, first, an in-group vis-à-vis two out-groups, Jews and Gentiles. Paul distinguishes his addressees from these out-groups in many ways, but on two occasions he does this explicitly by pointing out that what matters is neither circumcision nor uncircumcision but faith working through love (5:6) and the new creation which results (6:15). There are no more distinctions between Jew and Greek (3:28). As we will see, however, there is considerable tension among the Christ-followers; they do not comprise an harmonious group. Second, the Jews are an in-group in relation to two out-groups, Christ-followers and Gentiles; prior to Paul's arrival the Jews had encountered only the latter as an out-group. Third, the Gentiles are an in-group with respect to the Jews and Christ-followers, although we obtain no sense of their perspective on the situation in Galatia as we do for the other two groups.

The principal focus of Paul's concern in this letter is the boundary (as just explained) represented by the line AB, which separates his Christ-followers from the Jews, since the Gentiles among them are under intense pressure to be circumcised (6:12). Their succumbing to such pressure could be regarded in two ways. If all Gentile Christ-followers were circumcised the boundary would be dissolved altogether (5:2–3). If only some did, they would be regarded as having crossed the line and entered the Jewish group. The

Jewish members of his congregations, whom other Jews regarded with suspicion as located on the wrong side of boundary AB since the time they became members and entered into full table-fellowship with the Gentiles, are under pressure from the wider Jewish community (6:12–13) either to eliminate boundary AB altogether by securing the circumcision of the Gentile members or to cross back again by breaking off table-fellowship with them (4:17). The latter approach had previously been adopted by Peter, Barnabas and the other Jewish Christ-followers in Antioch (2:11–14), probably as a means of achieving the long-term goal of forcing the Gentiles to accept circumcision (Esler 1995b). We discern from this that the boundary AB is to some extent permeable, in allowing communication (especially attempted persuasion) across it, and to some extent impermeable, in marking off quite distinct practices with regard to table-fellowship and circumcision. We can be confident that Paul's (internal) sense of the boundary AB was a rich one, given the variegated identity of groups he had formed, whereas he must have been aware that Jews had a much more stereotyped (external) understanding of it, given their preoccupation with the issue of circumcision.

The line BD represents the critical boundary between Jews and Gentiles. First century CE Jews regarded Gentiles as sinners, mainly because of their involvement in various forms of idolatry; Paul's acceptance of this view, as a Jew himself, emerges clearly at Gal 2:15: 'We ourselves, who are Jews by birth and not Gentile sinners . . . '. The line CB is the boundary between the Christ-followers and the Gentiles. The Gentiles among the Pauline congregations had once been on the Gentile side of the boundary, engaged in various kinds of idolatrous practice, to which Paul refers in the letter (4:3, 8). Paul sees some of the Gentile Christ-followers as being at risk of crossing back over into the realm of Gentile idolatry (4:9).

Group identity and inter-group boundaries and conflict in Galatia

Given the nature of these three groups and the tensions, indeed conflict, between at least two of them, it is useful to introduce here some theoretical perspectives which will enable us to probe in more detail their inter-relationships in the context of a consideration of family language in Galatians as a whole. I have elsewhere employed a model drawn from the social psychology of Henri Tajfel (1978) to argue that a primary function of Gal 5:13 to 6:10 is to portray the identity of the Galatian congregations as distinct and as embodying the opposite of the life-style and ethical norms evident among out-groups (Esler 1996a).[7] There are seven aspects to this model and I will now briefly summarise them.

Identity and group membership

Our identity, our sense of who we are, is largely defined in terms of the groups to which we belong. There are three elements of group belonging:

- Recognition of belonging to a group ('cognitive')
- Positive or negative connotations of belonging ('evaluative')
- Attitudes towards insiders and outsiders ('emotional')

Family imagery figures prominently in Galatians in the establishment of group identity. There are five major ways in which Paul achieves this goal outside the confines of Gal 5:13 to 6:10. First of all, the members of the congregations experience God as father, a motif which begins as early as Gal 1:1–3, with two references to God in this role. They are all sons of God through faith in Christ Jesus (3:26); in baptism they have 'donned Christ' (3:27). Through Jesus, the son of God, they become God's adopted sons (4:1–7), a notion powerfully expressed in the statement: 'Because you are sons, God has sent out the Spirit of his Son into your hearts crying "Abba", that is, "father"' (4:6). Second, through Christ, the seed of Abraham (3:16), they too are sons (3:7) and seed of Abraham (3:29). This is a particularly audacious claim, since the Jews and Jewish Christ-followers in Galatia advocating circumcision were probably (and reasonably) proposing kinship with Abraham as one of the glittering prizes for taking that step. Paul redefines Abrahamic lineage as obtained by faith so as to draw upon its evident appeal, to enjoy the honour attached to having such an illustrious ancestor. Third, Paul actually portrays the Galatians as his children (4:19–20). Fourth, they are children of the promise made to Sarah (4:21–31); she is their mother (4:31). In this sense they are free, as opposed to the Jews, or more specifically the Jewish Christ-followers in Jerusalem, who are slaves (4:25). Lastly, all of these methods of asserting or creating parent–child or ancestor–descendant relationships between the Galatians provide a foundation for Paul's repeated designation of his addressees as brothers (*adelphoi*: 1:2, 11; 3:15; 4:12, 28, 31; 5:11, 13; 6:1, 18). Christ-followers who have opposed his message in the past are 'false brothers' (2:4).

Each of these five aspects of the cohesive pattern of the fictive kinship Paul creates among his congregations can be said to have cognitive, evaluative and emotional dimensions within Tajfel's model. As noted above, in the heavily group-oriented Mediterranean world of the first century, the family was the most significant group of all. The mere fact of knowing one belonged to a family (cognitive dimension) provided the main focus for identity and at the same time, if that family were regarded as honourable the members would have had a very positive attitude towards it (evaluative dimension). Both of these dimensions can be seen in Paul's use of family imagery, with sonship of God and Abraham being as high as one could reach. Finally, the third dimension ('emotional'), can generally be presupposed in the Mediterranean practice of having positive regard for one's family (as long as it is regarded as honourable) and negative feelings for outsiders, while it is explicitly present in the way Paul depicts the in-group as the zone of freedom, but the out-groups as those of slavery (2:4 and 4:25: Jews and Jewish Christ-followers; 4:8: Gentiles; 5:1).

Dialectical relationship between social setting and group belonging

The number and variety of social situations seen as relevant to group membership will increase the stronger a member's cognitive, evaluative and emotional connections with a group. Conversely, some social situations, such as persecution (of which there are signs in Galatians at Jewish hands (4:29; 5:11 and 6:12)), will force individuals to act in terms of group identification, however weak their initial connection. In terms of boundaries, one would say that the extent of the permeability between an in-group and an out-group may decrease as the members' connections with the group in these three areas are strengthened.

As we have just seen, Paul employs several varieties of fictive kinship in the letter, no doubt with the aim of promoting what we are calling the cognitive, evaluative and emotional dimensions of belonging to the Galatian congregations. That he needed to go to these lengths, however, may have been due to the fact that there were too many social situations which the Galatians did not relate to their membership of the congregations; that is, the boundaries between them and out-groups (represented by lines AB and BC on the diagram) were too permeable. I will return to this issue in the detailed discussion of Gal 5:13 to 6:10 below.

Group norms

Norms are values defining acceptable and unacceptable attitudes and behaviours for group members. Norms bring order and predictability to the environment, helping members to construe the world. They also point to appropriate behaviour in new and ambiguous situations. Norms enhance and maintain group identity – this is the critical point: in Tajfel's model norms are not treated as separate from group identity but as an integral aspect of it.

It is obvious how easily this aspect of the model can be related to first-century Mediterranean families, discussed above. The sense of group identity arising from family membership encompasses more than just acting in accordance with certain norms, pre-eminently those to do with honour. On the other hand, the very centrality of honour carried the continual risk that the identity of the family, especially in its evaluative and emotional dimensions, could be dealt a serious blow by a disgrace involving one of its members.

In this perspective, we should not fall into the mistake of simply cate-gorising Gal 5:13 to 6:10 as 'ethical' without considering whether normative material in this passage is really significant in the creation or protection of group identity rather than in the expression of an ethical view for its own sake.

Group conflict and inter-group behaviour

Our sense of belonging to one group is largely defined in relation to other groups to which we do not belong. In this context an important distinc-tion must be drawn between inter-individual and inter-group behaviour. Purely inter-individual behaviour is determined solely by reference to personal characteristics of those involved and not by reference to any social categories; it is difficult, in fact, to envisage any behaviour which is purely inter-individual. Purely inter-group behaviour is solely determined by membership of social groups which ignores individual differences and personal relationships; it is seen very clearly in a pilot releasing a load of bombs on an enemy population. All behaviour is capable of being situated somewhere on a continuum stretching from purely inter-individual behaviour at one end to purely inter-group behaviour at the other.

As we have seen, much of Paul's strategy in Galatians involves referring his audience to a number of fictive kinship groups (sons of God, sons of Abraham) to which they belong in contrast to other groups in their environ-ment. Moreover, Galatians reveals a strongly inter-group perspective with barely a sign of inter-individual conduct, except perhaps at 4:10. That Paul should follow this path is not surprising in a culture so strongly oriented around group-belonging.

Stereotyping the out-group

The closer behaviour is to the inter-group extreme, the greater the tendency to treat out-group members as undifferentiated items in a unified social category. This leads to a clear awareness of in-group–out-group dichotomy, the attribution to all members of the out-group of traits assumed to be common to their group as a whole ('stereotyping') and (usually negative) value judgments of those traits.

Stereotyping is central to the argument of Galatians, as Paul strives to draw the sharpest distinction between those who have faith in Christ Jesus and those who do not: 'Those who rely on keeping the law are under a curse' (3:10). And again: 'If you seek to be justified by law, you are severed from Christ and have fallen from grace' (5:4). From what we have already said, moreover, we would expect stereotyping in a Mediterranean context such as Galatia to involve the expression of negative attitudes towards outsiders on the strength of their membership of dishonourable families. This is precisely what we find in the allegory of Hagar and Sarah (4:21 to 5.1): the children of the slave-girl Hagar, the present Jerusalem, are slaves (4:24–25).

Social immobility and inter-group inferiority

Extreme forms of animosity towards out-group members usually require sharp boundaries between the two groups, so that movement from one to another is impossible ('social immobility'). Paul is doing all he can in Galatians to maintain an impermeable boundary between the members and the two out-groups. This explains the sharp animosity expressed at 1:9 (where he wishes that the proponents of the rival Gospel be accursed) and at 5:12 (where he wishes they would castrate themselves), but it also helps to account for his presentation of the opposition as members of a servile family (Hagar's).

Group differentiation through value inversion

A group which is subordinate to another in terms of power and status will frequently respond through forms of group differentiation which attack the basis for the perceived inferiority. This was probably the case in Galatia, where we may assume that the local Christian congregations were no match for the Jewish synagogues in terms of power and influence. Responses by the inferior group usually involve side-stepping the main dimensions of the comparison, either by changing those dimensions or inventing new ones. A common strategy is the assertion that the true positive values are the antithesis of those espoused by the dominant group or groups.

FAMILY IDENTITY AND THE *OIKOS* IN GAL 5:13 TO 6:10

As I have argued elsewhere (Esler 1996a), this model also helps us to explain the flesh/spirit contrast in the passage as an example of a situation where the identity of the in-group is characterised by norms which are the opposite of those of the dominant out-groups, in this case Jews or idolatrous Gentiles. My interest in this essay lies in the extent to which Paul's interest in the fictive kinship operative within the Christian congregations serves to achieve this purpose. I have explored above the five principal areas of imagery focusing on this subject in the letter. A further point of contact with Abraham in particular is that Paul links the experience of the Spirit, which is vital to his proof that justification is by faith and not the law (3:1–6), with the promise made to Abraham (3:14). Although there is a large measure of artificiality in this connection, the frequent references to the Spirit in 5:13 to 6:10 as characteristic of Christian identity – in contrast to the realm of the flesh – themselves evoke the quasi-kinship with Abraham which Paul is so determined to promote. No doubt the circumcising group were seeking to encourage a different (and more plausible) type of link with Abraham based on ethnicity and Paul must have regarded the fact that he could associate the Spirit with his version as a significant element in his argument. This familial theme, therefore, provides the general intra-textual context within which Paul proceeds to a more precise discussion in 5:13 to 6:10, where the somewhat lofty notions of sonship of Abraham and of God, which no doubt contribute greatly to sustaining the identity of his congregations, are developed further in the area of everyday experience. Yet there is another area of kinship language within Gal 5:13 to 6:10 – that related to the household (*oikos*) – which we must now address.

House and house members

The description of those belonging to the Galatian congregations as *oikeioi tês pisteôs* in 6:10 demands consideration of another important issue related to Paul's use of family imagery, namely, the ramifications of the fact that the context for their meetings was probably a house, *oikos*, owned by a member. On three occasions in his correspondence Paul uses the expression *kat' oikon ekklêsia*, 'house-church', to describe a congregation formed in and around, and convening in, a private household (1 Cor 16:19; Rom 16:5; Phlm 2; see Banks 1979). It is essential to note that these households were functioning families, containing family members and possibly slaves and visiting clients, not just the shells of houses taken over for meetings of the congregation. As a result, the congregations were actually swept up into the social realities, the roles, values and institutions, of particular families in the cities in which they were located. This fact had important consequences for the congregation, since it meant, for example, that the celebration of the eucharist could be distorted by local dining practices, as Gerd Theissen has argued (Theissen 1982: 145–74), and, perhaps more significantly, that the owner of the house, male or female, might well function as a patron to the rest of the membership (Bartchy 1992a). Paul does not say whether the Galatian *ekklêsiai* (1:2) were of this type, but it is a reasonable assumption that they were, given that Paul does not indicate any other type of context for his congregations.

A question of critical importance is how this type of social organisation differed from that which characterised Gentile and Jewish groups. Gentile groups can be dealt with fairly quickly. The main type of organisation was that of the *koinôniai* or *collegia*,[8] the associations either of those active in a particular craft or of poor people who wished to secure a proper burial for themselves. These had patrons and their own rooms or buildings for regular dining; they did not meet in the houses of one or more of their members. In general, however, the members were from the non-elite section of society and although they no doubt differed in levels of wealth they probably exhibited a reasonable degree of social homogeneity. There is evidence that the members did regard themselves as (fictive) brothers under a (fictive) father, their patron (Duling 1995: 163) and this may constitute a feature in Paul's social environment influencing his use of *adelphoi* with respect to the Christ-followers in his congregations. Pauline house-churches, however, differed from these in as much as they sometimes (as in Corinth) straddled elite and non-elite social strata, involved members in the actual social dynamics of family life, especially through the conjunction of meals with eucharistic table-fellowship, and they were provided with numerous strands of fictive imagery deriving from Abraham and so on which provided a rich context for a strong sense of family.

But what was the social setting in which Jews met in Diaspora cities? How did this differ from Christian house-churches? Here we must briefly enter the difficult area of the existence and nature of Jewish synagogues outside Palestine (for example, in the Galatian region) in the middle of the first century CE. At present a lively reassessment is underway into the origins of the synagogue and this has an important bearing on its existence in the Diaspora.[9] There seems little need, however, to doubt the existence of Jewish synagogues throughout the Diaspora in the first century. Although there is very little archaeological evidence,[10] the literary evidence for the existence of synagogues throughout the Diaspora is strong, with Acts of the Apostles being the most useful source. Luke describes Paul and other missionaries as entering synagogues (*synagôgai*) in nine cities throughout the eastern Mediterranean.[11] Although there is some doubt as to whether this is an excessively stereotyped picture for the benefit of Luke's readers rather than historical evidence of Paul's practice (Esler 1987: 42–43), it is most unlikely that the presence of synagogues in these cities is itself a Lucan invention. There is also other literary evidence in Josephus[12] and Philo.[13]

Our particular interest is in the extent, if any, to which the house context of the Pauline congregations differed from the synagogue. The particular pertinence of this question springs from the fact that some of the synagogues which have been excavated in the Diaspora, at Dura Europus (on the Euphrates), Priene (western Asia Minor) and Stobi (in the former Yugoslavia), began life as houses (Kraabel 1995: 99, 108, 112–15). In each case the synagogue began as a domestic dwelling and was gradually remodelled into a larger and more differentiated structure as time went on. Although these are later than the first century, there is no reason to think that the position would have been any different earlier. Accordingly, we must enquire whether there was a significant distinction between the architectural context of house-church and synagogue (where it met in a house) and or whether Lietzmann, with whom Hengel agreed, was right in suggesting that the Jewish synagogue in Stobi was equivalent to the *ekklêsia kat'oikon* of early Christianity (cited in Hengel 1966: 162). If this were the case, the distinctiveness of the Pauline congregations, including those in Galatia, based upon family identity, would be rather attenuated.

There are two arguments of a general nature for disagreeing with Hengel and Lietzmann. First, at a time when Paul was establishing small Christian groups in these cities it is probable that many of them already contained large and perhaps reasonably well-off Jewish communities which could not have been comfortably accommodated in someone's home. Second, there is the analogy with the history of the Christian house-church. Although in the first phase of Christianity (to about 150 CE) the communities did operate in functioning houses, during the period 150–250 CE private residences were renovated and dedicated exclusively for the use of the congregation (Blue 1994: 124–25), even if the outside of the building gave no sign of its alteration in function. This type of building is referred to as a *domus ecclesiae* (White 1990). The church at Dura Europus, which was built about 232/33 CE and renovated about 240/41, is a good case in point (Blue 1994: 166). It would be most surprising if a step taken by Christians as early as 150 CE, in spite of occasional persecution by Roman authorities, had not also been found necessary and practical by Jewish communities, who were not under such a threat, much earlier in their occupation of the Diaspora cities.

Moreover, a close examination of the evidence for the clearest case, at Stobi, reveals evidence of a specific type that Lietzmann and Hengel have uncharacteristically fallen into error here. There is extant from Stobi an inscription recording a gift of a house by one Polycharmos to the Jewish community to use as a synagogue, on condition that he and his heirs retain possession of all of the upper rooms, where they presumably continued to live (Kraabel 1995: 113). This makes it quite clear that the local Jewish community was to be given vacant possession of the rest of the house, so that there would be no on-going interaction between it and the family of Polycharmos such as typified the Christian house-church and enhanced the familial dimension of Christian identity. Accordingly, while it would make good sense for Christ-followers in Galatian cities gathering in the homes of one of their number and experiencing their everyday operations to address one another as 'brother', the local synagogue would probably have lacked this stimulus to the adoption of the language of kinship in its interrelationships. Accordingly, the ethos of the meetings of the two groups would have been quite different.

It is worth noting another important difference between a Jewish synagogue, even if meeting in what was once a domestic dwelling, and a house-church, namely, the prominence given in the former to the Law. There is no doubt that the reading of the Law every sabbath was characteristic of Jewish synagogues in the first century CE.[14] The emphasis given to this activity, its centrality in the meeting, no doubt reinforced by the fact that the scrolls were brought out from a side-room or store each sabbath for this purpose (Hengel 1966: 165) and placed on a special table, carries an architectural and social significance which served to differentiate the synagogue from the Christian house assemblies. In due course torah shrines were erected in synagogues, but this seems to have occurred only after 70 CE and would have had no relevance to the position in Galatia in the fifth decade of the first century when Paul wrote the letter.[15]

FAMILY HONOUR IN GALATIANS 5:13 TO 6:10

At the beginning of this passage Paul refers to his addressees as 'brothers', *adelphoi*, which can be translated (somewhat archaically) as 'brethren' to emphasise the inclusion of women in the congregations (3:28). This is the eighth instance of *adelphoi* in the letter in relation to members of the congregations and plainly constitutes a continuation of a significant strand of family imagery. Yet the theme of fictive kinship now assumes a new importance, since Paul proceeds to a different, although, as I have argued elsewhere (Esler 1996a), related dimension of his message – not the need to resist Jewish or Jewish-Christian pressure to be circumcised – but the necessity of having an identity appropriate to their new status, which includes treating one another properly. He begins with statements of principle:

> For you were called to freedom, brethren (*adelphoi*); only do not use your freedom as an opportunity for the flesh, but through love be slaves to one another. For the whole law is fulfilled in one word, 'You shall love your neighbour as yourself'.
>
> (5:13–14)

In verse 13 the loftiness of the initial proclamation of freedom is immediately qualified by mentioning that they are 'brothers', and then even more circumscribed by express restrictions, most notably that they are to be 'slaves to one another through love' (*agapê*). As a general matter of Mediterranean culture, this type of statement primarily evokes a domestic context, given that most slaves worked in families in urban settings (Bartchy 1992b: 68). In terms of the Tajfel model, however, whereas Paul has previously complained that it was the circumcisers who sought to enslave the Gentile Christians (Gal 2:4; 4:25) and that before their conversion they were enslaved 'under the elements of the world' (4:3), a description characterising both Jewish and Gentile out-groups (Betz 1979: 204–5), now, paradoxically, he advocates a form of intra-community enslavement of love, thereby redefining the concept away from its oppressive meaning current among those outsiders towards an entirely different reciprocal love relationship. Something very similar to this strategy continues in the next verse. Here Paul's point is not that Christians should adopt part of the Mosaic law, as some suggest,[16] but rather that the love which they must express as a consequence of their call to freedom as brothers, and which is the first gift the Spirit (5:22), gives them, albeit by an entirely different route, is the best the Law can provide.

Then comes the surprise, almost as great as that occasioned by Luke's sudden reference to conflict in the Jerusalem community in Acts 6:1:

But if you bite and devour one another take heed that you are not consumed by one another.

(5:15: Revised Standard Version)

Hitherto we have had no mention of internal disorder of such a kind, akin to the savagery of wild animals, among the congregations. Now we find, suddenly thrust before us, either a reference to behaviour of this type which has occurred, or at least a warning that the potential exists for it, although without learning the details. There is a striking disjunction between his addressing them as *adelphoi* in 5:13 (and elsewhere in the text) and the attribution to them of behaviour quite inappropriate between family members in 5:15. The force of the contrast depends upon the importance of family solidarity and honour in Mediterranean culture. Plutarch actually offers the hostility of wild animals toward one another in the search for food as an example of the behaviour which brothers should avoid (*Peri Philadelphias*, 486B). In verse 15 Paul is bent upon a course which is represented in the last aspect of the Tajfel model in that he warns them to avoid behaviour which is the antithesis of that mentioned in the previous two verses, behaviour no doubt meant to be regarded as characteristic of out-groups. Earlier in his career, in 1 Thess 4:9, Paul had identified the notion of loving one another (*to agapan allêllous*) with brotherly love (*philadelphia*) as if it was almost a matter of course. An admonition similar to that of 5:15, although couched in less extreme language, occurs at 5:26 and is discussed below.

Betz (1979: 276–77), followed by Dunn (1993: 293), counsels against taking the statement at 5:15 as relating to actual conduct in Galatia on the basis that it is typical of the style of the diatribe,[17] although Dunn allows the possibility that Paul has in mind a danger to be warned against even if not a situation to be rebuked. For the purposes of the argument in this essay it is sufficient that Paul faced merely the potential for divisiveness of such a type. Yet to the extent that one might have diatribal features here (and elsewhere in 5:13 to 6:10), we should not too easily discount the possibility that Paul has introduced them in response to actual problems in Galatia rather than as merely reflecting a fondness for the style of Hellenistic moralising. Paul is writing to congregations of whom he has received disturbing news after his departure, even to the extent of their turning to another Gospel (1:6–7). In this context, the abrupt introduction of the theme of internal dispute in 5:15 reads very naturally as his reaction to another element of the exigencies of the situation in Galatia, even if it is flavoured with diatribal style.

The next section (5:16–26) contains the protracted contrast between life in the Spirit and life in the flesh, which I have discussed elsewhere (Esler 1996a). In 5:19–21 he lists several social and personal delinquencies associated with the flesh: fornication (or incest), impurity, licentiousness, idolatry, sorcery, enmities, strife, jealousy, anger, selfishness, dissension, factions, envy (*phthonoi*), drunkenness, carousing. As just suggested, his Galatian addressees were probably either guilty of at least some of these, or on the verge of falling into them, which meant that they misunderstood the nature of Christian freedom (5:13). Most of these disorders, moreover, could be seen as being socially destructive within the description in 5:15. A little later he runs through the entirely different phenomena which characterise the Spirit (5:22–23). Paul's second list provides a vision of reality which is diametrically opposed to the values and practices of the first. Since the list at 5:19–21 characterises how people in this culture behaved towards outsiders (or how wayward brothers acted towards one another), while the second list (at 5:22–23) specifies the type of existence within a harmonious family, we can now see how this extended set of antitheses functions to provide normative content to a particular type of family identity in accord with the model from Tajfel. As noted by Betz, indeed, the two lists in 5:19–23 are actually related to two types of sons, similar to the contrast between the two sons of Abraham in Gal 4:21–31, who represent absolute opposites (Betz 1978: 252).

Yet the admonition at 5:26 – 'Let us not engage in empty boasting (*kenodoxoi*), challenging (*prokaloumenoi*) one another, envying (*phthonountes*) one another' – constitutes a remarkable crystallisation of what Paul sees as the exact opposite of the proper identity and behaviour of the congregations. What we have here is virtually a summary of Mediterranean man,[18] always envious of the success of others outside the family circle and seeking to provoke them to social contests of challenge and response in order to win honour and to be able to boast as a result. The model set out above suggests that, in urging his audience to distance themselves from such an outlook, Paul wants them to adopt a corporate identity appropriate to members of one family, who did not challenge each other to contests of honour. The proper course was for *adelphoi* to cooperate and defend one another's honour and it was quite scandalous, even sacrilegious, when they did not. Paul was to make almost exactly this point a little later in his career, in Rom 12:10, where he advised: 'Be affectionate toward one another in brotherly love (*philadelphia*); rate one another more highly in honour (*timê*).[19] Plutarch also expresses a similar sentiment at some length in *Peri Philadelphias*: 485 when, *inter alia*, he describes the need for brothers to do everything they can to avoid becoming envious of one another. At one point he makes the very revealing concession that if brothers find it impossible not to envy, they should at least direct their malice (for which he uses the word *baskanon*, referring to the baleful effect of the evil eye) to people outside the family (*trepein exô kai pros heterous apocheteuein to baskanon*), just like politicians who divert sedition by means of foreign wars (485E). Although the repeated word 'one another' in 5:26 might suggest that Paul comes close to this latter view of Plutarch, in as much as he seems mainly interested in his addressees eschewing such behaviour amongst themselves however they might treat outsiders, this possibility may conflict with the admonition at 6:10 to do good to outsiders, unless, as I suggest below, it is possibly unwise to place too much stress on such a sentiment.

Paul continues this theme of family honour in the next section, 6:1–10, which is actually framed with family imagery, beginning with an address to the brethren, *adelphoi*, in 6:1 and closing with a reference to the members of the household of faith, the *oikeioi tês pisteôs*, in 6:10. In 6:1 Paul urges the brothers (*adelphoi*), also described as *pneumatikoi*, gently to use influence on wayward members. Although Betz is right to say that the Galatians may have used the word *pneumatikoi* as a term of self-designation (1979: 297), we must add that in this letter it also carries the connotation of 'sons of Abraham' because of the connection, noted above, which Paul establishes between possession of the Spirit and descent from Abraham. We see in this verse, therefore, Paul recommending what is virtually sibling pressure being brought to bear on people to conform. This pressure stems ultimately from the desire in a strongly corporate culture to preserve group honour, especially where that group is a family. Furthermore, the domestic associations of this process are enhanced by the reference to the gentleness or 'mildness' (*prautês*) to be employed, since, as Hauck and Schulz point out, 'it is fitting to show mildness to one's own people', one's *oikeioi* (1968: 646). These views find corroboration in Plutarch, who also advises of the need for brothers to remonstrate with wayward brothers, frankly (*meta parrêsias*) pointing out their errors of commission and omission but with care and concern (*Peri Philadelphias*: 483A–B).

Next, in 6:2, he urges them to share one another's burdens, so that they will 'fulfil the law of Christ' (*nomon tou Christou*). The proximity of this verse to the exhortation to brothers in the verse before, coupled with the fact that cooperation was most commonly seen within families, suggests that here too he is seeking to establish a group identity rooted in family imagery. Plutarch treated it as a sign of a healthy relationship between brothers that they had in common their father's property and friends and slaves (*Peri Philadelphias*: 478C). The notion that it is with *philoi* that one should share one's burdens was popular in Greek popular philosophy (Betz 1979: 298–99), while in archaic Greek family ethics kinship (*syngeneia*) and friendship (*philia*) had been closely related (Betz 1978: 232). Moreover, '*philos* was a term with so broad a connotation as to embrace relatives as well as (the standard rendering) "friends"' (Whitehead 1986: 231). Aristotle actually commented at one point in the *Nichomachean Ethics* that 'Brothers have all things in common' (8.9.1–2). Thus the philosophic background does not preclude a familial nuance here. Paul's use of the expression 'the law of Christ' in this verse is noteworthy; this is the only time out of some thirty instances in Galatians that 'law' (*nomos*) is not used of the Jewish Law. My view, argued elsewhere (1996a: 237), is that Paul is employing 'the law of Christ' as a metaphor for the way in which love, originating in the Spirit, now becomes the guiding force in Christian life, so that his use of the word in Gal 6:2 represents the high-point of the inversion of the values of a major out-group troubling his communities.

In Gal 6:3 Paul reiterates the Mediterranean wisdom that it is foolish to esteem oneself without foundation, a condition aptly described as *kenodoxos* in 5:26. In verses 4–5 Paul, however, diverges from prevailing values, just as he had in 5:26, to suggest that his audience ditch a central aspect of their local culture, namely, the continual striving to measure oneself against others and to win the honour that came from being publicly adjudged superior to them, as asserted by boasting over someone else.[20] Although he does not say so explicitly, to jettison this activity means to act as one should properly behave towards one's relatives, with whom it is unseemly to engage in tussles over honour since this shames the whole family. Verse 5 confirms this point by reminding the members of the need to concentrate on their own responsibilities; in other words, they are to avoid pointing out how much better they are doing than others. There is a theme quite close to this in the *Peri Philadelphias* where Plutarch advises anyone who simply cannot control his envy for his brother at least to choose a separate field of activity to eliminate the possibility of comparison of the one with the other.[21]

In verse 6 Paul recommends that a pupil share what he has with his teacher, although the precise nature of what is to be shared is uncertain. Betz suggests that it reflects a practice whereby students and teachers shared 'in all good things', an adaptation of the Pythagorean saying *panta koina tôn philôn* (Betz 1979: 305). Nevertheless, it seems that in some circles at least this type of common sharing was recognised as being itself modelled on family life, as indicated by the following provision of the Hippocratic Covenant: 'to hold him who has taught me as equal to my parents and to live my life in partnership with him, and if he is in need of money to give him a share of mine' (Betz 1979: 305).

Paul changes tack in verses 7–9 by reminding his audience that there is another dimension to the choice to live according to the flesh or the Spirit, namely, the issue of one's ultimate destiny, which he refers to as 'eternal life'. This does not contradict the creation of a distinctive Christian identity in which he has hitherto been engaged, since a sense of where we are heading is very often an integral part of our sense of who we are. Moreover, to the extent that ethical norms do constitute an important dimension of this identity, he reminds the Galatians of the ultimate consequences for acting in defiance of them. Paul knows of no disjunction between faith and moral responsibility.

At last we come to verse 10: 'So then, as we have opportunity, let us do good to everyone, especially to the house members of the faith (*oikeioi tês pisteôs*).'[22] In the first clause Paul advocates doing good to everyone, which must here include those who are outside the congregations. Betz comments that this verse indicates that Paul was more universalistic in his ethics than

Plutarch, whose ethics were clearly focused on the family, while outsiders were of far less concern (Betz 1978: 255). Yet one wonders if Paul is really paying any more than lip-service to such sentiments here and if he can really be distinguished from Plutarch in this way. His manner of dividing the world into two such sharply contrasting zones of flesh and Spirit in Galatians raises doubts about the depth of his concern for outsiders, those who were of the flesh. On the other hand, Rom 12:14–21 shows that, admittedly at a later time and for another audience, he could be quite solicitous for the well-being of out-groups. In any context, our interest lies in the second clause, where Paul at last explicitly enunciates a theme which has been the implied context for much of the discussion since 5:13, that the Galatian believers are members of the one *oikos* of faith, relatives and, perhaps, slaves. It is quite possible, as Dunn suggests, that this expression is constructed in conscious contrast to the typical Old Testament phrase 'house of Israel'.[23] This contrast would then be the last of a series of redefinitions which have characterised the passage. Yet Paul's point extends far beyond the fact that this household is typified by faith and not just law. The developing strands of family imagery since 5:13 give substance to the fact that the household (in its distinctive Mediterranean sense) represents the most appropriate metaphor to express the unique identity of the Galatian Christians. The manner in which house-members should behave to one another as opposed to non-kin conveys for Paul a central feature of that identity.

CONTEMPORARY IMPLICATIONS

I have argued in this chapter that Paul enlists a variety of ways to create among his congregations social patterns analogous to those expected among family members in the ancient Mediterranean, thereby sharply differentiating their identity from that of the wider world, where competitiveness and striving to win honour reigned. Yet what has all this to do with our contemporary experience? One approach, which I have recently developed elsewhere, involves adopting the theology of George Lindbeck in seeking to make the story of the first Christian generations, critically understood, our story (Esler 1995a: 1–20). This is a process which can only take place in believing communities; it is not really a task for the academic theologian.

More specifically, it must be insisted that recognising the cultural gap that separates us from Paul, by utilising social-scientific insights to unravel the relationship between society and *kerygma* in the earliest period of the Church, does not result in a form of interpretation which is unable to assist with the contextualisation of Gospel truth in our own modern situations. It is a serious error to believe that a style of exegesis which fully acknowledges the differences between our culture and the culture (or counter-cultures) of the early Christian communities relegates their experience to a zone irrevocably distanced from us. For the first step in communicating with people from other cultures is to seek to understand their utterances in their formative contexts however alien they might seem; but that is only the first step. There is now an extensive literature on the phenomenon of 'inter-culturalism', which means the process of becoming familiar with another culture so that upon returning home we no longer see things in the same way but in a manner inevitably transformed by our foreign experience. This does not mean that we bring the values of the other culture directly to bear on our own, but as inter-cultural persons, with our feet planted in both cultures, as it were, we stand greatly enriched in vision and understanding compared with our previous mono-cultural state (Gudykunst and Kim 1992: 246–57). In a sense, our ancestors in faith, by whom and to whom Galatians was written, are strangers whom we may yet encounter through a process of historical investigation and from whom we may learn.

Paul's letter to the Galatians testifies to the need for his congregations, troubled by external and internal pressures, to adopt a model of group identity with the depth and resilience necessary to ensure that the members found legitimation of their existence in faith. In modern North Atlantic contexts prevailing cultural patterns throw up quite different models of social and familial relationships. The precise terms of the dichotomy Paul erects between kin and non-kin are not applicable in our situation. Nevertheless, we are capable of inter-cultural enrichment from the experience of the Pauline house members of the faith. In an era when an unjust distribution of the world's goods, corrupted political processes, population pressures, bureaucratisation and increasing pluralism in moral values contribute to our growing sense of depersonalisation and powerlessness, we are capable of being enriched by immersion in the familial intimacy and values advocated by Paul. The precise way in which this occurs will depend on the experience of each modern community of faith exposed to the Pauline model. Nevertheless, it is reasonable to believe that the Christian churches, in seeking to offer an alternative voice on these and other issues, might well consider that new forms of ecclesial existence which, for example, move away from the gun-barrel church with its heavily institutionalised roles and structures towards a more localised and small-scale *modus operandi*, offer responses to our condition which are closely analogous to the path Paul forged two millennia ago.

NOTES

1 It is disappointing that the importance of using social-scientific perspectives to clarify the meaning of basic terms in the discussion of Pauline and other early Christian views on family has not been recognised in recent books by Will Deming (1995) and Stephen Barton (1995). See the reviews of these books by Esler (1996b) and Moxnes (1997).

2 See, for example, Pomeroy 1975; Hallet 1984; Bradley 1991 and Rawson 1991. In addition, see the references in Halvor Moxnes' chapter in this volume.

3 To ward off the evil eye, especially at times of great happiness or exultation, such as at the birth of a child or when enjoying a triumph, when envy will be greatest, various types of amulets and other apotropaic devices are worn.

4 The play is helpfully discussed by Gratwick 1987.

5 Gratwick comments in connection with this surprising resolution: '*Senex lepidus* is really a shallow fool, true wisdom and right belong with *senex durus*' (1987: 29).

6 The word *philadelphia* does not appear in Hierocles' discussion, but it is used in the introduction to the extract of the passage in Stobaeus' *Anthologium* (4.27.20), for a translation of which see Malherbe 1986: 93–95. For relevant bibliography on Hierocles, see Kloppenborg 1993: 271.

7 Also helpful are Brown 1988 and Jones 1989.

8 The standard treatment of collegia is Waltzing 1895–1909. For a summary of some of the relevant issues, see Esler 1987: 173–75 and Duling 1995: 161–64.

9 The view that the synagogue originated in the time of the Babylonian exile and during the return to Palestine in the sixth century BC, which has been very popular from the sixteenth century until quite recently, has been subjected to heavy attack as resting on a virtually non-existent evidentiary basis (Urman and Flesher 1995: xx–xxiii). There is even evidence that synagogues only appeared in Palestine at all after the Maccabean revolt (Grabbe 1995: 19–23). Our earliest reliable evidence for synagogues comes from Egypt during the third and second centuries BC (Griffiths 1995), on the assumption that the expression *proseuchê*, originally meaning 'prayer' but used in this material with reference to a building, is actually an abbreviation for *oikos tês proseuchês*, 'house of prayer'. This is a reasonable view to take of the evidence. One of the Egyptian papyri referring to the *proseuchê*, from the second half of the first century BC, distinguishes it from the assembly of Jews itself, the *synagôgê* (Kasher 1995: 209). Hengel has made a good case for the proposal that *synagôgê* was actually used of the building itself in Palestine up to the first century CE (as in the Theodotus inscription) and thereafter largely supplanted *proseuchê* which had been employed in the Greek-speaking Diaspora (Hengel 1971: 171–80). This meant that the word which had originally referred to a Jewish group came to be applied to the building in which it met.

10 It is true that there is even less archaeological evidence for first-century synagogues outside Palestine than the little that exists for their presence in Palestine at this time (Flesher 1995; Grabbe 1995). Given the uncertainty as to whether the structures identified as synagogues at Masada and Herodium actually fulfilled that function (Flesher 1995: 34–38), the only archaeological evidence for first-century Palestinian synagogues is that referred to in the Theodotus inscription from Jerusalem and the remains from Gamala (Flesher 1995: 38–39) and Migdal (Groh 1995: 58–59), both in Galilee. Much of the archaeological evidence for the Diaspora synagogue has been surveyed in an important article by Kraabel, first published in 1979 (Kraabel 1995). Also see Kraabel 1981. Debate still rages as to whether the building on Delos identified by some as a synagogue, and which was in use during the first century CE, actually served that purpose (Kraabel 1995: 109–12).

11 (Acts 9.20 [Damascus]; 13.5 [Cyprus]; 13.14 and 43 [Pisidian Antioch]; 14.1 [Iconium]; 17.1 [Thessalonika]; 17.10 [Beroea]; 17.17 [Athens]; 18.4 and 7 [Corinth]; 18.19, 26 and 19.8 [Ephesus]). On the other hand, in Acts 16.13 Paul, Silas and Timothy, while visiting Philippi, went out of the town-gate on

the sabbath expecting to find a *proseuchê* beside a river. It is unclear if this is a building or merely a location, although at 16.16 the evangelists are said to be going 'into the *proseuchê*', which suggests a building. The word *proseuchê* is used of a building in Juvenal 3, 296.

12 Josephus: *Antiquities* 16.164–73; 19.300; *War* 2.285–89; 7.44; *Life* 277, 280, 293.

13 Philo: *Quod omnis probus liber sit* 81; *Flaccus* 45–48; *Spec. Leg.* 20, 132; *Embassy to Gaius* 156.

14 Acts 15.21 is the best evidence of this, but also cf Josephus, *JA* 16.43 (referring to the weekly assembly which was devoted to learning Jewish customs and law) and *Against Apion* 2.145; Philo, *Moses* 2.4–42 (referring to the reading of law on the sabbath) and *Embassy to Gaius* 156 (referring to the ancient custom of the Jews of assembling in their houses of prayer on the sabbath when they studied their ancestral wisdom). The Theodotus inscription relating to a pre-70 CE synagogue in Jerusalem states that it was erected for a number of purposes, the first one listed being the reading of the Law (Deissmann 1927: 440).

15 There seems no archaeological evidence for Torah shrines from the few pre-70 CE synagogues for which remains survive – see Flesher 1995 and Groh 1995 for the Palestinian examples. There was also no shrine found in the 'synagogue' in Delos (Kraabel 1981: 82). At first the repository for the scrolls was a small niche or *aedicula*, just large enough to hold a wooden ark, whereas later it took the form of a large apse (Seager 1981: 43).

16 As proposed by Barclay 1988: 141 and Dunn 1993: 288–91. *Contra*, Esler 1996a: 233.

17 For useful discussion of the diatribe, see Stowers 1981 and 1988.

18 The male gender is used deliberately. By and large, challenge and response was a social game played out between men in public, and incidents such as that recorded in 1 Sam1.4–28 involving Hannah's humiliation by Peninnah constitute an exception to the rule.

19 For an excellent discussion of 'brother' and 'family' in Rom 12.3–16, see Moxnes 1995.

20 The RSV misunderstands the point of 6.5: 'But let each one test his own work, and then his reason to boast will be in himself alone and not in his neighbor.'

21 *Peri Philadelphias*: 486D: 'Therefore those who cannot, by their very nature, share without envy their brothers' reputation and influence, should divert as far as possible from those of their brothers their own desires and ambitions, so that by their successes they may give pleasure to each other instead of pain' (trans. Helmbold 1939: 293– 95). Betz sees a similarity between the sentiments here and those in Gal 5.26 and Phil 2.1–4 (1978: 255).

22 The first clause illustrates a theme in early Christianity whose importance may have been underestimated according to Bruce Winter in a recent monograph, namely, the obligations of Christians as benefactors and citizens in their society (Winter 1994). Winter does not, surprisingly, comment on 6.10.

23 Dunn 1993: 333, citing Num 20.29; 2 Sam 1.12; Ezek 3.4; Judith 4.15; *Pss. Sol.* 17.42.

BIBLIOGRAPHY

Banks, Robert (1979) *Paul's Idea of Community: The Early House Churches in their Historical Setting*, Sydney: Anzea Publishers.

Barclay, John M. G. (1988) *Obeying the Truth: A Study of Paul's Ethics in Galatians*, Edinburgh: T. & T. Clark.

Bartchy, S. Scott (1992a) 'Philemon, Epistle to', *Anchor Bible Dictionary* 5: 305–10.

—— (1992b) 'Slavery (New Testament)', *Anchor Bible Dictionary* 6: 65–73.

Barth, Fredrik (ed.) (1969) *Ethnic Groups and Boundaries: The Social Organization of Culture Difference*, Boston: Little, Brown and Company.

Barton, Stephen C. (1994) *Discipleship and Family Ties in Mark and Matthew*, SNTS Monograph Series 80, Cambridge: Cambridge University Press.

Betz, Hans Dieter (ed.) (1978) *Plutarch's Ethical Writings and Early Christian Literature*, Leiden: E. J. Brill.

—— (1979) *Galatians: A Commentary on Paul's Letter to the Churches in Galatia*, Hermeneia Commentary, Philadelphia: Fortress Press.

Blue, Bradley (1994) 'Acts and the House Church', in D. Gill and C. Gempf (eds) *The Book of Acts in Its First-Century Setting, vol. 2. The Book of Acts in its Graeco-Roman Setting*, Grand Rapids, MI and Carlisle: William B. Eerdmans Publishing Company and The Paternoster Press: 119–222.

Bradley, Keith R. (1991) *Discovering the Roman Family: Studies in Roman Social History*, Oxford: Oxford University Press.

Brown, Rupert (1988) *Group Processes: Dynamics Within and Between Groups*, Oxford: Basil Blackwell.

Cohen, Anthony (1989) *The Symbolic Construction of Community*, London and New York: Routledge.

Deissmann, Adolf (1927) *Light from the Ancient East: The New Testament Illustrated by Recently Discovered Texts from the Graeco-Roman World*, English trans. Lionel R. M. Strachan, London: Hodder and Stoughton.

Deming, Will (1995) *Paul on Marriage and Celibacy: The Hellenistic Background of 1 Corinthians 7*, SNTS MS 83, Cambridge: Cambridge University Press.

Dibelius, Martin (1934) *From Tradition to Gospel*, English trans. Bertram Lee Woolf, London: Nicholson & Watson.

—— (1976) *A Commentary on the Epistle of James*, revised H. Greeven, Hermeneia Commentary, English trans. Michael A. Williams, Philadelphia: Fortress.

Duling, Dennis C. (1995) 'The Matthean Brotherhood and Marginal Scribal Leadership', in P. F. Esler *Modelling Early Christianity: Social-Scientific Studies of the New Testament in Its Context*, London and New York: Routledge: 159–82.

Dunn, James D. G. (1993) *The Epistle to the Galatians*, Black's New Testament Commentaries, Peabody, MA: Hendrickson.

Elliott, John H. (1988) 'The Fear of the Leer: The Evil Eye from the Bible to Li'l Abner', *Forum* 4: 42–71.

—— (1990) 'Paul, Galatians and the Evil Eye', *Currents in Theology and Mission* 17: 262–73.

—— (1991) 'The Evil Eye in the First Testament: The Ecology and Culture of a Pervasive Belief', in Norman K. Gottwald (ed.) *The Bible and the Politics of Exegesis*, Cleveland, OH: Pilgrim Press, 147–59.

Esler, Philip F. (1987) *Community and Gospel in Luke–Acts: The Social and Political Motivations of Lucan Theology*, Cambridge: Cambridge University Press.

—— (1994) *The First Christians in their Social Worlds: Social-Scientific Approaches to New Testament Interpretation*, London and New York: Routledge.

—— (ed.) (1995a) *Modelling Early Christianity: Social-Scientific Studies of the New Testament in Its Context*, London and New York: Routledge.

—— (1995b) 'Making and Breaking an Agreement Mediterranean Style: A New Reading of Galatians 2:1–4', *Biblical Interpretation* 3: 285–314.

—— (1996a) 'Group Boundaries and Inter-group Conflict in Galatians: A New Reading of Gal 5:13 to 6:10', in Mark Brett (ed.) *Ethnicity and the Bible*, Leiden: E. J. Brill: 215–40.

—— (1996b) Review of Deming 1995, in *The Expository Times* 107: 184.

Flesher, Paul. M. (1995) 'Palestinian Synagogues Before 70 CE: A Review of the Evidence', in Urman and Flesher (eds) *Ancient Synagogues: Historical Analysis and Archaeological Discovery*, vol. 1, Leiden: E. J. Brill: 27–39.

Gill, David W. J. and Gempf, Conrad (eds) (1994) *The Book of Acts in Its First-Century Setting, vol. 2. The Book of Acts in its Graeco-Roman Setting*, Grand Rapids, MI and Carlisle: William B. Eerdmans Publishing Company and The Paternoster Press.

Grabbe, Lester L. (1995) 'Synagogues in Pre-70 Palestine: A Re-Assessment', in Urman and Flesher (eds) op. cit.: 16–26, (reprinted from (1989) *JTS* 39: 401–10).

Gratwick, A. S. (1987) (ed.) *Terence: The Brothers*, Warminster: Aris and Phillips Ltd.

Griffiths, J. Gwyn (1995) 'Egypt and the Rise of the Synagogue', in Urman and Flesher (eds) op. cit.: 3–16, (reprinted from (1987) *JTS* 38: 1–15).

Groh, Dennis E. (1995) 'The Stratigraphic Chronology of the Galilean Synagogue from the Early Roman Period through the Early Byzantine Period (c. 420 CE)', in Urman and Flesher (eds) op. cit.: 51–69.

Gudykunst, William B. and Kim, Young Yun (1992) *Communicating with Strangers: An Approach to Intercultural Communication*, second edn, New York: McGraw-Hill, Inc.

Gutmann, Joseph (ed.) (1981) *Ancient Synagogues: The State of Research*, Brown Judaic Studies 22, Chico, CA: Scholars Press.

Hallett, Judith P. (1984) *Fathers and Daughters in Roman Society: Women and the Elite Family*, Princeton, NJ: Princeton University Press.

Hauck, Friedrich, and Schulz, Siegfried (1968) *'Praus, Prautēs'*, TDNT 6: 651.

Helmbold, W. C. (1939) *Plutarch's Moralia*, vol. 6 (of 14), Loeb Classical Library, London and Cambridge, MA: William Heinemann and Harvard University Press.

Hengel, Martin (1966) 'Die Synagogeninschrift von Stobi', ZNW 57: 145–83.

—— (1971) 'Proseuche und Synagoge: Jüdische Gemeinde, Gotteshaus und Gottesdienst in der Diaspora und in Palästina', in Gert Jeremias, Heinz-Wolfang Kuhn, and Hartmut Stegemann (eds) *Tradition und Glaube. Das frühe Christentum in seiner Umwelt. Festgabe für Karl Georg Kuhn zum 65. Geburtstag*, Göttingen: Vandenhoeck und Ruprecht: 157–84.

Howard, George (1979) *Paul: Crisis in Galatia: A Study in Early Christian Theology*, Cambridge: Cambridge University Press.

Jones, Edward E. (1989) 'Social Psychology,' in Adam Kuper and Jessica Kuper (eds) *The Social Science Encyclopedia*, London and New York: Routledge: 780–83.

Kasher, Aryeh (1995) 'Synagogues as "Houses of Prayer" and "Holy Places" in the Jewish Communities of Hellenistic and Roman Egypt', in Urman and Flesher (eds) op. cit.: 205–20, (reprinted from A. Kasher, A. Oppenheimer and U. Rappaport (1987) *Synagogues in Antiquity*, Jerusalem: 119–32 [in Hebrew]).

Kloppenborg, John S. (1993) *'Philadelphia, Theodidaktos* and the Disocuri: Rhetorical Engagement in 1 Thessalonians 4.9–12', NTS 39: 265–89.

Kraabel, Alf Thomas (1981) 'The Social Systems of Six Diaspora Synagogues', in J. Gutmann (ed.) *Ancient Synagogues: The State of Research*, Brown Judaic Studies 22, Chico, CA: Scholars Press: 70–91.

—— (1995) 'The Diaspora Synagogue: Archaeological and Epigraphic Evidence since Sukenik', in Urman and Flesher (eds) op. cit.: 95–126, (reprinted from

H. Temporini and W. Haase (eds) (1979) *Aufstieg und Niedergang der Römischen Welt: Principat, Religion (Judentum: Allgemeines; Palästinisches Judentum)*, vol. 19: 1, Berlin and New York: Walter de Gruyter & Co.: 477–510).

Lütgert, W. (1919) *Gesetz und Geist. Eine Untersuchung zur Vorgeschichte des Galaterbriefes*, Gütersloh: C. Bertelsmann.

Malherbe, Abraham J. (1986) *Moral Exhortation: A Greco-Roman Sourcebook*, Philadelphia: Westminster.

Malina, Bruce J. (1993) *The New Testament World: Insights from Cultural Anthropology*, revised edn, Louisville, KY: Westminster/John Knox Press.

Moxnes, Halvor (1995) 'The Quest for Honor and the Unity of the Community in Romans 12 and in the Orations of Dio Chrysostom', in T. Engberg-Pedersen (ed.) *Paul in His Hellenistic Context*, Edinburgh: T. & T. Clark: 203–30.

—— (1997) Review of Barton 1994, in *Biblical Interpretation* (forthcoming).

O'Neill, John C. (1972) *The Recovery of Paul's Letter to the Galatians*, London: SPCK.

Pomeroy, Sarah B. (1975) *Goddesses, Whores, Wives and Slaves: Women in Classical Antiquity*, New York: Schocken Books.

Rawson, Beryl (ed.) (1987) *The Family in Ancient Rome: New Perspectives*, Ithaca, NY: Cornell University Press.

Ropes, J. H. (1929) *The Singular Problem of the Epistle to the Galatians*, Cambridge, MA: Harvard University Press.

Seager, Andrew R. (1981) 'Ancient Synagogue Architecture: An Overview', in Gutmann (ed.) op. cit.: 39–47.

Stowers, Stanley K. (1981) *The Diatribe and Paul's Letter to the Romans*, SBLDS 57, Chico, CA: Scholars Press.

—— (1988) 'The Diatribe', in David E. Aune (ed.) *Greco-Roman Literature and the New Testament*, SBLSBS 21, Atlanta, GA: Scholars Press: 71–83.

Tajfel, Henri (1978) *Differentiation between Social Groups: Studies in the Social Psychology of Inter-group Relations*, London: Academic Press.

Theissen, Gerd (1982) *The Social Setting of Pauline Christianity*, English trans. John H. Schütz, Edinburgh: T. & T. Clark.

Urman, Dan, and Flesher, Paul V. M. (1995) (eds) *Ancient Synagogues: Historical Analysis and Archaeological Discovery*, vol. 1, Leiden: E. J. Brill.

Vellacott, Philip (1961) *Aeschylus: Prometheus Bound, The Suppliants, Seven Against Thebes and The Persians*, London: Penguin.

Waltzing, J.-P. (1895–1900) *Étude Historique sur les Corporations Professionelles chez les Romains*, 4 vols, Louvain: Charles Peeters.

White, L. M. (1990) *Building God's House in the Roman World. Architectural Adaptation among Pagans, Jews, and Christians*, The ASOR Library of Biblical and Near Eastern Archaeology, Baltimore, MD and London: Johns Hopkins.

Whitehead, David (1986) *The Demes of Attica: 508/7–c. 250 BC*, Princeton, NJ: Princeton University Press.

Winter, Bruce (1994) *Seek the Welfare of the City: Christians as Benefactors and Citizens*, Grand Rapids, MT: William B. Eerdmans.

8

EQUALITY WITHIN PATRIARCHAL STRUCTURES

Some New Testament perspectives on the Christian fellowship as a brother- or sisterhood and a family

Karl Olav Sandnes

INTRODUCTION

An ordinary reader of early Christian texts would be inclined to think that brotherhood and family terms belong together in a set of family metaphors. But it is not that simple, since household terms cover relationships between different members of a family, including the relationships between superior and subordinate, between genders, and the roles within the household, as well as the relationship between close and more distant relatives. Brotherhood terms, however, apply only to the relationship between siblings, who are usually considered to be equals, although there may be differences between younger and elder brothers.

The distinction between household and brotherhood (*philadelphia*) as separate models of fellowship has in recent years been urged by a number of New Testament scholars. Klaus Schäfer, in his monograph *Gemeinde als Bruderschaft* (1989), sets out to define the implications of the *philadelphia* nature of the church according to Paul's letters. He postulates a dichotomy between the fellowship as a brotherhood, and real family life, such that brotherhood becomes a theological symbol for an egalitarian fellowship. He considers household and brotherhood as contrasting models in Pauline ecclesiology: the household represents the patriarchal model, while brotherhood represents the egalitarian and participatory. Accordingly, he depicts the Christian church in Paul's perspective as '*Kontrastgesellschaft*' (Schäfer 1989: 19, 37, 353–55, 358, 369, 443–44). The Pauline churches he thus considers as antitypes of the family in Antiquity.

Schäfer's interpretation is basically shared by E. Schüssler Fiorenza in many of her contributions to early Christian history and theology. Her argument follows a theory of decline: in the beginning the early church was an egalitarian community with no patriarchal elements in it. This is witnessed in texts like Mark 3:31–35; par. Matt 23:8–10 and the baptismal confession in Gal 3:28. The egalitarian character of the Christian counter-cultural groups was destroyed as the church gradually replaced the egalitarian forms of community by patriarchal structures. This can be seen in the letters of the

New Testament in general, and in particular in the adaptation of the house-hold codes and in the Pastoral epistles.[1] A decline into household structures took place in early Christianity. The family terms are here interpreted within a framework of a specific reconstruction of the history of the early Church (Schüssler Fiorenza 1979: 46–49; 1983: 147–51).[2]

It is the achievement of Schäfer and Schüssler Fiorenza and others to have pointed out that the Christian fellowship was not just a copy of any other contemporary group. The Christian groups formed a fellowship of an entirely new type. It is, however, my conviction that the dichotomy they postulate between household and brotherhood goes beyond the evidence and beyond what is likely from a cultural-historical point of view.

My thesis is that in the family terms of the New Testament, old and new structures come together. There is a convergence of household and brother-hood structures. The New Testament bears evidence of the process by which new structures emerged from within the household structures. What we see in the New Testament is not an egalitarian community which is being replaced by patriarchal structures; the brotherhood-like nature of the Christian fellowship is in the making, embedded in household structures. The aim of this chapter is to substantiate this claim. Emphasis will be laid on Pauline texts.

THE SOCIAL CONTEXT OF THE FAMILY TERMS IN THE NEW TESTAMENT

In order to have a proper understanding of the family metaphors in the New Testament, it is necessary to bring together questions of texts or theology and questions of socio-historical context. To understand the implications of family terms, it is necessary to keep both text and context in view. Two factors were decisive in shaping the structure of primitive Christianity as family-like: the churches originated when households embraced the faith, and conversion of individuals often caused a family crisis.

Conversion of households

Making its way through the Roman Empire, Christianity left house-churches in its wake,[3] as we see in the letters of Paul: the Christians gathered in private homes (1 Cor 11:34; 14:35). In some texts Paul names the head of the household where the believers came together: 1 Cor 1:16; 16:15–16, 19; Rom 16:5 (cf Col 4:5). The role of the house of Stephanas is a revealing example: as head of his household he was baptised with his *oikos* (1 Cor 1:16). Paul calls his household the firstfruits (*aparchê*) of Achaia (1 Cor 16:15–16). This means that Paul considers this house to have embraced the Christian faith en bloc through the conversion of Stephanas. Furthermore, this household devoted itself to ministering (*diakonia*) to the church.

Although Paul does not specify the nature of this ministry, Stephanas' arrival in Ephesus indicated to Paul that the household was involved in Paul's mission (Ollrog 1979: 100; Gielen 1990: 94–98). People like Stephanas who were in charge of households were a primary conversion target for Paul. They were people of some social and economic standing, and he considered them key figures since they became the hosts of the congregations. Thus they provided the fellowship with a meeting-place, a starting point for organising church life. Thanks to the hospitality they provided, these households were essential to Paul's mission.

The nature of Paul's letters means that information on the Christian households is accidental and incomplete. A broader understanding of what Paul means may be found in the Acts of the Apostles. Regarding the role of the household in early Christianity, there is a considerable overlap between Paul's letters and the later Acts of the Apostles. The starting point of the churches was normally the conversion of the *paterfamilias*, who embraced the Christian faith together with his whole household. While visiting Jerusalem, Peter makes a report about the incident in Cornelius' house: 'he will give you a message by which you and your entire household (*pas ho oikos sou*) will be saved' (Acts 11:14). Cornelius, the *paterfamilias* and the patron, his family, kinsmen and close friends – all adopted the Christian faith. This picture emerges if this text is connected to Acts 10:24 where Cornelius is said to have invited all these people to his house. This means that the 'entire household' of Cornelius involved his extended family, who did not necessarily live in his house. This may well be an exaggeration, but it points to an important structural element in the history of Cornelius' house. Conversion is thus of a social nature. Some members of the household may well have been converted due to social relationships rather than out of personal conviction. Different levels of commitment or membership within the Christian household are therefore quite natural (Taylor 1995).

According to Acts 16:15 a similar event took place in Lydia's house. Lydia, probably a widow continuing her husband's business, was converted with her household: 'When she and her household were baptized she urged us, saying, "If you have judged me to be faithful to the Lord, come and stay at my home"'. Acts 16:40 says that Paul found Christian *adelphoi* gathered in Lydia's house. This is a good example of the conversion of the head of a household marking the genesis of a house-church. This description of how a church came into being is confirmed in Acts 16:31–34 and 18:8 (cf John 4:53).

It happens quite regularly in these conversion stories that the newly-converted share a meal with the missionary and his associates (Acts 10:48; 16:15, 34). This is more than simply a courteous gesture. In this meal the converts seek acceptance and friendship. The missionaries accept the invitations as a means of friendship; the common table is *philopoios*: friendship-making. This Greek word is used for instance by Plutarch to describe the end or purpose of a meal (Plut. *Mor.* (*Table Talks*) 612D; 621C). This gives these meals associated with conversion a symbolic meaning: the common table affirms and strengthens the relationship with the missionary and is a sign that the convert has been accepted into the Christian fellowship.[4]

The reliability of Acts is debatable. In its account of the conversion of households, however, Acts is reliable, since the same basic structure is alluded to also in Paul's letters. Furthermore, the information in Acts is what one would expect in a society dominated by the *paterfamilias*. In other words, the family-oriented society in which primitive Christianity took root provides the framework for what Acts tells us about the conversion of households. It is no surprise to find that the growth of the Christian faith ran on family lines in a family-oriented society.[5]

The starting point of the churches was normally the conversion of the *paterfamilias*, who embraced the Christian faith together with his whole household. Conversion of households fixes the character of the Christian fellowship; the embryo of the community was a family and the household is turned into a congregation. The social matrix of early Christianity was *oikos* and kinship. From the very beginning the movement was marked by kinship logic and precepts. In churches that originated in this way, it is reasonable to assume that traditional household roles – especially the leading role of the father – provided for some basic elements in their life. The role of being the host to the church is one such basic element.

Schäfer is, of course, aware of the existence of house-churches, but in practice his investigation entails a denial of their role. The significance of household and kinship is overlooked in his investigation.[6] Schüssler Fiorenza emphasises that the house-church was the beginning of the church in a city or place. But according to her description these churches ceased to be households, and became egalitarian associations or *collegia* (Schüssler Fiorenza 1983: 175–84). These scholars are thereby led to consider household and egalitarian brotherhood as contrasting models for life in early Christianity. No doubt, there are texts which indicate an egalitarian fellowship (see above). But this model was hardly implemented in full. In some texts (see below) we can see that it was in the making within the household structures. The egalitarian brother- or sisterhood is clearer as a model than it is in reality.

Conversion and family crisis

It is, however, evident that conversion did not always take place in connection with households. Sometimes only a husband converted, sometimes only a wife. The New Testament provides little information about the intra-familial tensions caused by the conversion of individuals. The New Testament writers clearly attest, however, that problems existed in marriages in which only one of the two was a Christian, and in households where only a slave was a believer. In particular this is witnessed in the Gospel traditions. Being a follower of Jesus affected family ties, but Jesus promised integration into his eschatological family (Mark 3:31–35; 10:28–31). The persecution and social ostracism suffered by the disciples is caused by members of their own households. Belonging to the household of Jesus brings separation and hostility from one's natural kin (Matt 10:34–36 par.) (Barton 1994).

That tensions and crisis arose in households because individuals joined the Christian faith is seen also in other New Testament literature, e.g. 1 Cor 7:12–17; 1 Pet 2:18–19 and 3:1–2 which mention the relationship between spouses and between master and slave.[7] The crisis within households is usually witnessed when a subordinate embraced the faith. Although the evidence is somewhat scattered, significance should be attached to this evidence of intra-familial tensions. This is suggested by Graeco-Roman texts as well as by anthropological material which sheds light on how a kinship society works in matters such as conversion.

In a filial piety-based society like the one in which primitive Christianity emerged, the conversion of the individual does not remain a personal or individual affair. Since family life is interwoven into the fabric of religion, the harmony and honour of the family is involved. The honour of the family is upheld by the agreement of the members in sharing the same traditions (McVann 1993; Neyrey 1995). A conversion is seen as challenging the stability within the family and the social system as well:

> The monotheistic exclusiveness of the Christians was believed to alienate the goodwill of the gods, to endanger what the Romans called the *pax deorum* (the right harmonious relationship between gods and men), and to be responsible for disasters which overtook the community.
>
> (Croix 1974: 238)

Religion was embedded in family life. This group identity has been labelled the dyadic personality of the Mediterranean population in the first century (Malina 1981: 51–93; Malina and Neyrey 1991).

Considering examples from cultural anthropology may help us to an adequate reading of the scattered New Testament evidence. The Finnish scholar and missionary Seppo Syrjänen has written a study on conversion to Christianity in Pakistani Muslim culture, based on interviews with former Muslims who have embraced the Christian faith (Syrjänen 1987). The family or clan orientation is strong. Connected with this also is respect for parents as well as the honour of the family. Syrjänen's work is quite illustrative of conversion in the early Church. Throughout, the interviewees say that their conversion caused a crisis or alienation from family and friends. Some experienced a dramatic clash with their relatives, while others suffered social ostracism. As an explanation of this reaction, Syrjänen says that it causes shame and dishonour to a family if children, whatever their age, abandon Muslim belief. The family is then not considered to have succeeded in bringing up its children. The honour of the family may only be restored by emphasising distance vis-à-vis those who have fallen away.[8] By means of material like this we are better equipped to form an adequate image or idea of the social forces implied in the scattered evidence on familial tensions within the New Testament.

In Antiquity social harmony was associated with people worshipping the same gods (Dio Chr. *Or.* 38.22; 41.10). There is a basic parallel between the *sacra publica* and the *sacra privata*. The fundamental assumption that the household is a city-state in microcosm means that domestic worship is seen in a political perspective. This is common thinking in Antiquity (e.g. Xen. *Mem.* 4:4.16; Philo *Spec. Leg.* 3:169–70; *Jos.* 38; Cic. *Amic.* 23), and represents a development of Aristotle's logic in his *Pol.* I.1252a–55b. What happens in the families may safeguard or endanger the harmony and well-being of the wider community. The main religious activity in Antiquity was therefore the family cult.[9] Hereby one safeguarded the members of the household, its property and its internal harmony. It is domestic worship that makes the home or family sacred (Cic. *Dom.* 109). The bond that keeps the family together and safeguards it is 'to share in common the same family traditions, the same forms of domestic worship, and the same ancestral tombs' (Cic. *Off.* 1.54–55). In his *Advice to Bride and Groom*, Plutarch describes harmony as the family ideal. This harmony is founded on husband and wife sharing the same worship:

> A wife ought not to make friends of her own, but to enjoy her husband's friends in common with him. The gods are the first and most important friends. Wherefore it is becoming for a wife to worship and to know only the gods that her husband believes in, and to shut the front door tight upon all queer rituals and outlandish superstition. For with no god do stealthy and secret rites performed by a woman find any favour.
>
> (Plut. *Mor.* 140D)

The ethnic affiliation involved when a Gentile turned to Judaism was not involved if the same person joined the Christian faith. Still, Judaism and early Christianity both belong to the same great tradition which demands a worship excluding other gods. In Juvenal's *Satire* 14 the deleterious effect of paternal example on offspring is presented by means of a father worshipping the Jewish God on the sabbath and abstaining from pork (14: 96–100). The upsetting thing is that this will necessarily lead to the son abandoning the Roman law for the Jewish one. It is, in other words, monotheistic exclusivity – found in both Judaism and Christianity – which challenged the Classical mind. Early Christianity was deeply embedded in Jewish tradition. This makes it relevant also to consider the hatred with which the Gentile environment regarded the Jews and proselytes as a relevant parallel to how Gentiles conceived of Christian converts.[10] Judaism was considered an anti-social religion (Tacitus *Annals* 15.44.3–8) because it made the proselytes 'despise all gods, to disown their country, and set at nought parents, children, and brethren' (Tacitus *Hist.* 5.5). This saying of the Roman historian is illuminating because he assumes the close bond between cult, state and household. The domestic, political and cultic sphere are not separated; on the contrary they are dependent upon each other.

The social context of primitive Christianity was concrete family life. Furthermore, there was a need for alternative households among the recent converts (Elliott 1981). The perspective of the recent convert in need of an alternative primary group suggests that there are some basic links of continuity between the church as a family and the family in society. Both observations suggest that a household model describing the nature of the Christian fellowship cannot be abandoned.

Talking about early Christianity in terms of a family and emphasising the distinction between household and brotherhood increases the danger of painting an over-idyllic picture of life in the early Church. The social reality was more patriarchal and household-like than most modern theologians are happy to admit. The household structures, however, underwent some modifications when they came into contact with the Christian gospel. We now turn to a chapter in the history of these modifications. This is what we can see in Paul's letter to Philemon. Within the context of a household, he wants a new reality to emerge.

PAUL'S LETTER TO PHILEMON

The story behind this letter is not easily defined. We are left with many questions concerning the precise nature of the situation. The most probable hypothesis is that Onesimus had been deliberately running to Paul as a friend of his master, hoping that he would intervene on his behalf. Paul is then given the role of *amicus domini* who holds a higher rank than the offended master (Lampe 1985; Rapske 1991). There is, however, hardly any doubt that the letter is concerned with Christian brother- and sisterhood; the master–slave relationship between Philemon and Onesimus was changed into a brotherhood relationship in all respects. This change is due to the conversion Onesimus experienced while visiting Paul in custody. The conversion is mentioned in two ways. Speaking of Onesimus in terms of his former and present life (*pote–nuni* in v. 11 and *ouketi* in v. 16) is conventional conversion language among both Jews and Christians. The change is spelled out in verse 16: 'no longer as a slave but more than a slave, a beloved brother – especially to me but how much more to you, both in the flesh and in the Lord'. Onesimus had become the brother of his master *en sarki kai en kyriô*.

In this sentence Paul is struggling to express the new identity of

Onesimus in relation to his master. First he denies that 'slave' is an appropriate word for this new relationship. Onesimus has become the brother of Philemon in every way. Both Philemon and Onesimus have a new status ascribed to them. They both owe their Christian faith to Paul, the apostle of Christ. The phrase *en kyriô* summarises their ascribed, non-earned status as believers. In the Lord, the master and his slave have entered a new relationship to God (vv. 3–4) on an equal basis, and also a new relationship to each other. They are now equal brothers. This is their new status in Paul's theological or eschatological perspective.

Paul's concept of the master and slave having a common identity thanks to Christ was meant to have practical consequences. The fact that Onesimus has become Philemon's brother in the flesh (*en sarki*) necessarily involves this. The question is therefore the following: do Paul's letters attest that this eschatological brotherhood of equality should have any effect on the life within the household, and if so, to what extent? The aim of the following section is to clarify the practical consequences Paul draws from this egalitarian brother- and sisterhood. Is Philemon's status as a master confirmed, questioned, challenged or modified? Norman R. Petersen has rightly pointed out that in this letter Paul is confronting Philemon with a challenge: how is he to deal with Onesimus as a brother? By returning Onesimus to the household of Philemon and by paying his debt to Philemon, Paul has terminated the crisis between the master and slave (Petersen 1985: 93–95). Now Paul expects Philemon to act in turn according to what Paul writes in his letter. As Petersen puts it, 'the spotlight now shifts to Philemon' (Petersen 1985: 98).

Paul's request to Philemon

Paul backs his concept of the common identity of master and slave as having practical consequences by putting social pressure upon Philemon. This social pressure is secured by different means. Since Paul is employing a collective form of address (v. 2) in this letter, we must assume that the context was known to the church members gathering in Philemon's house. The return of Onesimus must have caused much curiosity as to how Philemon would deal with the situation. The collective nature of the letter is also affirmed by the closing greetings (vv. 22–23). The rhetorical force of this public reference should not be underestimated; it is part of the rhetorical strategy of Paul's letter. The public nature of a letter dealing with a runaway slave, an issue which was usually for the master of the household to deal with by himself, is significant. Paul is making Philemon answerable to the Christian fellowship on the spot as well as to the trans-local fellowship of believers. It is not a private matter how Onesimus is welcomed. Paul has effectively pulled the issue of the returning slave out of the private sphere. A master would be considered to be responsible alone for his decision in such a matter. Paul does not accept the master's power when it comes to the question of the status of a recent convert. Philemon's position as the master of the household is accepted, but he is supposed to act according to the brotherhood-nature of the Christian fellowship. Paul is setting the church in Philemon's house to watch him as he finds his way in the matter of Onesimus. In doing this, Paul tacitly questions the autonomy and sovereignty of the master on the basis of the nature of the Christian fellowship. The social pressure upon Philemon is well presented by Petersen (1985: 98–102). He points out that Paul may even have endangered the fellowship, since Philemon is the host of the congregation. It is, however, not necessary to suppose that Philemon might be expelled from the fellowship.

The precise nature of Paul's request is not easily defined. This is due to Paul's skilful and rhetorical way of approaching a delicate matter, his respect for the integrity of Philemon, and also the fact that he may be in some doubt about the matter himself. We will approach the question of the nature of Paul's request by focusing on the texts where his request is relatively clearly articulated: first, Paul asks Philemon to receive Onesimus as he would receive Paul himself (v. 17). Second, Philemon is asked to comfort and help Paul in his deep concern for Onesimus (v. 20). Third, he is asked to be obedient (v. 21). Fourth, Paul wants him to prepare the guestroom since he will soon be on the spot; that is, to act as a friendly host to Paul (vv. 22–23).

Since Paul closes his letter by stating that he is confident that Philemon will be obedient, Paul himself is of the opinion that Philemon has received clear indications on what to do, or else the word 'obedience' would have no sense here. As far as Onesimus is concerned, the request is emphasising that he is to be welcomed back. Clearly, hospitality holds a key position in Paul's request as being a sign of friendship and acceptance. But this seems to be an immediate solution. The question which intrudes itself is: to what is he welcomed back?

A more permanent solution seems to be hinted at in two hidden pleas. In v. 18 the apostle urges Philemon to forgive his servant. Paul's saying that Onesimus formerly was useless to Philemon, indicates a story of harm related to the debt Paul paid for Onesimus.[11] We cannot here enter the question of what harm he had done to his master. Tacitly and indirectly Paul presents his own point of view in verses 13–14: his wish is to keep Onesimus for himself. This would be a great help while Paul is in custody, and also represents an opportunity for Philemon to demonstrate his goodwill towards Paul. Col 4:9 may indicate that the permanent solution was that Onesimus joined Paul in his mission work (similarly Schäfer 1989: 267; Marshall 1993: 184–85, 188). Before Paul receives Onesimus as his helper, he wants Philemon to welcome Onesimus.

Since Paul is backing his somewhat indefinite request with strong arguments, one might think that the argument as such should be included in his purpose in composing the letter. In a way, the whole of the letter is one long argument of love, good and partnership, aimed at elucidating the consequences of Onesimus' newly-obtained status. Paul seeks from the outset to praise Philemon in a way that prepares his request on behalf of Onesimus. This praise (vv. 4–7) is made up of the principles on which Paul will base his appeal: Philemon's love is well-known (vv. 5 and 7). It is this love Paul is appealing to (v. 9). Philemon is known to be acting out of his good will (v. 6). Paul asks him for a good deed (v. 14). Philemon is known to have practised love and good to his house-church which is the fellowship of faith (*koinônia tês pisteôs*: cf Gal 6:10). Paul is also his partner (*koinônos*: v. 17). Philemon's loving deeds to the house-church aimed at refreshing the heart of the saints (*ta splagchna tôn hagiôn anapepautai*) (v. 7). Now Paul is in a situation calling for Philemon to bestow his help upon him: 'Refresh my heart' (*anapauson mou ta splagchna*, v. 20). This repetition of key concepts gives coherence to Paul's argument (Church 1978: 22–24). The loving deeds that Philemon has been practising towards the saints should now include Onesimus in a special way.

Paul argues that Onesimus has become the brother of his master. This means that Philemon no longer has any claim on sovereignty in dealing with Onesimus. We have already seen that Paul presents the issue in front of the 'tribunal' of the whole congregation. Yet there is also another point which questions Philemon's power over Onesimus. Paul presents Onesimus as his own child. He has himself become his parent. The evocative term 'heart' (*ta splagchna*) used twice to describe Paul's relationship to Onesimus underscores this. He is a beloved brother especially to Paul and even more to Philemon. The remarkable statement of adding 'how much more' to the superlative means that Onesimus has a loyalty *both* to Paul and Philemon. This is explicitly stated in v. 11: 'he is indeed useful both to you and to me'. Thus, from two perspectives Philemon's autonomous role as a master vis-à-vis Onesimus is questioned.

Paul is not only making a request, he is formulating an argument as well: he wants Philemon to consider and re-think the status of Onesimus within his household. This also involves considering his role as a Christian master of the brothers and sisters in his house-church. To foster this process of re-thinking is part of the purpose of the letter.

The hospitable welcome – a symbolic act

Paul's immediate concern is, however, that Philemon welcomes Onesimus back. The significance of this request calls for some attention. Petersen has nicely worked out different maps of social relationships involved in this letter (Petersen 1985). The relationship which is of importance in order to have a proper understanding of the request in v. 17 is that between Paul and Philemon. Paul explicitly presents this relationship as a standard for how he wants Philemon to welcome Onesimus: 'So if you consider me your partner (*koinônos*), welcome him as you would welcome me (*proslabou auton hôs eme*: v. 17). In his relationship with Paul, Philemon is given a standard and an example from which to proceed in the case of Onesimus. Some manuscripts have *proslabou* also in v. 12. The verb *proslambanesthai* has a wide range of meaning. In the middle voice and followed by an accusative of person it often means to receive or accept someone into one's society or house (BAGD s.v. and Malherbe 1977). It is a term of hospitable welcome. By comparing the reception of Onesimus to the hospitable welcome Paul expects for himself, Paul provides a proper context for interpreting this verb. Paul wants Philemon to act like a host to Onesimus, and to welcome him as a respectable person into his household. Paul uses the same verb in middle voice followed by an accusative of person also in Rom 14:1, 3 and 15:7:

Rom 14:1   As for the man who is weak in faith, welcome him (*Ton asthenounta tê pistei proslambanesthe*)

Rom 14:3   for God has welcomed him (*ho theos gar auton proselabeto*)

Rom 15:7   Welcome one another, therefore, as Christ has welcomed you (*Dio proslambanesthe allêlous kathôs kai ho Christos proselabeto hymas*)

Paul here describes the act of salvation in terms of hospitality. From this he deduces how Christians in Rome should act towards each other. The attitudes of the different groups towards each other should reflect God's welcoming attitude. The use of the verb here may deliberately echo its use in Old Testament psalms. Psalm 26:10 (LXX) may serve as an example. Here it says that even if father and mother forsake one, 'the Lord has welcomed me' (*ho de kyrios proselabeto me*) (cf Ps 17:17; 64:5). The verb is here contrasted to forsaking or leaving behind, and it is compared to the loving care of parents; it even transcends their loving care. The verb thus has an aspect of 'taking care of'. Two instances in Acts may shed further light on the word chosen by Paul in Phlm 17. It says in Acts 18:26 that Priscilla and Aquilas *proselabonto* Apollos and explained to him the way of the Lord. This Christian couple did more to Apollos than just 'taking him aside', as a common translation goes (e.g. NRSV and BAGD s.v.). In Acts 28:2 the verb refers to a hospitable reception where the hosts provide for the shipwrecked companions of Paul. In sum, Paul wants Philemon to extend a hospitable welcome to Onesimus.

What does this actually mean? He must do this as a sign of Onesimus' new status as the brother of Philemon. The hospitable welcome of Onesimus has a symbolic value, it is a symbol of unity. As believers in Christ, Onesimus and Philemon are brothers on an equal footing. Their new relationship as well as their common identity in Christ is made visible in the symbolic act of the welcome.[12] The return and reception of Onesimus have in Paul's eyes a function resembling the symbolic significance of Jesus and Gentiles enjoying table-fellowship together (Gal 2:11, 16). This is Paul's immediate concern: Philemon is urged to make the new relationship and identity which he shares with Onesimus visible within his household.

Egalitarianism within inherited structures

When it comes to how this will affect daily life in Philemon's household beyond the hospitable reception, much remains unclear. We have seen that the verb *proslambanesthai* has a reference beyond the immediate welcome. Paul is not, however, setting a clear agenda on how the new identity of Onesimus should affect the daily routine of Philemon's house. He hints at a solution which seems to be a way out of a dilemma. Philemon is tacitly asked to let Paul have Onesimus as his companion in the mission. Paul is very careful in driving home this point. Paul is unable or unwilling to give Philemon clear directives. He was aware of the practical considerations involved for Philemon,[13] and therefore he made the suggestion of having Onesimus for himself on behalf of Philemon and his debt to Paul (vv. 13–14, 19). He has no intention of undermining Philemon's position as host and benefactor of the fellowship. The tacit plea to Philemon to send Onesimus to Paul after the friendly welcome may be a way out of a dilemma for Paul as well as for Philemon.

The very fact that Paul returns Onesimus to Philemon, and awaits his opinion, indicates that Onesimus is to submit to the decision being made. The problem Philemon may face by not complying with Paul's letter is not that Onesimus is turning rebellious, but that Philemon may jeopardise his relationship with Paul.

The relationship between Philemon and Onesimus, the master and his slave, is thus somewhat complex. They are brothers who have been ascribed a new identity in Christ on an equal footing. Paul appears more imprecise, however, when it comes to how this should be implemented in relation to their roles and function in the household. Again the relationship between Paul himself and Onesimus may guide our reading. Philemon is Paul's beloved brother and co-worker (vv. 1, 7, 20). He is Paul's *koinônos*. These are terms of equality: Paul and Philemon are brothers on equal terms. This brotherhood is, however, joined with another aspect: Paul is Philemon's superior. He is in a position to make demands on him (vv. 8–9). Philemon is expected to be obedient (v. 21), and he is Paul's debtor. On the other hand, Paul is approaching Philemon to act as his benefactor, to help him in his concern for Onesimus (v. 20), and to be his host (v. 22). The relationship between the two is therefore somewhat complex. Paul considers it possible to enjoy full brotherhood in the Lord within the context of a relationship which includes both demands and obedience, superiority and pleading for help. The brotherhood of Paul and Philemon is defined within a context of both equality and inequality. Thus it would be too simple to label their relationship without further ado as brotherhood between equals. Their relationship is complex.

There is an egalitarianism found within a structure which also embodies hierarchical relationships. Within this complexity, the primary issue for Paul is the ascribed identity which is common to both master and slave: 'Thus, Paul accepts a differentiation of roles and functions, but not a status differentiation' (Moxnes 1989: 105). Paul expects Onesimus to accept whatever decision Philemon will make: he is to submit. Paul beseeches instead of commands, he appeals to love and partnership; in so doing he sets an example for Onesimus. As for Philemon, however, he is left with a challenge, he has to rethink his relationship to Onesimus. He is challenged to consider him in the light of his new status which they both share. His position as master and head of the household is not questioned, indeed is rather taken for granted, but Philemon is challenged with respect to his relationship to Onesimus, challenged to bring this relationship into accordance with his status as a brother. Finally, Philemon's position is modified in that he is made answerable to the Christian community. This means that Philemon is now responsible for taking the consequences of the fact that he and Onesimus share a common ascribed identity in the Lord.

CONCLUSION

It is hardly possible to describe a life-style in early Christianity which is brotherly and not household-like. Reciprocity, sharing of resources and spending time together, may all be applied to both models. The family terminology, or the inclusive language, is not primarily aimed at arousing emotions or feelings. This language of kinship, within the context of Antiquity, says something about economic distribution. This terminology indicates a sharing of resources found among siblings as well as family members.

The New Testament writings leave us with a picture of ambiguity, or even tension: egalitarian structures are emerging within patriarchal household structures. It is misleading to consider the relationship between the brotherhood and household models as a decay from egalitarian structures into patriarchal structures. Within the context of households an egalitarian brother- and sisterhood is in the making. The new identity of the believers, i.e. that they were brothers and sisters on equal footing, involved, however, a modification of household structures. Paul's letter to Philemon is an example of this. Paul insists that the master and slave have become siblings. This siblingship is theologically or eschatologically based. He also insists that this new relationship should have some practical consequences. But Paul seems not to be able to describe this in the way he presented the Gentile–Jew relationship based on the new ascribed identity of believers in Christ. The new identity of Onesimus changed attitudes and perspectives, but not the social system of the household as such. Paul wants this to have social implications, but beyond the symbolic value of the hospitable welcome he is in doubt how to put the equality into practice. A way out of the dilemma may be for Philemon to let Paul have Onesimus as a mission worker.

The autonomy of the *paterfamilias* in dealing with Onesimus is questioned. Thus the authority of Philemon is modified, although not denied or abandoned. A new relationship based on equality is in the making. Paul's letter to Philemon bears witness to the model of eschatological equality among believers, but it also testifies that this model did not easily overcome the inherited structures of society, not even within a Christian household. The Christian fellowship as a family consisting of brothers and sisters was articulated and incarnated in dialogue with the cultural forces of a patriarchal society.

NOTES

1 Schäfer also questions Pauline authorship of these letters *inter alia* on grounds of the household metaphors in these letters; Schäfer 1989: 369. Similarly with Roloff 1988: 213–14.
2 Similarly Bassler 1984.
3 The literature on the house-churches is enormous; see the references in Klauck 1981; Branick 1989 and Sandnes 1994a: 93–105.
4 For further references on the friendship-making character of the table, see Sandnes 1994b.
5 The New Testament examples of kinship relations among some of the believers may be seen as a further indication; see Sandnes 1994a: 99–105.
6 At the very end of his investigation, in a note, Schäfer connects his findings to the role of the house-churches (1989: 718).
7 Further references in Barton 1994: 1–11; Sandnes 1994a: 22–27. Coyle 1981 lays emphasis on the patristic evidence.
8 This may also be illustrated by material from Confucian-based cultures in East Asia. For Chinese filial piety see Yu 1984; Khiok-Khug 1994. Further references in Sandnes 1994a: 3–5.
9 Further references and literature on family cults are found in Sandnes 1994a: 28–29.
10 On this Jewish perspective on Christian conversions see Sandnes 1994a: 26–28, 41–46. For more general references on how Gentiles saw Jews and proselytes see Whittaker 1984 and Lührmann 1986.
11 On this question see e.g. Stuhlmacher 1975: 51 and the discussion in Martin 1991: 329–33.
12 On hospitality as a means of friendship see Smith 1987; Sandnes 1994b; Holmberg 1995.
13 This dilemma is elaborated by Barclay 1991: 175–80.

BIBLIOGRAPHY

Barclay, J. M. G. (1991) 'Paul, Philemon and the Dilemma of Christian Slave-ownership', *NTS* 37: 161–86.

Barton, S. C. (1994) *Discipleship and Family Ties in Mark and Matthew*, SNTSMS 80, Cambridge: Cambridge University Press.

Bassler, J. M. (1984) 'The Widow's Tale: A Fresh Look at 1 Tim 5:13–16', *JBL* 103: 32–41.

Branick, V. P. (1989) *The House Church in the Writings of Paul*, Zacchaeus Studies: New Testament, Wilmington, DE: Glazier.

Church, F. F. (1978) 'Rhetorical Structure and Design in Paul's Letter to Philemon', *HTR* 71: 17–33.

Coyle, J. K. (1981) 'Empire and Eschaton, The Early Church and the Question of Domestic Relationships', *Eglise et Theologie* 12: 35–94.

Croix, G. E. M. de Ste (1974) 'Why were the Early Christians Persecuted?' in M. Finley (ed.) *Studies in Ancient Society*, London and Boston: Routledge and Kegan Paul: 210–49.

Elliott, J. H. (1981) *A Home for the Homeless, A Sociological Exegesis of 1 Peter, Its Situation and Strategy*, Philadelphia: Fortress Press.

Schüssler Fiorenza, E. (1979) 'The Study of Women in Early Christianity: Some Methodological Considerations', in T. J. Ryan (ed.) *Critical History and Biblical Faith, New Testament Perspectives*, Villanova: Villanova University: 30–58.

Gielen, M. (1986) 'Zur Interpretation der Paulinischen Formel, *hê kat oikon ekklêsia* ZNW 77: 109–25.

—— (1990) *Tradition und Theologie Neutestamentlicher Haustafelethik, Ein Beitrag zur Frage einer Christlichen Auseinandersetzung mit Gesellschaftlichen Normen*, BBB 75, Frankfurt: Anton Heim.

Holmberg, B. (1995) 'Paul and Commensality', in T. Fornberg and D. Hellhoem (eds) *Texts and Contexts, Biblical Texts in Their Textual and Situational Contexts*, in Honor of Lars Hartman, Oslo: Scandinavian University Press: 767–80.

Khiok-Khug Yeo (1994) 'The Rhetorical Hermeneutic of 1 Cor 8 and Chinese Ancestor Worship', *Biblical Interpretation* 2: 294–311.

Klauck, H. J. (1981) *Hausgemeinde und Hauskirche im Frühen Christentum*, SBS 103, Stuttgart: Katholisches Bibelwerk.

Lampe, P. (1985) 'Keine "Sklavenflukt" des Onesimus', *ZNW* 76: 135–37.

Lührmann, D. (1986) 'Superstitio – die Beurteilung des Frühen Christentums durch die Römer', *TZ* 42: 193–213.

McVann, M. (1993) 'Family-Centeredness', in J. Pilch and B. Malina (eds) *Biblical Social Values and their Meaning*, Peabody, MA: Hendrickson: 70–73.

Malherbe A. J. (1977) 'The Inhospitality of Diotrephes', in J. Jervell and W. A. Meeks (eds) *God's Christ and His People*, in Honour of N. A. Dahl, Oslo: Universitetsforlaget: 222–32.

Malina, B. J. (1981) *The New Testament World: Insights from Cultural Anthropology*, Louisville, KY: John Knox.

Malina, B. J. and Neyrey, J. H. (1991) 'First-Century Personality: Dyadic not Individual', in J. H. Neyrey (ed.) *The Social World of Luke–Acts, Models for Interpretation*, Peabody, MA: Hendrickson: 67–96.

Marshall, I. H. (1993) 'The Theology of Philemon', in K. P. Donfried and I. H. Marshall (eds) *The Theology of the Shorter Pauline Letters*, Cambridge: Cambridge University Press: 175–91.

Martin, C. J. (1991) 'The Rhetorical Function of Commercial Language in Paul's Letter to Philemon (Verse 18)', in D. F. Watson (ed.) *Persuasive Artistry, Studies in Rhetoric in Honor of George A. Kennedy*, JSNT Sup 50, Sheffield: Sheffield Academic Press: 321–37.

Moxnes, H. (1989) 'Social Integration and the Problem of Gender in St Paul's Letters', *ST* 43: 99–113.

164

Neyrey, J. H. (1995) 'Loss of Wealth, Loss of Family and Loss of Honour, The Cultural Context of the Original Makarisms in Q', in P. F. Esler (ed.) *Modelling Early Christianity, Social Scientific Studies of the New Testament in its Context*, London and New York: Routledge: 139–58.

Ollrog, Wolf-H. (1979) *Paulus und Seiner Mitarbeiter, Untersuchungen zu Theorie und Praxis*, WMANT 50, Neukirchen-Vluyn: Neukirchener.

Petersen, N. (1985) *Rediscovering Paul, Philemon and the Sociology of Paul's Narrative World*, Philadelphia: Fortress Press.

Pilch, J. J. and Malina B. J. (eds) (1993) *Biblical Social Values and their Meaning*, Peabody, MA: Hendrickson.

Rapske, B. M. (1991) 'The Prisoner Paul in the Eyes of Onesimus', *NTS* 37: 187–203.

Roloff, J. (1988) *Der Erste Brief an Timotheus*, EKKNT 15, Zürich/Benziger: Neukirchen-Vluyn.

Sandnes, K. O. (1994a) *A New Family, Conversion and Ecclesiology in the Early Church with Cross-Cultural Comparisons*, Studies in the Intercultural History of Christianity 91, Bern: Peter Lang.

—— (1994b) 'Omvendelse og Gjestevennskap, Et Bidrag til Noen Lukas–Acta Tekster', in R. Hvalvik and H. Kvalbein (eds) *Ad Acta, Studier til Apostlenes Gjerninger og Urkristendommens Historie*, in Honor of Edvin Larsson, Oslo: Verbum: 325–46.

Schäfer, K. (1989) *Gemeinde als 'Bruderschaft', Ein Beitrag zum Kirchenverständnis des Paulus*, Europeische Hochschulschriften XXIII/333, Bern: Peter Lang.

—— (1983) *In Memory of Her, A Feminist Theological Reconstruction of Christian Origins*, New York: Crossroad.

Smith, D. E. (1987) 'Table Fellowship as a Literary Motif in the Gospel of Luke', *JBL* 106: 613–38.

Stuhlmacher, P. (1975) *Der Brief an Philemon*, EKKNT 18, Zürich/Benziger: Neukirchen-Vluyn.

Syrjänen, S. (1987) *In Search of Meaning and Identity, Conversion to Christianity and Pakistani Muslim Culture*, Vammala: The Finnish Society for Missiology and Ecumenism.

Taylor, N. H. (1995) 'The Social Nature of Conversion in the Early Christian World', in P. F. Esler (ed.) *Modelling Early Christianity, Social-scientific Studies of the New Testament in its Context*, London and New York: Routledge: 128–36.

Whittaker, M. (1984) *Jews and Christians: Graeco-Roman Views*, Cambridge Commentaries on Writings of the Jewish and Christian World 200 BC to AD 200, vol. 6, Cambridge: Cambridge University Press.

Yu, Chi-Ping (1984) *Confucian and Biblical Concept of Filial Piety, Implications for Pastoral Care in the Chinese Church in Taiwan*, Boston: Boston University School of Theology Diss.

9

BROTHERHOOD IN PLUTARCH AND PAUL: ITS ROLE AND CHARACTER

Reidar Aasgaard

POSING THE PROBLEM

Paul frequently calls his co-Christians sisters and brothers (*adelphoi, adelphê,* and *adelphos*).[1] In fact, this is by far the most frequent designation Paul uses for Christians, and thus presumably one of the most important. Why does he use this terminology? How does it function in his letters? And what is the character of the 'brother' concept and of the brother relationship?

Surprisingly, this terminology and concept have not been much studied, and they are in need of closer and more extensive investigation.[2] Earlier research has described this Christian 'brotherhood' idea mainly in two ways. One has been to subordinate it under the wider concept of family/household, and to speak of the Christian communities as 'new families'. Two examples are Wayne A. Meeks (Meeks 1983) and Karl Olav Sandnes (Sandnes 1994). Another way has been to understand the Christian community as a brotherhood entity, with features developed on a more or less exclusively theological basis, e.g. the Christians as sisters and brothers through Christ. This is the case with Klaus Schäfer's monograph on the theme (Schäfer 1989).

Both these perspectives fall somewhat short, I believe, of depicting the role and character of brotherhood in Paul. The first becomes too general, and does not get hold of the particular character of Pauline brotherhood. The other is too theological: it does not take sufficiently into consideration the broader, socio-historical background of the concept. In my view we therefore have to investigate the brotherhood ideas more closely in Paul's letters, and try to understand them on the basis of their social context in society and family life in general.

In a short chapter it is not possible to discuss the relationship between brotherhood and family in Paul; nor can I treat the theological aspects of his brotherhood ideas. My aim here will instead be to use socio-historical material in order to illuminate his ideas of Christian brotherhood. The guiding question will be: what is the relationship between a general understanding of brotherhood in Antiquity and Paul's ideas of Christian brotherhood?[3] First I will present Plutarch's 'On Brotherly Love' as an important case-

166

study, then – more briefly – Paul's use of brotherhood ideas, and – finally – compare them with each other, focusing on common features.[4]

How do we come to grips with the characteristics of brotherhood and brotherly love according to Plutarch and Paul? I shall try to do it by showing how they conceptualise brotherhood, how they motivate it, and distinguish it from other relationships, how they structure it internally, what kind of brother conflicts they describe, and the ways they advise to solve problems. From these angles it will, I believe, be possible to draw a profile of brother relationships that will make some characteristics appear.

However, we also have to read Plutarch's and Paul's presentations of brotherhood with a special perspective in mind, though we cannot expand on it here: what reflects social reality, and what is ideal thinking, coloured by the widespread notion of decline in family life? Suzanne Dixon (Dixon 1991: 99–113; 1992: 19ff) has pointed to the notion which she calls the Roman 'sentimental family ideal'.[5] Within this ideal the family may aptly be described as a 'haven in a heartless world'. This was an ideal that gradually evolved: while former times seem to have emphasised obligations of family life, emotional aspects were instead underscored in later times, especially in the imperial era. The family was not only expected to fulfil material and social requirements, but also to meet the emotional needs of the individual. The family should support the individual loyally, particularly in times of hardship, and reciprocal, internal solidarity was highly evaluated. Moreover, this ideal focused not on the extended family, but on the nuclear, especially the relationships between wife and husband and between parents and children. Though Dixon does not treat sisters and brothers explicitly, the same ideal in my opinion is attached to this relationship within the nuclear unit. I believe that similar attitudes can be detected in Plutarch and Paul.

In addition, in Antiquity history was felt to be a time of decline, and especially moral decline (Betz 1978: 244; cf also 233–34). Plutarch is very much on a level with these general attitudes; in his introduction he explicitly consents to the notion: 'And according to my observation, brotherly love is as rare in our day as brotherly hatred was among the men of old' (478C). In 'On Brotherly Love' and elsewhere he thus approaches ethics not from a positive standpoint, but from a negative, restorative one. In order to recreate what has been destroyed 'it is fitting to cleanse away completely the hatred of brothers' (481B). Whether this idea of decline – also called the 'myth of the archaic Roman family' (Dixon 1992: 19ff) – was rooted in reality, cannot be discussed here, but it clearly belongs to the presuppositions of Plutarch (and maybe of Paul?).

PLUTARCH'S 'ON BROTHERLY LOVE'

Plutarch's (c. 50–120 AD) moral treatise *On Brotherly Love* (*Peri Philadelphias*) is the only complete text left from Antiquity that has the relationship between brothers as its main focus,[6] although the subject was much discussed in popular morality (Betz 1978: 231; Malherbe 1986: 93). Philosophically Plutarch leans on Platonic tradition, but also employs elements from Aristotelian and Stoic popular thinking. Though the treatise is strongly marked by Plutarch's background in the aristocratic, cultural elite, it still reflects widespread and approved attitudes towards the relationship between brothers; it reproduces a general mentality within current Hellenism. The treatise was meant to present its topic in an agreeable way for an 'informed' Greek-Hellenistic and Roman audience (Betz 1978: 4–8, 231f). *On Brotherly Love* is oriented towards theoretical (Chapters 2–6) as well as practical (Chapters 7–20) issues, and the essay thus informs us about the ideology as well as the practice – particularly the ideal practice – of brotherly relations.[7]

At the basis of Plutarch's thought is the idea of harmony: the human mind, the human body, social life, all should be in internal balance (478F: *eunoia, symphônia*; 479A: *homonoia, harmônia*), in accordance with the whole of creation (478D and elsewhere: *physis*). The goal of his advice is that harmony must be restored. In social life this is achieved by just behaviour towards all. But some are entitled to special honour (*timê, doxa*): parents (479C, 479F–480A) and brothers (491B). The task of Plutarch – as psychagogue – is to guide the souls of his readers to recover the upset harmony (cf 482D, and Betz 1978: 4, 6f; also Glad 1995).

Brotherly love as a concept

Plutarch clearly presents brotherhood and brotherly love as a concept with specific features, that is with characteristics, problems, and possibilities of its own.[8] This is apparent from the overall perspective of his treatise: Plutarch believes that the relationship between brothers needs, as well as is worthy of, a separate treatment (478A–D). To denote the content and profile of brother relations he uses the word *philadelphia*, 'brotherly love' (478B–C, 480 E–F, 491A and elsewhere). Apart from Plutarch and Paul, only a few occurrences (about ten) of the word and its closest cognates are known from Antiquity. Charles J. Brady mentions the most important, among them one each in Eratosthenes, Diodorus Siculus, Lucian of Samosata, and Babrius (Fabularum Scriptor), and in a couple of papyri (Brady 1961: 7ff).

Motivations for brotherly love

Plutarch gives one fundamental as well as several practical grounds for brotherly love. The fundamental and most important one is based on nature, namely that brothers have the same biological origin: 'Nature from one seed and one source has created two brothers, or three, or more, not for difference and opposition to each other, but that by being separate they might the more readily co-operate with one another' (478E). Thus brothers should love one another out of respect for their common parents (480A–C). A brother is the best gift parents can give (480D–E). And love of brothers is a proof of love of parents (480F). Love of brothers differs from many other kinds of love: you do not choose your brothers, but are born into community with them, and thus under obligation to love them (482B).

Brotherly love is also motivated out of everyday experience and common sense, since brothers through the whole span of life share so much: 'sacrifices and the family's sacred rites, (to) occupy the same sepulchre, and in life, perhaps, the same or a neighbouring habitation' (481D–E). Harmony between brothers is also a condition for the welfare of the whole family (479A). Brothers often have and ought to have the same friends (490A–91C), and even common enemies (490F).

Brotherhood, family, and friendship

Plutarch regards brotherly love as an important element within kinship ethics, and he therefore also discusses a brother's relationships towards others in the *family*. Human beings are of nature social, they are not supposed to live without close social relationships (479C); and the strongest social entity is the household or family (479A, C–D: *genos, oikos*). Kinship is here understood in the broad sense: sisters-in-law, nephews, nieces, and others are included (486E, 491D–92D).

Parents, and fathers in particular, stand at the centre of the family. Parents are due more honour than all others (479E–480A). Children should strive to live up to the expectations of their parents, one of the most important is that brothers should love each other (480A–C). And to criticise a brother is, indirectly, to criticise one's parents (480D). Plutarch also emphasises a brother's relationships towards others, e.g. one's spouse (486E) and the rest of the family (491D–92D: a brother's closest relatives), but these are not granted the same weight as the parent–child and the brother–brother relation (479C–D).

Plutarch seems to accentuate the parent–child and the brother–brother relations equally, and he also demonstrates how closely linked these two relationships are. Still he does not merely make them functions of each other, nor does he simply subsume brotherhood under a patriarchal kinship system. Being a brother implies special obligations and rights: one may even stand up for a brother against one's father (482F, 483B–C). One should also, if necessary, prefer the welfare of a brother rather than of one's own children, even in questions of life and death: 'rightly, then, did the Persian woman [cf Herodotus III.119] declare, when she chose to save her brother in place of her children, that she could get other children, but not another brother, since her parents were dead' (481E). According to Plutarch, then, brotherhood has a very central and a relatively autonomous role within the family.

Plutarch also discusses brotherhood in relation to *friendship*. Questions on relationships to friends are given ample room and much weight in the treatise (490A–91C), though he regards friends as being outside the family, and friendship as different and inferior to brotherhood: 'For most friendships are in reality shadows and imitations and images of that first friendship which Nature implanted in children towards parents and in brothers towards brothers' (479D, cf also 482B–C, 491B).

Hans Dieter Betz has contended that Plutarch's brotherhood ethics is primarily a combination of family and friendship ethics, and not distinguishable from these. Brotherhood would then be nearly identical, or at least a close, positive analogy to these. In my opinion this is not correct.[9] In the treatise brotherhood has a clearly distinctive character; this distinctiveness is in fact Plutarch's basic reason for writing the treatise at all. He takes great care in defining as well as describing it on its own terms; friendship serves partly as a contrast that throws the qualities of brotherhood into relief, partly as a means for welding ties between brothers. Whereas brotherhood is nature-given, friendship is developed over time; one sizes up another before he is chosen as a friend, and love of him only grows gradually (481C–D, 482A–C). Common friends are important instruments to strengthen brotherly bonds (491A–B). Brothers should not compete over the favour of common friends (490B). Friendships influence the relationship between brothers, and one must take great care that this does not divert them from each other (490E). In public settings honour should always be given to brothers first:

> But even if we feel an equal affection for a friend, we should always be careful to reserve for a brother the first place in public offices and administrations, and in invitations and introductions to distinguished men, and, in general, whenever we deal with occasions which in the eyes of the public give distinction and tend to confer honour, rendering thus to Nature the appropriate dignity and prerogative.
>
> (491B)

Thus, friendship here for Plutarch plays a minor role compared to brotherhood. Even though there are some connections between the two, there is no clear analogy, rather a contrast: their profiles are different, and should be judged accordingly. This is also confirmed in Plutarch's treatment of friendship elsewhere.[10]

Structures within brotherhood

At the outset, we should notice Plutarch's general emphasis on emotional aspects within kinship. His interest is not primarily in the formal and juridical side of relationships between kin or towards those outside, nor in the hierarchy or the power relationships among kin. Rather, he describes and prescribes what he regards as correct attitudes and feelings within these givens; to preserve good relationships emotionally, harmony in spite of differences, emerges as a fundamental ideal for the kinship group. The same also applies to brotherhood in particular.

Plutarch uses the human body as a model for brotherly relations. Many of the most important members are two 'brothers', or 'twins': hands, feet, eyes, ears, and nostrils. They are pairs in order to support one another and to cooperate, and not the opposite (478D–E, 481C and E). At the same time, however, the body is constructed in a way that gives its parts different functions and status (478E—F, 484B).[11] Plutarch thus uses the body metaphor partly to underscore brothers' mutual inter-dependence, but also to stress differences, and how to handle them. He does not criticise the fact that differences lead to the grading of persons, but rather approves of it. To get in touch with the particular qualities of brotherhood, we shall follow Plutarch's description a little further on this point: what kind of differences does he allow within the brother relationship, and in what way does he characterise these differences? Plutarch devotes a substantial part of the treatise to this issue (Chapters 12–17).

One criterion of distinction is *age*. Elder brothers ought not to behave in a fatherly way towards younger brothers, but should treat them in a way that is comradely and considerate. Younger brothers should treat the elder ones not as rivals, but as model persons, with respect and obedience (486F–87B). The distinction of age (as a power criterion) seems to be fundamental for Plutarch; but in the service of harmony the elder is expected to soften it, and the younger to display respect for it. From infancy on, the mentality of competition should be avoided (487E–F).

Another criterion stems from *nature*. Brothers are differently gifted by nature, or have their strengths in separate areas of life: they have different abilities and characters (484B–85A, 487E–88A). 'Against these inequalities we must be on our guard and must cure them, if they arise' (484D).

Plutarch also focuses on distinctions in *social roles and status*. One brother is often more successful socially or professionally than another; he may also have more, or more important friends. Problems which these distinctions cause must be met by inclusive behaviour, and sought to be bridged from both sides in order to attain harmony (488A–C, 490A–E).

Especially interesting is the overall perspective Plutarch seems to have for perceiving differences: he groups brothers, whether of different age, nature or sociability, as *'superior'* (484D, 485C: *hyperochê, hyperechôn*) and *'inferior'*

171

(485C: *ho leipomenos*), and approaches possible conflicts from this angle. In fact, he structures his text around this dichotomy: general advice to the superior is given in 484D–85C, to the inferior in 485C–86A. The superior brothers should give the inferior a share in their benefits and soften divisions (484D–E); the inferior ones should not unduly elevate the others (485C–E) or degrade themselves (485E–86A).

Conflict areas between brothers

Differences in age, disposition or social position can give rise to several kinds of problems, and Plutarch adduces many examples. Some of these conflict areas may be of interest, but do not appear very striking: they are presented in a rather general way. Slanderers, flatterers, and intriguing persons within and outside the household are also mentioned as threats against brotherly relations (479A, 486D–E). Are there, however, conflict areas that receive attention, and which seem to have been regarded as more problematic than others? In my opinion Plutarch's focus on conflicts over property and inheritance, which he addresses frequently and at length, is worth special mention.

In 479E he gives an example from his own experience as an arbitrator between two brothers. In 478C–D he mentions brothers cordially sharing an undivided inheritance, as a now lost ideal (cf also 483D). Brothers are the most precious gift and inheritance parents can give their children (480E, 483E). A father who hates his brothers is a bad example for children to inherit: 'For a man who has grown old in law-suits and quarrels and contentions with his brothers, and then exhorts his children to concord . . . weakens the force of his words by his own actions' (480F–81A). When conflicts (*pragmata*, cf also 1 Cor 6:1) arise, justice must prevail, and the case be settled as quickly as possible (488A–C).

Plutarch also treats the quarrels of brothers before the division of the father's goods, underscoring that the 'greatest and fairest of inheritances [is] their parents' goodwill' (482D–E), at the same time implying that inheritance is an important conflict area: 'But as the starting-point of my admonitions, let us take, not the division of the father's goods, *as other writers do*, but the misguided quarrels and jealousy of the children while the parents are yet alive' (482D). After some advice on this, almost the whole of the following chapter is devoted to how to handle inheritance (Chapter 11, 483D–84B): 'And when they seek to divide their father's goods, they should not first declare war on each other, as the majority do . . . ' (483D). Here he advises and mentions examples of wrong and right attitudes in dividing inheritance:

> 'by the lots of Justice', as Plato says, let them, as they give and take
> what is suitable to each and preferred by each, be of the opinion that it
> is the care and administration of the estate that is being distributed,

172

but that its use and ownership is left unassigned and undistributed for them all in common.

(483D)

Solving conflicts between brothers

When conflicts between brothers arise, it is preferable that they are solved internally, between those involved, and with Justice as judge (483D, 488B–89B). If necessary, others can be present, as arbitrators or witnesses, but these ought to be friends they have in common (483D, 490F–91A). Conflict in public obviously is to be avoided.

Plutarch recommends many remedies against brotherly discord, advice which displays much common sense and appears socially and psychologically well founded. Some are mentioned above; several others could have been mentioned. One remedy, however, is particularly important for Plutarch, and seems to summarise, or to be the basis of, the others. In his outline it is put at a central point (Chapter 7: 482A–C); it points back to his theoretical basis for brotherhood, but at the same time it also sounds the keynote for what follows: practical advice on brotherly behaviour. In addition it is the remedy for which he has the most explicit and fundamental reasons. His advice runs: brotherly love is characterised by mutual *leniency*. On the one hand a brother should be given freedom of movement, in general and towards his brothers: 'brothers one would prudently advise to put up with the evils with which they are most familiar rather than to make trial of unfamiliar ones' (482A: *ta oikeiotata tôn kakôn hypomenein mallon ê peirasthai tôn allotriôn*). A brother is given, not chosen; thus his weaknesses should be tolerated, and he should not be tested in the way friends are:

> No boon-companion or comrade-in-arms or guest 'is yoked in honour's bonds not forged by man', but he is who is of the same blood and upbringing, and born of the same father and mother. For such a kinsman it is altogether fitting to concede and allow some faults (*epichôrein enia kai pareikein*), saying to a brother when he errs (*examartanonta*), 'I cannot leave you in your wretchedness' and trouble and folly.

(482A)

One has to allow some faults on the part of a brother, and still remain loyal. His sins should not be severely judged (482B: *mê pikrous einai mêd akribeis tôn hamartêmatôn exetastas*), but tolerated: [Brothers should practise] 'the art of making mutual concessions, of learning to take defeat, and of taking pleasure in indulging brothers rather than in winning victories over them' (488A).

On the other hand, one should also display a strong motivation to forgive when something has gone wrong, trying to forget a day of quarrel with a kin member, and rather to remember all the good days together:

173

For either it is in vain and to no avail that Nature has given us gentleness (*praotêta*) and forbearance (*metriopatheias*), the child of restraint (*anexikakian*), or we should make the utmost use of these virtues in our relations with our relatives (*syggeneis*) and household (*oikeious*). And our asking and receiving forgiveness (*syggnômên*) for our own errors reveals goodwill and affection quite as much as granting it to others when they err. For this reason we should neither overlook the anger of others, nor be stubborn with them when they ask forgiveness, but, on the contrary, should try to forestall their anger, when we ourselves are time and again at fault, by begging forgiveness, and again, when we have been wronged, in our turn should forestall their request for forgiveness by granting it before being asked.

(489C–D)

Plutarch thus connects leniency and mutual forgiveness to family relationships, since these relations are based on nature. His advice is formulated generally, as valid for all kin. This implies that he does not see absolute distinctions between different family relations, but that he nevertheless gives this advice a special relevance for brothers. In the same chapter, the longest in the whole treatise (Chapter 18, 488C–90A), he substantiates this through numerous examples, all from the brother relationship.

In sum: in Plutarch's treatise brotherhood and brotherly love, though related to family and friendship, emerges as a concept of its own, and with its own characteristic features. Brotherly love is fundamentally motivated in nature, but also in common upbringing. Hierarchies among brothers exist, but should be mitigated. When conflicts arise, brothers ought to be lenient, more so towards each other than towards others.

PAUL AND CHRISTIAN BROTHERHOOD

We now turn to Paul for a brief investigation of brotherhood ideas in his letters. Paul uses brother/sister terms in several ways. Very often (more than sixty times) they occur as address (e.g. Rom 7:1: 'Do you not know, brothers and sisters . . . '; 12:1: 'I appeal to you therefore, brothers and sisters . . . '). Several times particular persons or more or less specified groups are named brother/sister or brothers: co-workers (e.g. Rom 16:1; 1 Cor 16:12) or a group (e.g. 1 Cor 16:11). Brother terms are also found in particular thematical contexts; some of these I will discuss below. The terms are very unevenly spread throughout Paul's letters. They are, for example, almost never used in 2 Cor, while they are very frequent in Rom, 1 Cor and 1 Thess. This seems to indicate that the role and function of these terms, and of the brotherhood ideas, vary in Paul's letters: Paul consciously emphasises and de-emphasises them when he finds it appropriate.

Brotherly love as a concept

Paul – like Plutarch – makes use of an idea of brotherhood, and of what it basically should be like. The relationship should be marked by love, and Paul also names this general attitude *philadelphia*. He uses the word in two texts. Rom 12:10: 'Love one another brotherly with mutual affection' (*tê philadelphia*) forms part of a number of loosely connected exhortations of traditional character. Together with the other 'imperatival' participles and adjectives of v. 9b–13 it may be regarded as an explication of the 'headline' in v. 9a: 'Let love (*agapê*) be genuine.' (cf Wilson 1991: 150–55 and 156–65). The *philadelphia* of v. 10 is introduced without any evident reference to the rest of the text, and its function here needs further analysis: is its meaning, for example, coloured by the rest of the text, or – conversely – do the other exhortations serve to deepen the idea of brotherly love? No answer can be given here, but the impression is left that the recipients of the letter knew well the idea of brotherly love among Christians, or at least that Paul presupposes that they do. They are expected to display brotherly affection, and to know what that means. The ideas of brotherhood and brotherly love thus seem to be familiar concepts for them; it is possible that it formed part of their fundamental Christian training, or of their primary catechetical knowledge.

This general impression is confirmed by another text, 1 Thess 4:9f: 'Now concerning love of the brothers and sisters (*peri de tês philadelphias*), you do not need to have anyone write to you, for you yourselves have been taught by God to love one another'. Also here Paul presupposes that they know and share the idea of brotherly love, and that they know what it implies. They have even been 'taught by God' (*theodidaktoi*). The precise meaning of this word, which is first and almost only known from Paul, is disputed (Holtz 1986:174f; Kloppenborg 1993: 278–81). It nevertheless indicates that the idea of brotherly love has been transmitted to them as a vital part of their basic Christian training, though the way this knowledge has been acquired is uncertain. In addition, brotherly relationship reaches beyond care for the individual brother or their own group of sisters and brothers: it also embraces those who belong to other Christian groups, even people with whom they are unfamiliar – 4:10: 'indeed you do love all the brothers and sisters throughout Macedonia'.

Motivations for brotherly love

Paul does not give the reasons for brotherhood and brotherly attitudes, but refers to it as well known, possibly even self-evident. He does not argue on the basis of a common origin for the Christians, e.g. that they are the children of God, and therefore one another's brothers and sisters. This idea may be close at hand (e.g. Rom 8; Gal 3:26 to 4:7), but it is nowhere explicitly mentioned or developed further. Nor does Paul introduce Christ as the one who turns believers into sisters and brothers, whether through baptism or through the Spirit.[12] Furthermore, Paul does not argue from experience in favour of the brotherhood concept. He gives no particular reasons from everyday life why Christians should act in a brotherly way towards one another. Brotherly relations are simply presupposed, and the lack of justification appears somewhat striking.

Brotherhood, family, and friendship

Paul uses several terms from kinship relationships (father/mother, old man, sons, children, sister/brother) when he describes relations within the Christian communities and towards God or Christ. The designations vary, even within the same letter, and no single, coherent pattern can be detected. Paul may, for example, call himself 'father' of the addressees, and in the same letter address them as '(sisters and) brothers' (e.g. 1 Cor 4:6 vs. 4:14ff; 1 Thess 2:1,14 vs. 2:11). At the same time, however, the sister/brother terminology and ideas have a rather independent function, as a concept of its own. In the texts with the strongest emphasis on brotherhood the concept appears unrelated to other kinship terms: only the brother terminology is used (e.g. Rom 14; 1 Cor 6 and 8; 1 Thess 4:9–12).

Paul scarcely uses terms connected to friends and friendship. It is striking that he never uses the word 'friend' (*philos*) for co-Christians. This cannot be accidental, but probably mirrors the fact that Paul regards the qualities of friendship to be different from brotherhood, and also not suitable to characterise the relationship between Christians (cf Sevenster 1954–55; Mitchell 1991: 1–9, 22f).[13]

Structures within Christian brotherhood

Paul does not give any general criteria for distinguishing between brothers. A few differences appear, nevertheless, but they are more or less occasioned by the context: Paul's co-workers seem to hold a particularly strong position as brothers (e.g. 1 Cor 1:1; 2 Cor 1:1). Paul calls co-Christians *his* brothers: he thus indirectly seems to figure himself as a brother. But he never names himself so; rather, when he describes his role in terms of kinship, he is a 'father' (e.g. 1 Cor 4:15), an 'old man' (e.g. Philem 9), a 'mother/nurse' (e.g. 1 Thess 2:7)! When he wants to imply distinctions, he does not do it within the brother concept, but by abandoning it, e.g. by using other kinship structures. Jesus is possibly understood as an older brother, the 'firstborn among many brothers' (Rom 8:29).

Two other texts need special mention, since they combine brother terminology and a description of differences. They appear to be the only texts of this kind. Though they occur in separate letters and rather diverse situations, they still display strikingly similar features, terminologically as well as in content. In Rom 14 and 1 Cor 8 brother terminology plays an important part, but at the same time Paul distinguishes between weak (Rom 14:1f; 15:1; 1 Cor 8:7, 9–12: *ho asthenôn*, *adynatoi*) and strong or free (Rom 15:1: *dynatoi*; 1 Cor 8:9: *hê exousia*; 9:1: *eleutheros*) parties or – possibly – persons. Both texts treat problems of behaviour connected to acceptable or illicit food; these problems are, however, also symptoms of underlying conflicts regarding internal status and power. What is interesting for us, is the way in which Paul depicts the conflict: he classifies those involved into two separate groups, and characterises them in terms of low and high status. This indicates that Paul, when he approaches problems related to Christian brotherhood, does so by utilising terms denoting some kind of hierarchy among Christian brothers. He seems, however, somewhat reluctant to approve such a structure; rather, he regards it a problem to be overcome.

Conflict areas between Christian brothers

Are there any particular conflict areas that can be related to the brotherhood concept? Above I hinted at one area: problems concerning food regulations, which also reflected structural conflicts. Another area surfaces in 1 Cor 6:1–11. Here Paul addresses a quarrel (v. 1: *pragma*) between Christians: persons within the community are suing each other at the public courts. Once again Paul strongly emphasises brotherhood ideas (vv. 5, 6, 8: 'and *brothers* at that'). He probably considers it especially shameful (v. 5: 'I say this to your shame') for Christians – since they are brothers – that they quarrel, and even in public, over worldly matters. Scholars hold different opinions as to the point at issue; most of them, however, maintain that it has to do with property of some kind (cf Schrage 1991: 402ff). One possible, but perhaps too speculative, interpretation of this passage is that Paul is speaking of persons who are both Christian and carnal brothers, and that the lawsuit is on inheritance. This concurs with Paul's argument in v. 9, that 'wrongdoers will not *inherit* the kingdom of God', which would then be an appropriate sarcasm or irony. And if this interpretation is wrong, Paul never-theless probably conveys the idea that Christian brothers who litigate against one another on property or the like, consequently disinherit them-selves from the kingdom of God. For Paul, then, there seems to be some kind of connection between brotherhood and inheritance.

Solving conflicts between Christian brothers

When conflicts arise between Christians, Paul enjoins that they should be done away with internally. He also prescribes a procedure for internal litiga-tion (1 Cor 5: a case of sexual immorality). This is even more urgent for him when their status as brothers is at stake. This is the case in 1 Cor 6:1–11. If they are not able to solve conflicts internally, that is as brothers, but have to appeal to public courts, they bring shame on the whole community.

What are Paul's guidelines for solving internal conflicts in cases where brotherhood is highlighted? Paul's advice in the relevant texts is very much the same: as brothers the Christians should not pass judgment on one another (Rom 14:10, 13; 12:10ff). The strong among them ought to put up with the failings of the weak, and not please themselves (Rom 15:1; 1 Cor 8:7, 12). The strong should refrain from what might make the weak stumble (Rom 14:15, 21; 1 Cor 8:11, 13). And they should all rather suffer wrongs than themselves do wrong (1 Cor 6:7f). When things go wrong, they ought to welcome and accept one another (1 Thess 5:14f), even across social borders (Philem 16f). The advice is to a certain extent general, but still has a characteristic profile: Christians are supposed to display generosity, to support each other, to try to bridge over differences of status, to be willing to renounce, and to forgive one another.

PLUTARCH AND PAUL

During the presentation of Plutarch and Paul some differences, but more similarities, have emerged. Though we should always beware of detecting too many similarities in such a comparison, several common features cannot be dismissed as merely accidental.

Both Plutarch and Paul focus strongly on a concept of brotherhood, with a force that is unusual in texts extant from Antiquity – though Plutarch, to be sure, treats carnal brotherhood and Paul some kind of spiritual brotherhood. Paul's idea of brotherhood seems more open: he also includes persons and groups that are geographically spread.

Both subsume the correct brotherly attitude under the heading of brotherly love (*philadelphia*), a term that seems to have a more prominent place in Plutarch and Paul than elsewhere. We should also observe that both approach brotherly attitudes very much from a practical side: they do not perceive of brotherhood from a theoretical, philosophical stance, but are interested in how it is implemented in practical, social life. They also both emphasise the emotional aspect of brotherly relations.

They differ, however, when they give reasons for the importance of brotherhood. Plutarch – due to the character of his treatise – takes great care to ground its character in nature as well as in practice, whereas Paul gives no such grounds: he simply presupposes its importance. On the part of Paul this may be accidental, but it is still worth observing that in several contexts he could easily have exploited the concept theologically, e.g. by arguing for brotherhood on the basis of God as their common father.

Both present brother relations as distinct from other relationships. Though brotherhood cannot be separated totally from other kinship relations, it is nevertheless perceived as a relationship of its own. It is allotted a predominant role, and functions in practice, for the most part, independently of the other relationships. The same is the case with the friendship relationship: Plutarch uses it as a contrast to brotherhood; Paul leaves friendship terms (and ideas?) almost completely out.

Both Plutarch (directly) and Paul (indirectly) hint at hierarchies of different kinds within the brother relationship. Plutarch explicitly and fundamentally approves of these, though he attempts to soften opposites, in the service of harmony. Paul, however, does not accept hierarchy within the brotherly relationship in the same way. Though he does not explicitly contradict it, he nevertheless seems to aim at a higher degree of equality than Plutarch does, at least when the Christians are viewed as brothers.[14]

Importantly, when there are problems within the brother relationship, Plutarch and Paul portray the conflicting parties in strikingly similar ways structurally. Both distribute brothers in two groups, which oppose each other. Both place them on different levels in a hierarchy: they are given different status. The hierarchies are characterised in related ways: Paul calls them 'weak' and 'strong' or 'free', Plutarch 'inferior' and 'superior'. The two may, however, display a certain difference in attitude towards hierarchy: whereas Plutarch directs his advice towards inferior and superior alike, Paul puts the responsibility for mending the brotherly relationships primarily on the strong.

For both of them, brotherhood is exposed to conflict, and such conflicts have several causes: for Plutarch age, nature and social status, for Paul probably social conditions and religious status. One conflict area receives special focus: brotherly quarrels over property or inheritance. The focus may be due to this actually being a widespread problem within the brother relationship in Antiquity, or alternatively to it reflecting a general mentality that brothers were suspected of quarrelling over property and inheritance (Hallett 1984: 198ff). For Plutarch this idea is an important motive for writing his treatise. With Paul it seems to lurk in the background: Christians, being brothers, should not fall into the notorious trap of mutual quarrels and litigation. They both seem to conceive of brotherhood as an ideal relationship, but a relationship that at the same time is seriously harmed (Plutarch) or threatened (Paul).

The way they handle conflict also has much in common. Both propose procedures to solve the problems internally; for both this is to avoid brothers (or their kin) being shamed in public. In their practical advice, both advocate tolerance. Brothers, since they *are* brothers, ought to be lenient towards one another, and indulge each other's weaknesses and mistakes. One should not be too rash to judge a brother and his sins. Such tolerance also implies that one should be willing to forgive a sinning brother, and also to ask for his forgiveness.

Such advice seems to be of a rather general character, and may – from our 'modern' point of view – be applied to most human relationships. But was this true in Antiquity? Or were Plutarch's and Paul's exhortations to leniency and mutual forgiveness indicative of general ideas on brotherhood and its particular character? In the honour and shame societies of Antiquity there were narrow limits for divergent behaviour. Was brotherhood the social relation that was the least regulated internally, and thus the one that rendered the greatest possibilities for individual differences, and at the same time for mutual tolerance and forgiveness?

Whatever may be the answer to this, there are in my opinion several close and striking parallels between Plutarch's presentation of carnal brotherhood and Paul's ideas of Christians as sisters and brothers. These parallels need to be investigated further in other sources, to see whether, how far, and in what ways there are connections between prevalent ideas on brotherhood in Antiquity and Paul's use of them in his letters.

NOTES

1 Words with the root *adelph*- occur about 100 times in Paul. Throughout this article I mostly use the terms 'brother(s)' and 'brotherhood'. Plutarch clearly has (almost) only brothers in view in his treatise, and not sisters, whereas Paul also uses *adelph*- terms for sisters. In this article I have to leave on one side the complicated questions on gender in Paul, Plutarch, and in Antiquity in general.

2 The aim of my doctoral dissertation (in progress) is to throw new light upon the background, role and character of brotherhood in Paul's letters. The material in this article is going to form part of a case-study in the dissertation.

3 By 'brotherhood' is meant here the relationship between carnal or social brothers (and sisters). There has been extremely little research on sibling relationships in Antiquity. Two exceptions are Hallett 1984: 150–210, and Cox 1988.

4 All citations are from 'On Brotherly Love' in Plutarch's *Moralia*, vol. VI, Loeb Classical Library 1970: 246–325, Cambridge, MA: Harvard University Press, and *The Holy Bible*, New Revised Standard Version 1989, Nashville: Thomas Nelson Publishers. When necessary, I have made some alterations on the basis of the Greek texts.

5 Dixon treats Roman tradition, but the ideal is in my opinion not limited to this: it is of a more general character, and also adequate for Hellenistic and Jewish traditions at that time. This, however, cannot be amplified here.

6 A fragment by the Stoic Hierocles (early second century AD) is also preserved, cf Malherbe 1986: 85–104, especially 93–95.

7 With some reserve, I support Betz' outline, cf Betz 1978: 234–36. Plutarch always has carnal brotherhood in mind, although he knows other (metaphorical) ways of using the brother terminology (479D). Betz also discusses the use of the brotherhood and family terminology in the New Testament, and assumes that it has entered early Christian literature through Hellenistic Judaism (Betz 1978: 232–33). His discussion is, however, very brief and general, and mostly restricted to references to NT texts. Several of these references are to Paul, but though Betz makes several valuable observations, he does not structure and assess the Pauline material in relation to Plutarch.

8 In interpreting Plutarch's treatise we should be aware that he runs the risk of

over-emphasising the particular characteristics of brotherhood: when it is made a special topic, differences, rather than similarities with other relationships (e.g. within the family, or between friends) tend to be stressed.

9 Betz 1978: 236f (cf also 231f, 234–36). Betz bases much of his outline and interpretation of the treatise on a close connection between brotherhood and friendship. Betz maintains, for example, that Plutarch defines brotherhood as derived from friendship (and family), regarding a passage in 478C–D as a definition of both:

> but all men of today, when they encounter brothers who are good to each other, wonder at them no less than at those famous sons of Molione, who, according to common belief, were born with their bodies grown together; and *to use in common a father's wealth and friends and slaves* is considered as incredible and portentous as *for one soul to make use of the hands and feet and eyes of two bodies*.

The first underscored text Betz considers a definition of brotherhood, and the second one of friendship. This interpretation is for several reasons very unlikely, reasons which, however, I cannot explicate in full here. In my opinion the second half of the period merely follows up the first half, that true brotherly love is as rare as the Molione twins. Betz also holds that brotherhood and friendship are 'intimately related "by nature"'. This, too, is incorrect. In 478C–D – and elsewhere – the two are differently defined in principle and are described with mutually exclusive features (cf my rendering of Plutarch's argument).

10 Cf O'Neil 1991. None of the terms Plutarch uses to characterise friendship is used of brotherhood; the only exception is *eunoia* which has a very general meaning.

11 The parallels with Paul are striking (Rom 12:4ff; 1 Cor 12:12ff). But there are significant differences in how the metaphor is applied; Plutarch, for example, uses the body metaphor to justify that not only the tasks and roles of brothers, but also their social status, may differ. They seem to have different points of departure and different intentions: Plutarch argues for the status quo, while Paul uses the metaphor for a re-evaluation of relations.

12 Baptism and Spirit make them children/sons of God, but not sisters and brothers. Paul's argument runs vertically (father–children/sons), not horizontally.

13 E.g. Marshall 1987 (1 Cor) and Stowers 1991: 105–21 (Phil), however, maintain that Paul approaches his co-Christians on the basis of friendship ideas. I believe that their viewpoints are rather problematical, but cannot discuss this here.

14 'Equality' is a very problematical word here, but I believe that it nonetheless signals a difference in Plutarch's and Paul's ways of thinking. It is, however, not possible to expand on this here.

BIBLIOGRAPHY

Betz, H. D. (ed.) (1978) *Plutarch's Ethical Writings and Early Christian Literature*, Studia ad Corpus Hellenisticum Novi Testamenti vol. 4, Leiden: E. J. Brill.

Brady, C. J. (1961) *Brotherly Love. A Study of the Word Philadelphia and its Contributions to the Biblical Theology of Brotherly Love*, unpublished dissertation, Fribourg.

Cox, C. A. (1988) 'Sibling Relationships in Classical Athens: Brother–Sister Ties', in *Journal of Family History* 13: 377–95.

Dixon, S. (1991) 'The Sentimental Ideal of the Roman Family', in B. Rawson (ed.) *Marriage, Divorce, and Children in Ancient Rome*, Canberra and Oxford: Humanities Research Center/Clarendon Press: 99–113.

—— (1992) *The Roman Family*, Baltimore and London: Johns Hopkins University Press.

Glad, C. E. (1995) *Paul and Philodemus. Adaptability in Epicurean and Early Christian Psychagogy*, NovTSup 81, Leiden: E. J. Brill.

Hallett, J. P. (1984) *Fathers and Daughters in Roman Society. Women and the Elite Family*, Princeton, NJ: Princeton University Press.

Holtz, T. (1986) *Der erste Brief an die Thessalonicher*, EKKNT 13, Zürich: Benziger/Neukirchener Verlag.

Kloppenborg, J. S. (1993) '*Philadelphia, theodidaktos* and the Dioscuri: Rhetorical Engagement in 1 Thessalonians 4:9–12', *NTS* 39: 265–89.

Malherbe, A. J. (1986) *Moral Exhortation: A Greco-Roman Sourcebook*, Philadelphia: Westminster Press.

Marshall, P. (1987) *Enmity in Corinth: Social Conventions in Paul's Relations with the Corinthians*, WUNT 2: 23, Tübingen: J. C. B. Mohr (Paul Siebeck).

Meeks, W. A. (1983) *The First Urban Christian. The Social World of the Apostle Paul*, New Haven: Yale University Press.

Mitchell, A. C. (1991) ' "Greet the Friends by Name": New Testament Evidence for the Greco-Roman Topos on Friendship', paper presented at the Hellenistic Moral Philosophy and Early Christianity Consultation on 'Friendship in Greek Authors and Sources', Annual Meeting of the Society of Biblical Literature.

O'Neil, E. N. (1991) 'Plutarch on Friendship', paper presented at the Hellenistic Moral Philosophy and Early Christianity Consultation on 'Friendship in Greek Authors and Sources', Annual Meeting of the Society of Biblical Literature.

Sandnes, K. O. (1994) *A New Family. Conversion and Ecclesiology in the Early Church with Cross-Cultural Comparisons*, Studies in the Intercultural History of Christianity 91, Bern: Peter Lang.

Schäfer, K. (1989) *Gemeinde als 'Bruderschaft'. Ein Beitrag zum Kirchenverständnis des Paulus*, Europäische Hochschulschriften Reihe XXIII Bd. 333, Frankfurt: Peter Lang.

Schrage, W. (1991) *Der erste Brief an die Korinther*, EKKNT 7:1, Zürich: Benzige/Neukirchener Verlag.

Sevenster, J. N. (1954–55) 'Waroom Spreekt Paulus Nooit Van Vrienden en Vriendschap', *NedTeolTijdschr* 9: 356–63.

Stowers, S. K. (1991) 'Friends and Enemies in the Politics of Heaven. Reading Theology in Philippians', in J. M. Bassler (ed.) *Pauline Theology. Volume I: Thessalonians, Philippians, Galatians, Philemon*, Minneapolis: Fortress Press: 105–21.

Wilson, W. T. (1991) *Love without Pretense*, WUNT 2: 46, Tübingen: J. C. Mohr (Paul Siebeck).

10

BROTHERHOOD IN CHRIST

A gender hermeneutical reading of 1 Thessalonians

Lone Fatum

This chapter is an example of what I would like to call a gender hermeneutical approach to the communication of Paul. First I shall present a reading of 1 Thess in which I do not really pretend to present anything new to those already familiar with narrative and rhetorical criticism. Then I shall examine the socio-sexual structure of Paul's symbolic universe, drawing on insights from sociology of knowledge, social history, and cultural anthropology. Finally I shall focus on the gender ideological implications of 1 Thess concerning the historical construction of the Pauline community after the model of the patriarchal family. How does Paul stage himself and his audience in 1 Thess, and how does he apply the hierarchic code of the family model to the Christian association? What are the implications for women converts of Paul's ideal of the eschatological brotherhood, and what may we conclude concerning the Thessalonian women from his effort to organise and administer the community as male kin, his dependent sons in Christ?

All interpretation takes place in a context. To focus on gender from a constructivist point of view in order to assess the workings and effective history of gender ideology is, of course, a modern hermeneutical project. In that sense, my critical feminist position is not defined primarily by Pauline Antiquity; it depends on the historical reflexivity so characteristic of late modernity (Giddens 1991). And yet, as regards gender bias and sexual discrimination on a basis of patriarchal order and a hierarchic code of androcentric social values, modernity does not seem very far or very different from Antiquity. In our present context it can actually still be debated whether women's rights are human rights, i.e. whether women are in fact fully human. Indeed, one issue which caused extremely heated and difficult encounters during the recent conference in Beijing, The Fourth World Conference on Women, September 1995, was the status of women as free and independent, socio-sexual agents. A gender hermeneutical reading of 1 Thess raises the question, whether women could in fact be fully Christian according to the androcentric values of Paul's socio-sexual communication. Were Thessalonian women converts actually among the recipients of 1 Thess? Are we to count them among the brothers as full members of the

Christian community and to see them, like male Christians, with a status as Christian agents?

THE PARAENETIC COMMUNICATION

In his address to the Thessalonians Paul is as gentle as a nurse towards her own children (Malherbe 1988: 61–94; 1989b: 35–48; Fowl 1990), but in order to exercise fully his apostolic authority as the founder and religious guide of the community and, most important, as the moral model (Castelli 1991: 89–136) for his converts, he casts himself both as father and as brother. Encouraging, exhorting and instructing his sons and brothers, Paul deliberately (Meeks 1983: 84–96; Petersen 1985: 124–63) employs a man-to-man language on a man-to-man stage setting in order to institutionalise a social pattern of fellowship and reciprocity. Thus the epistolary form and the paraenetic content constitute the specific character of 1 Thess. Both the letter and the community of recipients, who are to be strengthened by it in their mutual respect and concord, are defined by androcentric values and social conventions and organised in terms of the patriarchal structures so characteristic of urban society in Graeco-Roman Antiquity (Malina 1981: 71–90; Fatum 1989; 1995; Torjesen 1992).

Of course, neither androcentric bias nor patriarchal order originated with Christianity. But both have been mediated and institutionalised effectively as part and parcel of Christian tradition, not only in its historical presentation and relative social practice but in its religious and moral implications as well. 1 Thess is our earliest extant illustration of this and deserves to be recognised as such (Fatum 1994a; 1994b). All through the letter a communication is taking place in which Paul expresses his affectionate solidarity with a group of male Christians living their daily lives as craftsmen, artisans and tradesmen. Some of them may be heads of households, but all of them, apparently, must work manually for a living (Hock 1980: 11–49; Malherbe 1988: 5–33) in order to uphold their social status of honourable independence. Accordingly, they are to relate to each other and to non-Christians in all the necessary social engagements in a way that will demonstrate to their pagan neighbours as well as to themselves the extraordinary quality of their newly acquired collective identity as Christian converts belonging to God. Proper internal and external relations are important for maintaining the fellowship in Christ built on faith, love and hope (Holtz 1990: 131–40; Hyldahl 1994: 42, 56–57).

Compared with Paul's other letters, 1 Thess looks atypical; it seems to lack a thematic profile and appears as a letter in which Paul has no need to defend either his gospel and its implications or the legitimacy of his apostolic authority. In 1 Thess we are, literally, among friends; the letter is neither polemic nor apologetic, it is pastoral (Malherbe 1989b: 49–77; Chapa 1994), and the cause and motivation of Paul's writing is not conflict but the care and concern of friendship (Meeks 1983: 85–94; Marshall 1987: 1–34, 130–64; Malherbe 1988: 95–107). Thus, the immediate purpose of the letter is to replace Paul's personal presence among the new converts and to compensate for a face to face communication (2:17–20; 3:6–10). In this sense, 1 Thess is a straightforward and uncomplicated communication.

It falls into two parts: 1:2 to 3:13 appears as an extended thanksgiving· and 4:1 to 5:24 as applied paraenesis, characterising the whole of the letter as apostolic exhortation. Praising the Thessalonians for their work of faith, their laborious demonstration of love, and their perseverance in the hope of Christ (1:3), Paul defines the paraenetic pattern of his communication. The presupposition is that all three concepts, faith, love and hope, are inter-dependent, each qualifying the others and emphasising together the social commitment of the new conviction as well as the eschatological orientation of the new life. To become adherents of Christ is to become servants of the living and true God (1:9), thus committing oneself to a life of faith, demon-strated by love. Essentially, however, it means to believe in the resurrection of Jesus, thus committing oneself to a life of hope, demonstrated for the present by love and for the future by the expectation of the parousia of Jesus as the son of God and his deliverance of the Christians from the approaching wrath (1:10) (Gager 1975: 66–92; Longenecker 1985).

Paul's thanksgiving characterises the Thessalonians as a model commu-nity (1:7), and his appealing and very affective recollections of their willingness to accept his preaching and himself as their teacher and example (1:4–6; 2:1,13), and even to endure oppositions and personal hardship as the inevitable consequence of their new adherence, mark them in every respect as a fellowship, qualified by God himself to live the life of Christ (1:6; 2:14; 3:3–4; 4:9; 5:4–5). This is a life radically different from their immediate past (1:9) as well as from their present surroundings (4;5,12) because of the future for which they have been chosen (1:10; 4:13; 5:9–10). Consequently, hope is the decisive characteristic of their new status as Christian converts. Hope conveys spiritual affirmation (1:4–5; 2:13; 5:24) and, at the same time, implies social and moral obligation (3:13; 4:1–8,10–12; 5:6, 8, 12–23). Because they have hope, the Thessalonians are expected to demon-strate more faith and practise more love in order to appear holy before God at the parousia (3:9–13; 4:10). Thus, the extensive purpose of Paul's communication is to guide his new converts through a steady progress of moral improvement onward and upward to that state of pure holiness that is the goal of their election and conversion (4:7).

THE SOCIAL SETTING

But to be a community of newly converted is to be in the middle of a very critical progress of change and readjustment. In the urban society of Graeco-Roman Antiquity, defined by publicness and collectivity (MacMullen 1974:

57–87) and organised on the basis of family relations, of trade, craft and neighbourhood associations and memberships of clubs and cultic assemblies (Meeks 1983: 51–73; Donfried 1985), social identity is secured by group adherence, and status is maintained in a vertical pattern of social alliances and public loyalties (MacMullen 1974: 88–120; Banks 1980: 33–51, 142–70, Hendrix 1992). In such a society it is indeed a comprehensive and risky project to change one's faith and way of life; in a very literal sense it means a radical change of social identity in order to adjust to a new pattern of adherence and inter-dependence. Old bonds and alliances as well as natural relations break down or must be ignored; new ones have yet to be built, or lack the necessary stability. The converts experience opposition and exclusion (2:14) (Gilliard 1989); they are regarded with suspicion by family and friends, and at the same time their confidence in their new adherence may be faltering. The Christian community itself is perhaps not yet properly organised, and the loyalty and reliability of the new brothers not yet sufficiently reassuring.

This, at least to some extent, is a process of suffering (1:6), causing social insecurity and frustration as well as spiritual doubts and psychological weakness (Malherbe 1988: 61–94). At worst, the pressure from the surroundings becomes unbearable, and some lose courage altogether and relapse into their old life (3:3–5). The process is familiar to Paul, who values both opposition and personal hardship as the significant distinctions of Christian existence. But Paul is nonetheless apprehensive of the danger of defection. Accordingly, he has expressly prepared the Thessalonians for a time of sufferings (3:4) by pointing to his personal example (1:6; 2:2) and the *theologia crucis* paradigm of his soteriology (1:6; 2:14–16) (Wolter 1990). Yet the Thessalonian community is possibly only months old and already exposed to great pressure. Moreover, the new converts must deal with Paul's absence (2:17–18). At the time of writing, he regards them as very young children, his dependent sons, under age and immature, in need of their father's guiding presence (2:7–12,17; 3:1–5) (Malherbe 1990). Although he has been comforted by Timothy (3:6–9), he is still anxious to go to Thessalonica himself to instruct them face to face and exhort directly by his personal example in order to make good the deficiencies of their faith and to further their love (3:10–13), thus urging them onwards in their collective endeavours to reach the parousia in the ultimate state of holiness.

THE SOCIAL OBLIGATION OF HOPE

Although at the beginning of his thanksgiving (1:3) Paul emphasised faith and love and hope, he seems in his reference to Timothy's report deliberately to leave out hope (3:6). Apparently, doubts have arisen among the Thessalonians concerning the meaning and implications of the Christian hope, i.e. the implications of the belief in the resurrection of Jesus and his parousia concerning the future expectations of the Christians. Deaths seem to have occurred among them, and this seems to have caused unrest and uncertainty in the community (Holtz 1990: 182–208; Hyldahl 1994: 49–53). For consolation and exhortation together, Paul amplifies his teaching on the resurrection of the dead and the final union of all Christians with the Lord in the air at his parousia (4:13–18) (Sellin 1986: 37–49, 63–65). But, most important, in regard to the paraenetic purpose of the communication, he incorporates the teaching on the resurrection of the dead as part of his extensive exhortation in 4:1 to 5:24 concerning the social and moral behaviour of the living, thus affirming their present, everyday obligation to live in this world in accordance with their calling and their future expectations (1:1, 4; 5:23–24).

Thus, the purpose of 1 Thess is not to be found in the consolation concerning the dead or in the eschatological teaching *per se* (Schnelle 1986; Lautenschlager 1990). Rather, all through the letter, and 4:13–18 is no exception, Paul is concerned with the social and moral obligations of the living Christians and with the problems of their actual, everyday life. Consistently, he endeavours to guide his converts towards the ultimate goal of holiness, appropriate to their state of calling (4:7), and so he exhorts them to endure as well as to develop in order to signify more and more clearly that they are the sons of light and day (5:5). Together they constitute the community of life, qualified by hope, and this sets them apart from the rest of the world. Therefore, they must lead a life which is qualitatively different in order to maintain (Berger and Luckmann 1966: 149–93; Berger 1967: 29–51; MacDonald 1988: 46–60, 72–83) their exclusive status (4:3–8; 5:12–22). They must actually demonstrate their Christian status as the status of hope by their works of faith and love, faith and love being their breastplate or body armour, while the hope of salvation, characteristically, is their helmet (5:8) (Malina 1981: 60–64).

According to this reading, then, 1 Thess is a social and moral communication. Paul focuses on the practical implications of hope and not on hope *per se* in a theological or eschatological sense. And simply because he cannot, for the time being, convey his exhortation in person, demonstrating the implications of hope by his fatherly presence and guiding example, he resorts to writing. This explains why his personal example dominates his recollections in 1:2 to 3:13; but it also emphasises the impact of Paul's patriarchal authority on the social and moral identity of his new converts. Constantly appealing to memory as well as to knowledge and agreement of the Thessalonians (Meeks 1983: 114–15; Malherbe 1988: 61–81), Paul urges them to identify with him, imitating his apostolic behaviour (1:6; 2:1–12), in order that they may show progress in their everyday life of hope (4:10–12; 5:12–15). Thus, in the extended thanksgiving, he re-establishes the initial inter-dependence between the apostle and his converts, between father and sons. And through the recollections of their common past he confirms himself as their personal authority and model (Holmberg 1978: 72–95). On a secure basis of authority and imitation he then applies his social and moral paraenesis in 4:1 to 5:24.

In other words, Paul re-establishes his role of apostolic authority in 1:2 to 3:13 in order to exhort effectively in 4:1 to 5:2, thus, at the same time, re-establishing himself as the living demonstration of his paraenetic communication. The implications of Paul's personal example cannot be separated from the purpose of his teaching and exhortation; nor can the androcentric implications of his teaching and exhortation be separated from his consciousness of imitating Christ himself, personifying by his own behaviour the *theologia crucis* of his soteriology. To adhere to Paul's teaching of Christ implies, literally, to imitate the way Paul presents himself to his converts as the social and moral embodiment of his teaching (Schütz 1975: 204–32). This means, in the communication to the Thessalonians, that Paul is their model of social and moral behaviour, because he is himself the model of a man qualified in Christ to live the life of hope. To follow the example of Paul is in a practical sense to be guided on the basis of hope through the problems of everyday living (Best 1972: 355–58). In the ultimate sense, however, it is to follow the authorised way of the apostle towards the goal of holiness and the union with the risen Christ at his parousia.

THE ESCHATOLOGICAL IDENTITY OF THE BROTHERHOOD

Rhetorically, as it has been pointed out before, the whole of 1 Thess 4:1 to 5:24 may be seen as a coherent piece of paraclesis (Malherbe 1988: 88–94; 1990; Holtz 1990: 241–45), and Paul is pursuing his moral aim of unity and holiness among his sons and brothers along a double track of exhortation. One line of argumentation is apocalyptic and *explicitly* eschatological, conveying a message of consolation and encouragement. The other is social and *implicitly* eschatological, specifying the moral demands on the brothers to live in this world in accordance with their heavenly calling. The lines may be distinguished but not separated, for, consistent with his moral logic, Paul bases his social instructions on eschatological teaching, literally deducing moral obligation from his eschatological definition of Christian existence.

The apocalyptic line of argument (4:13 to 5:6) concerns the affinity of the brothers with the risen Christ and has, characteristically, a present as well as a future aspect. The fundamental hope of union with Christ (1:9–10; 5:9–10) defines the unity of the Christians already in this world and is to sustain their anticipation of a heavenly consummation at the time of salvation, including in the final resurrection all the brothers at once, notwithstanding that some will have died before the day of the parousia (4:15–16) (Best 1972: 179–202; Holtz 1990: 182–208; Hyldahl 1994: 49–53). So the brothers are qualified by their joint hope as an eschatological community, bound for a future with Christ and, therefore, fundamentally different from the world around them. But by the same token, i.e. the affinity with the risen Christ, Paul imposes on them the joint responsibility to uphold this brotherhood of eschatological difference through all the anxieties and challenges of the present life.

Consequently, the social line of argument (4:1–12; 5:7–14) concerns the responsibility of the newly converted to be morally superior to their non-Christian surroundings and to engage from within in the fortification of the brotherhood. The eschatological community is to prove unshakeable, self-reliant and non-offensive. In 5:8, the armour metaphor is one of resistance and self-protection, clearly conveying the defensive strategy of Paul's insistence on holiness (4:1–3, 7). The social terms are those of integrity, solidarity and long-suffering perseverance (5:12–22), and the brothers are not to depend on or in any way be indebted to the outside world (4:9–12) (Malherbe 1988: 95–109).

Because they are sons of light and day, the brothers are to behave with sobriety and watchful consideration (5:4–11). And, accordingly, because they have been called by God to share in the holiness of the risen Christ, they are to lead their everyday lives now in holiness and purification, answering to God's will as well as to the superior status of their calling with self-control and moral restraint in their socio-sexual activities (4:3–8).

Thus, eschatological and social arguments are correlated and, all through his paraclesis, Paul applies the moral obligation of brotherhood in order to create a strong group with a high grid (Douglas 1970; Malina 1986: 13–27). The brothers are, in other words, to form and uphold a tightly organised community of hierarchic inter-dependence inwardly, with weaker brothers giving their respect and loyal adherence to stronger ones and the stronger in turn their lenient guidance and support to the weaker, so that all of them together will put forth the image of a well-defined and honourable association.

THE ANDROCENTRIC IMPLICATIONS OF PAUL'S EXHORTATION

Though the Christian brotherhood is a voluntary grouping, based on a voluntary commitment, Paul seems intent on pressing upon it a binding commitment characteristic of the kinship group, defined as a non-voluntary association; he strives in fact to organise the brothers according to the social and moral institution of the *patriarchal family*.

In a general sense, Paul may present himself as a brother to his converts, i.e. as a member of the brotherhood in Christ. But in a very specific sense, as emphasised already, he exhorts the Thessalonians as a father his sons. In the role of exemplary father he is to them, the brothers, the representative of Christ. In other words, the vertical affinity with the risen Christ, mediated by Paul and his co-workers, defines and qualifies the horizontal relationship of the brothers in their local setting. Socially and morally they are inter-dependent, but they are not equal; on the contrary, just like the model family of Graeco-Roman Antiquity, their relationship is one of inequality and dissimilarity (Malina 1981: 71–90; Meeks 1983: 74–110; 1986: 97–123), held together by something more comprehensive than mutual social interest. Consequently, Paul wants them to build up a personal network of greater intimacy and inter-dependence than those of trade guilds or funeral societies. Like male kin, they are to be organised and administered according to the hierarchic code of the asymmetrical alliances of the patriarchal household.

Thus, Paul's frequent and ostentatious use of familial epithets and his highly affective expressions of fatherly concern and devotion carry a literal or invoking meaning (Petersen 1985: 17–30; Castelli 1991: 89–117). All through 1 Thess, Paul's emotional language has a social impact; but in the explicit paraclesis, especially, his relational appeals to the brothers function to console them as well as to bind them together and to himself. His direct calls upon the brothers in 4:1, 10, 13 and 5:1, 4, 12, 14 have a complementary effect. For the more his Thessalonian sons adhere to his fatherly authority and imitate his personal example, the more they will be united like brothers in their Christian development, and Paul will be affirmed in his patriarchal role as the mediator of Christ (Malina 1981: 53–60; Marshall 1987: 91–129; Hendrix 1992: 39–58). Again, vertical affinity has horizontal significance; bound by joint adherence, the brothers will be able to strengthen their shared social identity and will appear as a group with common boundaries and rules of behaviour – the functional equivalent, that is, of the male collective of the household family.

Unambiguously, then, Paul addresses male Christians in 1 Thess on the conditions of an androcentric ideology of gender values and virtues, self-evident, we must assume, to Paul himself as well as to his male audience, since this is in fact the basic ideology of patriarchal Antiquity. But how exclusively male Paul's exhortation actually is, is best illustrated by the specific instructions in 4:3–8, where Paul addresses the socio-sexual activities of the brothers.

Whether the instrumental reference to the tool or object in 4:4 is seen as a reference to the woman, perhaps the wife, or to the male body, viz. the male sexual organ (Whitton 1982), the moral message of 4:3–5 is quite clear. When marrying, or in his marital life, the Christian is to be restrained and self-composed in his sexual behaviour, since to Paul, the former Pharisee (Phil 3:4–6), illegitimate and uncontrolled sexuality is tantamount to ungodliness and pagan impurity, idolatry and fornication being virtually synonymous in traditional Jewish interpretation (Gal 5:19–21; 1 Cor 6:9–10, Rom 1:24–32). Paul's argument in vv. 3–5 is loaded with stereotyped Jewish contempt of non-Jews in its caricature of pagan licentiousness. By enjoining the former pagans to demonstrate their new Christian identity

190

in accordance with Mosaic rules of purity and superior exclusiveness, Paul reveals how comprehensive the influence of traditional Jewish interpretation has been on his formative Christian teaching, especially relating to gender and socio-sexual morality (Douglas 1966: 114–39; Malina 1981: 122–51).

The exhortation of 4:3–8 may be read as an equivalent to a Jewish paraenesis, based on the Decalogue (Ex 20:1–17 and Deut 5:6–21). And Paul is not just echoing the Commandments; rather, he applies them as his implicit moral reference and even maintains their thematic coherence in a way that demonstrates how he takes for granted the whole construction of symbolic reality, gender values and social order on which they are based and which, of course, in the Mosaic context, they are designed to legitimise (Berger and Luckmann 1966: 110–34; Geertz 1973: 87–125; Malherbe 1989a: 152–57). Thus, in his Christian paraenesis, Paul is not just using Mosaic tradition; he is actually authorising, viz. Christianising, the Mosaic code of socio-sexual meaning.

Under the joint heading of the holiness demand in v. 3, dependent on the First Commandment and emphasised with a warning in vv. 6b–8, Paul links together in vv. 4–6a the Sixth and the Tenth Commandments against fornication and the coveting of one's neighbour's house. Obviously, the moral concern is the establishment and maintenance of the patriarchal household; probably, in v. 4, Paul deals with the acquisition of a wife and, in thematic coherence, with the social integrity of the head of the household, the Greek equivalent of the Roman *paterfamilias*, in v. 6a. Since Paul's focus is defined by the head of the household and, generally, by the patriarchal organisation of male activity according to the social order of challenge and response (MacMullen 1974: 88–120; Malina 1981: 25–42), a social agent is to him a male agent, and the social territory of one agent, making up the social honour of the family, has to be defended against transgression and possible usurpation by other agents.

Consequently, and fully in accordance with the gender ideology and traditional patriarchal values of the Decalogue, a woman or wife is implied in v. 4 as the prerequisite for male social activity, just as in v. 6a she may be implied again as part of the household, not to be violated. But then this is actually the only indication at all in the whole of 1 Thess of female presence among the brothers; and in its own context it is neither a negative nor a positive indication. Rather, it conveys as a matter of fact what the socio-sexual conditions designed for women by patriarchal construction are, the power to interpret gender and to administer sexuality being generally accepted as a male prerogative (Torjesen 1993).

Obviously, gender is not the issue in 1 Thess and yet, all through the letter, Paul's address to his Thessalonian sons and brothers is, of course, gendered (Ortner and Whitehead 1988: 1–27; Castelli 1994; Nicholson 1994). But his bias is shared, apparently, by his male audience, allowing him to insist on the unity and holiness of the brotherhood on a basis of

191

androcentric congeniality and sympathetic understanding. Thus, the gender ideology implied by his teaching and exhortation does not have to be specified or qualified; the patriarchal pattern of social values and virtues is merely taken for granted as a common code of reference, and so is the androcentric orientation of the brothers' joint commitment to organise and develop their moral superiority and exclusiveness, vertically as well as horizontally, in imitation of Paul.

Summing up the implications of these conditions and presuppositions, Paul's communication in 1 Thess does not invite the conclusion that female presence among the brothers is synonymous with full and equal membership for women of the Christian brotherhood (Meeks 1974; Fiorenza 1983: 205–41; Eriksson 1995: 103–27). We may assume, of course, that women were also among the converts in Thessalonica. But were they also among the Christians, i.e. did they actually count, individually, as members of the community, the quorum of the brothers, identified with Christ? It must remain an open question how we are to imagine Christian women's social integration into the Thessalonian community, when the impact of Paul's exhortation seems merely to confirm their exclusion (Young 1994: 31–37).

MALES ONLY?

Historically we may assume, of course, as stated already, that women were among the converts in Thessalonica. The woman implied by 1 Thess 4:4, 6a may indeed be a Christian wife and Acts 17:4 refers to a considerable number of prominent women adding, it seems, a valuable contribution of nobility and affluence to the establishment of the local community.

Acts 17:1–13, however, is the Lucan version of Paul's Thessalonian mission and, in almost every respect, it is incompatible with the evidence of Paul himself (Haenchen 1968: 444–53). Thus, Acts 17:1–13 seems to represent a Lucan reconstruction, characterised by Lucan interests, and, as an integral part of his stereotyping, he inserts in v. 4 his ideal portrait of the local Christian patroness of high social status and influence. Both v. 4 and the duplicate in 17:12 are connected with the presentation of Lydia in 16:13–15 and with the idealisation in Luke 8:1–3 of the women supporting Jesus and his followers (Schürmann 1982: 444–48). With their economic assets and independent social activity, these women are staged by Luke according to the conditions of his own time and urban context (D'Angelo 1990). But, even so, they may be the products of wishful thinking and the Lucan strategy of social idealisation rather than reliable references to actual experience of affluent women's patronage. Thus, by means of utopian construction, staged and qualified as historical reconstruction, the Lucan author may be said to have anticipated the utopian reconstructivism of modern feminist/womanist hermeneutics of liberation (Portefaix 1988; Fiorenza 1992).

Anyhow, since we cannot rely on the information of Acts concerning the Thessalonian women of Paul's time, we have to be content with the evidence of Paul himself and 1 Thess. In other words, we have to come to grips with what seems to be the exclusion of women from the brotherhood of Christians, recognising at the outset that such an exclusion is not the result of Christian interpretation in particular but, rather, the established expression of patriarchal social custom in general (MacDonald 1990).

According to the social structure of the symbolic universe in which Paul communicates with his male audience, the lives of women are embedded in the lives of men, and women are defined and qualified by their dependence on men. Thus, women are not counted in 1 Thess among the members who, as social agents, constitute the Christian community. As a consequence of the patriarchal logic, we may indeed assume that women converts have not been integrated into the brotherhood, that is, into the quorum of the community. Rather, they have been attached to the faction of brothers through husbands or male heads of households with reference to their social roles as wife, daughter, mother or sister, since no proper or virtuous woman may appear and be acknowledged as a social agent in her own right and with her own purpose (Torjesen 1992).

Further, the gender ideology and patriarchal social order of Paul's universe illustrate a pattern of values and virtues according to which *male* means general or universal, wholly compatible with Paul's interpretation of the collective identification with Christ (Fatum 1989; 1995: 57–65), whereas *female* means special or gender specific, compatible only with the present life of the body, femaleness thus constituting one part or component of a man's world, the social world, that is, of male interaction. This is the evidence of 1 Thess 4:3–8. When a woman is visible to the male eye as the object of androcentric gender interpretation, woman is defined in a comprehensive sense by her socio-sexual functionality, and women's activities are qualified according to the purpose of men's activities (Bach 1993).

As emphasised already, Paul seems able to take for granted both the social institution of the household and the hierarchic order of the family, and we may assume that neither Paul nor his Thessalonian audience have a negative view on marriage and marital life at this point. Indeed, the eschatological ideal of virginity seems not to have become an issue yet and, therefore, the reason why women are virtually invisible in 1 Thess may well be that particular women are not yet seen as a challenge to established morality. In other words, married women are not dishonouring their husbands by disorderly conduct, and virgin women are not behaving like males, i.e. like Phoebe, the *diakonos* of Rom 16:1–2, performing a male role and acquiring a male social status (Fiorenza 1983: 168–84; Holtz 1990: 242).

The Thessalonian women converts at Paul's time of writing, which is probably 49–50 CE (Hyldahl 1986: 107–11) seem to make up a homogeneous group, conforming to patriarchal social custom and established gender ideology. Apparently, their Christian identity is not perceived to be incompatible with their ordinary socio-sexual identity, and so their conversion is not causing any dissonance with regard to behaviour or public appearance. In relation to the community of brothers, they are seen to be embedded in men's lives, just as in society in general women's lives are embedded in those of men.

We may conclude that women were among the converts in Thessalonica; but, in concord with patriarchal logic as conveyed by Paul, they are not among the brothers of Christ; individually they are not members of the new community. Because they are defined and qualified as women, they cannot also be seen and qualified eschatologically as Christians. Literally, therefore, they are invisible in Christ and, accordingly, their socio-sexual presence among the brothers is, virtually, a non-presence.

This conclusion may seem discouraging indeed, jeopardising the idea of human equality and women's affirmation as an essential part of Christian interpretation. However, Christian interpretation is androcentric interpretation and depends on patriarchal construction. If we want to confront the socio-sexual discrimination of our own time and context, we must be able to confront also, with critical consistency, the socio-sexual discrimination at the roots of our Christian tradition.

BIBLIOGRAPHY

Bach, Alice (1993) 'Signs of the Flesh: Characterization in the Bible', *Semeia* 63: 61–79.

Banks, Robert (1980) *Paul's Idea of Community. The Early House Churches in Their Historical Setting*, Exeter: Paternoster.

Berger, Peter L. (1967) *The Sacred Canopy*, New York: Anchor Books.

Berger, Peter L. and Luckmann, T (1966) *The Social Construction of Reality*, London: Penguin (1976).

Best, Ernest (1972) *A Commentary on the First and Second Epistles to the Thessalonians*, London: A. & C. Black.

Castelli, Elizabeth A. (1991) *Imitating Paul. A Discourse of Power*, Louisville, KY: Westminster/John Knox Press.

—— (1994) 'Heteroglossia, Hermeneutics, and History. A Review Essay Of Recent Feminist Studies of Early Christianity', *JFSR* 10, 2: 73–98.

Chapa, Juan (1994) 'Is First Thessalonians a Letter of Consolation?', *NTS* 40: 150–60.

D'Angelo, Mary Rose (1990) 'Women in Luke–Acts: A Redactional View', *JBL* 109: 441–61.

Donfried, K. P. (1985) 'The Cults of Thessalonica and the Thessalonian Correspondence', *NTS* 32: 336–56.

Douglas, Mary (1966) *Purity and Danger*, London, New York: Ark Paperbacks (1988).

—— (1970) *Natural Symbols*, New York: Vintage Books (1973).

Eriksson, Anne-Louise (1995) *The Meaning of Gender in Theology. Problems and Possibilities*, Uppsala: Uppsala University.

Fatum, Lone (1989) 'Women, Symbolic Universe and Structures of Silence. Challenges and Possibilities in Androcentric Texts', *ST* 43: 61–80.

—— (1994a) 'Broderskab i Kristus. Om Kønssymbolik og Socialmoral i 1 Thessalonikerbrev', in N. P. Lemche and Mogens Müller (eds) *Fra dybet*, FS John Strange, Copenhagen: Museum Tusculanums Forlag.

—— (1994b) '1 Thessalonians', in Elisabeth Schüssler Fiorenza (ed.) *Searching the Scriptures. Volume Two: A Feminist Commentary*, New York: Crossroad.

—— (1995) 'Image of God and Glory of Man: Women in the Pauline Congregations', in Kari Elisabeth Børresen (ed.) *The Image of God. Gender Models in Judaeo-Christian Tradition*, Minneapolis: Fortress Press. Oslo: Solum (1991): 56–137.

Fiorenza, Elisabeth Schüssler (1983) *In Memory of Her*, London: SCM Press.

—— (1992) 'Feminist Hermeneutics', *The Anchor Bible Dictionary* vol. 2: 783–91.

Fowl, Stephen (1990) 'A Metaphor in Distress. A Reading of NHPIOI in 1 Thessalonian 2.7', *NTS* 36: 469–73.

Gager, John G. (1975) *Kingdom and Community*, Englewood Cliffs, NJ: Prentice Hall.

Geertz, Clifford (1973) *The Interpretations of Cultures*, New York: Basic Books.

Giddens, Anthony (1991) *Modernity and Self-Identity. Self and Society in the Late Modern Age*, Cambridge: Polity Press.

Gilliard, F. (1989) 'The Problem of the Antisemitic Comma between 1 Thessalonians 2.14 and 15', *NTS* 35: 481–502.

Haenchen, Ernst (1968) *Die Apostelgeschichte*, Meyers Kommentar III Abt., Göttingen: Vandenhoeck & Ruprecht (1956).

Hendrix, Holland (1992) 'Benefactor/Patronage Networks in the Urban Environment: Evidence from Thessalonica', *Semeia* 56: 39–58.

Hock, Ronald F. (1980) *The Social Context of Paul's Ministry*, Philadelphia: Fortress Press.

Holmberg, Bengt (1978) *Paul and Power*, Lund: Gleerup.

Holtz, Traugott (1990) *Der erste Brief an die Thessalonicher*, EKKNT XIII, Zürich, Braunschweig: Benziger/Neukirchener (1986).

Hyldahl, Niels (1986) *Die Paulinische Chronologie*, Leiden: E. J. Brill.

—— (1994) *Første og Andet Thessalonikerbrev. Indledning og Fortolkning*, Copenhagen: Institute of Biblical Exegesis.

Kennedy, George A. (1984) *New Testament Interpretation through Rhetorical Criticism*, Chapel Hill and London: University of North Carolina Press.

Lautenschlager, Markus (1990) '*Eite Gregoromen eite Katheudomen*. Zum Verhältnis von Heilung und Heil in 1 Thessalonicherbrief 5,10', *ZNW* 81: 39–59.

Lefkowitz, Mary R. and Fant, Maureen B. (eds) (1992) *Women's Life in Greece and Rome. A Source Book in Translation*, Baltimore: John Hopkins University Press (1982).

Longenecker, R. N. (1985) 'The Nature of Paul's Early Eschatology', *NTS* 31: 85–95.

MacDonald, Margaret Y. (1988) *The Pauline Churches. A Sociohistorical Study of Institutionalization in the Pauline and Deutero-Pauline Writings*, Cambridge: Cambridge University Press.

—— (1990) 'Women Holy in Body and Spirit: The Social Setting of 1 Corinthians 7', *NTS* 36: 161–81.

MacMullen, Ramsay (1974) *Roman Social Relations. 50 BC to AD 284*, New Haven and London: Yale University Press.

Malbon, Elizabeth Struthers (1992) 'Narrative Criticism: How Does the Story Mean?', in Janice Capel Anderson and Stephen D. Moore (eds) *Mark and Method. New Approaches in Biblical Studies*, Minneapolis: Fortress Press: 23–49.

Malbon, Elizabeth Struthers and Anderson, Janice Capel (1993) 'Literary-Critical Methods', in Elisabeth Schüssler Fiorenza (ed.) *Searching the Scriptures. Volume One: A Feminist Introduction*, New York: Crossroad.

Malherbe, Abraham J. (1988) *Paul and the Thessalonians*, Philadelphia: Fortress Press (1987).

—— (1989a) *Moral Exhortation. A Greco-Roman Sourcebook*, Philadelphia: Westminster Press.

—— (1989b) *Paul and the Popular Philosophers*, Minneapolis: Fortress Press.

—— (1990) ' "Pastoral Care" in the Thessalonian Church', *NTS* 36: 375–91.

Malina, Bruce J. (1981) *The New Testament World. Insights from Cultural Anthropology*, Atlanta: John Knox Press.

—— (1986) *Christian Origins and Cultural Anthropology*, Atlanta: John Knox Press.

Marshall, Peter (1987) *Enmity in Corinth. Social Conventions in Paul's Relations with the Corinthians*, Tübingen: Mohr (Siebeck).

Meeks, Wayne A. (1974) 'The Image of the Androgyne: Some Uses of a Symbol in Earliest Christianity', *History of Religions* 13: 165–208.

—— (1983) *The First Urban Christians. The Social World of the Apostle Paul*, New Haven and London: Yale University Press.

—— (1986) *The Moral World of the First Christians*, Philadelphia: Westminster Press.

Nicholson, Linda (1994) 'Interpreting *Gender*', *Signs* 20: 79–105.

Ortner, Sherry B. and Whitehead, Harriet (eds) (1988) *Sexual Meanings. The Cultural Construction of Gender and Sexuality*, Cambridge: Cambridge University Press (1981).

Petersen, Norman R. (1985) *Rediscovering Paul. Philemon and the Sociology of Paul's Narrative World*, Philadelphia: Fortress Press.

Portefaix, Lilian (1988) *Sisters Rejoice. Paul's Letter to the Philippians and Luke–Acts as Received by First-Century Philippian Women*, Uppsala: Almqvist & Wiksell International.

Rhoads, David (1992) 'Social Criticism: Crossing Boundaries', in Janice Capel Anderson and Stephen D. Moore (eds) *Mark and Method. New Approaches in Biblical Studies*, Minneapolis: Fortress Press: 135–61.

Schnelle, Udo (1986) 'Der erste Thessalonicherbrief und die Entstehung der Paulinischen Anthropologie', *NTS* 32: 207–24.

Schürmann, Heinz (1982) *Das Lukasevangelium. Erster Teil*, Herders Theologischer Kommentar III, Freiburg/Basel/Vienna: Herder (1969).

Schütz, John H. (1975) *Paul and the Anatomy of Apostolic Authority*, Cambridge: Cambridge University Press.

Sellin, Gerhard (1986) *Der Streit um die Auferstehung der Toten*, Göttingen: Vandenhoeck & Ruprecht.

Theissen, Gerd (1974) 'Theorethische Probleme Religionssoziologischer Forschung und die Analyse des Urchristentums', in *Studien zur Soziologie des Urchristentums*, Tübingen: Mohr (Siebeck) (1979).

Tolbert, Mary Ann (1993) 'Social, Sociological, and Anthropological Methods', in Elisabeth Schüssler Fiorenza (ed.) *Searching the Scriptures. Volume One: A Feminist Introduction*, New York: Crossroad: 255–71.

Torjesen, Karen Jo (1992) 'In Praise of Noble Women: Asceticism, Patronage and Honor', *Semeia* 57: 41–64.

—— (1993) 'Reconstruction of Women's Early Christian History', in Elisabeth Schüssler Fiorenza (ed.) *Searching the Scriptures. Volume One: A Feminist Introduction*, New York: Crossroad.

Whitton, J. (1982) 'A Neglected Meaning for SKEUOS in 1 Thessalonians 4.4', *NTS* 28: 142–43.

Wolter, Michael (1990) 'Der Apostel und seine Gemeinde als Teilhaber am Leidensgeschick Jesu Christi: Beobachtungen zur Paulinischen Theologie', *NTS* 36 s: 535–57.

Young, Frances (1994) *The Theology of the Pastoral Letters*, Cambridge: Cambridge University Press.

Part III

FAMILY, SEXUALITY AND ASCETICISM IN EARLY CHRISTIANITY

11

PAUL WITHOUT PASSION

On Paul's rejection of desire in sex and marriage[1]

Dale B. Martin

Paul was apparently not a very romantic fellow. While most modern Christians consider marriage the proper sphere for the expression of desire (perhaps we should specify *heterosexual* desire), Paul considered marriage a mechanism by which desire could be extinguished. In Paul's view, unlike that of some other ascetic-oriented writers of his day, sex was not so much the problem as desire. And sexual intercourse within the bounds of marriage functioned to keep desire from happening. Sex within marriage was not the expression of desire, proper or improper; rather it was the prophylaxis against desire.[2]

Paul's particular brand of asceticism, the control of desire, is not exactly like other ancient attempts to control it. But a comparison with some of those other attempts shows, in the first place, that Paul was not absolutely peculiar in the ancient world in his belief that sexual desire could and should be completely extirpated, even by means of sexual intercourse if necessary. As other scholars have pointed out, Stoics also advocated sex without desire. In the second place, such a comparison shows that the precise structure of Paul's asceticism – his assumptions about its meanings, his reasons for it, and the ways he believes desire can and ought to be controlled – is different from that of others. This essay will compare Paul's rationality of desire and its avoidance with those of ancient medical writers, on the one hand, and Stoics, on the other. The control of desire was a common concern in the early Roman Empire, at least among many intellectuals, but the logics or rationalities underwriting such control differed among different social groups.

THE EXTIRPATION OF DESIRE IN PAUL'S WRITINGS

The key passage that brings out Paul's position is 1 Corinthians 7, which is devoted to the argument that people who are too weak for celibacy should get married, and that people who are strong enough for celibacy should remain unmarried and chaste. A central point in Paul's argument is an enigmatic statement in which he urges marriage for those who are 'out of control'. They should get married, he says, because 'it is better to marry than to burn' (1 Cor 7:9). Taking the 'burning' here as a reference to eschatological judgment is possible but not, in the end, compelling. Throughout the chapter Paul is concerned about the here and now of people who are having trouble controlling their sexual desires (7:2, 5, 9, 36). The theme of judgment, though playing a role elsewhere in 1 Corinthians, has not been mentioned in this section and plays little part in Chapter 7. Furthermore, as I have argued elsewhere, conceiving sexual desire as a 'burning' within the body, metaphorically and physically, was so common in Paul's day, as seen in medical, magical, physiological, philosophical, and 'artistic' texts, that it is unimaginable that Graeco-Roman readers would have missed such a reference here (Martin 1995a: 212–14). In fact, Paul elsewhere (as I will analyse further below) quite clearly speaks of sexual desire as a burning (Rom 1:27). Even if we decide that Paul's 'burning' of 1 Corinthians 7 includes a reference to eschatological judgment, we cannot exclude a reference here to sexual passion and desire.

This means, of course, that Paul believed that it was not only possible but preferable, in fact, *necessary* that Christians experience sexual intercourse only within the context of marriage and only in the absence of sexual passion and desire. As remarkable as this may be for modern people, it seems to be the case. Paul can, indeed, use the term 'desire' (*epithymia*) in a morally neutral sense, as when he says that he 'desires' to see someone or do something (Phil 1:23; 1 Thess 2:17). But whenever Paul broaches the subject of sex and the desire associated with it, he has nothing good to say about it. In 1 Corinthians 7, for example, Paul nowhere mentions a positive kind of desire as opposed to the 'burning' that he hopes marriage will quench. He says that sex within marriage functions to guard weak Christians from the pollution of *porneia* (7:2); it is a duty Christian spouses owe to one another (7:3); and it protects Christians from Satanic testing (7:5). The romanticism of modern Christian (especially Protestant) attitudes about marriage – that it functions as the 'fulfillment' of divinely created and 'healthy' human sexuality, or at least heterosexuality; that it is the 'normal' outcome of love between a man and a woman; that human beings were practically created *for it* – is strikingly, though not surprisingly, absent. Paul's either/or of 7:9, therefore, should be taken seriously: marriage is the option for weak Christians who cannot otherwise avoid desire.

This complete exclusion of sexual desire is reflected in other Pauline passages. In 1 Thessalonians 4, Paul says that the will of God is the 'holiness' or 'sanctification' of the Thessalonians (*ho hagiasmos*), and the first issue threatening that holiness Paul mentions is *porneia*. Christian men should 'possess' their wives *not* in the passion of desire (*en pathei epithymias*) like the Gentiles who do not know God. As in 1 Corinthians, Paul is concerned about *porneia*, which is taken to be the characteristic sin of the Gentile world 'outside' the closed boundary of the body of Christ. The passion of sexual desire is part of the polluting complex of the cosmos that threatens the

Church. The problem of *porneia* is that it is unclean (*akatharsia*: 4:7), as opposed to the holy *pneuma* of God that inhabits the Church. The passion of desire, therefore, is part of the dirty, polluted cosmos in opposition to God. The way to avoid the pollution is for men to possess and control their 'vessels' (their wives) as safe receptacles for their sexual overflow. But the idea that passion could be a part of that process is not entertained; in fact, it is excluded.

This connection of sexual desire with the Gentile world 'out there' is also important for Paul's interpretation of Numbers 11 in 1 Corinthians 10. The people of Israel, according to Paul's reading, pursued a catastrophic path from 'desire' (*epithymia*) to idolatry (v. 7) to *porneia* (v. 8) to 'testing Christ' and subsequent destruction (v. 9). Paul here stands in a long tradition of both Greek and Jewish placements of *epithymia* at the centre of the destructions wrought by the passions. For Paul, as for most Jewish writers on the subject, *epithymia* is linked particularly to idolatry. But for all sorts of writers, Greek, Roman, and Jewish, it was a problem. Moreover, as G. D. Collier has argued, in 1 Corinthians 10 *epithymia* 'is not merely one of the listed sins, but *the source* of sin to be explicated'. What follows in Paul's argument, his warning about idolatry, *porneia*, and rebellion, is simply a 'spelling out' of the passion of desire (Collier 1994: 71).

This 'downhill slide' from desire to destruction occurs also in Romans 1, which is again a place where the uncleanness of *porneia*, idolatry, Gentiles, and sexual passion are connected in Paul's argument. Many readers have taken Paul's comments in Romans 1 to refer only to homosexual desire. But this is a tendentious reading prompted by a modern urge to condemn homosexual desire while sparing heterosexual desire. Paul's argument actually does not differentiate between the two kinds of desire, which is understandable when we recognise that desire itself is the problem for Paul, not just what moderns call 'homosexual' desire.[3]

Whereas the sequence in 1 Corinthians 10 was from desire to idolatry to *porneia* to destruction, in Romans 1 the rebellion of idolatry comes first, which merely demonstrates that Paul is less concerned about the *order* of events than the general complex of idolatry, *porneia*, and passion, and their connection to the Gentile world that must be rejected by Christians. Due to their wilful rejection of the true God and preference for idolatry and polytheism, God 'gave up' the Gentiles 'in the desires [*epithymiai*] of their hearts into uncleanness' (1:24). That this reference to *epithymia* includes sexual passion is confirmed by the parallel statement in v. 26, where 'passions of dishonor' express themselves sexually. In v. 27 we have the reference to the 'burning' of the Gentiles' urge (*orexis*) for one another. Here as elsewhere, *epithymia* and *pathos*, when referring to sexual desires, are in a complex of idolatry, *porneia*, pollution, and the Gentile world from which Christians need protection.

Modern Christian interpreters of Paul, often wishing to find some Pauline support for modern notions of romance and marriage, read all these texts as condemning not sexual desire in general but illicit, unnatural, or excessive passions. Paul *must* have had, so the thinking goes, a notion of good, healthy, heterosexual desire; otherwise, why get married at all? Why have sex at all? But I argue that such appeals to what 'must' have been the case just beg the question. The worst historians and cultural anthropologists often appeal to 'common sense' or what 'must' be the case; even good scholars appeal to such arguments when they have no evidence.[4] But all such appeals are problematic. Rather than insisting on what 'must' have been the case based on modern common sense, we would do better to look for structures of plausibility in the ancient world by which the absence of sexual desire would be not only possible but preferable.

MEDICAL AND ARISTOTELIAN CONTROL OF DESIRE

The medical writers of Paul's day would have found his extreme position puzzling. They also viewed sexual desire as dangerous. They speak of it as a disease, in particular, a disease of burning, and they offer therapies and regimens to control the burning of desire. But they would have considered any absolute avoidance of desire to be impossible. For the medical doctors, the disease of desire sprang from the natural heat of the body, and any body, to be alive at all, had to have some heat. Health was the appropriate balance (dry and moist, hot and cold) of the constituents and dispositions of the body, usually including the body's elements, like the humours. What needed to be kept in balance was debated by doctors and scientists, but they pretty much all agreed that balance was health (Martin 1995a: 146–53, 216–17). A complete quenching of heat would mean death. Furthermore, the doctors were in service to those male heads-of-households who paid the bills, and those men were almost all interested, at least to some degree, in producing babies. According to the dominant theories of sex, the heat of desire was necessary for the concoction of sperm or semen. Some doctors understood semen as the foam from concocted blood and *pneuma*, the most powerful material of the body, that resulted from the natural coming together of these different corporeal elements. Others explained that semen came from the concoction of humours. Still others held that the friction of sex itself caused the foam. In all cases, however, the heat of desire, as either the compulsion towards friction or the friction that led to compulsion, was essential for ejaculation (and for most of the doctors, it seems, both men and women had to produce semen for pregnancy to result). No more heat would mean no more semen and no more progeny. And for a Graeco-Roman householder, that was usually unacceptable.

So doctors taught their patients how to control the heat of desire in themselves, and especially in their wives and daughters. Rufus, who lived perhaps slightly later than Paul, wrote an entire 'Regimen for Virgins' guaranteed to ensure that young girls would not get too hot before they reached marriageable age (12, for Rufus).[5] Soranus, another physician roughly contemporaneous with Paul, believed that the most healthy route for both men and women was the complete avoidance of sex. (He seems to have been in the minority on this.) This did not mean, however, that they could completely avoid the burning of desire. So Soranus gives advice and prescriptions intended to contain and control the disease of desire, the heat of passion.[6]

Physicians weren't the only ones with these beliefs. Plutarch, for example, follows the Aristotelian tradition that says that desires and appetites are placed in the body by nature to assure that the body will get what it needs. There are different kinds of desires, of course. Those that arise from the body and relate to simple urges like that for food or sex are natural and need only be controlled, not extirpated. Only the fantastic and unnatural desires that arise from the mind when undisciplined must be avoided entirely (*De tuenda sanitate praecepta*: *Mor.* 125B; Aristotle, *Nichomachean Ethics* 3.11.1, 1118b8; 7.2.6, 1146a10). Control and moderation are urged. To be most healthy, one should eat moderately, avoid working to exhaustion, and preserve one's 'spermatic substance' (129F; see also 129E; 125D). Plutarch even criticises those therapists, including perhaps the more strenuous Stoics, who are too rigorous, urging cold baths or periodic fasting on a fixed schedule. Little wonder, then, that Plutarch never advocates either the complete avoidance of sex or the extirpation of desire. As Plutarch says, people ought 'to preserve that natural constitution of our bodies, recognizing that every life has room for both disease and health' (135D; trans. F. C. Babbitt).[7]

THE STOIC CONTROL OF DESIRE

In her recent book *The Therapy of Desire*, Martha Nussbaum (1994) calls the view I have just outlined the Aristotelian or Peripatetic position. In quite self-conscious opposition to it, according to Nussbaum, were the Stoics. Rather than taking passion or emotion as a natural compulsion that arises out of necessity, the Stoics, in this case Zeno (according to Diogenes Laertius 7.110), took it as irrational and unnatural. Seneca admits that the wise man will experience 'shadows of passion' (*umbras affectuum*), but from passion itself he will be completely free (*De ira* 1.16.7). The Stoics also think of desire as disease, and so they mock the Peripatetics, who would then seem to suggest that one might be content to be just a *little* ill. No, a man with even a slight fever is still sick. If health is what we are after, we will seek complete freedom from the disease of desire, the complete extirpation of the passions (*Ep.* 85.3–4; 116).

Sexual love, Seneca explains, is particularly a state of disorder, as anyone who has experienced it can attest; it is a lack of control, like slavery (*Ep.* 116.5; see also Cicero, *Tusculan Disputations* 35.75; 4.11.25–7). Thus one must learn to have sex without love, without passion, without desire. And one *can* learn this. In fact, the real disagreement, according to Seneca, is about the *ability* of a human being to attain such a free, stable existence without the passions. Critics of the Stoics claim that such a state is against human nature. Seneca claims just the opposite: yes, we can! The real reason, according to Seneca, that Stoic ideas are rejected by other philosophers is because they are too enamoured of their vices. The nature of a human being is to be rational and free. Only with the extirpation of the passions, including sexual desire, can we be free and self-sufficient (see e.g. *Ep.* 116.7).

The Stoics, like Paul, do not think this means an end to marriage or sex. The goal, and they seem to believe it is attainable at least by the wise man, is to have sex without desire. A favourite slogan among later ascetic Christians like Jerome had its origin among the Stoics: 'The man who loves his wife too much is also an adulterer'.[8] The good Stoic will be a good citizen, a member of the community of humanity, and therefore he will marry, have children, participate in society. But he must do all of these things without suffering from *pathos* or *epithymia*. He must completely extirpate desires.

For the question, 'how could or why would a person have sex at all without any compulsion to do so?' the Stoics had an answer, following a lead from Aristotle. They taught that the natural compulsion for intercourse, like that for food, did spring from nature and that human beings shared these impulses with animals (who were not rational beings and therefore could not experience passions or emotions, which are 'misjudgments', and not possible for non-rational beings; see Diogenes Laertius 7.85, 110). But the natural impulse is not *pathos* or *epithymia*; it is *hormê*, which occurs in plants and animals as well as humans.[9] All living beings have an impulse to self-preservation placed there by nature. This includes hunger and an impulse towards self-propagation through sex. Giving in to such an impulse is no more immoral than scratching an itch. But this impulse must not be confused with that harmful and dangerous emotion that people experience when they fall in love or feel as if they can't live without that special someone. The line between 'impulse' and 'desire' is a fine but important one. The wise man may follow the natural, unemotional impulse to propagate, like, say, an impulse to defecate. But to get too involved in it is disgusting and harmful. In fact, it is 'sick'.

The Stoics offered a system of therapy, based on discussion, reasoning, self-questioning, analysis, and critique of conventional beliefs, by which anyone with a strong enough will could learn to control and finally extirpate the passions: grief, pleasure, anger, and desires of all kinds. They claimed to be able to teach people how to live lives of self-control and self-sufficiency. They offered *eudaimonia*, a word difficult to translate but meaning something like well-being, contentedness, happiness, the 'blessed' life. Furthermore, according to Nussbaum, the philosophers (the Stoics and other schools as well) offered their therapy as an alternative to other, perhaps more popular methods of attaining 'the good life', that is, therapies of desire practised by doctors, popular healers, astrologers, priests and other religious leaders, to mention a few.

DESIRE AND RATIONALITY(-IES)

As I hinted at the beginning of this chapter, Nussbaum's account of the Stoics' therapy of desire is important for me because it presents another system of thought in the Graeco-Roman world that advocated, and believed possible, the complete extirpation of sexual desire even within the sexual activities of marriage. What may appear highly improbable and perhaps impossible to modern readers, and to ancient doctors, was quite possible at least to some segment of ancient society. Nussbaum's account is also important because it helps us place Paul's position in relation to other therapies of desire in ancient culture. We have here, to simplify somewhat, three different understandings of desire and its treatment: the physicians', the Stoics', and Paul's.

All three treat desire like a disease and agree that it is dangerous. With the Stoics, Paul shares the belief that the complete extirpation of desire is both possible and preferable, even within sexual relations in marriage. But along with the doctors, Paul would doubtless reject the Stoics' doctrine that complete self-sufficiency is possible, since both Paul and the physicians take the self to be a part of its environment and too constituted by that environment to be able to achieve radical self-sufficiency. The Stoics and the medical writers, however, would share a belief that self-sufficiency is an *ideal* towards which people may strive. Only Paul's position, of these three, takes marriage to be a tool for guarding against desire. And Paul, against both other positions, would certainly reject self-sufficiency as an ideal towards which Christians should strive. This is such an important point that I will return to it later.

What are the more fundamental differences among these three therapies? How or why did these people arrive at these particular differences in understandings and treatments of desire? Nussbaum's answer to such questions is that the philosophical position (and I will concentrate on the Stoics as more important for Paul's position as well as the one given most attention by Nussbaum) differs from all other ancient therapies of desire because it is, well, philosophical. By that she means it is 'rational', it cures the patient by means of discourse rather than drugs, and by critical reasoning rather than miracles or salvation. For Nussbaum, philosophy is basically 'the pursuit of logical validity, intellectual coherence, and truth', and it will deliver 'freedom from the tyranny of custom and convention'. Religious and other therapies depend on dogma, conventional beliefs, or external agents, whether they be divinities, demons, doctors, or drugs. Only philosophy offers a therapy that depends on the rationality of the self; therefore it is *the* rational therapy.[10]

This argument about rationality is difficult to evaluate because, for one thing, Nussbaum actually uses 'rationality' in two different ways in the book. When attempting to define or describe philosophy or rationality, she concentrates on issues of procedure, not the actual content of beliefs. Thus, rationality or reason is the process of seeking truth by questioning; it is dialogical, open-ended with regard to results, free from custom and convention, non-dogmatic. It scrutinises assumptions and the self and is open to self-revision at every point. It avoids prejudice by employing critical thinking and examining every issue from every relevant perspective (see e.g. Nussbaum 1994: 148). This kind of definition, however, is unusable for comparative purposes, as can be seen when one notes the 'question begging' terms that inevitably occur in such definitions. For example, *how* open to any possible end must one be before being accepted as rational? *How* critical must one be of *how many* assumptions? In any actual situation, I would argue, no one can be truly open to *any* possible end nor completely critical of *all* assumptions, given our own contingency and finitude. The parameters of possibility are simply set to some extent. To cite another example, who gets to decide what is or is not a 'relevant' perspective? We would certainly have to admit that no one could consider *all* possible perspectives on an ethical issue, since perspective, as the very mathematical metaphor reveals, is as infinite as the number of possible fractions. These are only examples, but similar question-begging conditions occur in each section where Nussbaum tries to describe 'rationality' by concentrating purely on method in the abstract.

The other way Nussbaum speaks of rationality or reason is more revealing but just as problematic. Throughout the book Nussbaum uses these terms to refer not to a method for arriving at truths but to particular truths themselves.[11] There simply *are* beliefs that are rational, and most of the time Nussbaum makes no attempt to argue *for* the rationality of such beliefs from the ground up (e.g. ibid.: 353–54). A list of such cases is revealing. Rational positions are those that assume the existence of a stable individual self. Even though human beings live within society and should be part of it, they are individually free beings with free will and capable of free moral agency (ibid.: 326). Rationality will convince these free agents that they possess universal citizenship and have available to them universal rationality (ibid.: 318). That is, every human being of all places and times has the ability (at least) to reason alike, and if they would just do so they would arrive at the same truth (ibid.: 96, 325). Also rational is a belief in the equality of the sexes (ibid.: 324). Rationality is critical of cultural assumptions, society, and convention. It is naturalistic, which is to say that all things in the universe must be understood to operate by similar mechanisms, the mechanics of 'nature'. Thus rationality may admit a notion of religion or the divine, but only one that would not threaten the freedom of the individual. In fact, a rational belief in divinity (if any is needed) recognises the divine within the human person (ibid.: 160–61). The one exception permitted by Nussbaum to this free, stable self, open and visible to itself and subject to its own rule is the presence of the unconscious. But even the unconscious can be accessed and controlled to a great extent by procedures that sound remarkably like modern psychotherapy (ibid.: 133–34, 490). The existence of the unconscious therefore offers no real threat to the possibility of a stable, free self.

So whereas rationality sometimes refers to a method for arriving at truth, at other times it refers to actual truths with little or no attention given to the method by which these beliefs came to be accepted as true. There is, though, no contradiction here, because Nussbaum really believes that if human beings – any, anywhere, any time – pursued these methods they would arrive at these truths (see e.g. Nussbaum 1986: note on 11; 1994: 148). In my opinion, this is a 'faith statement' which, although it may be true, can be supported neither by empirical comparative evidence (experience) nor by some abstract argument that uses universal criteria of reasonableness ('rationality'). Indeed, Nussbaum seems to recognise that her position is more akin to faith than knowledge when she admits that someone like Michel Foucault would find her confidence that rationality can make us free, to be an illusion – but, she insists, she still *believes* it (Nussbaum 1994: 6).

As my comments reveal, I find this appeal to rationality insufficient for explaining the differences among Paul, the doctors, and the Stoics. I want to argue, rather, that each position is rational in a sense, and that we can see its rationality when we analyse the therapy in light of its different assumptions about the world and the self. Paul's position, for example, would be rejected by both the doctors and the Stoics as hopelessly uneducated and superstitious. As I have shown elsewhere, educated people in the Graeco-Roman world rejected fears of pollution from outside agents as superstition (Martin 1995a: 153–59). Rather than following a 'logic of invasion' when thinking about disease, they thought of disease along the lines of a 'logic of imbalance'; disease was the result of an imbalance of the body's normal states and elements. Thus all Paul's concerns in 1 Corinthians that the Church, the body of Christ, might be polluted by idol meat, *porneia*, or desire itself would have appeared ignorant and naive to them. Although the doctors would also have rejected the radical self-sufficiency advocated by the Stoics, they would have assumed that moderate self-sufficiency was a natural ideal. But to accept notions about polluting demons and invading diseases would have posed an unacceptable challenge to the secure, stable, sufficient self that was at least an ideal for upper-class intellectuals in general. Thus their therapies of desire are understandable within the context of their views of the body and the world. And within their system, Paul's fears are irrational.

We can only imagine how Paul would critique their view, especially the more radical Stoic view of self-sufficiency. For rhetorical purposes, Paul can claim self-sufficiency. He tells the Philippians, for instance, that he appreciates their gift but didn't exactly *need* it, since he is *autarkês* and lacks nothing (Phil 4:11). But this rhetoric carries none of the freight for Paul that it would for the philosophers (Sevenster 1961: 113–15). Paul readily admits his absolute dependence on God and explicitly rejects the notion that human beings can be self-sufficient: '*Not* that we are sufficient (*hikanoi*) of ourselves so that we could consider anything as really ours; rather our sufficiency comes from God' (2 Cor 3:5–6; note the emphatic placement of 'not' (*ouch*) at the beginning of the sentence). There is no attempt by Paul to establish or protect a stable, secure self. While Christians are 'at home in the body' they are 'away from their home that is the Lord' (2 Cor 5:6). Even Christ is not thought of as independent and self-sufficient. Note, for example, the thick inter-connections of being in Paul's statement that Christ 'died for all, so that those who live live no longer for themselves but with regard to the one who died and was raised for them' (2 Cor 5:15). Christ's existence is 'for' others; because of what he did 'for' them, the others no longer live 'for' themselves. Such frank admissions of mutual dependence would be scorned by the Stoics.

DESIRE, SELF-SUFFICIENCY, AND IDEOLOGY

The Stoics' rejection of the passions is based on their ideal of self-sufficiency and their belief that true well-being could be had only by exercising self-control. The passions threatened the perfect control over their bodies, and indeed, their world, for which they yearned. I would argue, moreover, that of the passions desire was in some ways a special threat because it was a constant signal of need – *in*sufficiency. According to both Aristotelian and early Stoic theory, the 'urge' for food and sex was placed by nature in the body to meet its 'needs'.[12] Desire arose from unnatural confusions surrounding those needs and urges. Desire, therefore, signifies 'lack', and this was a painful confession for Graeco-Roman philosophers. True nobility was self-sufficient, just like the ancient aristocratic ideal of the self-sufficient household which was capable of growing all its own food, making all its own clothes and utensils, and running its own day-to-day affairs with no interference of any kind. Like the southern American plantation owner of later times, the Graeco-Roman *paterfamilias* nourished an ideal of his own private community. And his body was a microcosm of that self-sufficient community. To recognise that he needed a woman to further his line was something of a shameful surprise, but it was, after all, part of 'nature'. The goal was to fill this lack in such a way as to demonstrate as little lack as possible within himself. Men had many ideological stratagems for getting over what appeared to be an insurmountable lack in nature and their bodies. One example is the Aristotelian theory, eventually rejected by perhaps most doctors, that all the requisite seed for the embryo came from the man, with the woman being only the fertile field in which the important substance was planted.[13] All such theories, in any case, were attempts to minimise the experience of lack, the sign that constantly pointed to the illusion of self-sufficiency.

The entire ideological complex of the self-sufficient man and the stable self is absent in Paul's writings. The reality of 'lack' is recognised all through his letters: Epaphroditus supplies what the Philippians lack (Phil 2:30); the abundance of the Corinthians supplies what other Christians lack (2 Cor 8:15); Paul wants to visit the Thessalonians to supply what they are lacking (1 Thess 3:10). Furthermore, Paul doubtless would have none of that 'moderation' so important to the philosophers. He constantly uses language celebrating both lack and abundance, even 'over-abundance'.[14] The philosophical idea, for example, that too much love is a bad thing would have struck Paul, as it doubtless struck most people in that society, as ridiculous.

But not only would Paul have rejected the *ideal* of self-sufficiency; he also would have believed it absolutely impossible. For Paul, every human being receives its identity by virtue of its place, either in 'this cosmos' or Christ. Christians live by the pneuma of Christ; non-Christians have only the pneuma of 'this world'. Furthermore, every self, even Christian ones, can be threatened by disintegration due to a variety of cosmic forces: the death-dealing of *sarx*, the pollution of *porneia*, even the poison that Christ's body becomes when eaten unworthily (Martin 1995a: 131–32, 170–74, 176–77, 190–97). Moreover, however we settle the tricky question of Paul's views on predestination or free will, no one can persuasively argue that Paul would have believed possible the radical kind of free choice so necessary for Stoic doctrine and therapy.[15] Paul can speak of human beings, even Christians, as predestined by God (Rom 9–11), as hopelessly deluded apart from God's grace and revelation (1 Cor 2:6–6; 3:18–23), or as hindered by Satan from carrying out their wills (1 Thess 2:18). Any part of this Pauline complex renders impossible the free will and free moral agency necessary for Stoicism. Thus both the ideal and the possibility of a stable self would be rejected by Paul as illusions.

What started out in this chapter as a comparison of beliefs about desire, sex, and marriage has become an analysis of complex ideological systems. But that is what I believe is necessary for an adequate interpretation of the ancient therapies of desire. Paul's position would doubtless have been rejected by the ancient philosophers and doctors as irrational. But for a modern scholar to be satisfied with that verdict is inadequate. Paul had very good reasons, given his own assumptions about the world and the human self, to fear sexual desire as a polluting force that threatened the health of the Christian's body and Christ's body. His insistence that desire must be excluded entirely, even within sex in marriage, was reasonable – just as reasonable, in fact, as the Stoics' radical position was within their own system, based as it was on a belief in the possibility of a stable self-sufficiency. Both systems, from different rationalities, taught that sexual desire, even within sex, must be extirpated.

One of Martha Nussbaum's goals in writing *The Therapy of Desire* (1994) was to convince modern readers, especially post-religious, liberal Americans, that ancient moral philosophy can provide a method and concepts useful for modern ethics. She finds the Stoics especially appealing, with the proviso that their insistence on complete self-sufficiency and the extirpation of desires is too radical (for a stronger questioning of their view of self-sufficiency, see Nussbaum 1986: 3). She would take up, to some extent, the Stoic cause, and she believes that cause to be a good one as long as one adds in a bit of compassion.

I don't believe that's such a good idea, mainly because it either ignores the ancient ideological context and function of their system, or it insists, wrongly I believe, that their therapeutic system can be divorced from the negative aspects of its ideological assumptions. Although Nussbaum begins by noting that ancient philosophy must be studied with a view to society and culture (1994: 7), there is actually very little attention to culture in this book and none to ideology.[16] And that is its problem. In my view, the ancient aristocratic ideal of self-sufficiency was possible only within a context of slavery and exploitation. Indeed, it is hard to imagine the conditions for the rise of that ideal except in a society where a small portion of the population could mask its own great dependence on other human beings by rendering them less human. The extent to which a *paterfamilias* could convince himself that he was or could be self-sufficient was the extent to which he could close his eyes to the thick matrices of economic and social systems on which he unavoidably depended. Self-sufficiency as an ideal requires just such ideological ignorance. The ancient philosophical therapies of desire depend on notions of self-sufficiency and fear of lack; the therapies don't make sense without such presupposed values. And these values are anything but democratic and egalitarian. Of course, from a Christian point of view, and I think this is not just Paul's view, self-sufficiency is neither possible nor desirable. I also find it hard to imagine how a philosopher these days can so confidently *assume* the existence of a stable integrated self capable of exercising free moral agency, given current biomedical and biochemical research, genetic engineering, post-structuralist psychological theories, philosophies of the mind based on artificial intelligence, and studies showing the disintegration of the self through pain and torture.[17]

In the end, I believe the myth of self-sufficiency is especially dangerous for Americans, with our tendency to splendid isolation and self-centredness and our uncanny ability to fail to notice our domination of and dependence on other countries and our own lower class. Americans, 'liberal' and 'conservative' alike, are already far too enamoured of the myth that social problems can be solved by individualism and volunteerism. I understand why a liberal democratic American philosopher like Nussbaum would find 'self-suffi-ciency' an appealing goal. But I also believe that it plays into the worst aspects of modernist individualism, capitalist ideology, and American lies about the self-saving self.

Is Paul's account of desire, sex, and marriage any better? Not for me, thanks. Given our own probably unshakeable modern assumptions about love, sex, romance, and desire, we perhaps could never wholeheartedly accept the possibility, much less the desirability, of sex without desire. It is signifi-cant that no modern Christian church has attempted even to recognise, let alone appropriate, Paul's ethics of sexuality here. And I would not advocate that it do so. Both Nussbaum's advocacy of ancient philosophy and some Christians' belief that our sexual ethics should come rather simplistically 'from the Bible' are just different forms of Classicism, which in my view is nostalgic and self-deluding.[18] I do not understand why modern persons would want to ground their own therapies of desire on either the ancient philosophers or Paul. I suppose I'm too much a post-modernist to find real Classicism alluring, whether in art, architecture, or morality.

NOTES

1 The writing of this essay as well as travel to and from the conference where it was originally presented were funded by the Alexander von Humboldt Foundation, Germany. I am grateful to the foundation as well as to my host in Tübingen, Professor Hubert Cancik, for their kind hospitality and gracious support.

2 I have offered a fuller argument on these issues in Martin 1995a. Indeed, most of the material in the first part of this essay is an abbreviated form of argu-ments mounted throughout that book and in Martin 1995b.

3 See my argument that the ancient world, and Paul as part of it, did not differ-entiate sexual desires by the gender of the object desired (Martin 1995b: 341–48). Whereas Paul does condemn same-sex intercourse, he has no notion of a particular desire (homosexual) that was a different *kind* of desire from 'normal' desire (heterosexual).

4 For one account of the cultural specificity of 'common sense', see Geertz 1983: 73–93.

5 Fragments of Rufus' text are found in the collection of medical texts made in late Antiquity by Oribasius. For the Greek, see Oribasius 1964: vol. 4, 106–9; Greek with French translation: Oribasius 1858.

6 See, for example, Soranus, *Gynecology* 1.7.31 and 1.8.33. Greek: Soranus 1927; English: Soranus 1956.

7 As I pointed out, this is an unremarkable representation of the traditional Aristotelian view. It seems to have been quite widespread among physicians and moral philosophers, though other, more rigorous views were also known. Aristotle believes that too much sex is damaging, but in moderation healthy; see, for example, his remarks about sex and young people: *Historia animalium* 581b9; 581b24–30.

8 Fragments of Seneca's *De matrimonio*, quoted by Jerome. See Haase 1872.

9 Diogenes Laertius 7.85; another term used for this 'urge' is *orexis*; see Nussbaum 1994: 86.

10 This picture is taken mainly from pp. 5–6, where Nussbaum criticises Foucault.

11 Charles Taylor identifies these two different uses of *rationality* (not, however, in reference to Nussbaum) as the use of the term to refer to *procedure*, on the one hand, and *content*, on the other (Taylor 1989: 86). I agree with Taylor's claim that the use of *rationality* to refer to particular beliefs (content) is more ancient than modern, whereas the use of the term to refer to *how* someone thinks (procedure) is more modern than ancient. Furthermore, the modern stress on 'procedural rationality' is bound up with the 'allegiance to modern freedom', that is, the Kantian notion that a truly moral choice (one that is 'rational') must be made free from the constraints of authority (such as that of religion or culture) or contingency.

12 Aristotle, *Politics* 1.1.4, 1252a25–30: the very root of community, in its simplest form male–female bonding, is in Aristotle's political theory *anagkê*, 'necessity, need'.

13 See the discussion of this issue, and suggestions about how to interpret apparent inconsistencies in Aristotle's own writings, in the footnote to Aristotle, *Historia animalium*, by D. M. Balme in the Loeb edition, book 10: 487–89. For Galen's arguments against the Aristotelian view, see his *On Semen* 1.9.15; 2.1; 2.4.5. This difference, of course, does not make Galen a feminist; he has many other ways of inscribing female inferiority into the female body.

14 See his frank admission, indeed celebration, of the utter *lack* of self-sufficiency in 2 Cor 1:8–11. For one instance of 'overabundance' (*hyperperisseuô*) see 2 Cor 7:4.

15 That is, although Paul can, of course, speak of choices, one cannot imagine him making the sort of claims as Epictetus, who can say to the tyrant, 'My leg you may bind, but my free will [ability to choose, *prohairesis*] even Zeus is not able to conquer!' (1.1.23; trans. mine).

16 Indeed, when culture and society make appearances in the book they are usually placed in simple opposition to other things taken as more 'real' or 'true'. For example, reason and the individual represent the 'rational' side of a dichotomy whose 'mere convention' side (irrational) is represented by culture and society (Nussbaum 1994: 328, 334); elsewhere 'nature' is opposed to 'the social' (ibid.: 497; we know from other statements that 'nature' is 'rational', ibid.: 160–63, 501).

17 Among the few studies that spring quickly to mind are: Hofstadler 1981; Deleuze and Guattari 1983; Scarry, 1985; Rorty 1989 (see especially Chapter 2); Dennett 1991; and of course the entire work of Foucault, against which Nussbaum is directing much of her fire. I believe Nussbaum is still too implicated in Kantian assumptions about ethics, the will, and rationality that, in my view, deserve the deconstruction to which they have already been subjected by other scholars. For one critique of the Kantian emphasis on radical freedom of the will from authority and contingency, a critique that I believe should also be turned against Nussbaum's views, see MacIntyre 1982.

18 For more criticism of Biblical *and* historicist 'foundationalism' in Christian ethical discussion, see Martin 1996.

BIBLIOGRAPHY

Collier, G. D. (1994) ' "That we might not crave evil." The Structure and Argument of 1 Corinthians 10:1–3', JSNT 55: 55–75.

Deleuze, G. and Guattari, F. (1983) *Anti-Oedipus: Capitalism and Schizophrenia*, Minneapolis: University of Minnesota Press.

Dennett, D. C. (1991) *Consciousness Explained*, Boston: Little, Brown, and Co.

Geertz, C. (1983) *Local Knowledge: Further Essays in Interpretive Anthropology*, New York: Basic Books.

Haase, F. (1872) *L. Annaei Senecae, Opera quae Supersunt*, vol. 3, Leipzig: Teubner.

Hofstadler, D. R. (1981) *The Mind's I: Fantasies and Reflections on Self and Soul*, New York: Basic Books.

MacIntyre, A. (1982) 'How Moral Agents Became Ghosts or Why the History of Ethics Diverged from that of the Philosophy of Mind', *Synthese* 53: 295–312.

Martin, D. B. (1995a) *The Corinthian Body*, New Haven: Yale University Press.

—— (1995b) 'Heterosexism and the Interpretation of Romans 1:18–32', *Biblical Interpretation* 3: 332–55.

—— (1996) '*Arsenokoitês* and *Malakos*: Meanings and Consequences', in R. L. Brawley (ed.) *Biblical Ethics and Homosexuality: Listening to Scripture*, Louisville, KY: Westminster, John Knox.

Nussbaum, M. C. (1986) *The Fragility of Goodness: Luck and Ethics in Greek Tragedy and Philosophy*, Cambridge: Cambridge University Press.

——(1994) *The Therapy of Desire: Theory and Practice in Hellenistic Ethics*, Princeton, NJ: Princeton University Press.

Oribasius (1858) *Oeuvres*, in C. Daremberg and U. C. Bussemaker (eds and trans.), Paris: Impr. Nationale.

—— (1964) *Oribasii Collectionum Medicarum Reliquiae*, Ioannes Raeder (ed.), Amsterdam: Adolf M. Hakkert.

Rorty, R. (1989) *Contingency, Irony, and Solidarity*, Cambridge: Cambridge University Press.

Scarry, E. (1985) *The Body in Pain: The Making and Unmaking of the World*, New York and Oxford: Oxford University Press.

Sevenster, J. N. (1961) *Paul and Seneca*, Leiden: E. J. Brill.

Soranus (1927) *Sorani Gynaeciorum libri IV, De Signis Fracturarum, De Fasciis, Vita Hippocratis Secundum Soranum*, Johannes Ilberg (ed.) Corpus Medicorum Graecorum 4, Leipzig: Teubner.

—— (1956) *Gynecology*, trans. Owsei Temkin, Baltimore: Johns Hopkins University Press.

Taylor, C. (1989) *Sources of the Self: The Making of the Modern Identity*, Cambridge: Harvard University Press.

12

ASCETICISM AND ANTI-FAMILIAL LANGUAGE IN THE *GOSPEL OF THOMAS*

Risto Uro

THOMAS AND EARLY CHRISTIAN ASCETICISM[1]

One of the most striking features of early Christian history is the vigorous growth of ascetic movements in various geographical and cultural contexts during the first centuries CE. Already in the second century there existed a number of sects and Christian leaders who taught a radical form of sexual asceticism, often called 'encratism' by scholars.[2] The most famous of such teachers were Marcion and Tatian, but it is apparent that the ideal of sexual abstinence was widespread in early Christianity and was represented with a variety of severity by church fathers as well as by their opponents.[3] Justin Martyr, for example, though a harsh critic of Marcion, praises Christian continence in his *Apology*, claiming that there are 'many, both men and women of the age of sixty or seventy years, who have been Christ's disciples from childhood', and yet 'remain in purity (*aphthoroi diamenousi*)'.[4]

The *Gospel of Thomas* has often been connected with radical sexual continence due to its world-denying ethos, asexual imagery and anti-familial language. Generally speaking, one can hardly deny that the *Gospel of Thomas* is an important document for the history of early Christian asceticism. Yet the nature of Thomas' ascetic traits as well as their relation to first-century Christian traditions are debated issues. To take but two extreme views, according to Gilles Quispel, *Thomas*' theology is unambiguously 'encratite', which means that the author rejected 'women, wine, meat, and therefore taught that only bachelors could go to heaven'.[5] An almost opposite view is represented by Stevan Davies, who argues that the 'abhorrence of sex' plays no, or at most a minimal, role in the gospel.[6] In his judgment, *Thomas* is less ascetic than, for example, the Q material, and consequently far less ascetic than the apocryphal Acts of the Apostles or the Desert fathers.[7]

Davies' position has not, however, received much following and the majority of scholars allow at least some degree of sexual asceticism for *Thomas*. A great number of scholars also suggest that the Gospel originated in eastern Syria, where ascetic tendencies flourished at an early stage among

Christian groups, and where traditions under the name of the apostle 'Judas Thomas (Didymos)' were transmitted.[8]

This general characterisation of the *Gospel of Thomas* as a representative of the ascetic 'Thomas' tradition is, however, in need of refinement. During the last two decades, there has been a growing interest in the study of asceticism, and scholars have become more conscious of the diversity of ascetic behaviour and its motives.[9] In this situation it is appropriate to pose the question of the *specific* nature of Thomas' asceticism and look into different sexual and gendered images used in the writing. Such analyses show, I will argue, that neither of the extreme views just mentioned does justice to the symbolic world presupposed in the Gospel. Ultimately, I hope, they will also lead to a more nuanced view of *Thomas'* ascetic language and its cultural background.

Thomas' asceticism covers a wide range of sayings as well as individual themes and symbols. In this chapter,[10] I will concentrate on one aspect, the anti-familial language of the Gospel, sometimes characterised as the ethos of 'homelessness'. The restriction is justified because this theme provides one of the major contexts for the language of 'family' in the Gospel. Moreover, focusing on the 'anti-familial' sayings allows us to make a comparison between the *Gospel of Thomas* and the Synoptic Gospels, in which a similar ethos can be found.

THE ETHOS OF 'HOMELESSNESS'

As is well known, the Synoptic Gospels include several sayings in which Jesus disregards conventional family piety and possessions and demands a wandering life from his disciples. Many of these sayings derive from the Sayings Gospel 'Q' (e.g. Q 9:57–60; 10:4–7; 12:22–34; 14:26),[11] and, since the seminal studies of Gerd Theissen, it has become customary to speak of 'itinerant radicalism' as a distinctive ethos of the early sayings tradition (Theissen 1973: 245–71 (or 1979: 70–105); see also Theissen 1978). Theissen has been criticised for undifferentiated reading of sources and for over-emphasising the role of the wandering charismatic in early Christianity, but the nucleus of his thesis has been widely acclaimed by scholars (see Uro 1987: 126–34). The *Gospel of Thomas* records many sayings which show a high valuation of 'homelessness' and disregard for family ties (*Gos. Thom.* 16; 42; 55; 79; 86; 99; 101; 105). Most of them have parallels in the Synoptic Gospels and the general tone of these sayings resembles one we can recognise already in Q. Jesus' message brings dissension upon earth (*Gos. Thom.* 16/Q 12:49–53). The 'son of man' has no place to lay his head (*Gos. Thom.* 86/Q 9:58). And disciples must be ready to hate father and mother to be worthy of Jesus (*Gos. Thom.* 55; 101; 105 and Q 14:26). As in Mark and the other Synoptics, but probably not in Q,[12] *Thomas* presents Jesus himself as expressing the same negative attitude towards his own family as he demands from his disciples (*Gos. Thom.* 79; 99; Mark 3:31–35 par.; Luke 11:27–28).

One should notice that the dissension within families anticipated in the *Gospel of Thomas* is never that between married couples, and this is probably true for the Q sayings on family relations as well. The reference to 'wife' is generally regarded as a Lucan redaction in Q 14:26.[13] In Luke's version of the parable of the Great Feast, marriage is one of the excuses presented by those invited (Luke 14:20). We cannot be quite certain about the Q form of the parable, since Matthew's version differs considerably from Luke's. In any case, it is interesting that the Thomasine version of the parable mentions the marriage only indirectly – the guest has to arrange his *friend's* wedding dinner, not his own – and the emphasis is on the business activities of those who receive the invitation (see *Gos. Thom.* 64).[14]

The similarity between Q and *Thomas* with respect to the ethos of 'home-lessness' has led scholars to assume similar social formations behind these two Sayings Gospels. Following such scholars as Arthur Vööbus (1958: 3–30) and Georg Kretschmar (1964: 27–67), they have often seen a direct social continuation between early Palestinian Christianity, distinguished by its charismatic wandering, and the second century (or post-70 CE) ascetic groups in Syria. In a recent book, Stephen J. Patterson has made a detailed argument for the view that the type of Christianity behind the *Gospel of Thomas* is best explained as a movement of wandering charismatics who have given up possessions and family ties (Patterson 1993: esp. 158–214).[15] While the Synoptic Gospels as well as such writings as the *Didache* were written from the perspective of 'settled communities', 'in the *Gospel of Thomas*, we encounter the product of the continuing tradition of wandering radicalism' (Patterson 1993: 166).

It is quite reasonable to suggest some kind of social continuation between those groups that transmitted radical sayings of Jesus in Palestine and were responsible for the collection of the Q materials, and those groups that later produced the *Gospel of Thomas*. Indeed, such a historical reconstruction may explain why a great number of Q sayings (and Synoptic materials in general)[16] found their way to *Thomas* largely untouched by the narrative frameworks of the Synoptic Gospels.[17] It is not impossible that the Jewish-Christian and Aramaic-speaking radical groups in Palestine could in the post-70 CE period extend their influence and mission to Edessa, where the *Gospel of Thomas* is usually located.[18]

However, the precise characterisation of Thomas Christianity as a move-ment of wandering charismatics is open to discussion. It is unlikely that the early Syrian Christianity in Edessa was entirely or even predominantly of Palestinian origin. There were close cultural links between Edessa and Antioch (see Drijvers 1985: 88–102; 1992: 124–46), and one must reckon with the influence of Greek-speaking and Gentile groups as originators of Christianity in Edessa. Moreover there is not much about 'wandering' in

Thomas. The mission instructions (Luke 10:1–16 and parallels), which, espe-cially in their Q form, provide the most important evidence for the 'itinerant radicalism', appear only in a short fragment (*Gos. Thom.* 14b: 'When you go into any land and walk about the districts . . . ')[19] as part of the Saying cluster against Jewish religious practices.[20] *Gos. Thom.* 42 ('Become passers-by') is too ambiguous for specific conclusions about the social formation of Thomas Christianity. The 'itinerant radicalism' need not be the only or even the most probable explanation for the appearance of the many anti-familial sayings in *Thomas* (see below). The final redaction of the Q document as well as Mark reflect the concerns of settled communities,[21] which indicates that collections of Jesus' sayings on 'homelessness' could be composed and used by non-itinerant Christians. Finally, one should remember that the *Wanderradikalismus*, at least in Theissen's definition, was a reform movement within pre-70 CE Judaism, whereas Thomas Christianity, with its negative attitude to Jewish religious obligations (cf. *Gos. Thom.* 6; 14; 53), seems to have made a good bit of progress in the 'parting of the ways'.[22] Even if wandering preachers were frequent in the social world of *Thomas*, we are here dealing with a quite different cultural and historical context.

TRUE MOTHERHOOD

The anti-familial language of *Thomas* focuses on the rejection of biological family and parenthood as a source of honour and replaces them with different sorts of family metaphors. There are two parallel sayings in Thomas, of which the latter seems to contrast ordinary parents with the idea of true 'motherhood'.

> Jesus said, 'Whoever does not hate his father and his mother cannot become a disciple to me. And whoever does not hate his brothers and sisters and take up his cross in my way will not be worthy of me'.
>
> (*Gos. Thom.* 55)

> [Jesus said] 'Whoever does not hate his [father] and his mother as I do cannot become a [disciple] to me. And whoever does [not] love his [father and] his mother as I do cannot become a [disciple to] me. For my mother [. . .], but [my] true [mother] gave me life'.[23]
>
> (*Gos. Thom.* 101)

The doublet is one of those cases which, according to Quispel, proves that *Thomas* used at least two written sources, one Jewish-Christian and the other encratite (see e.g. Quispel 1981: 224–25, 257). He thinks that the latter version of the saying, including the additional statement about 'mother', derives from the encratite source used by the author and should be under-stood as an injunction against procreation and marriage. Quispel refers to the encratites condemned by Clement of Alexandria in the third chapter of

Stromateis. According to Clement, they teach that one 'should not bring others . . . in this wretched world, nor give any sustenance to death' (*Strom.* 3.45). In the same context, Clement also attempts to prove that the encratites 'pervert the sense of books' by quoting a saying, which he elsewhere knows as a saying from the *Gospel of the Egyptians*:

> When Salome asked the Lord: 'How long shall death hold sway?' He
> answered: 'As long as you women bear children'.
> (Oulton & Chadwick 1954, trans. H. Chadwick)

This makes Quispel think that *Gos. Thom.* 101 also derives from the *Gospel of the Egyptians*. Both sayings reflect 'the same gloomy view, namely that man shall continue to die as long as women bring forth children' (Quispel 1981: 257).

The question of the numerous doublets of *Thomas* is certainly pertinent and may reveal different sources used in the process of the composition. But Quispel's identification of *Thomas*' encratite source as the gospel mentioned in Clement's *Stromateis* is speculative and has been criticized widely (see Fallon and Cameron 1988: 4216–219; De Conick 1996:175–80; Asgeirsson forthcoming). There are also problems in his 'encratite' reading of the additional material in *Gos. Thom.* 101. Quispel is compelled to fill the lacuna with words 'my mother [gave me death] . . . ' to create a better connection between *Thomas* and the teaching of the encratites mentioned by Clement, but there is no indication how this would work in Coptic. Moreover, the contrast between 'my mother' and '[my] true mother', rather than being a direct statement against marriage, reflects the idea of Jesus' (and the disciples') heavenly origin. *Gos. Thom.* 15 may indicate this kind of thinking:

> When you see one who was not born of women, prostrate yourselves on
> your faces and worship him. That one is your father.

The provoking saying in *Gos. Thom.* 105 ('He who knows the father and the mother will be called the son of a harlot') expresses this idea in a sharpened way. The language can be compared to other sayings which proclaim the true identity of the disciples as 'children of the living father' (e.g. *Gos. Thom.* 49; 50). In the *Gospel of Thomas*, the divine origin of Jesus is closely related to the true identity of the disciples, since the salvation is understood as a process of becoming 'like' Jesus, or even better, becoming him in a process of union (*Gos. Thom.* 108). This notion may explain why Jesus' rejection of his fleshly family plays such a central role in *Thomas*. Encratite theology is not, therefore, the only or major reason for the recurrence of this theme in the Gospel. The emphasis on the heavenly origin and the rejection of the biological family also demonstrates a difference from the idea of 'following', which is the dominant metaphor for discipleship in Q and the Synoptic Gospels.

BLESSED IS THE WOMB THAT HAS NOT CONCEIVED

Among the sayings that reflect the Synoptic ethos of 'homelessness', *Gos. Thom.* 79 presents an explicitly negative statement about childbearing.

A woman from the crowd said to him, 'Blessed are the womb which bore you and breasts which nourished you.' He said to [her], 'Blessed are those who have heard the word of the father and truly kept it. For there will be days when you (pl.) will say, "Blessed are the womb which has not conceived and the breasts which have not given milk".'

(*Gos. Thom.* 79)

The saying has two parallels in the Synoptic Gospels. The episode about a woman in the crowd is also found in Luke 11:27–28 (*Gos. Thom.* 79ab), material usually labelled peculiar to Luke. Scholars (e.g. Schürmann 1968: 231–32) have sometimes argued that The Woman in the Crowd was derived from Q and that Matthew omitted it and replaced it with the Markan story on True Relatives (Mark 3:31–35; Matt 12:46–50), but no waterproof arguments can be presented for this view.[24] The end of *Thomas'* saying (79c) has a parallel in the Lucan passion narrative (Luke 23:29) as part of the section which addresses the daughters of Jerusalem (23:27–31). This latter episode is also Luke's special material.

When compared with Luke, *Gos. Thom.* 79 appears to be a combination of these two traditions. Apparently, Luke did not create all of his parallel materials in 11:27–28 and 23:29, but it is unlikely that their connection in *Thomas* is original and that Luke split the materials into two different incidents. I rather take The Woman in the Crowd (Luke 11:27–28) as one thematic variant of the tradition on True Relatives (Mark 3:31–36 par.; *Gos. Thom.* 99) and the saying on the 'coming days' in Luke 23:29 and *Gos. Thom.* 79c as a separate tradition used by Luke in Jesus' pronouncement against the daughters of Jerusalem.[25] The catchwords 'blessed are the womb ... and the breasts' have given a formal reason for joining these two traditions. Whether or not the combination of the traditions is based on the Gospel of Luke is a matter of dispute. The specifically Lucan phraseology in v. 27a ('As he said this ... ') is lacking in *Thomas*, but on the other hand the words 'hear the word of God and keep it' has a Lucan flavour (cf Luke 8:21, see also 5:1; 8:11; Acts 6:2; 12:24; 13:5, 46; 17:13). The similar expression of *Thomas* may therefore reveal a Lucan redaction. The latter suggestion does not, however, solve the question of a possible independent tradition history behind the Thomasine saying, since the influence of the Lucan redaction may have occurred after the two units were joined.[26]

The above considerations only demonstrate how complicated the question of the literary relationship between the *Gospel of Thomas* and the Synoptic Gospels is. Apart from that question, we should ask whether the composition of *Gos. Thom.* 79abc reflects a definite stance for sexual asceticism and celibacy. Wolfgang Schrage argues that the omission of Luke's 'the barren' may reveal *Thomas*' intention to emphasise voluntary celibacy (Schrage 1964: 165, similarly Fitzmyer 1985: 1494). Peter Nagel, in turn, sees in *Gos. Thom.* 79 an early example of an ascetic interpretation of Jesus' apocalyptic word (cf Mark 13:17) (Nagel 1966: 26). One could also take notice of the word *menoun* in Luke 11:28, which has no equivalent in *Thomas*. This particle is probably to be understood in the corrective sense ('yes, but rather', Fitzmyer 1985: 928–29) and therefore has the effect of softening the contrast between maternal honour and true discipleship. In *Thomas*, biological motherhood is clearly contrasted with discipleship.

One can hardly deny that *Gos. Thom.* 79c (the blessedness of the infertile) adds an ascetic element to the story of The Woman in the Crowd. But we should be cautious about making this saying more 'encratite' than it is. The absence of 'the barren' in *Thomas* may be due simply to the parallelism between 79b and c ('Blessed ... the womb ... '), which makes further elements disturbing. Luke's 'softening' word (*menoun*) is to be ascribed to the evangelist's redaction,[27] and it may not have been preserved in or been part of the tradition that *Thomas* used.

More importantly, we should note that the eschatological language of Luke 23:29 (*idou erchontai hêmerai*) has not completely disappeared in the Thomasine saying, which similarly speaks of the 'coming days'. Of course, an apocalyptic or historical context, such as in Luke 23:27–31, is not present in *Thomas*, but the reference to a future situation leaves some possibility that the marriage and childbearing may be part of the *present* experience of *Thomas*' audience. In other words, even if the saying predicts that there will be a time when the disciples understand the preciousness of ascetic life, it is not an explicit exhortation to abolish marriage.

Although it would require a much longer discussion, we may briefly note here that the sayings on 'becoming a single one' or 'making the two one' are also ultimately eschatological or, perhaps better, protological statements (see *Gos. Thom.* 4; 22; 23; 106; note also 11). It is difficult to recognise what kind of mythology constitutes the symbolic world behind these sayings. It is often suggested that these sayings reflect the image of asexual Primordial Man based on Hellenistic Jewish exegesis of Gen 1–2, which can be found in Philo. The passage most often referred to is *Op. Mund.* 134, where Philo draws a contrast between the man formed of clay (Gen 2:7) and 'the man who came into being after the image of God' (Gen 1:27) being 'neither male nor female' (*out' arren oute thêly*).[28] Read against such a background, *Thomas* envisages the original realm of asexuality[29] as the final goal of human life. The idea of 'double creation' would also explain why the 'end' and the 'beginning' fall together in the Gospel (*Gos. Thom.* 18; see also 19; 49; 77). Such language could certainly motivate ascetic behaviour,[30] but one should not overlook the fact that similar protological ideas were frequent in early Christianity and do not always appear in strictly encratite traditions.[31] In any case, explicit statements against marriage are also lacking in this group of sayings in *Thomas*, and in many the final asexuality is still in the future. *Gos. Thom.* 4b is a good example of this futurist emphasis: 'For many who are first *will* come last, and they *will* become one and the same'.

The imaginary language of the much discussed saying in *Gos. Thom.* 22 ('when you make male and female into a single one') could also easily attract eschatological interpretations, even though the phrase 'entering the kingdom' is more open to a present reading than the reference to the 'coming of the kingdom' in the parallel in *Second Clement* (12:2).[32] The question of how logion 22 relates to the saying in *Gos. Thom.* 114, where Jesus promises to make Mary male, is difficult. The language of 'becoming one' and that of 'becoming male' can be used by the same author, as Philo demonstrates (Baer 1970: 51–55; Sly 1990: 55–56). On the other hand, it has often been argued that *Gos. Thom.* 114 is a later addition to the Gospel (Davies 1983: 152–55) and reflects a situation in which the presence of women has become a problem for the male members of the community (for the latter argument, see Marjanen 1995: 37–46). If the latter view is correct, one may suggest that *Gos. Thom.* 114 presupposes a more encratite situation than logion 22.

'REALISED ESCHATOLOGY' IN THE GOSPEL OF THOMAS?

One may readily object to the 'eschatological' interpretation here proposed. In light of the many references to the presence of the 'kingdom' or resurrection (e.g. *Gos. Thom.* 3; 51; 113), it has often been argued that *Thomas*' eschatology is 'realised' and spiritualised and there is no real future eschatological expectation in the Gospel (De Conick and Fossum 1991: 134; cf also Patterson 1993: 170). Since Jesus in *Thomas* claims that the resurrection 'has already come' (*Gos. Thom.* 51), it has been concluded that the asexuality expected in the Gospel is also seen as realised in the present situation of *Thomas*' group, for example, through baptism (see especially *Gos. Thom.* 37).[33] However true this may be, the categorisation of *Thomas*' symbolic world merely by the concept of 'realised eschatology' is one-sided and must be complemented by further definition. It is clear that *Thomas*, at least in its present form,[34] does not assume the doctrine of a physical resurrection (Riley 1995) and even ridicules those who teach that the kingdom will be some concrete reality within the visible world (*Gos. Thom.* 3). But on the other hand, there are a surprising number of future expressions with respect to the final 'salvation' in *Thomas*, which may not all be explained as purely rhetorical language or 'logical' futures (see e.g. *Gos. Thom.* 4; 11; 18; 23; 27; 44; 49; 57; 60; 70; 75; 79; 106; 111). This demonstrates that the tension between present and future is not eliminated.[35] Rather, the eschatological language of *Thomas* bears an ambiguity which can be compared to many other early Christian writings. *Thomas*' peculiarity is that 'salvation' is understood as a *process* of 'seeking and finding', a pattern that has its roots in wisdom literature.[36] *Thomas'* emphasis is individualistic and certainly non-apocalyptic.[37] But the present situation of *Thomas'* audience can be characterised as a state of being 'in-between' rather than one of final consummation. This observation must be taken into account when the social world of the gospel and the nature of *Thomas'* asceticism are depicted.

STANDING SOLITARY

> Jesus said, 'Men think, perhaps, that it is peace which I have come to cast upon the world. They do not know that it is dissension which I have come to cast upon the earth: fire, sword, and war. For there will be five in a house: three will be against two and two against three, the father against the son, and the son against the father. And they will stand solitary'.
>
> (*Gos. Thom.* 16)

The above saying on the Division in the Household has a parallel in Q 12:51–53 (the saying in 12:49 appears in *Gos. Thom.* 10). The version in *Thomas* is closer to Luke's form of the Q saying in that it contains a reference to numerals ('five in the house'), whereas Matthew's version of the Division follows closely the OT prophecy in Micah 7:6. As in many other sayings, the question of whether *Thomas* reflects the redaction of the canonical Gospels divides scholars into different camps.[38] For my purposes, the most interesting question is, what is the meaning of the phrase 'and they will stand solitary', which is specifically Thomasine (cf *Gos. Thom.* 49; 75; see also 18; 23) and can therefore give some information about how this Synoptic tradition was interpreted in *Thomas'* context.

The meaning of the term 'solitary' (*monachos*) has been discussed in numerous studies.[39] In addition to the present passage, it appears twice in *Thomas*, once as a parallel to 'elect' (*Gos. Thom.* 49) and once as a characterisation of those who 'enter the bridal chamber' (75). The word was not used as a noun by Classical Greek writers and it does not appear in Philo or in the Septuagint (note, however, the appearance of the word in the Greek translations of the Old Testament by Aquila, Symmachus and Theodotion).[40] Later, it came to mean 'monk' in the monastic terminology of Athanasius and Pachomius.[41] According to the common interpretation, the use of *monachos* in *Thomas* should be interpreted in light of the Syriac word *îhîdāyă*,[42] which as used by fourth-century Syrian writers[43] to denote consecrated celibates, both male and female, living in Christian communities (see Vööbus 1958: 220–21; Griffith 1995: 223). This interpretation would give a rather definite meaning to the phrase in *Gos. Thom.* 16: only virgins can remain faithful. *Gos. Thom.* 75 would then sound like a strictly 'encratite' statement: only the person who is unattached or single can enter the bridal chamber.

Whatever the meaning of the 'bridal chamber' is in *Gos. Thom.* 75,[44] it is obvious that *monachos* characterises the true disciple, who is also called the 'elect', 'child of the light/father', 'child', 'single one', and many other terms in the Gospel. Is then the true disciple celibate according to *Thomas*? There are two reasons that make me hesitant about the clear-cut encratite reading of *Gos. Thom.* 75. First, it seems wise not to read all of the later technical meanings of *îhîdāyă* into the *monachos* of the *Gospel of Thomas*, which by any dating is much earlier than the Syriac texts using this word.[45] Second, the 'bridal chamber' is as difficult to interpret as the term *monachos*, and this leaves us with a double difficulty in understanding the saying in *Gos. Thom.* 75. There is no indication of a specific sacramental interpretation of the symbol in *Thomas*, and that renders uncertain the suggestion that we are dealing with an initiation rite (baptism?) through which only celibate persons could enter the community. If the image is taken as eschatological, we are faced with ambiguity similar to that of *Gos. Thom.* 79.

The only clear hint we can obtain from *Thomas*' own context is that *monachos* is used with reference to those involved in conflicts within their households (*Gos. Thom.* 16). As we have seen, this theme is related to the question of the disciples' true identity as the 'children of the light' (*Gos. Thom.* 50). One can therefore easily imagine several ways of understanding the word *monachos* as referring to those who have been compelled to break away from family to become followers of Jesus in *Thomas*' community.[46] In a social context where such conflicts were frequent, 'solitary' could become, by way of generalisation, an honorary title for those who regard themselves as the 'elect of the living father' and who do not consider themselves as belonging to this world (cf 'poor' in *Gos. Thom.* 54). In this sense, *monachos* has indisputable anti-familial and ascetic overtones, but a clear-cut encratite interpretation does not do justice to the multi-dimensional imagery of the Gospel.

It should be noted that a similar openness remains in the *Dialogue of the Savior*, where the word *monachos* appears twice together with 'elect' (120:26; 121:18–20) in striking parallel to *Gos. Thom.* 49.[47] The dialogue presents a treatise on eschatology and the dissolution of bodily existence, creating a tension between present and future,[48] not unlike what we have found in the *Gospel of Thomas*. The writing does not have an overall encratite character, even though it discusses the Lord's words on 'praying in the place where there is no woman' (144, 15ff) in a way reminiscent of Jesus' saying in the *Gospel of Egyptians* (see above).

The Lord said, 'Pray in the place where there is no woman'. Matthew said: 'Pray in the place where there is [no woman]', he tells us, meaning, 'Destroy the works of womanhood', not because there is any other [manner of birth], but because they will cease [giving birth]'.

Mary said, 'They will never be obliterated'. The Lord said, '[Who] knows that they will [not] dissolve and . . . '

(trans. Emmel 1984)

Unfortunately the Lord's response to Mary's comment (or question) is badly damaged, which leaves the final interpretation of the saying open. In any case, the 'dissolution of the works of womanhood' is explained to mean that women 'will cease [giving birth]'. This may, of course, indicate sexual asceticism. But given the tension between present and future eschatology in the *Dialogue of the Savior*, it is not clear whether the author intends the cessation of childbearing to be part of the final 'dissolution' or whether it was meant to be an exhortation to the author's contemporary audience.[49] In any case, read as a whole, the *Dialogue of the Savior* is clearly less encratite than, say, the *Book of Thomas* or the *Acts of Thomas*. It is worth noting that the term *monachos* does not appear in the strongly ascetic *Book of Thomas*, and in the Syriac *Acts îhîdāyǎ* occurs only once as a reference to Christ.[50]

CONCLUSIONS

The examination of the anti-familial sayings has revealed a certain ambiguity in the ascetic language of the gospel. This means that we cannot always be sure whether the state of asexuality presupposed by *Thomas* is a matter of the final destination or whether it is anticipated by means of an unconditioned demand for sexual abstinence and the rejection of marriage. In my judgment, the ambiguity is best explained by the suggestion that *Thomas* does not derive from a strictly encratite sect in which celibacy was the condition of entrance to the community, even though ascetic tendencies must have been prevalent in *Thomas'* environment. But ascetic proclivities of various degrees had been popular among many Christian groups since the time of the apostle Paul. As Dale Martin has recently demonstrated, sexual abstinence was widely admired in the Graeco-Roman world, and a negative attitude towards sexual desire and the human body was a commonplace at least in many educated circles (Martin 1995). *Thomas'* ascetic language must be set against this general background.

The ethos of 'homelessness' shared with the Synoptic Gospels and Q is used to illustrate the theme of the 'true identity' of the disciple, which *Thomas* connects with the Christological notion of Jesus' heavenly origin. One can follow a trajectory from the early 'itinerant radicalism' of Q to *Thomas* Christianity, as Stephen Patterson has done (Patterson 1993: 158–214). However, *Thomas* is at the crossroads of different trajectories, of which that from Q is only one. The Hellenistic-Alexandrian background, for example, is certainly an important item on the agenda for future Thomasine studies.[51]

The ambiguity with respect to sexual asceticism I have described is in accord with some other traits of the Gospel. In *Thomas*, the cosmos appears as a worthless but threatening reality (e.g. 21; 27; 56; 80; 111). On the other hand, creation is not considered 'fallen' (cf 12; 89) and it can serve as a stage for Jesus' appearance 'in flesh' (28).[52] Nor has the 'body' been completely demonicised, even though it may be disparaged as 'poverty' (cf 29) and said to be 'wretched' (cf 87), if dependent upon a 'body' (the visible world?). The different emphases or inconsistencies may, of course, be considered in terms of redaction criticism and separate layers. They can also give a reason for a completely 'atomistic' reading of the *Gospel of Thomas*.[53]

I have taken a different approach, by which I hope to do justice to the regular multivalence of religious language and symbols. Finally, the ambiguous situation of the *Gospel of Thomas* may also shed new light on the development of Syrian Christianity, which later produced other books, radically encratite in character, in the name of the apostle Judas Thomas.

NOTES

1 There are several colleagues who have helped me in developing the ideas presented in this essay. I would particularly like to thank Karen King, who read an early version of the paper, and Dale Martin, who revised my English and suggested a great number of improvements.

2 The term is somewhat difficult to define accurately. According to a recent dictionary of Biblical studies (*The Anchor Bible Dictionary*), 'encratism' is defined as 'the advocacy of a harsh discipline of the body, especially in regard to sexual activity, diet, and the use of alcoholic beverages' (Edwards 1992: 506). More specifically the term can refer to a sect founded by Tatian; see Irenaeus, *Adv. haer.* 1.28. This chapter focuses on sexual asceticism only. The question of dietary regulations in *Thomas* is not discussed.

3 The most comprehensive study of sexual renunciation in early Christianity up to the time of Augustine is Brown 1988. For the church fathers, see also van Eijk 1972: 209–35.

4 Justin,'*Apology* I. 15.5. Translation from Roberts and Donaldson (eds) 1967: 167 (with minor modifications).

5 Quispel 1981: 234. The view of *Thomas* as an encratite writing is repeated in several publications by Quispel; note esp. 1967 and 1985: 35–81. Quispel is followed by De Conick 1996 (esp. 3–7). Puech (1963: 306) thought that the first, 'more orthodox', version of *Thomas* derived from encratite Christianity.

6 Davies 1983: 21–22. This position is repeated in 1992: 674 with reference to *Thomas*' disapproval of fasting (Sayings 14, 104).

7 Davies 1983: 22. Davies' main concern is to argue that the *Gospel of Thomas* is not a 'Gnostic' document and that it derives from the first century of Christianity.

8 For a discussion of the *Gospel of Thomas* as a source of early Syrian Christianity, see e.g. Klijn 1965: 64–82. For Syrian asceticism, see Beck 1956: 254–67; Vööbus 1958; Brock 1973: 1–19; Murray 1974–75: 59–80; Griffith 1995: 220–45.

9 Wimbush 1993: 462. The diversity and richness of ascetic traditions in Christianity as well as in other religions have been aptly demonstrated in a recent massive collection of articles edited by Wimbush and Valantasis (1995).

For other recent volumes on asceticism, see Bianchi (ed.) 1985 and Wimbush (ed.) 1992.

10 For a more comprehensive analysis of *Thomas'* asceticism, see my article in R. Uro (ed.) forthcoming.

11 According to the prevalent convention, Q texts are cited by their Lucan chapter and verse numeration, without implying that the Lucan wording and order is nearer to those of Q than is the case with Matthew.

12 This is true in particular if Luke 11:27–28 does not derive from Q (see below note 24). A closer comparison between the anti-familial material in Mark and Q reveals other differences too. In a recent study, Peter Kristen (1995) observes that Mark reflects Christian egalitarian communities, in which the followers could receive 'a hundredfold . . . houses and brothers and sisters and mothers and children . . . ' (Mark 10:31) already in *this life*. According to Kristen, this type of social formation differs from the itinerant radicalism presupposed in the early Q tradition.

13 Cf. Luke 18:29, where Luke has similarly redacted Mark 8:29.

14 The Lucan version of the parable was used by the encratites criticised by Clement of Alexandria in *Strom.* 3.12.90. Balch (1972: 351–64) has argued that Q shows some tendency toward virginity and celibacy in 14:15–24; 14:26f and 17:27, but it is more reasonable to attribute this proclivity to Luke (for such an argument, see Seim 1989: 125–40; 1994: 185–260).

15 Patterson does not stress that the wandering charismatics were celibate, even though he seems to imply this (see 1993: 153). For De Conick (1996), the followers of *Thomas* are clearly those who 'were abstaining from the world and were renouncing it completely by becoming poor wandering celibates with restricted diets' (1996: 135).

16 Roughly half of the Saying units in *Thomas* have parallels in the Synoptic Gospels and more than half of these parallels derive from Q. For a list of the parallels, see Koester 1990: 87–89.

17 This is not to say that echoes of the redaction of the canonical Gospels do not appear in *Thomas*. For the argument that such redactional elements can sometimes be explained by the phenomenon of 'secondary orality', see Uro 1996.

18 Cf Patterson 1993: 167–68. Patterson has no specific mention of a post-70 CE situation.

19 Here as elsewhere in this chapter I cite the translation by T. O. Lambdin in Layton 1989.

20 For the analysis of this saying, see Uro 1996.

21 For such an argument, see Uro 1987, and (for Q and Mark) Kristen 1995 (see above note 12).

22 *Gos. Thom.* 27b and 104b appear to contradict the explicitly negative statements in 6, 14, and 53, but neither of the first mentioned expresses an unequivocal command to keep the Jewish obligations. For the analysis, see the essay by A. Marjanen on 'Thomas and Jewish Religious Practices', in R. Uro (ed.) forthcoming. For a different reading of *Gos. Thom.* 27, see De Conick 1996:127–43.

23 Unfortunately the last sentence of *Gos. Thom.* 101 is partially damaged and remains defective, but the words '[my] true [mother]' are based on a well-grounded reconstruction. A possible reconstruction of the preceding lacuna is given with hesitation by Layton (1989: 88; in consultation with S. Emmel) and can be translated 'For my mother [gave falsehood]'.

24 The International Q Project (a group of more than thirty scholars who worked for the reconstruction of Q in the context of the SBL during the period of

1989–94), though sensitive to parallels in *Thomas* in general, concluded that the inclusion of this section cannot be decided with certainty (see Moreland and Robinson 1995: 475–85).

25 For Luke's composition of different traditions in Luke 23:27–32, see e.g. Neyrey 1983: 74–86.

26 An argument for the independence of *Gos. Thom.* 79 has been made by Patterson 1993: 59–60.

27 Cf the Lucan redaction in Luke 8:19–21, where Luke similarly makes it clear that Jesus' own family is not excluded from God's family.

28 Although Philo can occasionally suggest the myth of androgynous man (see *Op. Mund.* 151–52), the man after the image of God is to be understood more in terms of asexuality than of bisexuality or androgyneity (see Baer 1970: 14–44).

29 Since the *Gospel of Thomas* is lacking in explicit androgynous language (such as in Plato's *Symposium* 189C–93D or *Poimandres* 18), it is better to use the term 'asexual' than 'androgynous', even though the latter is often suggested with respect to *Thomas* (see Klijn 1962, 271–78; Meeks 1974, 165–208; MacDonald 1987).

30 For the idea of 'double creation' as a justification for encraticism, see e.g. Gasparro 1995: 134–69.

31 For example, such Valentinian texts as the *Gospel of Philip* or the *Excerpts from Theodotus* include ideas of the original unity of sexes (e.g. *Gos. Phil.* 68:23–27) or that of the union of the 'elect' with the 'male' angelic counterpart (*Exc.* 21–22). Neither of the texts represent an unambiguous encratite stance, however. For the discussion and further literature, see Marjanen 1995: 133–38. The idea of 'the two becoming one' appears metaphorically in the *Hymn of the Pearl* in the description of the son's reunion with the 'glittering robe' (*Acts Thom.* 112) without any sexual images.

32 For a comparison between *Gos. Thom.* 22; 2 Clem 12 and the saying from the *Gospel of the Egyptians* preserved in the *Strom.* 3.12.92, see Baarda 1982: 529–56; Dautzenberg 1982: 181–206; MacDonald 1987: 17–63.

33 *Gos. Thom.* 37 has widely been connected with baptismal setting since J. Z. Smith's influential article (1978: 1–23). Note, however, the criticism by De Conick and Fossum 1991: 123–50.

34 The Greek version of saying 5 (P. Oxy. 654: 31) may, however, indicate the resurrection of the dead: '[For there is nothing] hidden which [will] not [become], nor buried (*thethammenon*) that [will not be raised]' (the reconstruction by Attridge in Layton 1989).

35 *Pace* Koester 1971: 173. Note the critique of Koester in Davies 1983: 47–48.

36 Kloppenborg calls this a process of 'sapiential research' (1987: 307).

37 Temporal cosmological eschatology is not, however, completely absent in *Thomas* (cf logion 11).

38 For the discussion, see Schrage 1964: 57–61 (arguing for the dependence) and Sieber 1965: 113–17; Patterson 1993: 25–26 (arguing for the independence).

39 For the discussion on the origin of *monachos* (and *îhîdāyă*)   , see Adam 1953–54: 209–39; Beck 1956: 254–67; Harl 1960: 464–74; Klijn 1962: 272 n. 3; Quispel 1967: 26–28; 1981: 237–38; Morard 1973: 332–411; 1975: 242–46; 1980: 395–401; Judge 1977: 72–89; Griffith 1995: 223–29.

40 For the use of the word by later Greek Bible translators, see the helpful table in Morard 1973: 348. The most discussed passages are Gen 2:18, in which Aquila and Symmachus use the word *monachos* for Hebrew *lěbad*; and Ps 68:7, in which Symmachus and Theodotion use the same Greek word as an equivalent of *yāhid*. The latter ('solitary') has been understood by the rabbis to refer

to bachelors and the verse in Ps 68:7 was interpreted (under the influence of Aquila's translation) to refer to consecrated celibates by church fathers (see Morard 1973: 352–53). Since Symmachus and Theodotion are said to have been Ebionites, Quispel argues that *yāhid* 'was used to indicate the bachelor in Jewish Christian circles' (1981: 238). However, the Jewish-Christian background of Symmachus is uncertain, and Theodotion's origins even more obscure.

41 The earliest known use of *monachos* in the sense of 'monk' is found in a papyrus containing a petition of Aurelius Isidorus of Karanis, dated to June 324 CE (P. Coll. Youtie 77). For the text, see Judge 1977: 72–89.

42 Later it came to mean also 'monk'. A clear example of the equation of the Greek and Syriac terms is the fact that according to Field's edition, the Syro-Hexapla (seventh century) translates Symmachus' *monachos* in Ps 68:6 by using the word *îhîdāyă* (Morard 1973: 352). However, the early uses of the words and their precise relationship to each other are a matter of debate. For the discussion, see Adam 1953–54: 209–39; Vööbus 1958: 106–8; Griffith 1995: 223–29.

43 The earliest texts which give such a technical meaning to *îhîdāyă* are the Demonstrations of Aphrahat (died c. 345 CE) and the hymns and homilies of Ephraem the Syrian (d. 373 CE).

44 Cf also *Gos. Thom.* 104, where the Greek word *nymphon* is used. References to 'bridal chamber' are found also in the *Dialogue of the Savior* (138:14–20), *Gospel of Philip* (67:30; 69:1, 26–28; 70:18–19; 81:34 to 82:25; 86:4–19), (see Gaffron 1969: 212–391; Buckley 1980: 569–81; Valantasis 1995: 380–93), *Tripartite Tractate* (128:33), *Acts of Thomas* (12, cf 14 and 15), see also *Exc.Theod.* 63–64; Ireneus, *Ad. haer.* 1.8.4; *Val. Exp.* 31.37.

45 The date of the *Gospel of Thomas* is notoriously difficult to establish, but most suggestions fall into a period from the late first to the middle second century.

46 Quispel (1967:108) thinks that *Thomas* in logion 16 eliminated the female members of the family included in his Jewish-Christian source (cf Luke 12:51 and Matt 10:34–35), because he was thinking of father and son, who had rejected their wives and lived celibate. But why is the three–two dimension left, and what is the cause of the dissension, if both father and son are celibate Christians?

47 For *monachos* in the *Dialogue of the Savior*, see Morard 1980: 395–401.

48 This tension has been emphasised by Koester and Pagels 1984: 11–15.

49 Cf Koester and Pagels (1984: 15), who argue that 'the author's interpretation of the 'dissolution of the works womanhood' does not suggest a metaphysically motivated sexual asceticism', although on somewhat different grounds. Wisse (1988: 301–2), referring to the *Testimony of Truth* (30:18 to 31:5), supports a strongly encratite reading of the passage, but it would be more reasonable to interpret the saying in the context of the *Dialogue of the Savior*. For an ascetic reading of the dialogue, see also Perkins 1980: 107–12.

50 See *Acts Thom.* 7 (the so-called *epithalamion* hymn). The doxology (lines 52–54), in which the word appears, is lacking in the Greek version and is probably secondary (see Murray 1974–75: 74).

51 For the nearness of *Thomas* to the Philonic theology, see Davies 1992: 663–82.

52 See Marjanen's essay 'Thomas and the World' in Uro (ed.) forthcoming.

53 For such an approach, see Davies 1994, which signifies a drastic change of opinion as compared to his earlier studies on *Thomas*. Note also Wisse 1988: 304–5.

BIBLIOGRAPHY

Adam, A. (1953–54) 'Grundbegriffe des Mönchtums in Sprachlicher Sicht', *Zeitschrift für Kirchengeschichte* 65: 209–39.

Asgeirsson, J. Ma (forthcoming) 'The Double Sayings in Thomas', in R. Uro (ed.) *Thomas at the Crossroads: Scandinavian Essays on the Gospel of Thomas*.

Baarda, T. (1982) '2 Clem 12 and the Sayings of Jesus', in J. Delobel (ed.) *Logia. Les Paroles de Jésus – The Sayings of Jesus*, Leuven: Peeters & Leuven University Press: 529–56.

Baer, R. A. (1970) *Philo's Use of the Categories Male and Female*, ALGHJ 3, Leiden: E. J. Brill.

Balch, D. L. (1972) 'Backgrounds of I Cor VII: Sayings of the Lord in Q; Moses as an Ascetic THEIOS ANR in II Cor III', *NTS* 18: 351–64.

Beck, E. (1956) 'Ein Beitrag zur Terminologie des Ältesten Syrischen Mönchtums', *Studia Anselmiana* 38: 254–67.

Bianchi, U. (1985) 'La Tradition de l'Enkrateia: Motivations Ontologiques et Protologiques', in U. Bianchi (ed.) *La Tradizione dell'Enkrateia: Motivazioni Ontologiche e Protologiche. Atti del Colloquio Internazionale Milano, 20–23 April 1982*, Rome: Edizioni dell'Ateneo: 293–314.

Brock, S. P. (1973) 'Early Syrian Asceticism', *Numen* 20: 1–19.

Brown, P. (1988) *The Body and Society: Men, Women, and Sexual Renunciation in Early Christianity*, New York: Columbia University Press.

Buckley, J. J. (1980) 'A Cult-Mystery in the Gospel of Philip', *JBL* 99: 569–81.

Dautzenberg, G. (1982) ' "Da ist nicht Männlich und Weiblich": Zur Interpretation von Gal 3:28', *Kairos* 24: 181–206.

Davies, S. L. (1983) *The Gospel of Thomas and Christian Wisdom*, New York: The Seabury Press.

—— (1992) 'The Christology and Protology of the Gospel of Thomas', *JBL* 111: 663–82.

—— (1994): 'The Oracles of the Gospel of Thomas', Paper Read at the Annual Meeting of the Society of Biblical Literature, 19–22 November 1994, Chicago.

De Conick, A. D. (1996) *Seek to See Him: Ascent and Vision Mysticism in the Gospel of Thomas*, Supplements to Vigiliae Christianae, vol. 33, Leiden: E. J. Brill.

De Conick, A. and Fossum, J. (1991) 'Stripped Before God: A New Interpretation of Logion 37 in the Gospel of Thomas', *Vigiliae Christianae* 45: 123–50.

Drijvers, H. J. W. (1985) 'Jews and Christians in Edessa', *Journal of Jewish Studies* 36: 88–102.

—— (1992) 'Syrian Christianity and Judaism', in J. Lieu, J. North, and T. Rajak (eds) *The Jews Among Pagans and Christians in the Roman Empire*, London and New York: Routledge: 124–46.

Edwards, O. C. Jr (1992) 'Encratism', in N. Freedman (ed.) *Anchor Bible Dictionary*, vol. 2, New York: Doubleday, 506–7.

Emmel, S. (ed.) (1984) *Nag Hammadi Codex III.5: The Dialogue of the Savior*, NHS 26, Leiden: E. J. Brill.

Fallon, F. T. and Cameron, R. (1988) 'The Gospel of Thomas: A Forschungsbericht and Analysis', *Aufstieg und Niedergang der Römischen Welt* II:25,6: 4195–251.

Fitzmyer, J. A. (1985) *The Gospel According to St. Luke, X–XXIV. Introduction, Translation and Notes*, AB 28b, Garden City, NY: Doubleday.

Gaffron, H.-G. (1969) 'Studien zum Koptischen Philippusevangelium unter Besonderer Berücksichtigung der Sakramente', ThD Thesis, Rheinishce Friedrich-Wilhelms-Universität, Bonn.

Gasparro, G. S. (1995) 'Asceticism and Anthropology: Enkrateia and "Double

Creation" in Early Christianity', in V. L. Wimbush and R. Valantasis (eds) *Asceticism*, New York and Oxford: Oxford University Press: 127–56.

Griffith, S. H. (1995) 'Asceticism in the Church of Syria: The Hermeneutics of Early Syrian Monasticism', in V. L. Wimbush and R. Valantasis (eds) *Asceticism*, New York and Oxford: Oxford University Press: 220–45.

Harl, M. (1960) 'A Propos des Logia de Jésus: Le Sens du Mot Monachos', *Revue des Études Grecques* 73: 464–74.

Judge, E. A. (1977) 'The Earliest Use of Monachos for "Monk" (P. Coll.Youtie 77) and the Origins of Monasticism', *Jahrbuch für Antike und Christentum* 20: 72–89.

Klijn, A. F. J. (1962) 'The "Single One" in the Gospel of Thomas', *JBL* 81: 271–78.

—— (1965) *Edessa, die Stadt des Apostels Thomas. Das Älteste Christentum in Syrien*, Neukirchener Studienbücher Band 4, Neukirchen-Vluyn: Neukirchener Verlag.

Kloppenborg, J. S. (1987) *The Formation of Q: Trajectories in Ancient Wisdom Collections*, Studies in Antiquity and Christianity, Philadelphia: Fortress.

Koester, H. (1971) 'One Jesus and Four Primitive Gospels', in J. M. Robinson and H. Koester (eds) *Trajectories through Early Christianity*, Philadelphia: Fortress Press: 158–204.

—— (1990) *Ancient Christian Gospels: Their History and Development*, London/Philadelphia: SCM Press/Trinity Press International.

Koester, H. and Pagels, E. (1984) 'Introduction', in S. Emmel (ed.) *Nag Hammadi Codex III.5: The Dialogue of the Savior*, NHS 26, Leiden: E. J. Brill: 1–17.

Kretschmar, G. (1964) 'Ein Beitrag zur Frage nach dem Ursprung Frühchristlicher Askese', *Zeitschrift für Theologie und Kirche* 61: 27–67.

Kristen, P. (1995) *Familie, Kreutz und Leben: Nachfolge Jesus nach Q und Markusevangelium*, Marburger Theologische Studien 42, Marburg: NG Elwert Verlag Marburg.

Layton, B. (ed.) (1989) *Nag Hammadi Codex II.2–7*, vol. 1, NHS 20, Leiden: E. J. Brill.

MacDonald, D. R. (1987) *There is No Male and Female*, HDR 20, Philadelphia: Fortress Press.

Marjanen, A. (1995) 'The Woman Jesus Loved: Mary Magdalene in the Nag Hammadi Library and Related Documents', ThD Thesis, University of Helsinki.

—— (forthcoming) 'Cosmos in the Gospel of Thomas', in R. Uro (ed.) *Thomas at the Crossroads: Scandinavian Essays on the Gospel of Thomas*.

Martin, D. B. (1995) *The Corinthian Body*, New Haven and London: Yale University Press.

Meeks, W. A. (1974) 'The Image of Androgyne: Some Uses of a Symbol in Earliest Christianity', *History of Religions* 13: 165–208.

Morard, F.-E. (1973) 'Monachos, Moine: Histoire du Terme Grec Jusqu'au 4e Siècle', *Freiburger Zeitschrift für Philosophie und Theologie* 20: 332–411.

—— (1975) 'Monachos: une Importation Sémitique en Egypte?': 242–46 in E. A. Livingstone (ed.) *Papers Presented to the Sixth International Conference on Patristic Studies held in Oxford 1971*, TU 115, Berlin: Akademie Verlag.

—— (1980) 'Encore Quelques Réflexions sur Monachos', *Vigiliae Christianae* 34: 395–401.

Moreland, M. C. and Robinson, J. M. (1995) 'The International Q Project Work Sessions 23–27 May, 22–26 August, 17–18 November 1994', *JBL* 114: 475–85.

Murray, R. (1974–75) 'The Exhortation to Candidates for Ascetical Vows at Baptism in the Ancient Syriac Church', *NTS* 21: 59–80.

Nagel, P. (1966) *Die Motivierung der Askese in der Alten Kirche und der Ursprung des Mönchtums*, TU 95, Berlin: Akademie-Verlag.

Neyrey, J. H. (1983) 'Jesus' Address to the Women of Jerusalem (Luke 23:27–31) – A Prophetic Judgment Oracle', *NTS* 29: 74–86.

Oulton, J. E. L. and Chadwick, H. (1954) *Alexandrian Christianity: Selected Translations of Clement and Origen with Introductions and Notes*, LCC, vol. 2, Philadelphia: The Westminster Press.

Patterson, S. J. (1993) *The Gospel of Thomas and Jesus*, Sonoma, CA: Polebridge Press.

Perkins, P. (1980) *The Gnostic Dialogue. The Early Church and the Crisis of Gnosticism*, Theological Enquiries, New York: Paulist Press.

Puech, H.-C. (1963) 'Gnostic Gospels and Related Documents', in E. Hennecke and W. Schneemelcher (eds) *New Testament Apocrypha*, vol. 1, London: SCM Press: 231–362.

Quispel, G. (1967) *Makarius, das Thomasevangelium und das Lied von der Perle*, NovTSup 15, Leiden: E. J. Brill.

—— (1981) 'The Gospel of Thomas Revisited', in B. Barc (ed.) *Colloque International sur les Textes de Nag Hammadi*, Bibliothéque Copte de Nag Hammadi Section 'Études', Québec/ Louvain: Les Presses de l'Université Laval/ Peeters: 218–66.

—— (1985) 'The Study of Encratism: A Historical Survey', in U. Bianchi (ed.) *La Tradizione dell'Enkrateia: Motivazioni Ontologiche e Protologiche. Atti del Colloquio Internazionale Milano, 20–23 April 1982*, Roma: Edizioni dell'Ateneo: 35–81.

Riley, G. J. (1995) *Resurrection Reconsidered: Thomas and John in Controversy*, Minneapolis: Fortress Press.

Roberts, A. and Donaldson, J. (1967) *Ante-Nicene Fathers. Translations of the Writings of the Fathers down to AD 325*, vol. 1, Grand Rapids, MI: Eerdmans.

Schrage, W. (1964) *Das Verhältnis des Thomas–Evangeliums zur Synoptischen Tradition und zu den Koptischen Evangelienübersetzungen*, BZNW 29, Berlin: Verlag Alfred Töpelmann.

Schürmann, H. (1968) *Traditionsgeschichtliche Untersuchungen*, Düsseldorf: Patmos.

Seim, T. K. (1989) 'Ascetic Autonomy? New Perspectives on Single Women in the Early Church', *ST* 43: 125–40.

—— (1994) *The Double Message: Patterns of Gender in Luke and Acts*, Nashville: Abingdon Press.

Sieber, J. H. (1965) 'Redactional Analysis of the Synoptic Gospels with regard to the Question of the Sources of the Gospel According to Thomas', PhD Dissertation, Claremont Graduate School.

Sly, D. (1990) *Philo's Perception of Women*, Brown Judaic Studies 209, Atlanta: Scholars Press.

Smith, J. Z. (1978) 'The Garments of Shame', in J. Z. Smith *Map Is Not Territory. Studies in the History of Religions*, Studies in Judaism in Late Antiquity 23, Leiden: E. J. Brill: 1–23.

Theissen, G. (1973) 'Wanderradikalismus. Literatursoziologische Aspekte der Überlieferung von Worten Jesu im Urchristentum', *Zeitschrift für Theologie und Kirche* 70: 245–71.

—— (1978) *The First Followers of Jesus*, London: SCM Press.

—— (1979) *Studien zur Soziologie des Urchristentums*, WUNT 19, Tübingen: J. C. B. Mohr (Paul Siebeck).

Uro, R. (1987) *Sheep Among the Wolves: A Study on the Mission Instructions of Q*, Annales Academiae Scientiarum Fennicae. Dissertationes Humanorum Litterarum 47, Helsinki: Suomalainen Tiedeakatemia.

—— (1996) ' "Secondary Orality" in the Gospel of Thomas? Logion 14 as a Test Case', *Forum* 9 (forthcoming).

—— (forthcoming) 'Sexual Asceticism in Thomas', in R. Uro (ed.) *Thomas at the Crossroads: Scandinavian Essays on the Gospel of Thomas*.

—— (ed.) (forthcoming) *Thomas at the Crossroads: Scandinavian Essays on the Gospel of Thomas*.

Valantasis, R. (1995) 'The Nuptial Chamber Revisited: The Acts of Thomas and Cultural Intertextuality', *SBLSP* 34: 380–93.

Van Eijk, T. H. C. (1972) 'Marriage and Virginity, Death and Immortality', in J. Fontain and C. Kannengiesser (eds) *Epektasis. Mélanges Patristiques Offerts au Cardinal Jean Daniélou*, Paris: Beauchesne: 209–35.

Vööbus, A. (1958) *History of Asceticism in the Syrian Orient. I. The Origin of Asceticism, Early Monasticism in Persia*, Corpus Scriptorum Christianorum Orientalium, vol. 184, Louvain: Van den Bempt.

Wimbush, V. L. (ed.) (1992) *Discursive Formations, Ascetic Piety and the Interpretation of Early Christian Literature*, Semeia 55: 1–2, Atlanta: Scholars Press.

—— (1993) 'The Ascetic Impulse in Early Christianity: Some Methodological Challenges', in E. Livingstone (ed.) *Papers Presented at the 11th International Conference on Patristic Studies held in Oxford 1991*, Studia Patristica 25, Leuven: Peeters: 262–478.

Wimbush, V. L. and Valantasis, R. (eds) (1995) *Asceticism*, New York and Oxford: Oxford University Press.

Wisse, F. (1988) 'Flee Feminity: Antifeminity in Gnostic Texts and the Question of Social Milieu', in K. L. King (ed.) *Images of the Feminine in Gnosticism*, Studies in Antiquity and Christianity, Philadelphia: Fortress Press: 297–307.

13

FAMILY STRUCTURES IN GNOSTIC RELIGION

Ingvild Sælid Gilhus

THE GNOSTIC RELIGION

Gnosticism was a complex movement within early Christianity. It flourished in the second and third centuries when its advocates were resourceful contributors to Christian discourse. Family structures in Gnosticism are clearly visible and rather prominent as mythological configurations. But little is known of Gnostic social life, and the family as a social category is elusive. In this chapter the stress will be laid on the Gnostic mythological world, with some suggestions to be made about Gnostic family life.

Gnostic religion is mythologically rich and seems to have been constantly developing. All the same, the themes of this mythology are limited, its cast of main characters is short, and its heroes in no way take part in the entire field of human experience; on the contrary, they have some specialised interests. These interests are mainly concerned with the acquisition of knowledge and the process of salvation. A consequence of this rather limited range of interests is that the mythological entities suffer from a lack of personality and appear more like functions than persons. All the same, the connections between them are described in terms of family relations. They are mothers and fathers, daughters and sons. However, their relationships are often bizarre, as when androgyne mothers bear monstrous offspring or when Christ is the fruit of a triadic parentship consisting of the Father, the Son of Man and the First Woman. These mythological families are used as cognitive tools shaped to carve out Gnostic thinking about the nature of human beings and the process of their salvation. In other words, family relations are used as mythical paradigms and metaphors.

Because family relations are close to human experience and symbolically rich it is to be expected that the semantic potential of the family used as a symbol is always greater than its realisation in the actual texts: connotations will occur abundantly on a subtextual level and contribute to making family a fruitful religious symbol. Further, it is probable that when mythological family structures transcend normal family relationships they will have more power in generating religious meaning.

The theme of the present article is to describe and interpret mythological family structures as they appear in some of the so-called 'Sethian' Gnostic texts. 'Sethian' is here used about texts which have certain mythological themes in common and where usually Seth, the son of Adam and Eve, or his sister Norea (not mentioned in the Old Testament) play a leading role.[1] I will concentrate mainly on *The Hypostasis of the Archons*, *The Origin of the World*, *Trimorphic Protennoia* and *The Apocryphon of John*.[2] These texts were found at Nag Hammadi in Egypt. They were copied about 350 AD, but their content is older. They represent different approaches to a shared world-view and have a partly overlapping mythology.[3] Together they provide us with an impression of how Gnostics used family structures to describe the relationship between human beings on the one hand and these human beings' relationships with God and the world on the other. Since the Gnostic concern was primarily the process of salvation, one important function of the family structures is to appear as soteriological paradigms or models to be imitated or rejected in the salvatory process of the individual. Male and female values are described as relational in terms of kin-roles and have complementary functions in the process of salvation. The theme of mytho-logical families is played out on different levels: in the emanation and organisation of the spiritual world; at the fall and creation of the material world; in the organisation of human life on earth; and in the salvation of the elect. Thus family symbolism is used to describe the salvation process of the individual by means of which knowledge was gained, and to explain the relationship between the Gnostic individual and the group of believers.

What sort of life did these individuals live? Were they married, did they raise children? How the mythological world was related to 'real' life is diffi-cult to comment on because our knowledge of the social life of the Gnostics is scant. The Sethian texts describe spiritual life not social life. Indirectly, however, the use of family metaphors will also reflect ideals and practices of human life. But what these ideals were and how they were brought to life are elusive and seem to have varied considerably. The primary sources show a preference for an ascetic life. But when we consult the church fathers, the picture looks different. While their anti-heretical works mention the ideal of continence and an ascetic life, they also tell of orgies and promiscuity. Especially Epiphanius, bishop of Salamis (365–403), who had been educated in Egypt in his youth, reveals shocking cultic practices and immorality among a group of Egyptian Gnostics. However, the difficulty of using Epiphanius' information is that it does not fit very well with the original texts. On the other hand, the pious bishop boasts of first-hand knowledge of Gnostic groups in Egypt. When we view the ideology of the original texts together with Epiphanius' anti-heretical work, *Panarion*, one possible conclusion is that different types of family life could be led supported by related texts.

This chapter will discuss the following questions: what is the structure of the mythological families in Sethian Gnostic texts? What processes are played out by means of these families? What implications concerning Gnostic family life can be drawn from the Gnostics' own texts and from the texts of the church fathers?

THE FAMILY AS METAPHOR

In general there are many possibilities for using family relationships as metaphors and mythological paradigms. Different sorts of relationships are possible, for instance: mother–daughter; mother–son; father–daughter; father–son; sister–sister; sister–brother; brother–brother, husband–wife. In mainstream Christianity, the dominant model has been a father–son relationship. The female element has either been weak, as in the case of the Holy Spirit, whose femininity was bloodless and soon wiped out, or the female element has been played out on a subordinate level, in the paradoxical form of Mary, eternal mother and virgin.

The Gnostic Christian texts bear a certain likeness to mainstream Christianity's way of conceptualising a divine family; on the one hand a strong male connection, on the other hand a subordinate female element. In the Sethian texts the father–son relation is predominant. But in contrast to mainstream Christianity, the female element was necessary for the dynamics of the mythological systems and in some of the Sethian texts a concept of God the Mother is developed. However, the female element seldom escaped an ambivalent position. Being a bridge between the material and the spiritual, one of its main functions was to express ambiguity.

Another difference between the texts of mainstream Christianity and those of the Sethians is that all the relationships which were listed above exist in one form or another in the divine world: mother–daughter; husband–wife; brother–brother, etc. Some of these relationships are prominent, others are used only rarely. In the texts, family structures are motive powers in a symbolic web where the dynamics of gender polarity, relations between family members, and genealogical connections are used to bring movement into the mythology and give it a direction.

Typical for Gnosticism is that family metaphors are often hiding places for processes other than those usually connected with the family. It is striking how the Gnostic systems mix family metaphors with metaphors of speech and audition. The ear is on the verge of becoming a sexual organ and the Word is born through an act of spiritual copulation. In Gnostic mythology, family life has a strong sensual grounding in a metaphorical language of sexuality and birth, but its ideological meanings are most of all about spiritual creation and communication. It seems as if the process of attaining knowledge has been strongly eroticised. When we hold the Gnostic symbolic language – where sexual relationships play a prominent part – together with its speakers' alleged ascetic inclinations, we have an interesting tension which has probably worked as one important emotional impetus in the production of the Gnostic texts.

THE SPIRITUAL FAMILY

The dynamics of the original spiritual family are elaborately described in *Trimorphic Protennoia* and *The Apocryphon of John*.

The Trimorphic Protennoia is a spiritual redeemer as well as the female aspect of the transcendent godhead. She is part of a triad consisting of the unbegotten Father, the only-begotten Son and herself, the Mother. This patriarchal nuclear family is the original divine triad, known in related variants from several Sethian texts. This Sethian primal triad is manifested on lower levels of the creation. The text describes Protennoia's three descents into the world in a mixture of linguistic and patriarchal metaphors. Father Voice is perceptible through Mother Speech, who has within herself the Son – the Word. All successful creative activity has its ultimate source in the unbegotten Father. The female principle is secondary, derived from him; she is both the Father's wife and daughter, and appears first and foremost as a mediator between the creator and the creation. In the end the Son completes the process of salvation (Gilhus 1994).

It seems as if the construct of this spiritual mother in *Tri. Prot.* is the result of a systematic philosophical thought combined with longing for the maternal origin. The construct is made even more complex by a strong effort to make the mother androgynous and male: Protennoia is designated Mother, but also 'male virgin'. In *Ap. John*, the female aspect of the Father is characterised as follows:

> This is the first thought, his image; she became the womb of everything for it is she who is prior to them all, the Mother-Father, the first man, the holy Spirit, the thrice-male, the thrice-powerful, the thrice-named androgynous one, and the eternal aeon among the invisible ones, and the first to come forth.
>
> (CG II.1 5:4–11; Robinson 1988: 107)

A general characteristic of the Sethian triad is that the female element has a tendency to be conceived of as male and androgynous. This self-contradictory language must be seen in relation to ruling symbolic values in the Gnostic world-view, where maleness and androgynity are frequently conceived of as spiritual qualities, while femaleness is a quality connected with the material world. One of the most anti-feminine Sethian treatises, *Zostrianos*, says it bluntly: 'Flee from the madness and the bondage of femaleness and choose for yourselves the salvation of maleness' (CG VIII:1. 131:5–8; Robinson 1988: 430; Wisse 1988). Thus we have the paradox of a spiritual mother who is not female, a paradox which reflects her adherents' need for the mother on the one hand, and their horror of femaleness on the other.

THE FALL AND THE FAULTY FAMILY

It should come as no surprise that a female spiritual entity is responsible for the fall. The transgressor is Sophia, who wanted to create out of herself without her male consort. Her creation, however, is unsuccessful because it is a female conception with no male participant.[4] This result is in line with Aristotle's views and with common medical knowledge, according to which the male contributed form and the female matter at the conception of the child.[5] This knowledge is implicit in the following quotation from *Ap. John*:

> She wanted to bring forth a likeness out of herself without the consent of the Spirit – he had not approved – and without her consort, and without his consideration. And though the person of her maleness had not approved, and she had not found her agreement, and she had thought without the consent of the Spirit and the knowledge of her agreement, (yet) she brought forth.
>
> (CG II.1 9:29–35; Robinson 1988: 110)

As is stated twice in these lines, two things were wrong with Sophia's conception. It took place without the Father's permission, and it took place without the contribution of her male consort. Both are grave errors against the patriarchal order of things – a female acting against her father and against her husband in such an important matter as the begetting of children. Sophia is, according to the text, ashamed of herself, grieving and repenting, because what she has done cannot be undone. She gives birth to the world-creator Ialdabaoth, the Gnostic answer to Jahweh. Ialdabaoth is described as a mixture of man and beast. He is the originator of the material world and the creator of Adam and Eve.

Sophia stands at the boundary of the spiritual world. She is a 'daughter' of the Father. Christ characterises her as his 'sister', and as the 'mother' of the world-creator. 'Mother', 'sister', 'daughter', are relational terms within a patriarchal universe (King 1990). Ialdabaoth is described in relation to his mother as an abortion. Together Sophia and her son make an incomplete and therefore pathological family. This pathological family unit is a chief mythological expression for the fall.

THE FIRST HUMAN FAMILY AND ITS PROBLEMS

Characteristic for several of the Gnostic texts is how the process of physical procreation and the process of developing spiritual knowledge are interconnected. However, while sexual desire is used as a symbol for spiritual attraction, the sexual act is often, but not always, a symbol for spiritual contamination. The ambivalent use of sexuality is especially played out in the mythology of the first human husband–wife configuration, Adam and Eve.

Eve appears in two variants, both as a spiritual entity and as a carnal woman. Adam on his part is accompanied by Ialdabaoth when he approaches his wife intimately. But which wife are we talking about? When it comes to the first human couple, the Gnostic mythology exploits an ambiguous sexual symbolism where sexual desire becomes a perverted form of spiritual attraction.[6] In this game it is crucial to discern between that which is spiritual and that which is material, and not to mix spiritual desire with carnal desire. Because they are blind and stupid, the archons do not fully realise the difference between the spiritual and the material. They desperately want to mix their seed with the spiritual Eve and through the offspring of this union to bind the spiritual elements to their material world. But they make a mistake, the spiritual woman escapes and they end up procreating children with the carnal woman. In *Orig. World*, Ialdabaoth is the father of Cain (CG II.5 117:15–18; Robinson 1988: 183). In *Hyp.Arch.*, Ialdabaoth is the father of both Cain and Abel, while Seth and his sister Norea are fathered by Adam and mothered by the spiritual Eve (CG II.4 89:17–30; 91:11–92:3, Robinson 1988: 164–66). That makes at least two different groups of human beings: one has an archontic origin, the other a spiritual origin.

The mythology of the first human family expresses two soteriological concerns, on the one hand to describe spiritual intimacy, on the other, to establish spiritual genealogy. Concerning spiritual intimacy, the smallest possible configuration, husband–wife/male–female, is used as an image of the relationship between human beings and the spiritual world. The paradigmatic ideal is Adam and the spiritual Eve. In *Orig. World* the relation between Adam and the spiritual Eve is described in this way: 'and he loved his female counterpart and condemned the other, alien likenesses and loathed them' (CG II.5 110:34–111:1; Robinson 1988: 179).

The Coptic term which is translated 'his female counterpart' is *tef-shr-eine*. This word is used in related ways in *Orig. World* and *Hyp. Arch.* where Adam is described as the male counterpart of the image of God.[7] The Spirit/Eve is described as the female counterpart of Adam,[8] while the carnal Eve is described as the female counterpart of the archons.[9] This use of the concept 'counterpart' reflects a strong tendency in these texts to let spiritual entities, as well as archontic forces, come in pairs. A spiritual entity is not complete without its spiritual counterpart, salvation being dependent on being connected to one's spiritual half. An archontic or material entity has no spiritual counterpart – consequently, it cannot be saved.

This tendency to make mythological pairs is also prominent in relation to the spiritual world above where Sophia's sin consisted in her creating without her consort (*pesconf*). The stress on spiritual relationships works in two ways. We saw in the case of Adam how he was incomplete without his spiritual counterpart. The other side of the coin is that the value of Adam's mundane spouse (the carnal Eve) is *nil* compared to his spiritual half. When this mythology is translated to bear on human life it could easily act as a background for arguments against marriage. The relationship with one's spiritual counterpart and the development of one's spiritual life could take the place of marriage and physical relationships, which could be conceived of as disturbing elements in the Gnostic process of salvation.

THE GNOSTIC GENEALOGICAL UNIVERSE

Genealogies play an important role in the Gnostic universe and have a special purpose in establishing this universe. According to the Macmillan Dictionary of Anthropology: 'Genealogies are important in lineage or descent-based kinship-systems, since they provide the basis for membership in kin groups' (Seymour-Smith 1988: 130). Concerning the Gnostics, we are talking about genealogical fiction to suit the interests of certain spiritually oriented groups. Genealogical kinship is used to describe spiritual origin and status. In the introduction to his work, *Adversus haereses* (c. 180 AD), Irenaeus, bishop of Lyon, describes the Gnostics in this way: 'Certain people are discarding the Truth and introducing deceitful and endless genealogies'. In other words, Irenaeus saw genealogy as a chief characteristic of the Gnostic religion in contrast to mainstream Christianity. Two hundred years later, Epiphanius of Salamis says similar things about what he calls the Sethian school of thought (*haeresis*), 'for they suppose that there are mothers above, and females and males, and almost speak of kinships and patriarchal lineages' (*Panarion* 39,2,3, quoted from Layton 1987: 188).

In the Sethian texts, genealogies appear both on the spiritual and the mundane levels of being. In the spiritual world, genealogy is used as an instrument to establish as many entities as possible (or practical) between the Father and the material world, and thus relieve the Father of all blame concerning Sophia's fall and its result – the creation of the material world. On the mundane level, genealogy is used with the purpose of establishing lineages. Here several actors virtually queue up to procreate children by Eve – Adam, Ialdabaoth and his archons and angels. These actors are the originators of different lineages and these lineages could be combined with efforts making the development of spiritual knowledge dependent on one's origin.

The mundane level is the most interesting in our connection. The line of Seth is contrasted with that of the rest of mankind. The descendants of Seth are frequently called 'his seed' (*sperma*) or 'his race' (*genos*) (Martin 1990). Seth appears in Gnostic texts as a revealer and a saviour; sometimes he is identified with Christ. That the spiritual ancestry of the race of the elect is male is not surprising. In the Mediterranean world the male line of descent was all-important and the descent system was patrilineal (Malina 1981). But some Sethian texts also reflect a type of matrilineal descent. *The Hypostasis of the Archons* traces the descent of the elect from Seth's sister Norea, and she plays a role which is usually taken by Seth. The archons try to rape Norea, but she is saved by spiritual intervention. She is described as a virgin and her children are those that will eventually be saved. The angel Eleleth says to Norea: 'You, together with your offspring, are from the primeval father; from above, out of the imperishable light, their souls are come' (CG II.4 96:19–22).

But even if the text implies a female line of descent, the final saviour will be the Son. He will teach the sons of Norea everything and anoint them with the unction of life eternal. According to interpolations in the text, everything happens according to the will of the Father of the All (Gilhus 1985: 14–17). So Norea may well be an originator of a Gnostic race, but the significance of this trait for the promotion of female values is counteracted by the references to the all mighty Father. Norea is designated 'virgin' (*parthenos*) (CG II.4 91:35 to 92:3); she has not been raped by the archons – on the contrary, she has been protected by her father. As pointed out by Karen King, this protection is in correspondence with the father's role in an ideal patriarchal family. In such a family, the father controls the sexuality of his women and in this way guards his and his family's honour. Thus the text reflects and reproduces the values of a traditional patriarchal family (King 1990:18).

It is a little puzzling that the virginal Norea simultaneously appears as having offspring. However, what are described in the texts seem to have been spiritual relationships more than biological. The designations 'children of Norea', 'the seed of Seth' and 'the race of Seth' were types of idealised kinship systems in which biology was either not involved or was subordinate.[10] That we are talking primarily of spiritual relationships is also supported by the fact that the genealogies of the Sethian texts are not *real* genealogies – they are not spelled out, only suggested in sweeping statements like 'the seed of Seth' or 'the children of Norea'. These designations suggested a general spiritual connection, but also connections to specific religious groups. Those outside the spiritual group could be described as the race of Cain.[11] In other words, genealogy is used by Gnostic groups to describe connection to a spiritual community, a strong group identity, and difference from Christians who do not share the group's religious conviction.

FROM MYTHOLOGICAL TO SOCIAL FAMILY

The texts do not discuss family structures as social realities. We must therefore take a more cautious approach and ask what consequences the ideologies of these systems could have for family life. What do the roles and values of mythological families in Gnosticism imply for the roles and values of the social family? What is the significance of sexuality?

As we have seen, family structure plays an important role in Gnostic mythology, but just as the texts include spiritual fathers, mothers and sons, the family units of the divine mythological entities are also transcended. One example is found in *Orig. World* where Eve says: 'It is my husband who bore me; And it is I who am his mother, And it is he who is my father and my lord (CG II.5 114:11–13; Robinson 1988:181).[12]

The speaker is one who both shares in and unites the different kinship roles of women. A parallel way of thinking about the individual in relation to family roles is found in *Ap. John* where John has a vision: the heavens open and everything is flooded in light. John sees a child, but this child is at the same time an old man filled with light. The figure says that he is the Father, the Mother and the Son, in other words he transcends family roles as well as age roles and sex roles. This vision is a direct reflection of how the divine Sethian triad ultimately is conceived of as a unity in which all social roles disappear. Consequently, one message mediated by these texts is that individual human beings are not complete in any of the traditional family roles, they are only fragments of a unity, which – paradoxically – is frequently described as a patriarchal nuclear family, Father, Mother, and Son.

So while the users of the Sethian texts expressed their thoughts by means of a mythological world of family relations – divine and human, spiritual and material, perfect and pathological – the individual mythological people in these relations seem to have been of less importance than the functions and the processes in which they were involved. The spiritual messenger Zoe, a variant of the spiritual Eve, is the daughter of the Spirit, but she is also a reflection of the Father's thought, called alternatively Protennoia or Barbelo. The personalities are fleeting; they are reflections and images of each other.

In relation to a perfect divine family unit, the Gnostic individual was incomplete. The individual had to be incorporated in a family-relation of spiritual beings, mythologically conceived of as a male–female connection or as a father–son connection. We saw that Adam found his spiritual counterpart in Eve. In the same way human beings on earth lack their spiritual counterparts and are therefore incomplete. In their material and psychical state they are ultimately the fruit of a female and therefore faulty conception, they are only children of the mother. Because of this lack they have to gain knowledge, complete the Gnostic rituals, and thus become sons of the Father. These texts breath an ardent wish that their readers should be united with their spiritual counterparts and/or become spiritual sons of the Father.

While it was a strong Gnostic ideal to become a son, it was not a corresponding ideal to beget sons. Mundane family life seems not to have been the most obvious context for the Gnostic individual on the way to spiritual fulfilment. On the contrary, family life and the production of children implied a further fragmentation of the original perfect spiritual family. The texts frequently speak against sexual desire and the begetting of children. One example is *The Apocryphon of John*. In *Ap. John*, sexuality is created and ruled over by the archons. The great archon sets the example for procreation, being the first to procreate children by Eve. In *Ap. John* desire (*epithymia*) is a quality connected with the world of the archons (CG II.1 18:6, 27; III. 17:6; BG 40:20), and the archons give Adam desire as part of his equipment (CG

II.1 21:4–14; III. 26:13–25; BG 55:2–13). Desire is connected with the Tree of Life. Because procreation leads to the human cycles of life and death, desire is redefined as a desire of death (CG II.1 21:35; III. 28:3; BG 57:4–5). The serpent teaches sexual desire to Adam or Eve, and a desire for procreation is planted in either Adam or in Eve (CG II.1 24:26–31; III. 31:21–32:3; BG 63:1–9). The function and purpose of intercourse is to make the light dilute and spread, for each time a child is born the spiritual element caught in this world is diminished and it will be increasingly difficult to save all the spiritual elements. The archontic strategy of procreation is further developed when evil angels are sent down to 'the daughters of men' to beget children with them and mix the scattered light still more with darkness.[13] Consequently, when human beings beget children, they are assisting the archons and act as instruments for them.

Ap. John can hardly be interpreted in any other way than that it takes a strong stand against the procreation of children. Sexual desire is part of human nature, created by the archons and linked with reproduction. The demonising of sexuality is one of the most significant examples of how the Gnostics turned a Biblical command upside down and made it into a weapon against its originator, the Old Testament God. While Jahweh bade human beings to multiply and fill the earth, Ialdabaoth uses sexual procreation as a chief device to enslave human beings. The authors of *Ap. John* have turned vehemently against the Biblical obligation to reproduce.

There is an unmistakable disgust for procreation and carnal relationships in *Ap. John*. Successful births on earth only occur in *Ap. John* when Adam fathers Seth with the spiritual Eve; in *Hyp. Arch.* also when he fathers Norea. But how these conceptions, not to mention births, really took place is not clear; their technical aspects are left deliberately vague. One solution could be to interpret these procreations as being consummated without passion. They are procreations without desire whose only purpose was to make spiritual ancestors for the Gnostic race. Otherwise reproduction stood in the context of death. In the *Orig. World*, the connection between sexuality and death is stressed when sensual pleasure is linked to Eros and the earth. From Eros and the earth as its centre, a vicious circle consisting of woman, marriage, birth and death evolves:

> Just as from the midpoint of light and darkness Eros appeared and at the midpoint of the angels and mankind the sexual union of Eros was consummated, so out of the earth the primal pleasure blossomed. The woman followed earth. And marriage followed woman. Birth followed marriage. Dissolution followed birth.
>
> (CG II.5 109:16–25; Robinson 1988: 178)

Nevertheless, it is not certain that the strong stand taken against procreation in *Ap. John* is absolutely valid for all texts, even if a connection is made between sexuality and death. Special comments on Gen 1:28a and 6:1a in

Orig. World and in *Hyp. Arch.* of how the earth was filled by human beings reflect that reproduction could also be used as part of a spiritual offensive against the archontic forces.[14] In *Hyp. Arch.* the multiplication of human beings follows the birth of Norea and is a positive consequence of this birth: 'Then mankind began to multiply and improve'(CG II.4 92:3–4). In *Orig. World*, the souls of the elect are told: 'Multiply and improve! Be lord over all creatures' (CG II.5 114:19). These quotations reflect that procreation in connection with the spiritual race also could be regarded as positive.

EPIPHANIUS AND 'THESE DEADLY WOMEN'[15]

Up to this point we have been dealing with texts whose creators seem either to have taken an ascetic stand, a stand which agrees well with a general trend in late Antiquity to combine spiritual life with sexual renunciation, or who permitted procreation when it served spiritual interests. These texts come from the Nag Hammadi library, and this library was found in the vicinity of a Pachomian monastery, with bills from the monastery inside the bindings of the books. The suggestion has been made that Pachomian monks read and copied the Gnostics texts and used them as edifying litera- ture.[16] It is not difficult to imagine how such a society of monks could get spiritual and ideological nourishment from these texts, as well as a certain support for that misogyny which usually thrives in that type of all-male society.

However, when we proceed to Epiphanius' *Panarion* the picture becomes more complicated and our fantasy of how Gnostics lived their lives has to be expanded, for Epiphanius has left us a picture of Gnostic life not fit for pious and ascetic monks. Astonishing as this church father's testimony is, it cannot so easily be brushed aside. For one thing Epiphanius visited Egypt in his youth, roughly at the same time as the Nag Hammadi library was finally stored away, which means that we are dealing with an eye witness, who, according to his own narrative, was instructed by exactly the same people he accuses of the most shocking libertinism. A second point, which also makes Epiphanius highly relevant, is that the mythologies he reproduces are similar to those we have met in the texts we have examined, especially *Ap. John* and *Hyp. Arch.*. When he wrote his *Panarion*, Epiphanius was appar- ently combining his own personal memories with texts he had at hand. However, he manages to make these two sources interlock, and to reveal some new possibilities for how cultic and social life could be constructed on a basis of a traditional Gnostic mythology nourished by sexual symbolism and metaphors of divine families.

In short, what Epiphanius tells us is connected with a group he calls alternatively Gnostics, Borborites and Phibionites.[17] Characteristic of this group was the way it indulged in different types of sexual activities in a cultic setting, heterosexual as well as homosexual. According to the group's mythology the spiritual elements of the Mother were bound to human sperm and menstrual blood. The members of the group practiced *coitus interruptus* and collected the spiritual elements through male and female emissions. This was done sacramentally and the male sperm and the menstrual blood were identified with the Lord's Supper. Childbearing was forbidden. If anybody conceived a child, the foetus was aborted, made into a ritual meal and eaten (*Panarion* 26,1–26,9).

What is striking about this group is how the paradoxical language of other Gnostic texts is discarded. Sperm is no longer only a metaphor for spirit, an identification is made between spirit and sperm. Sperm must not go to waste; the demons are lying in wait to catch it and bear their mixed children. For instance, this point is illustrated by how the prophet Elijah, according to the interpretation of these Gnostics, was unable to ascend to heaven because a female demon claimed that she had had children by him: 'Oh yes, often while you were dreaming dreams you had nocturnal emissions, and it was I who partook of your sperm and bore your children' (*Panarion* 26,13,5; Layton 1987: 213).

Ap. John and Epiphanius' Gnostics have a preoccupation with spiritual origin and seed and an opposition to childbearing in common, but the connection between sexual desire, intercourse and childbirth, so inevitable in *Ap. John*, has been deliberately broken in the group described by Epiphanius. According to Epiphanius' description, the members of the group were married couples. However, the purpose of their marriages was not to procreate children, alternative sexual practices were introduced that did not lead to childbirth. This separation between sexual practice and childbirth created a new matrix for the production of symbols and experimental cultic practices where sexual desire was used as an instrument for spiritual perfection. It seems as if Epiphanius' Gnostics had started to beat the archons on their own ground.

The bishop of Salamis certainly gives us a new alternative regarding Christian family life. He also gives an alternative to our impression that Gnostic groups were male-dominated (Goehring 1988). According to the bishop, the women were the ones who actively tried to entice him into their group, by using erotic narratives and playing on their beauty. Young Epiphanius at last broke loose from this 'flirty fishing' and retributed by reporting the Gnostics to the bishop. The result was that eighty persons 'who were hidden within the church' were expelled from the city (*Panarion* 26,17,9), thus implying that alternative ways of living in this case were combined with an apparently traditional Christian life.

We cannot be sure that Epiphanius was correct in what he wrote about Gnostic practice. He could be exaggerating, he could even be fabricating stories on the basis of the mythology he read in the texts. Remember, Epiphanius was writing in Cyprus about forty years after the scandalous events of his youth. He was deeply hostile to the Gnostics, a defender of the eternal virginity of Mary, and an advocate of the continent life. But even if we take an over-cautious approach to his narrative, at least it shows how the connection between Gnostic mythology and Gnostic practice is not absolute. It is possible to draw entirely different conclusions from the traditional Gnostic mythology than those leading to sexual renunciation.

CONCLUSION

In Sethian texts, the ideal mythological family was a divine triad of father, mother and son, a typical patriarchal family. The fall is conceived of as a violation of this archetypical triad by a female entity creating a son without the father's permission and with no male contribution at the conception.

Family relations and genealogical connections are used to describe the process of salvation of the individual, and to characterise the connection between the individual and the spiritual group. Thus the intimacy of family life is translated into spiritual relationships, where the soul appears as a son of the father or is connected to a female spiritual counterpart. This sort of translation implies that the individual is incomplete, and that completeness is achieved by inclusion into a spiritual family unit. The use of family metaphors to describe the relationship between God and the saved gives intimacy to the god–man relation, but at the same time renders inferior the relationships within families in flesh.

As for the procreation of children, the message of the Sethian texts and the secondary sources diverge and various options occur. One ideal is to be continent, and sexuality and the procreation of children are regarded as evil. Another possibility is that procreation is allowed to multiply the spiritual race, but not sexual desire. The third possibility is that sexuality is allowed, but not to bear children. This last option has a certain logic to it if the connection between seed and the spiritual elements is such that the spiritual elements are diminished when humans multiply.

If we take a look at the wider Egyptian Christian context of the Sethian texts, there was a variety of possible ways to live a Christian life in the fourth century. We encounter solitary ascetic desert dwellers, Pachomian monks staying in monasteries in villages, urban study-groups where men and women were living together in collective celibacy, mystery associations with original teaching and practices, as well as householders and family life. Though in retreat in relation to mainstream Christianity, Gnostics were still found. The Sethian texts and their mythological use of family structures could have had something to say to several of the Christian ways of living. But taking into consideration that the codes of the world were radically revised in the Gnostic texts, these texts had perhaps least to say to those living in ordinary patriarchal families.

NOTES

1 The characteristic 'Sethian' designates a certain family-likeness existing between several texts in the Nag Hammadi library. It does not imply that there existed a specific Sethian group, nor that there was a clear-cut Sethian system. For discussion about Sethian Gnosticism, see Turner 1976; Wisse 1981; van den Broek 1983; Pearson 1990: 2–83.

2 For the Coptic texts, see Layton 1974; Layton 1976; Layton 1982; Janssens 1978; Waldstein and Wisse 1995.

3 How influential and important these texts have been in Gnostic circles is difficult to know. The *Apocryphon of John* was found in three copies in the Nag Hammadi library. One more copy is known (BG). In addition, we have a description of a system similar to that of the *Apocryphon of John* in Irenaeus, *Adversus haereses* 1,30,1. The different copies of *Ap. John* suggest that this text at least must have been well known. Two copies are known of the *Orig. World*, while *Tri. Prot.* and *Hyp. Arch.* exist in one copy each.

4 This mythologeme is present in *Ap. John* and *Hyp. Arch.*. It is briefly touched in *Tri. Prot.*, but exists in a more complicated version in *Orig. World*.

5 For a discussion of this topic, see Smith 1988.

6 This point is prominent in *Orig. World*, *Hyp. Arch.* and *Ap. John*.

7 *pef-shr-eine* 'its male counterpart' (CG II.4 87:35).

8 *tef-shr-eine* 'his female counterpart' (CG II.4 89:19; 91:31; CG II.5 110:34).

9 *tetn-shr-eine* 'their counterpart' (CG II.4 92:24–25).

10 That kinship was not always based on biology in Roman society, is exemplified by the widespread practice of adoption. Adoption was a legal fiction that permitted a family tie to be artificially created, cf Martin 1990: 29–32.

11 Birger Pearson (1990: 95–107) has discussed and turned down the possible presence of real Cainite groups within the Gnostic movement as stated by some of the church fathers.

12 A similar language is found in *Hyp. Arch.*. It is also prominent in another Nag Hammadi text called *The Thunder: Perfect Mind* (CG VI.2).

13 This is a Gnostic exegesis of Gen 6:1–4. Cf Stroumsa 1984: 31ff.

14 The other comments on Gen 1:28a (6:1a) in *Orig. World*, are more like historical references to the multitude of human beings who had been born from Adam (CG II.5 114:19–20; 118:2–3).

15 *Panarion* 26,17,6.

16 Cf van den Broek 1983: 47. Though the hypothesis of a Pachomian origin for the Nag Hammadi library has many spokesmen, it has also opponents. For a recent discussion, see Khosroyev 1995: 61ff.

17 *Panarion* 25–26. Cf also Gero 1976.

BIBLIOGRAPHY

Broek, R. van den (1983) 'The Present State of Gnostic Research', *Vigiliae Christianae* 37: 41–71.

Gero, S. (1976) 'With Walter Bauer on the Tigris: Encratite Orthodoxy and Libertine Heresy in Syro-Mesopotamian Christianity', in C. W. Hedrick and R. Hodgson Jr (eds) *Nag Hammadi, Gnosticism and Early Christianity*, Peabody, MA: Hendrickson: 287–307.

Gilhus, I. S. (1985) *The Nature of the Archons: a Study in the Soteriology of a Gnostic Treatise from Nag Hammadi (CG II. 4)*, Wiesbaden: Otto Harrassowitz.

—— (1994) 'Trimorphic Protennoia', in E. S. Fiorenza (ed.) *Searching the Scriptures*, vol. 2, New York: Crossroad: 55–65.

Goehring, J. E. (1988) 'Libertine or Liberated: Women in the So–called Libertine Gnostic Communities', in K. L. King (ed.) *Images of the Feminine in Gnosticism*, Philadelphia: Fortress Press: 297–307.

Janssens, Y. (1978) *La Protennoia Trimorphe* (Bibliothèque Copte de Nag Hammadi, Section 'Textes', 4), Québec: Les Presses de l'Université Laval.

Khosroyev, A. (1995) *Die Bibliothek von Nag Hammadi: Einige Probleme des Christentums in Ägypten Während der Ersten Jahrhunderte*, Altenberge: Oros Verlag.

King, K. L. (1990) 'Ridicule and Rape, Rule and Rebellion: the Hypostasis of the Archons', in J. Goehrin, C. W. Hedrick, J. T. Sanders and H. D. Betz (eds) *Gnosticism and the Early Christian World*, Sonoma, CA: Polebridge Press: 3–24.

Layton, B. (1974) 'The Hypostasis of the Archons, or the Reality of the Rulers' (Part 1), *HTR*, 67: 351–425.

—— (1976) 'The Hypostasis of the Archons, or the Reality of the Rulers' (Part 2), *HTR*, 69: 31–101.

—— (1982) (ed.) *Nag Hammadi Codex II: 2–7*, vol. 2, (Nag Hammadi Studies vol. 21), Leiden: E. J. Brill.

—— (1987) *The Gnostic Scriptures: A New Translation with Annotations and Introductions*, New York: SCM Press.

Malina, B. (1981) *The New Testament World: Insights from Cultural Anthropology*, London: SCM Press.

Martin, L. (1990) 'Genealogy and Sociology in the Apocalypse of Adam', in J. Goehring, C. W. Hedrick, J. T. Sanders, and H. D. Betz (eds) *Gnosticism and the Early Christian World*, Sonoma, CA: Polebridge Press: 25–36.

Pearson, B. (1990) *Gnosticism, Judaism, and Egyptian Christianity*, Minneapolis: Fortress Press.

Robinson, J. M. (ed.) (1988) *The Nag Hammadi Library in English*, Leiden: E. J. Brill.

Seymour-Smith, C. (1988) *Macmillan Dictionary of Anthropology*, London: Macmillan Press.

Smith, R. (1988) 'Sex Education in Gnostic Schools', in K. L. King (ed.) *Images of the Feminine in Gnosticism*, Philadelphia: Fortress Press: 345–60.

Stroumsa, G. A. G. (1984) *Another Seed: Studies in Gnostic Mythology*, Leiden: E. J. Brill.

Turner, J. D. (1976) 'Sethian Gnosticism: a Literary History', in C. W. Hedrick and R. Hodgson Jr (eds) *Nag Hammadi, Gnosticism, and Early Christianity*, Peabody, MA: Hendrickson: 5–86.

Waldstein, M. and Wisse, F. (1995) *The Apocryphon of John: Synopsis of Nag Hammadi Codices II.1; III.1; and IV.1 with BG 8502, 2*, (Nag Hammadi and Manichaean Studies 33), Leiden: E. J. Brill.

Wisse, F. (1981) 'Stalking those Elusive Sethians', in B. Layton (ed.) *The Rediscovery of Gnosticism*, vol. 2, Leiden: E. J. Brill: 563–676.

—— (1988) 'Flee Femininity: Antifemininity in Gnostic Texts and the Question of Social Milieu', in K. L. King (ed.) *Images of the Feminine in Gnosticism*, Philadelphia: Fortress Press: 297–307.

INDEX OF ANCIENT SOURCES

APOCRYPHA AND PSEUDEPIGRAPHA

QUMRAN

JOSEPHUS

PHILO

RABBINIC LITERATURE

INDEX OF MODERN AUTHORS